The Imperishable Dominion

The Imperishable Dominion

The Bahá'í Faith and the Future of Mankind

'Thou art My dominion and My dominion perisheth not, wherefore fearest thou thy perishing?' Bahá'u'lláh

Udo Schaefer

Translated from the German by
Janet Rawling-Keitel, David Hopper and Patricia Crampton

ꝫ

George Ronald · Oxford

George Ronald, Publisher
46 High Street, Kidlington, Oxford OX5 2DN

Original German-language edition
Der Bahá'í in der modernen Welt © Copyright Bahá'í-Verlag GmbH Hofheim-Langenhain 1981
2nd revised edition
This translation © George Ronald 1983
Reprinted 1986

ISBN 0 85398 142 6 (paper)

Printed in Great Britain at the Alden Press, Oxford

Contents

To my dear wife

Sigrun

without whose help I would never have been able
to write this book

Thus have the mighty verses of Thy Lord been again sent down unto thee, that thou mayest arise to remember God, the Creator of earth and heaven, in these days when all the tribes of the earth have mourned, and the foundations of the cities have trembled, and the dust of irreligion hath enwrapped all men, except such as God, the All-Knowing, the All-Wise, was pleased to spare. Say: He Who is the Unconditioned is come, in the clouds of light, that He may quicken all created things with the breeze of His Name, the Most Merciful, and unify the world, and gather all men around this Table which hath been sent down from heaven.

Bahá'u'lláh, Tablet to Napoleon III

O King! I was but a man like others, asleep upon My couch, when lo, the breezes of the All-Glorious were wafted over Me, and taught Me the knowledge of all that hath been. This thing is not from Me, but from One Who is Almighty and All-Knowing. And He bade Me lift up My voice between earth and heaven, and for this there befell Me what hath caused the tears of every man of understanding to flow. The learning current amongst men I studied not; their schools I entered not. Ask of the city wherein I dwelt, that thou mayest be well assured that I am not of them who speak falsely. This is but a leaf which the winds of the will of thy Lord, the Almighty, the All-Praised, have stirred. Can it be still when the tempestuous winds are blowing?

Bahá'u'lláh, Tablet to Náṣiri'd-Dín Sháh

O Pope! Rend the veils asunder. He Who is the Lord of Lords is come over-shadowed with clouds, and the decree hath been fulfilled by God, the Almighty, the Unrestrained . . . Verily, the day of ingathering is come, and all things have been separated from each other. He hath stored away that which He chose in the vessels of justice, and cast into fire that which befitteth it. Thus hath it been decreed by your Lord, the Mighty, the Loving, in this promised Day. He, verily, ordaineth what He pleaseth.

Bahá'u'lláh, Tablet to Pope Pius IX

We exhort mankind in these days when the countenance of Justice is soiled with dust, when the flames of unbelief are burning high and the robe of wisdom rent asunder, when tranquillity and faithfulness have ebbed away and trials and tribulations have waxed severe, when covenants are broken and ties are severed, when no man knoweth how to discern light and darkness or to distinguish guidance from error.

Bahá'u'lláh, Lawḥ-i-Ḥikmat

Foreword

This book is a courageous book. Its author, Dr Schaefer, certainly has the courage of his convictions. It takes a brave man, nowadays, to go against the current and dare call a spade a spade. One of the paradoxes of the so-called permissive society is that it does not permit anyone to question its legitimacy. The permissive society is intolerant of critics, for they give it a guilty conscience. It feels no qualms about using against the upholders of 'old-fashioned' morality and common decency the sophisticated weapons of intellectual terrorism. The religious believer, the responsible parent, the dutiful child, the loving wife, the faithful husband, the law-abiding citizen, the conscientious workman, the student who really studies, the educator who really educates, the priest who prays, and above all the moralist who persists in distinguishing between good and evil, all are derided, ridiculed, summarily dismissed as irrelevant fossils. 'Not with it' is the final verdict condemning such benighted heretics. They can call themselves fortunate when they are not actually reviled or even threatened: didn't Sartre brand those who disagreed with his views as 'salauds' (bastards)? Well, Dr Schaefer is certainly 'not with it' . . .and he does not intend to be. The permissive society is his favourite target. He does not mince his words when denouncing its noxiousness.

Of all kinds of tyranny, the tyranny of fashion – and more particularly intellectual fashion – is perhaps the most ruthless. Philosophical ideas are seldom assessed according to their intrinsic value, but rather according to their degree of 'modernity'. It no longer matters whether they are 'true' or 'wise', but it does matter a great deal whether they are in keeping with the prevailing fashions and moods of a certain self-appointed intelligentsia. Nietzsche's famous pronouncement about the alleged death of God, for instance, was uncritically swallowed as a genuine piece of information by countless people, as if they had read it as actual news in their newspaper. Another and more recent slogan, aptly quoted in Dr Schaefer's book, is the anonymous 'Il est interdit d'interdire' (Taboos are taboo), which probably sets an all-time record in nonsensical aphorisms.

And yet, thousands of people have eagerly adopted it as the backbone of their philosophy, without realizing the inherent contradiction in this witty maxim, and the inconsistency in their own outlawing of some taboos – preferably other people's taboos – while *they* create scores of new taboos of their own? Dr Schaefer has little patience with such fads. He rightly sees that a decadent society can produce but a decadent philosophy and decadent ways of life, and that decadence is not in any way redeemed by modernity.

Not everything modern or fashionable is necessarily good, true, or admirable. Not everything that is praised to the skies by the small set of professional judges of wisdom is necessarily praiseworthy, even if crowds of unthinking people blindly trust and follow such judges. As Dr Schaefer puts it: '. . . the truth of an idea is independent of the size of its following. Number is not a criterion of truth.' Nor, should we be tempted to add, is 'modernity' or temporary popularity. A far more reliable criterion would be common sense, and Dr Schaefer amply demonstrates that he possesses this now rather uncommon gift to a high degree.

Dr Schaefer is a lawyer. As a lawyer, he naturally believes that laws are superior to anarchy, and wise laws to foolish ones. Ideally, the best possible laws would have a divine rather than human origin. All the great religions of the past have declared that such divinely-inspired laws existed, that they were repeatedly given to mankind through various seers, prophets, and revelators, in the long course of human history. However, the established churches that eventually constituted themselves as sole heirs and proprietors of such ancient messages from above were only too inclined to resent the intrusion of outsiders who claimed that God's voice was still to be heard, and that new messages still came down from heaven. The sheer notion of a *new* revelation, of an *additional* heavenly message, was anathema to the professional priestly caste, for they felt it would cause a sort of devaluation of the older message, which they hoarded as their personal property. Their monopoly seemed jeopardized each time a newcomer said he had re-established the interrupted communication between the Deity and the human race. Hence the recurrent priestly opposition to any allusion to the possibility of a new prophetic cycle, with revelation taking place outside the 'appropriate channels'. All the great established churches in turns have fought against new prophets, and branded new prophecy as heretical. It is an all-too-familar story: the Pharisees saw the early Christians as heretics, the Catholics saw the Protestants as heretics, the Protestants saw the Mormons as heretics, and the Muslims saw the Bahá'ís as heretics, to give only a few notorious instances of a universal and time-honoured ecclesiastical policy. Established churches are prone to see divine revelation as a sealed book. Truly religious people, on the other hand, always expect fresh outpourings from what Swedenborg called 'divine love and wisdom'. They are not satisfied with mere records, however admirable. What they

want is the Logos . . . live! Likewise, lawyers know that laws have to be
revised, reworded and reinvigorated periodically, lest they lose their
relevance or their efficiency.

Many years ago, Dr Schaefer realized that the 'old' divine laws were no
longer understood and obeyed. He saw that mankind needed a new set of
laws, as well as a new Covenant with the divine lawmaker. He looked for a
faith that could satisfy this need, and he discovered the Bahá'í Faith.

The Bahá'í Faith is a little-known religion, at least in Europe. It is also a
relatively recent one, although it purports to be nothing else than the per-
ennial monotheistic religion, the religion of Zoroaster and Abraham and
Melchizedek and Moses and Jesus and Muḥammad. To the established
churches, which readily forget their own beginnings as obscure cults, a new
religious movement is usually ridiculed as 'a mere sect', which should accordingly be despised, persecuted, and if possible annihilated. The world
has perhaps forgotten the barbarous tortures and massacres which befell
the early Bábís and Bahá'ís in the mid-nineteenth century, but the recent
persecutions inflicted on their great-grandchildren in Imám Khomeini's
Iran have hit the headlines. Hundreds, maybe thousands of innocent
people have been savagely humiliated and murdered because they refused
to believe that God was Hatred, and God's laws spelt intolerance,
chauvinism, slavery for women, and institutionalized obscurantism and
bigotry.

Such dreadful outbursts of modern savagery, along with the general
spread of terrorism, cruelty, vandalism and wanton violence, only
demonstrate how right Dr Schaefer is when he expresses the opinion that
an urgently-needed new religion should provide the men and women of
today with an ideology and a legislation capable of fostering a new world
civilization. The sad truth is that large portions of modern society are no
longer *civilized* in any sense of the word. In a remote past, Judaism,
Christianity, Islám, Hinduism, Taoism, Buddhism and other religious
systems did much to civilize people, or help them civilize themselves.
Unfortunately, with the possible exception of some latter-day versions of
these ancient creeds, none of them is in its prime any more. The divine
message has to be heard again. According to the Bhagavad Gîta, 'every
time the dharma fades away, and injustice becomes prevalent, I (= i.e. the
"avatar", God's manifestation in the human form . . .) am born again.
For the liberation of righteous people, for the destruction of evil doers, to
restore Justice to her throne, I am born again and again, from generation to
generation.' To see Justice restored to her throne is certainly Dr Schaefer's
most fervent wish. He believes that Bahá'u'lláh, the prophet of the Bahá'í
Faith, is the latest heavenly messenger. He expounds the Bahá'í Cause
with remarkable clarity, in a forceful and yet logical and even Cartesian
way. He defends it convincingly, with great intelligence. This book is
probably among the very few that make the Bahá'í religion really

intelligible to non-Orientals. Its reasoning is quite fascinating, and the reader feels grateful for being offered this fast-disappearing commodity: reasonable grounds for hope, in a seemingly hopeless world.

Dr Jacques CHOULEUR
Professor at the University of Avignon, France

Preface

No one can seriously deny that we live in a time of global upheaval. All aspects of our existence are being overturned and revolutionized. The manifold symptoms of a spiritual crisis, unprecedented in the annals of history, are all too obvious. What is the cause of this sinister process and where is it leading us?

This book springs from the conviction that the destruction and violence which surround us, and the dangers, now clearly visible, which loom ahead and darken the horizon of our future have their roots in a spiritual event which is still largely unknown to the world. It is the advent of the *Kairos*, the time prophesied in past ages and now fulfilled by the coming of Bahá'u'lláh. It is the appointed time at which the eternal, the unconditioned, has again intersected the flow of history and intervened in the world of transience. This event, by which the 'world's equilibrium hath been upset' (Bahá'u'lláh, Kitáb-i-Aqdas, *Synopsis*, No. 20), will prove to be a turning-point in history: the old order has been shaken and is gradually vanishing; a new reality is dawning.

Beginning with a description (inevitably sketchy and fragmentary) of the decline of religion and the overthrow of time-honoured values (in other words, a description of our rapidly changing, secular world), this book attempts to compare the essential features of this new reality with the attitudes prevailing in present-day society. Such a comparison which occasionally brings traditional Christian concepts into focus will enable the reader to reach a deeper understanding of the message of Bahá'u'lláh.

The religion of Bahá'u'lláh differs in many respects from the views, ideas, values and theories which are prevalent in present-day society; indeed, it is the very opposite of many of these. Just as light only acquires its colour by means of the object on to which it falls, so the unsounded depths of the new Word of God are revealed by means of a confrontation with ways of thinking that are far removed from the 'blossoms of true knowledge and wisdom' (Bahá'u'lláh, *Kitáb-i-Íqán*, p. 46). Thus the writer cannot avoid taking a firm stand, because, in a world that has lost its orientation and in an age which prefers blunt language, nobody would be helped by a lukewarm, colourless comparison. Confrontation rather than mere comparison is necessary, even if this process occasionally proves the truth of Lichtenberg's observation: 'It is almost impossible to carry the torch of truth through a crowd without somebody's beard getting singed.'

A few words should be said about the quotations, for the reader may wonder why there is such a profusion of them. The reason is that in a critique of a theological, cultural, or social kind, it seems advisable to let the relevant authors speak for themselves. At the same time, it allows this author to counter the objection that the results he has arrived at are a highly subjective interpretation of his attempts to prove what he already believes: namely, that the sands of the old era have run out. In those places where the Bahá'í Faith is the subject of discourse, it seemed to the author that mere reference to the original texts would not suffice since many readers have no access to these. Moreover, there is no better way of conveying a direct and unbroken impression of the spirit pervading the revelation of Bahá'u'lláh than to allow the revealed text to speak for itself.

This book is the outcome of the revision of an article published some years ago. ('What it means to be a Bahá'í', in *The Light Shineth in Darkness*, pp. 19 – 52.) As it offers only a minimum of information on the history of the Bahá'í Faith it is not intended to be an introduction to it. But the reader is referred throughout the book to various sources of Bahá'í literature. It would also be to his advantage if he were to acquaint himself with the essentials of Bahá'í teachings, such as are presented in a number of short but comprehensive works (e.g. J. E. Esslemont, *Bahá'u'lláh and the New Era*, 4th rev. edn 1974; John Huddleston, *The Earth is But One Country*, London 1976.)

At the request of the publisher, and with the aim of increasing the readability of the book, translations of foreign idioms and quotations have been included in an appendix. Quotations from the Bible are in the King James version; quotations from the Qur'án are in Rodwell's translation. References to quotations from the widely used compilation *Gleanings from the Writings of Bahá'u'lláh* are by chapter and paragraph rather than by page number, as this Bahá'í book exists in several different editions.

Finally, I would like to thank all those who, by their criticism and stimulus, have contributed to the style and content of this book: Ulrich Gollmer, Dr Ihsan Halabi, Foad Kazemzadeh, Peter Mühlschlegel, Dr Badi Panahi and Joachim Reitz. I am also particularly indebted to Gottfried Lemberg, Judge of the Baden-Württemberg Higher Administrative Court, for his critical reading of the manuscript and valuable ideas. I should like to thank all those who have helped in the preparation of this English edition: the translators, Janet Rawling-Keitel, David Hopper and Patricia Crampton, with the assistance of Cornelia Meseke, Mathy Thimm-

Bellows, Gerald Keil and Peter Terry; the editor, May Ballerio, and the staff of George Ronald; the reviewers on behalf of the National Spiritual Assembly of the Bahá'ís of the United Kingdom; and the proof-readers. Not least, I am deeply grateful to my wife for patiently typing the many versions of the text and for finding the English editions of the many quotations.

Heidelberg   U. SCHAEFER
  Autumn 1982

1. Is Religion Finished?

The Secularization of our World

Anyone who nowadays confesses to belief in a revealed religion will be looked upon, even by churchmen, as an 'interesting exception',[1] and anyone who actually professes to be the follower of a new religion and is actively committed to it will be regarded by his contemporaries, almost without exception, as an exotic outsider. Religious thinking is considered by many a relic of past ages, outmoded, doomed to extinction, a poetic creation of the human intellect which accompanied mankind only so long as a scientific explanation of the world, based upon reason and logic, was lacking. In our enlightened world, one which is moulded by reason and science, religion has become superfluous. Once the most profound principle of our existence, it is now being pushed into the background. For the twentieth century God is no longer 'a determining force in our earthly existence, but merely a pretext, an empty word for clothing other interests. He exists only as a subject of debate and not as a vital force in life.'[2] God has vanished from the horizon and become a 'foreign word'.[3]

We live in a new era, an 'age of technology', an 'atomic age', a 'cosmic age', or whatever term one likes to employ to express the fact that it bears the imprint of forces which are profane in character, namely science and technology. Man has split the atom and is now trying to solve the mysteries

1. At a conference of French bishops in Lourdes, 1975, Archbishop Etchegaray of Marseilles said: 'The interesting exception nowadays is no longer the disbeliever but the believer.' (*Süddeutsche Zeitung*, 31.10.1975.)
2. Max Müller, 'Weisen der Sinnerfahrung des Menschen von heute', p.28.
3. 'Gott ein Fremdwort' (God a Foreign Word) is the title of an article in the *Frankfurter Allgemeine Zeitung* of 11.9.1974. The article reports the results of an informative questionnaire conducted on 550 junior school children by Hahn, a theologian from Giessen. For most of the children, concepts such as God, Christ, etc., were completely foreign.

of the microstructure of matter; he has landed on the moon and made space probes as far as the distant planets of our solar system; in the operating theatre the throbbing human heart has been replaced for a few hours by a machine; biochemists have deciphered the building plans of animate matter and are getting ready to alter them. It is no longer sufficient to call our time the 'technical age' – it is the 'age of technocracy': 'Technology has become the subject of history, in which we are only "co-historical".'[4]

Our modern world has its roots in that Copernican revolution in thought which banished resort to authoritative sources of the past (a method which the Middle Ages practised as a science) and replaced it by a mode of investigating nature which is grounded in experiment and rational theory and is independent of earlier precedents. The modern world operates according to Galileo's maxim: 'Measure everything that is measurable and make measurable everything that is immeasurable.' This new attitude of mind, implying as it does a liberation from prejudice and preconceived ideas and at the same time a commitment to methodological discipline and absolute objectivity, was felt to be the ideal for man in his newly-attained state of independence and maturity.

The onward march of science signalled the retreat of religion. This led to the secularization[5] of the world and the development of a secular concept of man, one which regarded him as an autonomous individual: 'Belief has prevailed for a thousand years, but now doubt has taken its place . . . Doubt is cast on time-honoured truths and what always used to be taken for granted is now questioned.'[6] Scientific progress and the loss of transcendence are, as it were, the two sides of one coin, the inseparable components of the same historical process which has led to our modern world. With the emergence of science there opened up a disastrous hiatus between religion and science, between belief and knowledge, because the Church also made claims to truth in areas that lay outside her authority, namely those of empirical science.[7] Scientific thinking and religious belief were from now on the two poles of a divided modern consciousness.

The great spiritual movement of modern Europe which led to the secularization of society was the Enlightenment, which began in the seventeenth century and flourished in the eighteenth. This movement was 'es-

---

4. Günther Anders, *Die Antiquiertheit des Menschen*, Vol.II, p.9.

5. cf. David Martin, *A General Theory of Secularization*; Heinz Horst Schrey (ed), *Säkularisierung*.

6. Bertolt Brecht, *Galileo*, scene i.

7. Hans Küng points out that the sentence passed on Galileo at the hands of Pope Urban VIII and the later opposition on the part of the Church to Darwin's theory of evolution only appeared to be a defence of belief in God. In fact the Church was really defending traditional Greco-Medieval cosmology and her own authority in all questions of science and human life. It was this opposition which has continued to poison the relationship between religion and science right up to the present day: 'The gap between the Church and modern culture, which has by no means yet been bridged, is based to a large extent on these facts.' (*Existiert Gott?*, p.89.)

sentially revolutionary, directed against the authority of intellectual and religious tradition. The positive force at its core was a determined assertion of the freedom of the individual – freedom in affairs social and political, intellectual and religious. This spirit expressed itself most emphatically in a new and extravagant belief in the power of reason. Faith in the old presuppositions and authorities, for so long considered valid beyond question, gave way to a spirit of criticism. Faith was now sought exclusively by the path of argument; logical demonstration, like that found in Euclid, was considered the sole adequate basis for conviction; reason claimed to be autonomous and set itself up as the unique court of appeal. And with reason thus ensconced, the mysterious depths of life, the indefinable and incalculable, received scant recognition or appreciation. To strictly religious values the age was for the most part blind. Whatever, from the point of view of reason, had about it an air of mystery fell under suspicion; man's feelings, passions, and sentiments were in ill repute. Thus the movement took on an austere and barren coldness, which was welcomed in the beginning as is the first breath of mountain air after the suffocating heat of the plains; in time, however, it chilled men through and drove them back to a new appreciation of the sunnier and warmer sides of human life.'[8] The chief concern of the Enlightenment which followed 'close upon the heels of religious wars in France and Germany' was humanity: 'It was marked, consequently, by a revulsion against the intolerance and persecution which had characterized those conflicts.'[9]

Increasingly faith went into decline; doubt was cast upon the Christian Revelation, turning it into a subject for dispute, until the atheism of modern times reached its first zenith with the Age of Enlightenment in eighteenth-century France. In the works of the rationalists d'Holbach, Helvétius, Diderot and Voltaire, Reason assumed the throne which Revelation till then had occupied. In 1793 in Notre Dame, Paris, God was publicly 'dethroned'. Atheism became a political movement. At first it was a bourgeois–liberal kind of atheism, but it was followed later by a proletarian–socialistic form which is nowadays the dominant ingredient of state doctrine in communist countries.

The conflict between religion and science came to a head in the nineteenth century. These trends intensified and accelerated, culminating on the one hand in the great discoveries of science and on the other in the philosophical dissection of religion, the shattering of the religious conception of life, and in the emergence of an atheistic ideology. The nineteenth century is the true beginning of the present age – in an even deeper sense, as we shall see. Just as our modern life and technological world is based on those things which the nineteenth century discovered and

8. Theodor M. Greene, 'The Historical Context and Religious Significance of Kant's "Religion"', p.ix.
9. op.cit., p.x.

conceived, so the prevailing atheistic thinking of today has its roots in the ideas which the outstanding philosophers of the nineteenth century thought and taught. The cry 'God is dead!' echoes through that century and has done more than anything else to mould the physiognomy of our times. The thinkers who, in the final phase of the religions of the Adamic Cycle, in the 'time of the end',[10] laid the philosophical foundations of what constitutes today the creed of a systematic disbelief, were Ludwig Feuerbach, Karl Marx, Sigmund Freud and Friedrich Nietzsche.

'God is Dead!'

Ludwig Feuerbach was intent upon demonstrating that God is merely a reflection of man. According to Feuerbach the relationship between man and God is in reality a relationship between man and his own self, his *alter ego*, on which he has conferred the highest attributes of his species: 'What a man declares concerning God, he in truth declares concerning himself.'[11] Religion is 'human nature reflected, mirrored in itself', 'God is the mirror of man'.[12] It follows that 'the future life is the present in the mirror of the imagination'.[13] 'The beginning, middle and end of religion is man.'[14] Reversing the Biblical account of creation, Feuerbach says: 'Man first unconsciously and involuntarily creates God in his own image, and after this God consciously and voluntarily creates man in his own image.'[15] In reality man has his 'highest being, his God, within himself'.[16] 'Thus man is the God of man':[17] *Homo homini Deus*, says Feuerbach[18] and adds that this realization was the turning-point in the history of the world.[19] Essentially anthropology is therefore 'the Mystery of Christian Theology'.[20] For Feuerbach, religion is a degrading form of alienation, an estrangement of man from himself.[21]

In his critique of religion, Karl Marx goes one step further than Feuerbach by declaring that religion is determined by and dependent on social influences. The roots of religion are planted in the soil of conflicting economic interests; if the conflict is eliminated, religion will die out. The aim of his critique is to expose God and religion as an ideology, a 'useful invention' and an ideological superstructure of the ruling class. Religion is the self-assurance of man who is enslaved and alienated from himself. It

10. cf. Matt. 24:14; 2 Tim. 3:1–9.
11. *The Essence of Christianity*, p.28.
12. ibid. p.62.
13. ibid. p.181.
14. ibid. p.183.
15. ibid. p.117.
16. ibid. p.275.
17. ibid. p.82.
18. apparently alluding to Hobbes, cf. p.142 n.85.
19. ibid. p.268.
20. ibid. p.337.
21. ibid. p.43.

grows out of the soil of poverty and exploitation: 'The wretchedness of religion is at once an expression of and a protest against real wretchedness. Religion is the sigh of the oppressed creature, the heart of a heartless world and the soul of soulless conditions. It is the opium of the people.'[22] According to Marx, religion is one form of escape from social misery into an 'illusory happiness'. Thus the critique of religion 'is the critique in embryo of the vale of tears of which religion is the halo . . . The critique of heaven is transformed into the critique of the earth, the critique of religion into the critique of law, the critique of theology into the critique of politics.'[23] Marx believed too that God must die so that man could live[24] and throw away the crutches of religion. His critique also leads to the conclusion that man is the highest of beings and one capable of steering history on a positive course, provided he is able to grasp the historical factors which have hindered him from making free decisions, in particular the misleading idea that God is the lord of history. Once he has freed himself from such deceptions, he will be in a position to take the rudder decisively into his own hands. Belief in God will disappear as soon as exploitation and proletarian poverty have been eliminated and the 'Realm of Freedom' is established. 'Atheism first, and communism second, are the preconditions of human self-emancipation and self-recovery.'[25]

Next to Karl Marx, the thinker who has played so decisive a part in changing the face of our modern world is Sigmund Freud, one of the Church Fathers of modern social science. He lived in this century and yet his ideas were entirely moulded by the nineteenth. He too was one of the 'exposers' of religion. As Walter Dirks points out,[26] Freud's theory of the super-ego attacks religion perhaps even more radically than Marx. In his work *The Future of an Illusion*,[27] he traces the origin of religion back to the helplessness of the child. He regards religion as the outcome of infantile desires in adults who long for the shelter of childhood. According to Freud, God is an apotheosized father figure, and consistent with this idea is the fact that people address their prayers to 'Our Father'. Psychoanalysis reveals a close connection between the father-complex and belief in God. It teaches that 'a personal God is, psychologically, nothing other than an exalted father'.[28] Freud regards religion as a 'hallucinatory delusion' or 'a universal obsessional neurosis' which, with the help of science, mankind will be able to eradicate.[29]

22. *Critique of Hegel's 'Philosophy of Right'*, p.131.
23. ibid. pp.131 and 132.
24. See Vitezslav Gardavský, *God is not yet Dead*, Penguin Books, 1973.
25. J. L. Talmon, *Political Messianism*, p.214.
26. 'Gottesglaube und Ideologiekritik', p.226.
27. *The Standard Edition of the Complete Psychological Works of Sigmund Freud*, Vol.XXI, London, 1910.
28. 'Leonardo da Vinci and a Memory of His Childhood', p.123.
29. 'Obsessive Acts and Religious Practices', p.34. In more detail: Badi Panahi, 'Die Bedeutung der Psychoanalyse für die Sozialwissenschaften', pp.138ff. Moreover, Hans Küng (*Existiert Gott?*,

What was for the poet Jean Paul a nightmare,[30] was for Nietzsche a certainty. With 'captivating force of language' and 'radicality of thought'[31] he announced the death of God. The expression 'God is dead', which has since developed into a catch-phrase, originated from him. He describes the 'madman' looking for God with a lantern in broad daylight: ' "Where is God gone?" he called out. "I mean to tell you! We have killed him, – you and I!" ' He proclaims the death of God and celebrates a requiem for him in churches, which in his view have become nothing other than tombs and sepulchres for this God. That God is dead, that 'the belief in the Christian God has become unworthy of belief' is 'the most important of more recent events'.[32] Man wishes to live without restrictions and even exercise control over the eternity which is attributed to heaven. He strives to become godlike himself, to attain the 'superman' ideal, and wishes therefore to depose God. God must die so that man can live. Belief in the after-life is something for the 'sick and perishing'. They 'invented the heavenly . . . From their misery they sought escape, and the stars were too remote for them. Then they sighed: "O that there were heavenly paths by which to steal into another existence and into happiness!" Then they contrived for themselves their bypaths and bloody draughts!'[33]

And yet the madman who proclaims the death of God intones no song of joy. His words awaken fear and horror over what has taken place: 'What did we do when we loosened this earth from its sun? Whither does it move now? Whither do we move? Away from all suns? Do we not dash on unceasingly? Backwards, sideways, forwards, in all directions? Is there still an above and below? Do we not stray, as through infinite nothingness? Does not empty space breathe upon us? Has it not become colder? Does not night come on continually, darker and darker? Shall we not have to light lanterns in the morning?'[34]

Nietzsche, the Cassandra of modern culture, prophesied the consequences of the death of God, the abdication of transcendence, this 'period of gloom and eclipse, the like of which has probably never taken place on earth before',[35] and predicted: 'What must all collapse now that this belief [has been] undermined, – because so much [is] built upon it, so much [rests] upon it, and [has] become one with it: for example our entire

pp.299–63) deals with the question of psychoanalytical atheism. His main criticism is that the existence of wish-projection can in no way answer the question whether the projection exists or not. The 'replacement' of religion by atheistic science, which Freud had expected, and the belief that this science can solve all problems, is nowadays regarded by many as an illusion.

30. 'Siebenkäs. Rede des toten Christus', *Selections from the Works of Jean Paul Friedrich Richter*, New York, American Book Company, 1898.

31. Heinrich Fries, *Gott ist tot?*, p.25.

32. *The Joyful Wisdom*, Nos.125, 343.

33. *Thus Spake Zarathustra*, Part I: 'Backworldsmen', pp.30–31.

34. *The Joyful Wisdom*, No.125.

35. ibid. No.343.

European morality.'[36] He clearly recognized that the death of God was inseparable from the overthrow of our values: 'Nihilism stands at the door: whence comes this uncanniest of all guests?'[37] His definition of nihilism is 'That the highest values devaluate themselves. The aim is lacking; "Why?" finds no answer.'[38] The supreme values of the Christian ethic such as love, humility, generosity, submission and compassion are cast down and replaced by the new values of domination and the will to power. In concrete terms Nietzsche foresaw the consequences this would have for mankind: a 'lengthy, vast and uninterrupted process of crumbling, destruction, ruin and overthrow which is now imminent'.[39] He also realized that the abdication of transcendence was a slow process whose nadir would only be reached in the future. The madman says: 'I come too early . . . I am not yet at the right time. This prodigious event is still on its way, and is travelling, – it has not yet reached men's ears. Lightning and thunder need time, the light of the stars needs time, deeds need time, even after they are done, to be seen and heard.'[40]

Religious Traditions Torn Down

The 'monstrous happening', the 'greatest darkness' announced by Nietzsche is becoming visible today. Traditional belief in God has become unacceptable. As the Jesuit General Arrupe lamented,[41] atheism has become a 'worldwide phenomenon'.[42] The notion of Providence has been expelled and that of 'Progress' has taken its place; belief in Revelation has been replaced by belief in Science, a substitute religion which people 'serve' and 'make sacrifices for'. Knowledge based on reason has taken the place of the redemptive knowledge of religion. Reason is taking the place of Tradition and becoming a determining factor of history. All problems which cannot be tackled empirically and expressed mathematically, or otherwise solved by the methods of modern science – for example the purpose of life, the goal of history – are exposed as 'apparent problems', as symptoms of a 'spiritual migraine',[43] and written off as meaningless. The world has been stripped of its magic, been made rational and technical

36. ibid. No.343.
37. *The Will to Power*, 'Toward an Outline', 1.
38. *The Will to Power*, I, 2.
39. *The Joyful Wisdom*, No.343.
40. ibid. No.125.
41. at the 83rd German Catholic Day in Trier, 1970.
42. The general scepticism towards religion was considerably strengthened through the revolution in scientific thinking brought about by Darwin's theory of evolution. This was a revolution 'whose implications were no less than those which we associate with the name of Copernicus'. (Josef Ratzinger, 'Schöpfungsglaube und Evolutionstheorie', p.232.) Belief in creation and the theory of evolution seemed to be incompatible ways of thinking.
43. according to the Viennese physicist Ludwig Boltzmann (1844–1906). This positivism was opposed by the hermeneutics school of philosophy, in particular the Heidelberg philosopher Hans-Georg Gadamer in *Wahrheit und Methode* (Truth and Method), 3rd edn 1972.

and, as a consequence, utilitarian. What remains is a vast emptiness in which man is cut off from his metaphysical origins and left impoverished with merely the 'affairs of this world' to care about: 'discovery, invention, progress, achievement, production, consumption.'[44]

The belief that only those things which can be understood rationally, measured or scientifically proved are relevant to human life, together with the conviction that science 'should doubtless be able by rational means to create from nothing an entire culture and everything that goes with it' misleads people into 'throwing overboard the vast treasury of knowledge and wisdom which is contained in the traditions of every ancient culture and in the teachings of the great world religions'.[45] Science has largely become an authoritative institution, a 'substitute religion', tending to replace transcendental religious systems. Its rationality threatens to swing over into irrational ideology in which it is no longer simply descriptive but also prescriptive, in which it wishes to have the final say in all questions, even such as concern the purpose of life, and in which it claims for itself the right of autonomy, the right to possess moral and political authority.[46] The dominant role which science has assumed in modern society has tended to turn religious conviction into a private matter and expel it from the socio-political sphere: 'In this way, methodological atheism with all its consequences becomes the moulding force of the political and social order'.[47]

The transcendental is experienced less and less as a meaningful reality,[48] while the conviction that God is irrelevant becomes more and more entrenched. Our scientifically-defined world view 'no longer requires the concept, the "hypothesis", of God . . . self-help and organized progress

44. Marion Gräfin Dönhoff, 'Leben ohne Glauben'.

45. Konrad Lorenz, *Civilized Man's Eight Deadly Sins*, pp.63–4.

46. e.g. the well-known French neurophysiologist Paul Chauchard who wants to determine and define the essential nature of man – how it corresponds to the psychobiological nature of human life, and who derives moral standards from biological data: 'La nouvelle biologie humaine n'est plus seulement descriptive, mais tend à être *normative*, c'est-à-dire à définir dans toutes les conduites humaines ce qui est humain, conforme à la nature psychobiologique de l'être humain, ou plutôt ce qui est humanisant va dans le sens de l'épanouissement des possibilités de cette nature, et ce qui est inhumain, déshumanisant.' (*Biologie et Morale*, p.22.) Many representatives of other human sciences also believe that anything which they cannot investigate by scientific methods is irrelevant or non-existent.

47. Hugo Staudinger, 'Atheismus als politisches Problem', p.10. Hermann Boventer's essay 'Gott, Demokratie und politische Bildung. Sind Grundwerte verfassungswidrig?' (God, Democracy and Political Education. Are Basic Values Unconstitutional?) in *Aus Politik und Zeitgeschichte* (From Politics and Contemporary History), Supplement 33–34/80 to the weekly magazine *Das Parlament* of 16.8.1980, which deals with methodological atheism, and Christian Graf von Krockow's assertion that democratic politics is only possible within the context of disbelief ('Ethik und Politik', in R. v. Voss, *Ethik und Politik*, Cologne 1980), together with von Krockow's reply ('Glaube, Demokratie und Politische Bildung', in *Aus Politik und Zeitgeschichte*, Supplement 33–34/80, pp.81ff.) could not, on account of printing deadlines, be taken into consideration. The reader is referred to these highly interesting and readable articles which lead right to the heart of the discussion on fundamental values.

48. Those who still think it has some relevance 'find themselves in the status of a minority'. (Peter Berger, *A Rumor of Angels*, p. 7.)

appear to be more reliable guarantees of a tolerable future than religious practices'. [49] Even to question whether God exists or not seems to be outdated, just as Auguste Comte had already prophesied in the last century: 'God will vanish without even leaving the trace of a question behind Him.' [50]

Our century has been a century without God. Jean Améry arrives at this justifiable verdict by pointing out that the great philosophers of our time, from Husserl to Sartre, from Carnap to Heidegger, and most writers of significance, such as Proust, Joyce, Mann and Beckett, 'wanted nothing to do with God': 'The great intellectual movements which characterize this century are devoid of religious faith.' [51] Améry aptly illustrates the secularization of central Christian ideas through the spirit of modernism by considering such things as eschatology and the concept of 'soul': 'Psychoanalysis has destroyed the myth of the soul and into its place has stepped the psyche, [52] which, being anchored in a material foundation, has itself become a purely physical phenomenon. Marxism, the intellectual pillar of modernism, has demythologized and secularized eschatology and millennial expectation. It is not God, an unknown quantity about which there is nothing to say, who has a hand in history, but rather man: a known quantity.' [53]

It is not simply the Exodus from the Church [54] that symptomizes the decay of Christendom; it is rather the loss of religious consciousness and the tearing down of tradition. In a book about an opinion poll sponsored by the United Synod of the bishoprics of West Germany, Gerhard Schmidtchen, a sociologist of religion, spoke of a silent process 'whose significance is not to be found in the decline in Church membership – however important this evidence may be – but in an analysis of the structures of consciousness. Here in these structures, in what people think and feel, is the entire monstrosity of their existence; this is the scene of the religious drama in which the Church finds itself.' [55] 'To a

49. Max Seckler, 'Kommt der christliche Glaube ohne Gott aus?', p.182.
50. Quoted from Karl Lehmann, 'Vom Sinn der christlichen Existenz zwischen Enthusiasmus und Institution', p.47.
51. 'Provokationen des Atheismus', p.215.
52. cf. also Wilhelm J. Revers, 'Die szientistische Einäugigkeit des modernen Realitätsbewußtseins'.
53. Jean Améry, 'Provokationen des Atheismus', p.215.
54. In 1974 in West Germany 83,277 Catholics and 210,000 Protestants resigned from church membership. (*Süddeutsche Zeitung*, 15.10.1975.) The extent to which church membership has fallen in many countries is shown in a newspaper article according to which the Swedish archbishop Ingmar Ström found the emptiness in the churches of Stockholm as oppressive as the atmosphere of a mausoleum. He therefore advised the state church to sell the houses of God or transform them into dance-halls, exhibition rooms, concert halls or swimming baths. The bishop complains that in the main services on Sundays the congregation often consists of no more than the vicar's wife and a few inhabitants of the neighbouring old-age home – a very discouraging situation for both the minister and the organist. (*Süddeutsche Zeitung*, 16.3.1982.)
55. 'Befragte Katholiken – Zur Zukunft von Glaube und Kirche', p.164. According to a survey

colossal extent' modern man is in the process of 'spiritually abandoning the shelter of traditional ties. He has set out once again to experiment on himself and to probe the potentialities that lie within him, without knowing whether they are constructive or destructive.'[56] In this way, tradition, or the handing down of belief, is broken. In most families religious belief is no longer discussed. As the previously-mentioned experiment by the theologian Hahn impressively demonstrates, the enfeebled faith of today's parents is no longer adequate for instilling a religious consciousness into their children. And ecclesiastical 'confirmation', which is intended to strengthen the young person in his belief, mostly leads to his withdrawal from the Church: the 'salutatory benediction' becomes a 'valedictory blessing'.

Of course we can still find nowadays living witnesses of religious revival and genuine piety, and such will always exist. Those who do not want to admit that belief in God is dying out will always cling to such examples and find comfort in them. But these are now only islands of religious faith in the ocean of a godless world, oases of transcendence upon which the desert of unbelief is continually encroaching.[57] As Paul Tillich observed, modern man in fact retains 'only the remnants of a world-view, or even none at all'[58] and he is 'no longer affected by the Christian message'.[59] H.-J. Schoeps speaks of a 'post-Christian world situation' in which even interest in polemical argument between religionists and their critics has died out.[60] Active ungodliness 'has been supplanted by a paralysing godlessness and indifference'.[61] Modern society has put utopia in the place of religion – 'utopia not as a transcendental ideal, but one to be realized through history (progress, rationality, science) with the nutrients of technology and the midwifery of revolution'.[62]

Secular Salvation

Into the vacuum which the gradually-dying Christianity leaves behind, a new secular form of religiosity is infiltrating: a salvationist belief of a socialistic kind. This modern, worldly religion can be traced back to the teachings of eighteenth-century French philosophers who were convinced that their ideas were 'destined to supplant the Christian dispensation,

conducted by the Institute for Market and Social Research, Traunstein, and sponsored by the Catholic News Agency, only one in three inhabitants of West Germany can, according to the criteria laid down by the Churches, be considered a Christian. (*Süddeutsche Zeitung*, 23.12.1979.)

56. Gottlieb Hild und Helmut Aichelin, 'Staat–Kirche–Gesellschaft', p.15.
57. Peter Berger speaks of islands of immunity from the spirit of modernism 'especially in geographical or social areas that are relatively sheltered from modern mass communications'. (*A Rumor of Angels*, p.17.)
58. Quoted in Heinz Zahrnt, *The Question of God*, p.298.
59. loc. cit.
60. *Jüdisch–christliches Religionsgespräch*, p.54.
61. H.-R. Müller-Schwefe, *Atheismus*, p.30.
62. Daniel Bell, *The Cultural Contradictions of Capitalism*, p.28.

undo the evil religion had engendered (or according to some make good the pledge given but unfulfilled by religion), and as it were start history upon its real course'.[63] They considered it their mission to rescue man from his self-contempt and mistaken belief that he is incapable of ever attaining salvation by his own exertions. Triumphantly they asserted that man had no need of a higher authority to subdue his natural drives, because they claimed to have made the revolutionary discovery 'that social integration was dependent on the degree of individual self-expression, and man's freedom was commensurate with the advance of social cohesion. For individual frustration was the root cause of all social disorder, and social incoherence the reason for personal maladjustment.'[64] The aim was to tear down the old religious system, Christendom, and to lay waste the foundations of the 'ancient palace of imposture, founded one thousand seven hundred and seventy-five years ago'[65]: 'The axe is laid to the root of the tree.'[66]

These eighteenth-century philosophers never doubted 'that they were preaching a new religion'.[67] Spurred on by the French Revolution which brought the masses into contact with the abstract ideas of these few philosophers, this secular religion changed from primarily an ethical theory 'into a social and economic doctrine, based on ethical premises. The postulate of salvation . . . came to signify to the masses stirred by the Revolution a message of social salvation before all.' The ideology of the rising middle class was 'transformed into that of the proletariat'.[68] Whereas the driving force of the Chiliastic sects was the Word of God and the hope of direct, non-institutional salvation, by contrast 'modern Messianism has always aimed at a revolution in society as a whole'.[69] Its point of reference is 'man's reason and will, and its aim happiness on earth, achieved by a social transformation. The point of reference is temporal, but the claims are absolute.'[70]

Prominent in this chain of prophets of the Enlightenment is Karl Marx.[71]

63. J. L. Talmon, *Political Messianism*, p.506.
64. ibid.
65. Voltaire, letter dated 3rd August 1775 to Frederick II, King of Prussia. *Letters of Voltaire and Frederick the Great*, p.365.
66. Frederick the Great to Voltaire, letter dated 5th May 1767, op. cit., p.293.
67. J. L. Talmon, *The Origins of Totalitarian Democracy*, p.21. Cf. also Jean Servier, *Histoire de l'Utopie*.
68. J. L. Talmon, *The Origins of Totalitarian Democracy*, pp.5,6.
69. ibid. p.9.
70. ibid. p.10.
71. H. Schelsky regards the replacement of transcendental, redemptive religion by the new social religion as a major breach in world history. He remarks sarcastically that 'in the birth and evolution of the new social religion of salvation we find ourselves, as it were, in the second or third centuries *post Marxum natum*, and thus Hegel and the Enlightenment occupy a position analogous to that of John the Baptist or the other prophets'. (*Die Arbeit tun die anderen*, p.100.)

He has reduced the entire history of mankind to 'an economic process moving toward a final world revolution'.[72] His aim is profoundly messianic: he wishes to create the liberated society and the liberated man. The 'Realm of Necessity' is to be replaced by a 'Realm of Freedom': a 'Kingdom of God' without God. The germ of the new man is the proletarian, and in the proletariat Marx sees 'the world-historical instrument for achieving the eschatological aim of all history by a world revolution. The proletariat is the chosen people of historical materialism.'[73]

The striking parallels between the Jewish–Christian belief in salvation and this political messianism are numerous and take on many forms. There is the class consisting of the children of darkness and that of the children of light; there is the Last Judgement, the final crisis of the bourgeois capitalistic world, and the root evil of this aeon, namely the exploitation which corrupts man's moral and spiritual capacities.[74] The *Communist Manifesto*, as Löwith aptly puts it, is primarily a 'prophetic document, a judgement, and a call to action and not at all a purely scientific statement based on the empirical evidence of tangible facts'.[75] This manifesto holds fast to the main feature of religious faith: 'to the "assurance of things to be hoped for"'.[76]

Further parallels: that the ultimate struggle between the bourgeoisie and the proletariat corresponds to the ultimate struggle between Christ and Antichrist, that the universal salvation of the oppressed class corresponds to 'the religious pattern of Cross and Resurrection, that the ultimate transformation of the realm of necessity into a realm of freedom corresponds to the transformation of the *civitas Terrena* into a *civitas Dei*, and that the whole process of history as outlined in the *Communist Manifesto* corresponds to the general scheme of the Jewish–Christian interpretation of history as a providential advance toward a final goal'. Historical materialism is 'a history of fulfilment and salvation in terms of social economy', the Communist creed 'a pseudo-morphosis of Jewish–Christian messianism'.[77] Modern Marxist philosophers have expressed the belief that most people are incapable by their own intelligence of recognizing what is true and good, and that the living conditions of late capitalism have spoilt and deformed people to the extent where they can no longer see what is good for them. These philosophers are therefore convinced that the masses who live helplessly in spiritual darkness need to be governed by an élite avant-garde – a secular and political priesthood – in order 'to find their way from false to true consciousness, from their immediate to their real

72. Karl Löwith, *Meaning in History*, p.33.
73. ibid. p.37.
74. More details in Löwith, *Meaning in History*, pp.42–51.
75. ibid. p.43.
76. ibid. p.44; cf. in this connection Heb. 11:1.
77. Karl Löwith, *Meaning in History*, pp.44ff.

interest'.[78] Even this belief is nothing other than the secularization of the Christian concept 'of the state of sin in which the powers of discernment are clouded and the will is weakened, of the need for redemption, and of the mediation of salvation through the priests of the true teachings'.[79] Talmon's verdict is: 'The distinctive appeal of political Messianism . . . lies . . . in its having become a religion.'[80]

Clothed in the mantle of science, this new social religion is in the process of supplanting the old transcendental, saving religions. The promise of salvation in a world-to-come is being replaced by a promise which concerns this world, namely, the promise of a 'social order of harmony and justice, of equality and personal fulfilment. In other words, heavenly socialism has assumed the position previously occupied by the Christian promise of salvation in the life hereafter.'[81] Whereas Christianity promised that in the world-to-come men would be redeemed from the guilt of sin, and freed from earthly anxiety and suffering, the 'social religion' promises an ultimate condition of society 'in which fear, pain, violence, cruel blows of fate, degradation, abuse, poverty, sickness and tyranny no longer exist or occur (in the process of achieving this end, the fact of unavoidable death is systematically eradicated)'.[82] Teachings concerning 'transcendence in the hereafter' and the 'salvation of the soul' 'are reversed to "transcendence in this world"', that is to say, perfection of the individual and society in the foreseeable future'.[83] In this community of belief the word 'salvation' is replaced by the word 'revolution', representing 'a secularized version of "Judgement Day" on which and thereafter man is saved'.[84]

This social religion of salvation, as Talmon defines it, is 'a complex mixture of ideas, mystical faith, volition, passion, emotion, Messianic hope and error';[85] and it is precisely these ingredients which make it attractive because, as Löwith so aptly puts it,[86] the mere presentation of facts and scientific proofs does nothing to arouse the enthusiasm of the masses. The

---

78. Herbert Marcuse, *One-Dimensional Man*, p.xiii.
79. Wolfgang Brezinka, *Erziehung und Kulturrevolution*, p.117.
80. *The Origins of Totalitarian Democracy*, p.254. Concerning the morphological similarity between Christianity and Marxism, the reader is also referred to David Martin, 'Marxism: Functional Equivalent of Religion?' in *The Dilemmas of Contemporary Religion*, pp.79ff. Martin writes, 'It is a paradox that a system which claimed that the beginning of all criticism was the criticism of religion should have ended up with a form of religion which was the end of all criticism . . . The manipulators of this system are intellectuals who have transformed themselves into priests.' (pp.88–9.)
81. Helmut Schelsky, *Die Arbeit tun die anderen*, p.53. Heinrich Heine celebrates this here-and-now religion of salvation: 'I will write you a new, a sweeter song;/You shall sing it without a quaver;/We will build the kingdom of heaven on earth – /'Tis a better plan and a braver./ . . ./And angels and sparrows may have our share/Of the vague delights of heaven.' ('Germany. Romancero', 1844, *The Poetical Prose Works of Heinrich Heine*, Vol.III, pp.6–7.)
82. Helmut Schelsky, *Die Arbeit tun die anderen*, p.102.
83. ibid. p.220.
84. ibid. p.183.
85. *The Origins of Totalitarian Democracy*, pp.168–9.
86. *Meaning in History*, pp.44–5.

essential character of this political Messianism, which has been the determining factor of history for the last 150 years, is 'faith in a single and final
cause of and answer to all evils the world over; the belief that the secret has
at last been found, that humanity is heading in an irresistible march for
some denouement, a violent break-through to a preordained, perfect and
ultimate scheme of things'. [87]

Schelsky has provided a thorough description of this new religion of
social salvation, which has also found a footing in Western industrial
countries and has infiltrated and undermined contemporary institutions.
He has presented a shrewd analysis of its demands for power and its complex machinery of influence. His analysis clearly shows how the re-
interpretation of Christian teachings and the promise of a social paradise
through the 'gratifying elimination of all life's burdens', [88] under the ban-
ners of 'emancipation' and 'revolution', are quenching the thirst of the
modern, transcendentally-homeless individual. The sense of purpose once
provided by religion has been replaced by a sociological interpretation of
existence. The individual, who now sees himself merely as a 'social being'
and no longer as one created by God, is only concerned with his social
salvation, while the question of the soul and its salvation no longer has any
relevance for him. The modern spirit 'of unrestricted worldliness, of labor,
business, and acquisitiveness' is indifferent to the notion of salvation in a
future world and despises every form of spiritual discipline. [89] For in the
consciousness of modern secularism man and the world have 'their basis,
their centre, their purpose and meaning in themselves; relationship to a
transcendent reality does not exist'. [90]

The discarding of belief in personal salvation after death in favour of a
programme for securing happiness in this world led to far-reaching changes
in the structure of the modern state. The state became the 'organizer of
secular religious energy', [91] the champion of progress and guarantor of personal happiness: 'As the worldly counterpart of the Church, the state is
required to fulfil social demands, satisfy emotional desires and provide for
happiness. This leads to permanent overstrain which is magnified by the
expectation that everything seems possible, not only in the field of science
and technology but in that of society and politics as well.' [92] Debased to a
technical apparatus for administering services, the state becomes more
vulnerable to crisis: 'For every small failure, every disappointed expectation
and every forfeiture of welfare is regarded as a catastrophe beyond all com-

87. *The Origins of Totalitarian Democracy*, p.170.
88. Helmut Schelsky, *Die Arbeit tun die anderen*, p.193.
89. cf. Karl Löwith, *Meaning in History*, p.29.
90. Alfons Auer, *Autonome Moral und christlicher Glaube*, p.21.
91. Reiner Schmidt, 'Der geforderte Staat', p.161.
92. ibid. p.162.

pensation.'[93] Here we see how the breakdown of religion 'aggravates the instability of political systems' and how the state, 'as the bearer of and substitute for spiritualized values' becomes 'a hypersensitive structure'.[94] The ungovernability of Western industrial nations[95] often complained about has its roots in this fact.

The Crisis in Theology

The acuteness of the crisis in religion has its basis in the crisis into which theology has been plunged. The loss of ground which religion outwardly suffers is accompanied by a loss of identity which threatens religious faith from within. Doubt has moved in, the old truths and certainties have been shaken. What was for centuries regarded as constant and immovable is questioned and challenged. The process of disintegration, 'from which Christianity is not exempted', is rooted in the fact 'that the reality from which Christianity originates, and to which it continually refers, has become questionable'.[96] Even the central themes of the Bible and Church doctrine such as God, Christ, Church and Revelation 'have been called into question' amongst theologians and laymen alike.[97]

As pointed out elsewhere,[98] Christianity, since the Reformation, has split itself into an ever-growing number of separate and mutually-exclusive schools of thought, culminating in present-day theological pluralism in which, even in fundamental questions of belief, there is no common denominator left. Hermann Diem, Professor of Theology at the University of Tübingen, considers that among Protestant university theologians 'there is hardly any common ground on which the contestants can reach any understanding'.[99] The debate within Protestantism rages on; one speaks of the 'end of theology'.[100] This crisis cuts across all the traditional religious subdivisions of Western culture,[101] although it has afflicted Protestantism the longest. With Schleiermacher's famous publication in 1799, entitled *On Religion; Speeches to its Cultured Despisers*, began the process of adaptation with concessions to an ever-growing number of 'cultured despisers', that is, to 'the liberal-minded', the scientists and the divergent

---

93. ibid. p.161.
94. ibid. p.162. In the Lawḥ-i-Dunyā, Bahá'u'lláh revealed: 'Were man to strictly observe that which the Pen of the Most High hath revealed . . . they could then well afford to dispense with the regulations which prevail in the world.' (*Tablets*, p.90.)
95. In this connection: Paul Noack, *Ist die Demokratie noch regierbar?* (Is Democracy still Governable?), Munich 1980; W. Hennis, *Regierbarkeit, Studien zu ihrer Problematisierung* (Govern-ability: A Study of its Problems), Stuttgart 1977.
96. Max Seckler, 'Kommt der christliche Glaube ohne Gott aus?', p.185.
97. Paul Tillich, quoted from H. Zahrnt, *The Question of God*, p.299 with reference.
98. U. Schaefer, *The Light Shineth in Darkness*, pp.88ff. and ibid. n.224, p.79.
99. *Dogmatics*, author's Foreword.
100. Gerhard Petry, 'Das Ende der Theologie?', p.17.
101. Peter Berger, *A Rumor of Angels*, p.11.

schools of thought.[102] There was also a shift of emphasis away from the notion of life after death. Liberal theology alone, which dominated Christendom from the nineteenth century to the First World War, assisted the drastic eradication of the transcendental content from the Christian message. In his neo-orthodoxy, Karl Barth appealed for a return to the unconditional religious faith characteristic of the Reformation, a faith based solely on revelation and not on reason and experience, but this was an intermezzo which merely interrupted but did not arrest the process of secularization. Paul Tillich and Rudolf Bultmann, who together with Karl Barth make up the great trio of distinguished twentieth-century Protestant theologians, continued the liberal tradition and regarded the 'Correlation', that is, the harmonizing of Christian doctrine with philosophy, as the prime task of theology in making the Christian message acceptable to modern man.

The pains taken to adapt the Christian message to the spirit of the age and to integrate belief into a century hostile towards religion is the outcome of the correct realization that Christianity, within its historically-evolved, dogmatic and legal framework, has ceased to be a living force. As the Word of God made flesh, religion is essentially dynamic and not static, and thus adaptation to altered conditions is proper and necessary. But this adaptation becomes dangerous when relentlessly pursued in the hope of recovering lost ground, when pursued with the intention of 'jumping on the last train leaving the ghetto of religious belief'.[103] If prevailing trends of thought are constantly assimilated and legitimatized as binding truths, then the danger of losing identity becomes acute. Then religion gradually becomes an empty formula of indefinite meaning. Peter Berger speaks of the 'curious vulnerability' of Protestant theologians to the spirit of the age and describes the result as 'a profound erosion of the traditional religious contents, in extreme cases to the point where nothing is left but hollow rhetoric. Of late it seems more and more as if the extreme has become the norm[104] . . . it is as if the believer or theologian were standing in a landscape of smoldering ruins.'[105]

Political Theology

The extent to which Christianity has compromised with the world and the degree to which theologians have grasped the 'coat-tails of progress'[106] and

---

102. cf. Berger, op.cit., p.12.
103. Friedrich Tenbruck, 'Ethos und Religion in einer zukünftigen Gesellschaft', p.42.
104. Peter Berger, *A Rumor of Angels*, p.12.
105. ibid. p.11.
106. Nikolaus Lobkowicz, 'Vom Esel, der aufs Eis ging und dem Christen, der es ihm nachmacht' (Concerning the Donkey Who Went on to the Ice and the Christian Who Did the Same), *Am Ende aller Religion?*, p.15.

borne Christianity to its grave are manifest in the emergence of 'political theology', 'the theology of revolution', 'the theology of freedom' and, particularly in German-speaking and Anglo-Saxon countries, 'God-is-dead theology'.

For centuries Christianity, especially the Protestant form, regarded itself as 'the straight path' to God. The soul thirsting for grace and yearning for liberation from the guilt of sin was the main theme of the Church's teachings. Christianity was a religion of intimate, private and personal concern – a religion which confined itself to the individual in his relationship with God.[107] Christianity had few or no intentions regarding society. In the face of this Christian salvationary individualism with its remarkable blindness to social realities and the claims of a humane society, Karl Marx developed his critique of religion, namely, that religion condemned the individual to passivity and resignation; it comforted him with promises of a better life hereafter and thus paralysed his determination to take his fate into his own hands; it was therefore the opium of the people. Understandable as his verdict was, it is nevertheless false: on the basis of a particular development in Christianity Marx drew an *a priori* conclusion about the nature of religion as a whole.

Under the influence of Marxist principles a change has taken place in Protestant and Catholic theology during the last decades. 'The future' as a decisive component of Christian belief was rediscovered; the horizontal dimension was taken into consideration. In opposition to Luther's teaching of the two kingdoms, the Protestant theologian Jürgen Moltmann, by building up the eschatological structure of Jesus' message, arrives at a theology which incorporates political aspects. This sentence of his is reminiscent of Karl Marx: 'The theologian is not concerned merely to supply a different interpretation of the world, of history and of human nature, but to transform them in expectation of a divine transformation.'[108]

In the 'political theology' which he himself developed, the Catholic theologian Johann Baptist Metz, using the methods of modern hermeneutics, has attempted to disclose the socio-political content of the Gospel message and 'to formulate the eschatological message under the conditions of the present situation of society'.[109] Observing that the complete abandonment of the world to secular powers is diametrically opposed to the inward quality of faith, Metz wishes to see Christians placing greater emphasis on their duties towards the world.[110] Hans Maier raises the objec-

107. more details on pp.127ff.
108. *Theology of Hope*, p.84; cf. also Moltmann, 'Die Zukunft als neues Paradigma der Transzendenz' (The Future as a Paradigm of Transcendence), *Internationaler Dialog*, Zeitschrift 2, 1969, pp.2ff.
109. *Theology of the World*, pp.107,111.
110. Literature: J. B. Metz, 'The Church and the World in the Light of a "Political Theology"',

tion that in this respect the 'current Marxist interpretations, uncritically adopted' and the idea of 'Karl Marx as the new Aristotle of theology' are being put on a pedestal and bowed down to.[111] The exponents of 'political theology' apparently in no way deny the substance of this accusation. Despite the warnings of Scripture,[112] E. Höflich quite openly asks whether the 'philosophical ideas' of Karl Marx should serve not only as discussion material for the dialogue between Christians and Marxists, but also 'as medicine for the therapeutic rejuvenation of the Church'. In this way Höflich hopes for 'a regeneration of the teachings and social functions of the Church'.[113]

Political theology is a matter of considerable dispute within the Church.[114] Stigmatized by conservative Christians as 'devastation of the Lord's Vineyard', political theology is heading for the equating of eschatology with historical revolution.[115] This is the more 'moderate version' of the 'theology of revolution'[116] or the 'theology of liberation',[117] which emerged against the social background of exploitation and oppression in the feudal structures of Latin American countries. The brutal way in which freedom, rights and human dignity have been trampled on in many countries has led to the new conviction – a complete departure from traditional theology – that redemption is no longer to be sought primarily in the forgiveness of sins, but in the transformation of the world we live in. Salvation is no longer a goal for the hereafter but rather a political objective in the here-and-now. The theoretical instrument of the 'theology of revolution' is Marxist social analysis, its method is the radical elimination of the existing system of property ownership, its goal is the 'new man', the new classless society. Class war is the 'concrete form of love'

Theology of the World; H. Peukert (ed), 'Diskussion zur politischen Theologie'; Hans Maier, 'Kritik der politischen Theologie'; J. B. Metz, *Jenseits bürgerlicher Religion. Reden über die Zukunft des Christentums* (Beyond Bourgeois Religion. Essays on the Future of Christianity), Munich 1980.

111. 'Kritik der politischen Theologie', pp.34 and 53.

112. Matt. 6:24; 2 Cor. 6:14–16.

113. J. B. Metz and E. Höflich, 'Karl Marx für die Kirche. Eine Antwort auf Hans Maiers Polemik gegen die politische Theologie'.

114. Hans Maier's article 'Kritik der politischen Theologie' and J. B. Metz's replies ('Politische Theologie', *Stimmen der Zeit*, Vol.134, Freiburg 1969, pp.289ff; 'Erlösung und Emanzipation', *Stimmen der Zeit*, Vol.191, 1973, pp.171ff) provide a background to the discussion.

115. For Metz 'love' is a 'socio-critical dynamism' which, under certain circumstances, could even demand 'actions of a revolutionary violence' (*Theology of the World*, pp.119 and 120). See also Hans Maier, op.cit., p.80.

116. Hans Maier, op.cit., p.65.

117. Literature: Trutz R. Rendtorff and H. E. Tödt, *Theologie der Revolution*; H.-E. Bahr (ed), *Weltfrieden und Revolution. Neun politisch-theologische Analysen* (World Peace and Revolution. Nine polito-theological Analyses), Hamburg 1968; E. Feil and R. Weht (ed), *Diskussion zur 'Theologie der Revolution'* (Discussion of the 'Theology of Revolution'), Munich, Mainz 1969; R. Shaull and C. Oglesby, *Containment and Change*; Norbert Greinacher, *Die Kirche der Armen. Zur Theologie der Befreiung* (The Church of the Poor. The Theology of Liberation), Munich, Zürich 1980.

by which the whole of mankind will be redeemed. Revolution is the only way to change society for the better. According to this theology, therefore, the participation of the Christian in political struggle is prescribed. Redemption is henceforth something qualitatively different: those who change the world, or who fight against poverty and exploitation, are taking part in the work of redemption. The American theologian Shaull describes it as follows: 'In the course of human history God assumed human form and called us to follow Him, if we wish to be the salt of the earth (Matt. 5:13–14). In this context the Christian is called to take part in the revolution as it develops. Only at the centre of it can we observe what God is doing, understand what form the fight for humanization is taking and serve as agents of the atonement.'[118] Many theologians are convinced that if Jesus came again, he would carry a rifle.

Religion does indeed have a responsibility for this world, for the here-and-now and the structure of society. However, the realization that this responsibility was shamefully neglected for centuries and that religion has a horizontal as well as a vertical dimension is leading to widespread assimilation and approval of Marxist aims and principles, and consequently the degradation of the Gospel Message to a set of political instructions. The same religion, which for centuries confined itself to individual soul saving, is now reducing its focus to the here-and-now, to matters of purely secular concern; religion has become an instrument of politics. This development threatens to swing religion over to the other extreme: the notion of life hereafter has been displaced by the concept of this world and its future development. So strong is the emphasis on 'forward transcendence' (Ernst Bloch) that upward transcendence is getting forgotten. Theology is reduced to anthropology and social theory; Jesus is turned into a social revolutionary, an opponent of the Establishment; His Message regarded as a social gospel for this earthly life alone; and the 'Exodus' story interpreted as a classic model in the history of social liberation. At the same time, Marx and Freud are elevated to the rank of saints.[119]

The Glad Tidings have become the Social Message. Through the Christian theologians, who were among the most enthusiastic followers of the social salvation teachings as initially presented, the theology of redemption has been turned into a theory of social salvation which is confined to the here-and-now. As Schelsky points out, the extent to which the philosophy of emancipation and social critique has been adopted is shown by the fact that in both denominations, Catholicism and Protestantism, this new 'theology of the world' has absorbed 'the entire argumentation potential of the pseudo-salvationary, pseudo-religious sociology – it is

---

118. 'Revolution in theologischer Perspektive', in Rendtorff and Tödt, op. cit. pp.117ff.
119. Regarding the re-interpretation of the Buddha and of Muḥammad as social revolutionaries, cf.

swarming with expressions such as emancipation, maturity, manipulation, terror, structural violence, exploitation, repression, frustration and, over and over again, criticism, criticism, criticism'.[120]

This adoption of secular theories and their assimilation into the body of Christian teachings, this violent synthesis of disparate substances has direct, practical effects: hell-fire sermons aimed at drawing attention to individual guilt have given way to indictments of society in order to expose sources of social and political guilt. Clergymen who used to care for souls have now turned into social preachers and social engineers. The frivolous unconcern with which people are now throwing off the ballast of a centuries-old, evolved and established theology and adopting the principles of an atheistic and materialistic doctrine makes it difficult to resist a sarcastic comment: 'One recognizes them by their protruding tongues and their nagging cry of "We too, we too!"'

Cardinal König, Archbishop of Vienna, has made a critical study of this development[121] and he points out that 'a belief totally divest of mystery' cannot satisfy man's primal religious needs. Nevertheless, it is obvious that he regards this development as a fashionable trend within the Church or a transitory condition in the pendular swing between emotive faith and rational belief. The sociologist Schelsky shows a more penetrating insight when he writes: 'The waters of Christianity are not surging back and forth like the tide, rather they are ebbing away altogether.'[122] In the Great Adoption of the social philosophy of salvation and the theory of life put forward by the sociologists, he sees the danger of the Church sinking to the level of a 'sect': 'To a sect whose motivation is specifically Christian and which possesses conventional Christian terminology, but still only a sect within the matrix of a general, humanitarian social religion . . . by which it will in the course of time be absorbed.'[123]

Christian Atheism

In the footsteps of the philosophers, the theologians too are now proclaiming the death of God. Herbert Braun, for example, considers that God is now nothing more than a mere cipher for 'love-thy-neighbour'. In the First Epistle of John it is stated that 'God is love'; for Braun the statement is also true when reversed: 'Love – that is God.' In other words: 'Man as man, man with his brotherly love, implies God.'[124] In an essay

Peter Gerlitz, *Die Religionen und die neue Moral*, p.135.
  120. *Die Arbeit tun die anderen*, p.429.
  121. 'Für ein Lächeln von Marx', *Deutsche Zeitung* of 30.8.1974.
  122. *Die Arbeit tun die anderen*, p.432.
  123. Schelsky, p.435. Concerning the secularization of Catholic moral theology, cf. the presentation on pp.224ff.
  124. *Gesammelte Studien zum neuen Testament und seiner Umwelt*, p.325.

('Believing in God Atheistically') Dorothee Sölle proposes a form of religious belief which 'will perhaps have to relinquish the name of God', a belief which she regards as 'a lifestyle which has no need of supernatural, unearthly concepts of a heavenly Being'.[125] For the Hamburg pastor Paul Schulz (in the meantime he has been removed from office) God is 'a projection of human thought'. When man speaks of God 'he is really speaking of himself'.[126] God as an active entity in heaven directing the affairs of man in this world does not exist. God is the 'principle of love'. He does not exist, he happens: 'Wherever men come together in love, God happens in this process of loving.'[127] For Schulz, being a Christian does not necessarily mean being religious. Whereas in the past it was the task of religion to render transcendental reality comprehensible to man with the aid of mythical and symbolic illustration, nowadays science supplies the diagrams and formulae which enable us to understand reality. In the evolution of human consciousness, science, with its qualitatively different methods, is the continuation of religion and theology. Accordingly the Bible is 'not the Word from God, but the Word to God'.[128] It follows that death is only 'something quite natural'. What happens 'in human dying is nothing other than what happens during the perpetual disintegration of all natural phenomena. Life is before death.'[129] Schulz's view is also that 'after death man disintegrates, not only as body, but also as consciousness'.[130] This then is the end of orthodox Christian belief: all paths lead to immanentism. Thomas Altizer, a prominent American representative of the God-is-dead theology, calls for the solemn admission 'that the death of God is a historical event, that God has died in our cosmos, in our history, in our existence'.[131] Summing up, Berger, a sociologist of religion, says: 'the self-liquidation of the theological enterprise is undertaken with an enthusiasm that verges on the bizarre, culminating in the reduction to absurdity of the "God-is-dead theology" and "Christian atheism".'[132]

For a long time the Roman Catholic Church resisted the spirit of the age. In the *Syllabus of Errors* (1864) Pope Pius IX (and in the decree *Lamentabili* and the encyclicals *Pascendi* (1907) and *Humani generis*

---

125. The confirmed atheist Jean Améry finds outrageous this assimilation of Marxist ideas into Christian theology; he dismisses, for example, the current proposal that the Marxist philosopher Ernst Bloch is the greatest theologian of our time as an 'empty slogan', and speaks of the 'self-secularization of Christianity'. (*Provokationen des Atheismus*, pp.212ff.) Helmut Gollwitzer raises the objection that 'It is a case of resolving theology into humanism which differs from other forms of humanism only in its different philosophical basis and terminology'. (*The Existence of God as Confessed by Faith*, p.50.)
126. This way of putting it could have been derived from Ludwig Feuerbach.
127. *Ist Gott eine mathematische Formel?*, p.32.
128. ibid. p.143.
129. ibid. p.236.
130. ibid. p.233.
131. Thomas J. Altizer and William Hamilton, *Radical Theology and the Death of God*, p.26.
132. *A Rumor of Angels*, p.14.

(1950) the Popes Pius X and Pius XII) defiantly opposed it. Until the Second Vatican Council, the Church was able to suppress the rise of modernistic tendencies to adaptation. But since the Council, not even the rock of the Roman Church has been able to hold back the rising tide of change. The struggle for pluralism has flared up and the liquidation of once-sacrosanct structures begun.[133] Berger reports announcements from intellectual Catholic circles in recent times that are 'of a fearful modernity sufficient to put the most "radical" Protestant to shame'.[134] At the 1975 French Bishops' Conference in Lourdes it became apparent that 'it is not merely the administrative framework, the hierarchical discipline and liturgical traditions that are questioned by young priests nowadays,[135] but even religious belief itself. The extent to which the latter has been shaken to its foundations is shown in an essay by the Dominican father, Anselm Hertz,[136] in which he declares the 'ancient Christian form' of religion to be doomed to destruction. According to Hertz we can no longer pray to a 'Saving God', a Creator and Ruler of the World, because we know only too well that it is not God but the laws of nature, and man himself, that determine the multifarious occurrences of this world. Religion, as a public and private unifying force within society and between the individual and God, is dead; all that is left to man in his search for the meaning of existence is the possibility, indeed the responsibility, 'of transcending himself'.[137] Nikolaus Lobkowicz, a lecturer in political science and philosophy at the University of Munich, in a debate with Father Hertz, castigated the

133. As is shown by the teaching ban imposed on the theologians Küng, Halbfas, Holl, Denzler and others on the one hand and the protest made by the conservative Archbishop Lefebvre against the modernistic innovations of the Second Vatican Council on the other. The conflicts are becoming severer and more polemical. The *missio canonica* was withdrawn from Horst Hermann, a lecturer in church law at the University of Münster, for publishing two works – *Ehe und Recht* (Marriage and Law) in 1972 and *Ein unmoralisches Verhältnis* (An Immoral Relationship) in 1974 – without first obtaining episcopal imprimatur, for describing the Catholic Church as 'a society of wolves' and 'a system of injustice' and for having accused the Church of 'deprivation of Biblical pastoral care' as well as 'perversion under a Christian veneer'. Rudolf Krämer-Badoni scathingly criticizes the 'liberalistic twaddle' of the Second Vatican Council, while describing Pope Paul VI as an 'intellectual mediocrity' and labelling him a 'New Year's Speech Maker'. (*Revolution in der Kirche. Lefebvre und Rom* (Revolution in the Church, Lefebvre and Rome), Berlin, München 1980.) In an interview with the magazine *Der Spiegel*, Norbert Greinacher, a Catholic theologian at the University of Tübingen, expressed his doubts whether Jesus would be a member of the Catholic Church, were he to be alive today. In view of the threat to the official Church presented by internal criticism, Cardinal Joseph Höffner admitted to the full assembly of the German Bishops' Conference in Fulda in September 1982, that he was fully aware that many Catholics nowadays identified only partly with the Church. He commented: 'Lack of full commitment to the teachings on belief and morals will lead ultimately to schism.' (*Rhein-Neckar-Zeitung* of 29.9.1982.)

134. *A Rumor of Angels*, p.17. He quotes the English sociologist of religion David Martin: 'But for those only lately inured to clear and distinct ideas like Thomism or to the firm exercise of authority, the effect is startling. Just as Catholics who cease to be conservative often become Marxists so those who cease to be Thomist easily embrace the most extreme existentialist fashion.'

135. Klaus Arnsperger, in *Süddeutsche Zeitung* of 31.10.75.

136. 'Sind wir am Ende aller Religion?' (Are We at the End of All Religion?), Lobkowicz and Hertz, *Am Ende aller Religion*, pp.19ff.

137. loc. cit., p.27.

theologians and asserted that the decline of religion can scarcely be remedied by tearing the 'old' religion to shreds and then trying to give comfort to people by saying: 'Now transcend yourselves!' [138] He claims that the decline of religion is spurred on by those 'who should actually know better – from among the supposedly enlightened theologians. They, and not the believers, listen intently at the bosom of the world so that they may be the first to hear how far the world spirit has advanced; it was they, and not the believers, who were informed by auscultation that God is no longer there to help us, but survives merely as an anonymous transcendence and may even be already dead.' [139] According to Erich Kellner, Catholic theologian and founder of the Paulus Society, [140] 'Christianity is presently going through the severest crisis in its history. All the foundations seem to have been shaken. Those things which Christians have clung to and re-garded as true and reliable for two thousand years, the beliefs and hopes for which they lived and perished, are now as though dead and buried . . . Christianity has lost its identity.' [141] And Mario von Galli, Jesuit and former Council Advisor, announced in December 1976 at a Catholic gathering in Münster that 'the Church in its present form will die; it is already breathing its last.' [142]

We have only considered Christianity, which was the first religion to be confronted with the spirit of modernism and the one most likely to be plunged into a crisis. But it should be mentioned that not one of the civilizations of the major Asiatic religions has remained immune to the trends of secularization; in their case, the conflict between traditional and modern thinking broke out later, but it was equally as violent. [143]

A Future without Religion?

Has religion come to an end? [144] The theologian Dietrich Bonhoeffer believed that the advance of intellectualization and the secularization of

---

138. loc. cit., p.29.

139. loc. cit., p.36. In his New Year's Sermon of 1977, Cardinal Ratzinger criticized Christians for their 'childish complacency towards everything which the spirit of the age extols as modern and fashionable'. (*Süddeutsche Zeitung* of 2.1.1978.)

140. An association of scientists and theologians of international repute which was founded in 1956 and has its headquarters in Mondsee, Austria. It is concerned with the role of religious belief in a scientific age and wishes, by means of a rational dialogue between world ideologies, to create a univer-sal form of humanism. It cherishes the hope that Christianity will survive its present crisis, so entering a new and vital phase of stability in the long-term process 'of assimilation and repulsion of historical elements' (Erich Kellner, *Experiment eines kritischen Christentums*, p.10) and appeals not for the 'democratization of ecclesiastical Christianity but the de-institutionalization of the whole Church ap-paratus. A Church presenting itself as a system of officebearers and dignitaries, which stifles and crushes by virtue of its organization, power and wealth, can only be abolished, not modernized'. (Kellner, loc. cit., p.28.)

141. *Experiment eines kritischen Christentums*, Foreword.

142. Quoted from *Süddeutsche Zeitung* of 23.12.1976.

143. Peter Gerlitz deals with this question in *Die Religionen und die neue Moral. Wirkungen einer weltweiten Säkularisation*.

144. In the sense of a transcendental belief in God.

the modern world could no longer be reversed: 'We are moving towards a completely religionless time; people as they are now simply cannot be religious any more.'[145] Looking into the future, Friedrich Tenbruck also sees no place for transcendence 'in the sense of a supernatural, higher order which has been prescribed for man' and believes that 'if we extrapolate the process of secularization, we will either arrive at a church which is entirely of this world and devoid of God or we will come to the fringe sects which wish to cling to a supernatural order.'[146]

Thus we experience 'a situation which has no precedent or parallel'.[147] The theologian Heinz Zahrnt sums it up as follows: 'What is new in our position in the history of religion is that what is taking place is not the disintegration of one particular religion, accompanied as in the past by the transition from an old religion to a new, but the destruction of the very essence of religion. Something has really come to its final end in our times. Things will never again be as they were.'[148]

145. *Letters and Papers from Prison*, p.279.
146. 'Ethos und Religion in einer zukünftigen Gesellschaft', p.34.
147. Gerhard Ebeling, 'Die nicht-religiöse Interpretation biblischer Begriffe', p.331.
148. *The Question of God*, p.139.

2. The Physiognomy of our Secular World

Things will never again be the way they were, nor are we overcome by feelings of nostalgia or longing for the restoration of what has been. The wheel of history cannot be turned back. Nevertheless, the question arises as to whether a religious thinking has simply become absolutely impossible, or whether it is only the historical religions that have had their day. One thing is certain: if God and religion are dead, then the only formative sources of knowledge and creativity with which man can survive on this planet are reason and science.

Apocalypse Now?

This prospect is by no means as encouraging as many think. Although human knowledge has doubled during the successive intervals 1800 to 1900, 1900 to 1950 and 1950 to the present day, the question as to whether man has become more humane and happier must be answered in the negative. Scientific progress has not only brought blessings. Today it is generally realized just what a double-headed Janus this progress is and what dangers and risks it involves, dangers and risks that threaten our very existence. This realization has led to a remarkably ambivalent attitude towards science. On the one hand there is the above-mentioned uncritical belief in science which considers everything that bears the label 'scientific' as true. On the other hand there is scepticism, even hostility towards science, culminating in the accusation that science, by exploiting nature and blindly applying every scientific and technical possibility, is responsible for our ecological crisis.

In any case the material progress of mankind will be confronted in the foreseeable future with limits which we could not even have dreamt of

twenty years ago. The great promise of unlimited economic growth and
material plenty for everybody is not going to be fulfilled. The futurologists' vision of a life spent in a paradise of abundance has been dreamed
out: 'The future is not what it used to be.'[1] We will not live with a profusion of goods but, at best, with a scarcity of them.

Happy confidence in progress[2] suffered a shock after the First World
War, and Oswald Spengler made a stir in the twenties with his theory of
the ageing of cultures and his vision of the decline of the West. Today it is
in a forceful tone with numbers, figures and statistics that the planet-wide
catastrophe is being predicted, unless a complete change in thinking and
consciousness takes place and a radical change of course occurs. By March
1976 the world population had exceeded the four thousand million mark.
Every day the inhabitants of this planet increase by two hundred thousand.
In fifty-four years, if the rate of increase remains the same, the number of
people on the earth will have tripled and will have grown to twelve thousand million. This population explosion, which had already been described
by the English biologist Gordon R. Taylor in 1969,[3] and which was confirmed by the prognosis of the Washington Research Institute 'World
Watch', will have consequences in many areas, for instance: growing illit-
eracy,[4] mass unemployment, increasing destitution, ever poorer living
conditions in the cities,[5] world-wide famine aggravated by the increasing
shortage of food throughout the world.[6] Today a thousand million people
are starving in Asia, Africa and Latin America. Four hundred and fifty
million are simply vegetating, wavering between life and death. Every year
millions in the Third World die of malnutrition, whereas in the industrial
countries of the West there is a surplus of food: one of the most frequent
causes of illness is overeating.[7] In addition the dilemma of the future is

1. Arthur Clarke, quoted in Taylor, *How to Avoid the Future*, p.3.
2. See Iring Fetcher, 'Ursprung und Ende des neuzeitlichen Fortschrittsbegriffs' (Origin and End
of the Modern Concept of Progress), in O. Schatz (ed), *Hoffnung in der Überlebenskrise?* (Hope in
the Survival Crisis?), pp.88ff; Ernst Benz, 'Die uneingelöste Verheißung des Fortschritts als
Herausforderung für die Religion' (The Unfulfilled Promise of Progress as a Challenge for Religion),
op. cit., pp.106ff; Malte Buschbeck, 'Was ersetzt uns den Fortschrittsglauben? Vom therapeutischen
Nutzen der Apokalypse für die säkulare Gesellschaft' (What do we have as a Substitute for the Belief in
Progress? On the Therapeutic Benefit of the Apocalypse for the Secular Society), in *Süddeutsche
Zeitung* of 14–15.6.1980.
3. *The Biological Time-Bomb*, London, Thames and Hudson, 1968.
4. Today there are already 800 million people who are illiterate.
5. According to a study published in 1981 by the United Nations Conference on Human Settlement (Habitat) two-thirds of the urban population of developing countries live in slums.
6. Even today the grain reserves of the world can only satisfy a need of 30 days. See Taylor, *How to
Avoid the Future*, pp.255ff.
7. Report in *Süddeutsche Zeitung* of 24.5.1980 on the occasion of the conference of ministers of
the World Food Council (WFC) of the United Nations in Arusha, Tanzania from 3rd to 6th June. According to the 1980 report of the Federal Government of Germany on nourishment in the Federal
Republic of Germany every third citizen is overweight.

characterized by the raw materials crisis, of which the energy crisis[8] is only one aspect, by the advancing destruction of the environment threatening ecological catastrophe, by the chaos in the world currency system with the danger of a financial catastrophe that would mean the end of our world economy,[9] and above all by the menacing danger of collective mass suicide in the case of a nuclear war of the great powers.[10] Furthermore, millions of human beings are excluded from the blessings of progress. The industrial states have taken possession of the wealth of the earth and exploit it with intelligence and brutal egoism.[11] The result is a class war on a world-wide scale.

The command given in the Creation Story of Genesis, 'and replenish the earth and subdue it',[12] has long been fulfilled. Man has ransacked the earth with unbridled greed and is about to transform it into a desert.[13] Industry, efficient but short-sighted in its production, threatens to destroy our environment and the very basis of our existence. We must seriously ask ourselves what the result for future generations will be: will they not be left

8. If the world energy consumption increases annually by only 3% – the necessary rate in the opinion of national economists to maintain the stability of the present system – then the reserves which according to present calculations can be economically obtained will last only 23 years (mineral oil), 32 years (gas) and 63 years (coal) (*Süddeutsche Zeitung* of 25.1.1980). Although these figures are known to politicians and economy experts, the unbridled exploitation of resources and the irresponsible waste of energy are continued.

9. The world economy is going through its worst crisis since World War II. According to a report of the North-South Commission for International Development, it is not only individual nations which are threatened with bankruptcy, but whole groups of nations as well.

10. The Stockholm International Peace Research Institute (SIPRI) estimates the explosive force of the nuclear weapons which are in the arsenals of the nuclear powers to be equivalent to twenty thousand million tons of conventional explosives. This corresponds to a million bombs of the type used at Hiroshima. In spite of that the arms race goes on. The branch of the economy with the largest growth rate is the armaments industry. According to the annual report of the Executive Director of the U.N. Environment Programme, mankind spends almost one million dollars every minute for its own mutual military destruction (*Süddeutsche Zeitung* of 10.6.1980). Cf. *Abrüstung und Weltfrieden* (Disarmament and World Peace), A Declaration of the International Bahá'í Community with an introduction by Ulrich Gollmer, Hofheim-Langenhain 1980. One of the most remarkable studies on the horrors of an atomic war is Jonathan Schell's apocalyptic analysis, *The Fate of the Earth* (New York 1982). The book rose to the top of the best-seller lists immediately after it was published and has since caused a dispute between scientists, politicians and journalists.

11. The average economic distance between the developing countries and the industrial countries has increased from 1 : 1.7 (1850) to 1 : 9 (1960). Cf. Surendra Patel, 'The Economic Distance between Nations: Its Origin, Measurement and Outlook', *Economic Journal*, 1964, pp.122ff.

12. Gen. 1:28.

13. Year after year virgin forest areas are cut down and burnt at a rate of 20 hectares (about 50 acres) a minute, areas that correspond in size over one year to Denmark, Holland and Belgium combined. Sulphurous waste gases from the central European industrial countries, which descend in the form of sulphuric acid rain, have caused forests to die in the whole of Europe, even in Scandinavia. Canada and even some of the tropical countries have the same problem. The climate is changing, the desert is constantly gaining ground and enormous regions are becoming barren land. In the course of a century 69 kinds of mammals became extinct; 200 kinds are threatened by extinction (*Heidelberger Tageblatt*, 19.4.1979); 30 million square kilometres (i.e. 19%) of the earth's land surface are endangered through erosion, salination, deforestation, mining or industrial use (report of the United Nations Environmental Organization, *Süddeutsche Zeitung*, 19.6.1981.)

with a planet that has been plundered and devastated by human hands?

The catastrophe has been programmed; the apocalyptic aspects of the future cannot be ignored. Prominent futurologists who ten years ago still thought that alternatives and solutions could be found have become apocalyptic in their attitudes. They now believe that catastrophes rather than positive developments will determine the next fifty years.[14] Grover Foley, an American futurologist, wrote: 'The world is getting ready for the end.'[15] Hans Schuster wrote in an essay: 'The Apocalypse, the Last Judgement, no longer seems to be a dark, faraway myth, but a probability, historical in nature and measurable in figures',[16] and the philosopher Günther Anders satirized Robert Jungks's *The Future has already begun*[17] in the sub-title 'The Future has already ended'.[18] Such warnings are still dismissed by the majority of politicians and for the most part by the public media as idle crisis talk and irresponsible panic-making. Most people are only all too willing to share this view because they shrink from the far-reaching economic and social changes which are offered as alternatives. People are still prepared 'to endanger through the satisfaction of short-term interests their long-term living prospects – to say nothing of the prospects of future generations, whom no one thinks of anyway'.[19] Nevertheless, renowned scientists, philosophers, and theologians in increasing numbers are raising their Cassandra cries to warn us of the threatening breakdown.[20]

The whole extent of the crisis is emerging more and more clearly. The physicist Klaus Müller sees a 'world crisis which profoundly endangers the existence of all the more highly developed creatures on our earth', so that

---

14. 'The future, not to put too fine a point on it, promises to be dire: more violent than anything we can remember, more unstable socially, and more insecure. Life will be more inconvenient and frustrating, the material standard of living will fall, there will be financial disasters and whole classes will be wiped out. Food and resources will be in short supply, noise and pollution will be worse. There will be famines and no doubt wars, both civil and uncivil. It will also be much colder. Unless, of course, we all take drastic action to avoid this, starting *now*.' (Taylor, *How to Avoid the Future*, Foreword.)

15. 'Sind wir am Ende?', p.741.

16. 'Planetarische Schreckensvision' (A Planetary Nightmare Vision), in *Süddeutsche Zeitung* of 30.12.1975.

17. *Die Zukunft hat schon begonnen. Amerikas Allmacht und Ohnmacht.*

18. *Die Antiquiertheit des Menschen*, Vol.II, p.278.

19. O. Schatz, *Hoffnung in der Überlebenskrise?*, Foreword, p.9.

20. The Ninth Salzburg Humanism Symposium organized by Austrian Radio from 24–9 September 1978 was entitled 'Hope in the Survival Crisis? The Burdensome Consequences of Progress as a Challenge to Religion and Science.' The contributions of internationally renowned scientists, philosophers, theologians and sociologists have been collected in a volume edited by Oskar Schatz, *Hoffnung in der Überlebenskrise?* (Salzburger Humanismus-Gespräche. Graz, Vienna, Cologne 1979.) At a conference of the *Civitas* society in the spring of 1980 renowned philosophers and scientists both from Germany and elsewhere held talks on 'Scientific and Technological Development – Progress or Dead-End?' The subject of discussion was chosen because of concern that technological progress is developing an uncanny dynamism of its own, is threatening to slip away out of human

'everything we could previously rely on can now be called in question'.[21] The geneticist Carsten Bresch sees in humanity's present crisis 'the culmination of a fundamental process of evolution which has its only parallel four thousand million years ago. No analysis of cultural history can fully do it justice. It can only be understood in all its consequences from the viewpoint of a comprehensive theory of evolution.'[22] Günter Altner, a scientist and theologian, sees an 'epoch of collapse and unprecedented suffering' coming upon us.[23] The crisis of our scientific and technical civilization enables us to realize, for the first time in history, the collective death of the species, man, as a 'possibility that can be scientifically foreseen'.[24] The philosopher Günther Anders puts it in this way: 'The statement "all men are mortal" has nowadays been replaced by the assertion "mankind as a whole can be wiped out".'[25] These are not the mere theories of academic circles. The evidence of the crisis is not based 'at all on questionable, futurological prognoses, but on very concrete developments occurring before the eyes of us all and heading with increasing acceleration towards the great catastrophe. And this is all coming upon a humanity which is still torn with inner strife and is without inner peace'.[26]

These warnings to make an about-face have been unsuccessful to a large extent. Our political systems have proved to be, for reasons that are obvious, incapable of persuading the voters to take upon themselves the heavy restrictions and sacrifice which would necessarily be connected with a radical change in course. Economic circles (in both East and West!) whose main interest is the maximum short-term profit and the continuance of an economic system based on economic growth, rather than the future of later generations, resist vehemently the increasingly vociferous criticism. They

---

control and is leading straight into a dead-end. The biochemist Erwin Chargaff, who lives in New York, said: 'I live in the epicentre of the decay, but New York is merely a particularly glaring example of the development of the civilized world. We are surrounded on all sides by contradictions which are the result of a mechanization of the world, a process that is driven madly by our research. The researchers themselves, at least many of them, know quite well that they are caught in a trap.' (Quoted in Malte Buschbeck, 'Was ersetzt uns den Fortschrittsglauben?' in *Süddeutsche Zeitung* of 14–15.6.1980.) The enchanted broomstick which Goethe brought to life in his ballad, 'Der Zauberlehrling' (The Sorcerer's Apprentice) as an 'adventurous and exceptional incident, is now happening to us uninterruptedly'. The 'autonomous "broomsticks"', i.e. the technical apparati of atomic power-stations, nuclear missiles, gigantic industrial installations all of which render us increasingly dependent through their conferred power and independence, these are the controlling constituents of our world: 'Whereas Goethe showed us a single, lonely broomstick (and later a pair) acting with insane autonomy, today we are living in a dense and thickening forest of "broomsticks". And since there is no possibility of cutting this forest down or escaping from it, it is the world in which we must live.' (Günther Anders, *Die Antiquiertheit des Menschen*, Vol.II, pp.402–3.)

21. Quoted in O. Schatz, *Hoffnung in der Überlebenskrise?*, Foreword, p.9.
22. 'Die Menschheit an der zweiten Schwelle der Evolution', in O. Schatz (ed), op. cit., p.44.
23. *Zwischen Natur und Menschengeschichte*, p.161.
24. O. Schatz, op. cit., Foreword, p.11.
25. *Die Antiquiertheit des Menschen*, Vol.I, p.242.
26. O. Schatz, op. cit., Foreword, p.11.

call the irritating admonishers 'prophets of doom' and their theories 'bloodcurdling fantasies'. Günther Anders describes the contemporary attitude towards nuclear armaments as 'Apocalypse-Blindness'.[27] In this manner we inexorably create our own downfall and rush impetuously and with increasing speed towards the catastrophe.[28] There is little hope that man on his own can control the crisis and introduce a timely process of change to preserve us from ruin.

The Nation State – an Anachronism

This is not the place for a detailed discussion of all the unsolved world problems which threaten our existence.[29] One thing is certain: because of these problems we have only one alternative to destruction – resolute action by all peoples together. It has long been evident that the problems of world economy[30] and the dangers caused by environmental destruction, world-wide famine, the scarcity of raw materials and energy, the atomic armaments race, the wider dispersion of atomic weapons, hijackings, terrorism and the like, are beyond the control of individual nation states. The nation state, a historical achievement in the progressive development of mankind towards higher forms of order, has become a dangerous anachronism today. The 'principle of autarky', long associated with the

27. *Die Antiquiertheit des Menschen*, Vol.I, pp.235–324.

28. In this insight and the realization that a deadline has been fixed for mankind is, as it were, the *leitmotiv* of the above-cited work by the philosopher Günther Anders, whose second volume was published in 1980. (cf. Bahá'u'lláh, *Gleanings* 108: 'We have a fixed time for you, O peoples. If ye fail, at the appointed hour, to turn towards God, He, verily, will lay violent hold on you, and will cause grievous afflictions to assail you from every direction.')

29. On the whole topic: Denis and Donella Meadows, *The Limits to Growth. A Report to the Club of Rome's Project on the Predicament of Mankind*, New York, Universe Books, 1972; Herbert Gruhl, *Ein Planet wird geplündert. Die Schreckensbilanz unserer Politik*, Frankfurt 1976; Gordon Rattray Taylor, *How to Avoid the Future*, London, Secker & Warburg, 1975; Mihajlo Mesarović and Eduard Pestel, *Mankind at the Turning-Point. The Second Report of the Club of Rome*, London, Hutchinson, 1975; E. F. Schumacher, *Small is Beautiful; Economics as if People Mattered*, New York, Harper & Row, 1973; E. Küng, 'Die Krise der Wohlstandsgesellschaft und die notwendige Neuorientierung – Grenzen des wirtschaftlichen Wachstums' (The Crisis of the Affluent Society and the Necessary Re-Orientation – Limits of Economic Growth), *Universitas*, 27 (1972); *Sind wir noch zu retten? Schöpfungsglaube und Verantwortung für unsere Erde* (Can We still be Saved? Faith in Creation and Responsibility for Our Earth), Regensburg 1978. This publication of the Catholic Academy of Bavaria contains six contributions on the topic from a theological, philosophical, economical, and socio-ethical viewpoint; Adolf Geprägs, 'Die Weltreligionen und die ökologische Krise – Alternativen zum westlichen Denken' (The World Religions and the Ecological Crisis – Alternatives to Western Thought), published by the Lutheran Head Office for Ideological Questions, Stuttgart (Arbeitstexte, No. 20, XI/79); 'Ein anderer "Way of Life"' – Ist der Fortschritt noch ein Fortschritt?', *Bergedorfer Gesprächskreis zu Fragen der freien industriellen Gesellschaft, Protokoll*, No. 56, 1977; 'Wachstum und Lebenssinn – Alternative Rationalitäten?, *Bergedorfer Gesprächskreis, Protokoll*, No. 61, 1978; Pierre Chaunu and Georges Suffert, *La Peste blanche. Comment éviter le suicide de l'Occident*, Paris, Gallimard, 1976; H. A. Pestalozzi, *Nach uns die Zukunft. Von der positiven Subversion*, Bern 1979.

30. Daniel Bell, *The Cultural Contradictions of Capitalism*, pp.206ff, 212ff.

concept of sovereignty, 'from the very beginning of Western ideas on the nature of the state, has long been replaced by the phenomenon of the "importation and interweaving of problems". There are no suitable instruments for controlling the interdependencies.'[31] Humanity still has no international law that can be effectively enforced, because there is no higher authority to which the sovereign states would have to submit.

The peoples of the world, short-sighted and still incapable of seeing where their own advantage lies, stick to a form of politics that furthers only the interests of the nation states. Rarely has the topic of state sovereignty been discussed before an international forum as much as at the World Population Conference which took place in Bucharest in 1974. As one journalist commented:[32] 'Some states apparently would rather perish as sovereign states than sacrifice just one little bit of their sovereignty for the interests . . . of the whole.' Some years ago at a congress on international law, the Belgian lawyer Dautricourt said with bitter sarcasm that the collective consciousness of mankind would be formed – 'at the latest after an atomic war'.[33]

In their second report to the Club of Rome on the world situation, Mesarović and Pestel concluded from their scientific analyses that the problems of the world can be solved only by world co-operation. Thus they call for the development of a world consciousness 'through which every individual realizes his role as a member of the world community. Famine in tropical Africa should be considered as relevant and as disturbing to a citizen of Germany as famine in Bavaria.'[34] Furthermore, 'children starting first grade today will hardly become real operating members of the society before the year 2000. The twenty-first century is not that far away when you think in terms of basic education.'[35] If we do not manage to weld the world together into a co-operative global system, 'the only alternatives are division and conflict, hate and destruction[36] . . . The

31. Reiner Schmidt, 'Der geforderte Staat', p.160. Schmidt points out in another context that in economics and currency the network of international relationships which is to be penetrated is 'almost abominably impenetrable' and that one 'can hardly see the nation state anymore', neither economically nor from a legal point of view. Economic theory and jurisprudence have not kept pace with the dynamics of what is happening in international economics and currency: 'Even today the world economic situation is still comprehended simply as the sum of the activities of the sovereign national states.' ('Der Verfassungsstaat im Geflecht der internationalen Beziehungen', pp.67–71, 105.) On the problem of world-wide interdependence, cf. Hans Huber, 'Weltweite Interdependenzen' (World-wide Interdependences), in Hans Huber, *Rechtstheorie, Verfassungsrecht, Völkerrecht. Ausgewählte Aufsätze* (Theory of Law, Constitutional Law, International Law. Selected Essays), Berne 1971, pp.601ff.
32. Klaus Natorp in the *Frankfurter Allgemeine Zeitung* of 22.11.1974.
33. *Süddeutsche Zeitung* of 3–4.11.1979.
34. *Mankind at the Turning-Point*, p.147.
35. op. cit., p.148.
36. op. cit., p.157.

disparities in the world will eventually drive mankind over the brink into final destruction.'[37] In spite of the many cultural differences and varieties of political outlook, the peoples of the world share one thing in common: they are subject to the same fate, the same threat to existence in the face of which – so one would expect – all differences and conflicts ought to die away. If this common fate does not impel men to overcome the antagonisms which divide them and strive for solidarity, then the approaching calamity can no longer be averted.

In the face of these threatening dangers and the increasing instability of the world, Henry Kissinger, the former US Secretary of State, declared in 1974 before the US Senate and the United Nations in two highly-regarded speeches that the world was on the razor's edge and that western civilization would 'very likely fall into ruin, if we do not acknowledge our mutual dependency'. At the same time he spoke of the 'birthpangs of a new world order': the old order was breaking up, and a new one, still difficult for us to imagine, was emerging.

Disintegration of Value Systems

For people to work together there must first be a common goal and common values. Our dilemma is that we have neither the one nor the other. Science, which enables us to land on the moon, proves to be remarkably ineffective in the realm of man's social activity. The belief that science can cure all evils is, according to the Swiss sociologist Theodor Leuenberger, a 'superstition'.[38] Science is almost powerless against the irrational forces that are increasingly menacing mankind. It has little or nothing to set up against the phenomenon of growing criminality and drug abuse, and there is not even a satisfactory and generally acceptable theory explaining the causes of these problems. The integration of all peoples into a unified body capable of action is becoming recognized as absolutely vital, because the problems of man's existence can only be solved on a world-wide basis or not at all. But at the same time we are confronted with a new danger which threatens to rob us of the capacity for unified action: society is rapidly disintegrating and losing its structure. Living together with others is becoming more difficult every day, more and more conflicts arise, and the bonds which hold society together are becoming weaker. The material problems of mankind cannot be solved by a society which is being torn

37. op. cit., p.xii.
38. Stated at the conference entitled 'Faith, Science, and the Future' at the Massachusetts Institute of Technology from 12–24 July 1979 organized by the Ecumenical Council of Churches (*Süddeutsche Zeitung* of 18.7.1979). Cf. also the essay by Günter Altner, 'Zwischen zerbrochenen Ideologien', in *Der Überblick. Zeitschrift für ökumenische Begegnung und internationale Zusammenarbeit*, September 1979, pp.2–9.

apart by its self-contradictions and is losing its coherence. Of all the menacing dangers this is certainly the most serious, because it hampers our ability to act.[39] What is the reason for this process, and what are its symptoms?

The reason for the decline of our society is to be found in the decline of our system of values. Within a few decades a change has taken place with almost breathtaking speed in the way people think. It can certainly be described as a cultural revolution when one considers its far-reaching consequences. Norms and values which had been established by religion, which had been handed on and kept alive and considered absolutely valid for over two thousand years and were even recognized by the rationalists of the Enlightenment in the eighteenth century as rational values,[40] were swept away within a few decades and replaced by a pluralism of new and varied value concepts.

Just as in the course of a disease there are two components which work together – the susceptibility of the organism under attack and the germ causing the disease – so there are two conditions in which the reason for the cultural disintegration is to be found: on the one hand the weakness of the existing system of values which has lost its transcendental basis and has thus laid itself open to critical questioning, and on the other hand a one-dimensional rationalism,[41] an attitude which does not allow anything to have validity unless it can be established by empirical reason. This form of thinking, which has proved its worth in the field of science and technology and which ensures our material requirements, becomes problematic when applied to cultural values and norms. Brezinka has described the features of 'one-dimensional rationalism' thus: 'Rational thinking is critical, utilitarian and individualistic. It queries the traditional forms of sovereignty, religion, law, morality, ethics and custom. It deprives every non-rational *Weltanschauung* of its binding nature. It loosens the emotional ties to the conventional order of life, to its ideals and to the bearers of its authority. On the one hand this is experienced as liberation, as a gain in knowledge and in scope for action, or as intellectual and moral progress. But on the other hand, man has the need for a stable view of life and the world, for emotional security in a community of like-minded souls, for certainty concerning the state of his soul and for a clear-cut purpose in life – and a rationalist attitude leaves this need unsatisfied.'[42]

If rational proof is the only gauge for evaluating an ethical norm, then a

---

39. Taylor also sees the central problem in 'social cohesion'. (*How to Avoid the Future*, p.31.)
40. Even Pierre Joseph Proudhon (1809–65) wrote: 'L'homme est destiné à vivre sans religion . . . La loi morale . . . est éternelle et absolue. . . Eh! qui donc aujourd'hui oserait attaquer la morale?' (*De la création de l'ordre dans l'humanité ou principes d'organisation politique*, p.38, No. 60.) Today it is no longer daring to attack morals.
41. D. Bell, *The Cultural Contradictions of Capitalism*, p.4.
42. *Erziehung und Kulturrevolution*, p.15.

norm that commands positive action can only be recognized if it is proved
to be of advantage to everyone, and a norm that has a prohibitive function
can only be recognized when the social harmfulness of the prohibited act is
evident to all. [43] This 'critical attitude of the mind', which recognizes none
but rational values will automatically reject the notion of unconditional
duty and the existence of generally binding norms. Every human being is
then the supreme judge of the norms of his life-style and of the social
order. That is the meaning of the new ideal of 'self-determination' and
'maturity', whereas the recognition of an authority which cannot be questioned and the observance of its commandments is contemptuously
dismissed as 'immaturity': 'The illusion is cherished that everyone by
means of his own mental efforts will be able to realize what he should do
and will be capable of making a free choice for or against what should be
done . . . Thus the individual with his subjective desires, his chance experiences, his restricted knowledge and his limited understanding is
granted the right to consider himself the measure of all things,' says
Brezinka. He describes the consequences: 'The belief in absolute duties is
replaced by calculating adaptation to the contingencies of the day. The
love for ideals which demand that man overcome his egocentricity cannot
emerge in a society in which it is considered "progressive" to doubt
everything. As this love dwindles, so does the motivation to exert oneself in
ethical areas and the energy to devote oneself unselfishly to greater tasks
. . . In such a spiritual climate, the growth of egotism is accompanied by
the spread of pessimism and the foreboding of destruction. One becomes
indifferent to the welfare of others and is only concerned to get the best for
oneself as long as this is still possible.' [44]

In addition to this the 'normative power of actual facts' [45] has also had its
effect on moral standards: after it had been realized how large was the gap
between the acknowledged moral code and the actual practice of it, [46] the
conclusion was drawn that the prevailing code of morals demanded too
much of people and could therefore lay no claim to validity. After
ethnology and sociology had demonstrated the relativity of moral values and
concepts, such time-honoured virtues as decency, humility, obedience,
respect, modesty, self-discipline, politeness, self-denial, trustworthiness,
integrity and the like were 'exposed' under the slogan 'Emancipation' [47] as

43. This peculiar state of mind was the most important change that occurred in the eighteenth century: 'The rationalistic idea substituted social utility for tradition as the main criterion of social institutions and values . . . It thus postulated a single valid system, which would come into existence when
everything not accounted for by reason and utility had been removed.' (J. L. Talmon, *The Origins of
Totalitarian Democracy*, pp.3ff.) In fact the opposite happened.
44. *Erziehung und Kulturrevolution*, pp.16ff.
45. The phrase was coined by Georg Jellinek, a teacher of constitutional law at the University of
Heidelberg.
46. As in the investigations of the Kinsey report, for instance.
47. With reference to this term see W. Brezinka, op. cit., pp.151ff, 158; also Hans Maier in

the morality of the exploiting class and the terms were banished from the general vocabulary. [48] The education of children according to these ideals was dismissed as 'conditioning', 'drilling', and 'parental determination'. [49] The family [50] was denounced as a worn-out and outdated form of domination, as the 'authoritarian establishment of social domination', as the 'bourgeois dictatorial family', as a 'pedagogic vacuum', as 'completely putrefied'; it must be replaced by 'alternative forms of partnership'. Marriage was declared to be a hindrance to a genuine love-relationship [51] and should be put away 'in a museum, like the spinning-wheel': 'An institution for grey geese, not for people.' [52] The sexual relationship

Protokoll 41, *Bergedorfer Gesprächskreis*, p.9; Karl Steinbuch, *Maßlos informiert*, p.190; Hans Jochen Gamm, 'Emanzipation: Schlüsselproblem der Erziehung' (Emancipation: Key Problem of Education), *Die deutsche Schule* (The German School), Vol.65, 1973, pp.675–83.

48. See examples of undesirable words in W. Brezinka, op. cit., p.56.

49. An aggressive anti-education programme advocates freedom from education. Every kind of education is accordingly 'deception', 'child abuse', a 'crime' and must therefore be 'abolished': 'Educators are like drug dealers, who first of all get their victims addicted – and then they are genuinely dependent. But it was all unnecessary, and as soon as one has seen through it, one can make a withdrawal cure.' (Ekkehard v. Braunmühl in a pamphlet published by the German Association for the Protection of Children and entitled 'Erziehung? Nein danke!' (Education? No thanks!)

50. Haensch maintains that 'from an anti-authoritarian and sexual-economic position', the bourgeois marriage and family present 'a microcosm of the authoritarian society; they force the people living within it from childhood on to adapt to authoritarian conditions'. In his opinion the family prevents children, youth and adults 'from developing their genitality freely' and thus limits 'their vital life-needs', transforming them into 'submissive subjects who fear authority'. He is of the opinion that the family turns children into 'objects of sexual oppression' as a result of which these children later oppress others: 'Sexual oppression reduces the ability to criticize and conditions the mind to accept ideals which are actually opposed to the real interests of the individual.' (*Repressive Familienpolitik*, pp.37ff.) W. Brezinka (p.126) points out that according to this sexual-anarchistic interpretation of family upbringing only 'a radical break with the traditional structure of the family as realized in the "extended family", "family communities", "communes" etc.' can lead to 'forms of collective living' which 'aim at creating a new human being in a revolutionary society'. (Bookhagen, *Kindererziehung in der Kommune* (The Education of Children in the Commune); for further references see W. Brezinka, op. cit., pp.126 and 185.) A network of intimate friendships, of close friends who form a nucleus, and of friends who are attached to the group, is to replace the family. This formation will 'in time shape the new social structure'. (Rolf Schwendter, *Theorie der Subkultur*, p.412, with reference to James W. Ramey.) An investigation in the USA shows just how far the decline of the family has progressed. Only 37% of the population live in families. In the Federal Republic of Germany the willingness to marry is also declining. According to a statement by the Federal Office of Statistics in Wiesbaden there were only 370,265 marriages celebrated in 1974 compared with 530,640 in 1962. In the same period the number of divorces increased from 49,580 to 98,584. (*Rhein-Neckar-Zeitung* of 17.10.1979.)

51. 'Only those who were broken to a certain degree in their childhood are at all willing, ready or able to enter into a marriage. But in the marriage they are then completely broken, for in marriage, once the novelty and the first intoxication are gone, they can no longer realize their sexual needs and desires.' Thus marriage is equated with a 'voluntary amputation of sexual needs' (Herbert Amend, *Sexfront*, p.78). Edward Shorter describes the decline of marriage in the Western world in *The Making of the Modern Family*, New York, Basic Books, 1975.

52. Rolf Schwendter, *Theorie der Subkultur*, p.218. Whereas the institution of marriage is increasingly replaced by concubinage, this in turn will be superseded by a new development. Solitude is the catchword. People no longer want to take the trouble upon themselves that living with someone else entails. They live, but do not sleep, alone. They are called 'singles'. The result of this way of life

was no longer confined to marriage,[53] and in accordance with the motto 'Your body belongs to you!' the gratification of the sexual drive was declared to be entirely a private affair. The natural ranking order between people, such as in the parent–child[54] or teacher–pupil relationship, was condemned as an obstacle frustrating all warmer emotions. Any form of institutionalization of moral values was labelled repression: 'The dominant morality is the morality of those who dominate.'

Views, value concepts, and behavioural patterns developed by behavioural psychologists and sociologists have been put in the place of norms established by religion. The schools, in which emancipatory education is in the process of liberating young people from the commitment to certain norms and religious convictions, are to act as a lever for the desired social change. They are to liberate the young people in order to lead them towards self-determination, maturity,[55] autonomy and freedom without commitment to traditions and institutions, without acknowledgement of the bearers of authority. Such an education also aspires to prepare young people for living in an emancipated society in which everyone decides for himself but in which social coherence is nevertheless guaranteed, or, where the illusion of the autonomous self-determining person is not thought much of, this form of education aims to bind the person to new bearers of

---

'without conflict': loneliness and boredom. Recently, however, opinions have been voiced which indicate a different trend. Quite a number of people have begun to realize that promiscuity leads not to happiness but frustration, because, as Erich Fromm has already pointed out, promiscuity is only another form of escape and an addiction like alcohol or drugs (cf. Gabrielle Brown, *The New Celibacy*, New York, McGraw Hill, 1979).

53: After the prohibition of concubinage was revoked in the German states during the sixties, the way is now being paved for granting concubinage the same legal status as marriage. In a decision of 15.1.1980 the administrative tribunal in Berlin awarded civil servants living in circumstances similar to marriage an increase in pay normally granted under the federal wage laws to married people. The decision is based on a change in opinion over the last decade: the decision to live together with someone in a permanent relationship without a formal contract of marriage is being accepted as the personal decision of the partners concerned (*Neue Juristische Wochenschrift*, Heft 19, 1980, p. vi).

54. The extent to which the attack on traditional values already determines educational objectives is shown by the school readers approved by educational authorities in many of the states of the German Federal Republic. In the workbook for social studies for the seventh to ninth grades (ed. K. G. Fischer, 2nd edn, Stuttgart 1973) the following quotation can be found on pages 99ff. in the chapter 'The Family': 'The nuclear family is an institution which wastes a tremendous amount of time and money . . . You have to have experienced it to realize how lousy and stupid it is. This feeling of being bound . . .' A poem on Advent in *Fischer-Taschenbuch 1147* (pp.300ff), recommended as material for the secondary level I in accordance with the guidelines of one of the German states, reads: 'Advent, Advent, die Stube brennt,/mit Teppich und Gardinen./Der Papi brennt, die Mami brennt/und ich fress Apfelsinen./Papili und Mamili,/die wollten mich enterben,/der Tierverein soll Erbe sein,/drum müssen sie jetzt sterben./Ich hatte schon als lieber Sohn/mir oft gewünscht im Stillen,/bei Gelegenheit – zur Weihnachtszeit/ – die Eltern wie Hühner zu grillen' (Advent, advent, the room is burning, with its carpets and curtains. Daddy is burning, Mummy is burning, and I'm eating oranges. Daddy and Mummy wanted to disinherit me; the society for the protection of animals was to be their heir, so now they must die. As their dear son I had often secretly wanted, when the occasion should arise – at Christmas – to grill my parents like chickens.)

55. Cf. W. Brezinka, *Erziehung und Kulturrevolution*, p.148. For more on this concept see p.38.

authority.[56] Instead of giving basic orientation and forming the conscience according to certain norms, a form of education which describes itself as 'anti-authoritarian'[57] teaches profound scepticism towards traditional values, and permanent mistrust of society[58] and of every kind of standard, institution and authority which imposes limitations on our individual freedom. The basic principles of all 'progressive' education state that authority is 'just as harmful to the perfect society as it is to the development of the individual'.[59] However, the result of all this is insecurity, lack of orientation, destruction of values, arrogance on the part of those so educated,[60] 'new conflicts of conscience, new feelings of inferiority, a new fear of living – all these symptoms can be observed among a large proportion of older schoolchildren and university students,'[61] and they lead to the moral decomposition of society. The simple truth about education is no longer perceived: 'Only when a person has experienced a long period of obedience to authority, has been forced to sacrifice the satisfaction of his basic drives, has obeyed, and has experienced reward and punishment, is he able to acquire an independent conscience and the capacity for self-determination.'[62]

Linguistic Revolution

The 'revaluation of all values' (Nietzsche) is accompanied by the 'revaluation of all words' which form the basis of our state and society. This 'semantic deception . . . strips words of colloquial speech of their accustomed meaning and cunningly uses them in a different way'.[63] Language thus becomes a means of political struggle. According to Schelsky,[64] who has examined the methodical infiltration of language as critically as has Brezinka,[65] 'the fight for domination and the class struggle occur in the

56. On the whole topic see Cl. Günzler, *Anthropologische und ethische Dimensionen der Schule*, Freiburg, Munich 1976.

57. See W. Brezinka, op. cit., pp.166ff; Monika Seifert demands that children be permitted 'to grow up without guilt feelings, i.e. free of what we call morality'. ('Antiautoritäre Erziehung (Antiautoritarian Education), in S. H. Fraiberg, *Das verstandene Kind*, p.306.)

58. This criticism of authority springs from the direct experience of an authority that is outdated and therefore not real, and the technocratic utilization of man for the purpose of the economic machine. (See H. Marcuse, *One-Dimensional Man*.)

59. H. Schelsky, *Die Arbeit tun die anderen*, p.411.

60. The products of this type of education are 'young people who take it for granted that self-determination' can be achieved 'without having to work on oneself'. (H. Schelsky, op. cit., p.414.)

61. H. Schelsky, op. cit., p.411; see also p.71 n.247. Linked with this are the increasing drug dependency, the escape into a chemically stimulated inner world, and the threatening rise in the consumption of alcohol (cf. p.62).

62. W. Brezinka, *Erziehung und Kulturrevolution*, p.169.

63. Karl Steinbuch, *Maßlos informiert*, pp.299–300. George Orwell in *Nineteen Eighty-Four* calls this 'Newspeak'.

64. *Die Arbeit tun die anderen*, p.318.

65. *Erziehung und Kulturrevolution*, pp.54ff, 73, 108, 156.

Federal Republic of Germany today mainly in the form of a fight for words and concepts'. The constancy of terms and the common understanding of their meanings that could be expected just a few decades ago in the confrontation of different social and political opinions, are gradually being lost; an 'anarchy of language',[66] a 'deliberate Babylonian confusion of language'[67] remains. The loosening up of terms has consequences similar to those of the thoughtless and careless loosening up of structures: 'Without a reliable foundation of terms and structures there is no progress – when terms and structures lose their stability, we find ourselves sinking in the swamp.'[68]

There is a wealth of literature about the ideological control of language, and consequently of man himself. It exposes the clever mechanisms which are used.[69] Brezinka illustrates this using the terms of 'self-determination' and 'maturity' as examples:

By 'ability for self-determination' is meant 'the ability to free oneself from dependence', and 'to exist as a liberated person'.[70] This term is also used today to mean the exact opposite of what was previously meant by the moral concept of self-determination: 'The ability to control oneself, to overcome one's self-centredness and covetousness, to bridle one's passions and to voluntarily submit to the moral code.'[71] Even in antiquity (Seneca), in the Enlightenment and during the period of German classicism, self-

---

66. Wilhelm Hennis, in *Bergedorfer Gesprächskreis, Protokoll*, No. 41, pp. 20 and 21.

67. Karl Steinbuch, *Maßlos informiert*, p.202.

68. Karl Steinbuch, op. cit., p.191.

69. On the whole topic see Harald Weinreich, *Linguistik der Lüge. Kann Sprache die Gedanken verbergen?* (The Linguistics of Lying. Can Language Conceal Thoughts?), Heidelberg 1966; *Bergedorfer Gesprächskreis*: 'Sprache und Politik. Können Begriffe die Gesellschaft verändern?', *Protokoll*, No. 41 with a large number of references to further literature (pp.66–8); Hermann Lübbe, 'Der Streit um Worte. Sprache und Politik' (The Dispute about Words. Language and Politics), in Hermann Lübbe, *Bewußtsein in Geschichten* (Consciousness in Stories), Freiburg 1972, pp.132ff; Wolfgang Brüggemann, 'Didaktische Reflexionen zur politischen Sprache' (Didactic Reflections on Political Language), in *Zeitschrift für Gesellschaft, Staat, Erziehung*, August 1972; Herbert Marcuse, *An Essay on Liberation*, Boston, Beacon Press 1972; O. Roegele, *Kleine Anatomie politischer Schlagworte* (Small Anatomy of Political Slogans), Osnabrück 1972; W. Eberle and W. Schlaffke, *Gesellschaftskritik von A–Z* (Social Criticism from A to Z), Tübingen, Basel, Vienna 1972; Martin Greiffenhagen (ed), *Kampf um Wörter? Politische Begriffe im Meinungsstreit* (Fight for Words? Controversy over Political Concepts), Bonn 1980 (*Schriftenreihe der Bundeszentrale für politische Bildung*). Herbert Marcuse, in *Soviet Marxism: a Critical Analysis*, New York, Columbia University Press, 1958, sharply criticizes the ideological use of language in Soviet society. The same author in *One-Dimensional Man*, pp.13ff, 85–104, 168, gives a penetrating criticism of the tendency to 'reification' turning human beings into mere things. Associated with this is the banning of all elements which contradict a materialistic and conservative understanding of enlightenment and which cannot be verified by plain materialism. This is carried out under the pretext of purifying the language (for instance, Ludwig Wittgenstein, 'Wiener Kreis' (Vienna Circle), Ernst Topitsch, the Behaviourists, Karl R. Popper, Hans Albert, *Traktat über die kritische Vernunft* (Tract on Critical Reason), Tübingen 1968; Wilhelm Kamlah. Religion has been faded out of their thinking).

70. See Brezinka, *Erziehung und Kulturrevolution*, p.154.

71. Brezinka, op. cit., p.156.

determination was esteemed a moral virtue: 'the ability to control oneself, to overcome oneself to the point of selflessness'. According to the modern definition it has become the very opposite, namely 'the ability to enjoy oneself instead of to conquer oneself, the readiness to rebel against moral norms rather than to obey them, the disposition to demand happiness from society and to make use of any chance of self-gratification instead of serving and purifying oneself'. [72]

Whereas the phrase 'maturity' used to mean the ability 'to get along independently in society as it is, conscious of one's moral responsibility', today the concept 'maturity' is defined as the emotional disposition 'to subject society as it is to radical criticism and to help in the work of changing it according to the opposite socialistic ideal of society as it should be'. [73]

One technique of the dialectical re-interpretation of language is the connection of conceptual opposites with negative meanings, such as Herbert Marcuse's 'repressive tolerance', the 'creative hatred' of the theologian Dorothee Sölle, or the re-definition of terms such as 'violence', [74] 'critical', 'bourgeois', etc. The falsifying of political key words, the linguistic forgery which destroys original meanings and then employs the redefined terms as a Trojan horse, plays a considerable part in the process of social decomposition that we are experiencing today. The Chinese sages knew the profound connection between language and the order of the state: 'Premature death, collapse, and ruin do not arise of themselves but through the confusion of terms.' [75] Confucius describes the causal chain that occurs when language is corrupted and weakened:

> If terms be incorrect,
> then statements do not accord with facts;
> and when statements and facts do not accord,
> then business is not properly executed;
> when business is not properly executed,
> order and harmony do not flourish;
> when order and harmony do not flourish,
> then justice becomes arbitrary;
> and when justice becomes arbitrary,
> the people do not know how to move hand or foot.
> Hence, whatever a wise man states he can always define,
> and what he so defines, he can always carry into practice;
> for the wise man will on no account
> have anything remiss in his definitions. [76]

72. Brezinka, op. cit., p.157, with references to further literature.
73. Brezinka, op. cit., p.148. Günther Ebersold, *Mündigkeit – Zur Geschichte eines Begriffs* (Coming of Age – The History of a Concept), Frankfurt 1980.
74. Cf. the remarks on p.69.
75. Lü Bu We (232 B.C.) in H. Tieck (ed), *Wenn ein Blatt sich bewegt*, p.82.
76. *The Analects*, Vol. VII, Book XIII, ch. III, 4–6.

Elsewhere Confucius said: 'I hate the way in which sharp tongues over-throw both states and families.'[77] A statement by the French philosopher Claude Adrien Helvétius shows that this is evidently a phenomenon that appears in different historical epochs: 'He that would instruct and not deceive mankind, should speak their language.'[78]

The Utopia of an Anarchistic Society

In the secular code of values freedom rates highest. It is indeed a funda-mental value, for without freedom the individual cannot develop his per-sonality. The opposite pole to freedom is order. The individual cannot live without this either, for unlimited freedom is the end of all security; it brings chaos. Order is the twin sister of freedom and the sworn enemy of arbitrary will. The relationship between freedom and order is one of ten-sion – a not uncommon situation between brothers and sisters – and the problem to be solved concerns the principles of authority and structure on which a society should be founded in order that these categories come together in a harmonious and balanced relationship.

Today this view no longer seems to be the *communis opinio*. People have witnessed the excessive cult of the state, the unlimited exercise of power and total loss of freedom in the fascist state, and the consequence is that law and order have fallen into disrepute. For Dahrendorf, the sociologist, it is not 'conflict and change but stability and order that are the pathological special case in life'.[79] For many, the terms law and order seem to be the political slogans of a state that suppresses freedom, for many they are part of an inhuman vocabulary, and thus the theory of anarchy, which has its roots in extreme liberalism and must not be equated with the terror-ism of our times, is happily revived.[80] For some years not only have specific forms of rule been under attack but the very existence of rule itself. It is maintained that the rule of men over men is not a natural thing but the still effective consequence of the Fall of Man, by which Paradise's innocent natural condition of freedom from domination, a condition to which an-archists of all ages would return, was lost. Those who think in this way regard the state as the 'ruling terrorist'.

---

77. *The Analects*, Vol. VII, Book XVII, ch. XVIII.

78. *A Treatise on Man: His Intellectual Faculties and His Education* (1774), Vol. I, p.75, fn.6.

79. *Gesellschaft und Freiheit*, p.81.

80. The most extreme precursor of today's anti-authoritarian and emancipatory education was Max Stirner (1806–56). In his book *The Ego and His Own*, published in 1844, he called for the 'free man' (p.126) and the liberation from all authority (pp.129ff, 227ff, 235ff, 238ff). For him God, freedom, morality, justice, virtue, humaneness were 'fixed ideas' (p.43) or 'fancies' (p.44) and the person who had made these concepts part of his life was simply their prisoner. He considered conscience to be an 'inward servitude', an 'inner police' (p.89). People were educated to 'self-abasement' (p.81) before moral norms which were nothing but 'ghosts' (p.82). 'State, religion, conscience, these despots, make

Herbert Marcuse and others consider every form of sovereignty to be illegal. They demand the completely unhindered development of all human beings, and proclaim a form of communal living – free of rule, anarchistic in the literal sense with no binding restrictions by any encroaching legal institutions – as the only acceptable form of society. Thus they aspire to a form of society in which the 'rule of men over other men' and thus the exploitation of people by others is stopped, in which a 'pacific existence'[81] and a 'successful life'[82] will be possible. This utopian concept envisages a society without want or poverty, a society in which everyone is freed 'from the daily struggle for existence, from earning a living',[83] and in which, therefore, work is abolished. In this land of idleness and luxury a higher degree of rationalism, justice, freedom, beauty, happiness and humaneness will exist, and man will be able to attain 'to authentic self-determination'.[84] The goal is the new man, who has grown up without authority and who is spontaneously creative. This postulate that men should not rule over other men can ultimately be understood as man's wish for infinity, as the wish to be like God: God is *anarchos*, submissive to the will of none.

But the anarchistic concept, i.e. the establishment of a society without domination and without the rule of men over men, is an illusory dream.[85] Max Stirner has written on the unbridled striving for freedom: 'Everything turns on the question, how free must man be? That man must be free, in this all believe; therefore all are liberal too. But the un-man[86] who is something in every individual, how is he blocked? How can it be arranged not to leave the un-man free at the same time with man?'[87] It is not poss-

me a slave' (p.107). Thus one cannot improve the state and society, which can only be 'abrogated, annihilated, done away with, not reformed' (p.235). For Stirner there is no 'destiny' outside man himself (p.326); man is 'called to nothing' and has no 'calling' (p.326) in life: 'My concern is neither the divine nor the human, not the true, good, just, free etc., but solely what is *mine*, and it is not a general one, but is – unique, as I am unique' (p.5).

See also James Joll, *The Anarchists*, London, Eyre & Spottiswoode, 1964 (New York, Grosset & Dunlap 1966); Michael Bakunin, *God and the State*, Glasgow, The Bakunin Press, 1920 (New York, Dover Publication, 1970); Martin Buber, *Der utopische Sozialismus* (Utopian Socialism), Hegner-Bücherei 1967; Jan Cattepoel, *Der Anarchismus. Gestalten, Geschichte, Probleme* (Anarchism. Personalities, History, Problems), Munich 1979; Edith Eucken-Erdsiek, *Magie der Extreme. Von der Schwierigkeit einer geistigen Orientierung* (Magic of the Extremes. On the difficulties of spiritual orientation), Freiburg 1981.

81. Herbert Marcuse, *One-Dimensional Man*, p.235.
82. Jürgen Habermas, 'Erkenntnis und Interesse', p.164.
83. Herbert Marcuse, *One-Dimensional Man*, p.4.
84. Herbert Marcuse, op. cit., p.251.
85. One can seriously ask why it is that believing in God should be considered implausible, whereas believing in the realization of this goal is considered plausible.
86. [Translators note: It should be remembered that to be an 'Unmensch' (un-man) one must be a man. The word means an inhuman or unhuman man, a man who is not man. A tiger, an avalanche, a drought, a cabbage, is not an un-man.]
87. *The Ego and His Own*, II C3, pp.139–40.

ible for people to live together without political order or without ruling institutions, for when people live together and influence each other there is a
constant danger of conflict. This danger of conflict, which could not be
averted even in an affluent society whose members shared the same
interests, derives from the exercise of 'free will, combined with shared
living space'.[88] Conflict becomes a threat to man, because, when the
innate, automatic inhibition to kill is lacking, the settlement of the conflict
can lead to a life-and-death struggle: 'As long as there are practical
reasoning beings influencing each other in a shared living space and acting
without public justice but simply according to what they think is good and
right, then neither individuals nor groups nor whole peoples are safe from
conflicts with each other or acts of violence against each other.'[89]
Communal living without rule leads to *bellum omnium contra omnes* and
'the "right to do everything" turns out on closer analysis to be the right to
do nothing'.[90] Freedom has inherent limits. If freedom is not limited and
ensured by general laws, if there is no binding established law based on
political power, if there is no ruling order, then 'individual freedom is constantly in danger of being reduced to nothing'.[91] The need for rule is a
primal need of man, and the drive for power, like every other drive, has to
be refined. The sense and purpose of rule by the state is to make the use of
violence the exception and living together in peace the norm.

The Permissive Society

The idea of communal living without ruling institutions is the fantastic
dream of a misguided minority. But on the whole contemporary society
tends to break down or push back barriers so as to extend the freedom of
the individual. 'L'imagination au pouvoir!' was one of the political slogans
of the 1968 students' revolution. That the undertaking also entailed
risks – who was worried about that? The prohibition signs toppled
– except for one: 'Prohibition prohibited!' – Taboos taboo!

With sovereign unconcern the permissive society now permits modes of
behaviour that have been taboo for thousands of years, and still the call for
more freedom is raised. 'Our world echoes with the demand for pleasure
and freedom.'[92] Our Western civilization seems to be turning gradually
into a happy 'Mahagonny'[93] where the free development of the personality is expressed in doing everything one wants to.

---

88. Otfried Höffe, 'Herrschaftsfreiheit oder gerechte Herrschaft?'
89. ibid.
90. ibid.
91. ibid.
92. Hans Schaefer, 'Die Sexualität und die Medizin', p.725.
93. *The Rise and Fall of the City of Mahagonny*, opera by Bertolt Brecht and Kurt Weill (1929). In
the city of Mahagonny everything is allowed except having no money.

First and foremost is the demand for freedom *in sexualibus*. Sigmund Freud's psychoanalytical doctrine, according to which repression of sexuality makes one neurotic, sick, miserable and base, has led to the converse message of salvation whereby one only needs to free sex from the traditional, antiquated morality in order to become healthy, happy and good. The English biologist Alex Comfort calls for 'a mentality in which the word "problem" is banished permanently in favour of "enjoyment"'; in his opinion chastity is no more a virtue than malnutrition.[94] Under the influence of this popular psychology a new perspective towards man has developed: nowadays man regards himself as a 'being who seeks pleasure and has a right to obtain it',[95] as one who can claim for himself short-term happiness through orgasm and sexual potency. Maximum satisfaction of one's desires and needs is considered the natural right of man. When one accepts this view of man as merely a biological being, every social influence that restricts and disciplines sexuality appears to be 'unnatural'. Demonstrating that actual sexual behaviour does not at all correspond to the established norms of sexual morality, Kinsey would like to change sexual morality in such a way that the biological facts themselves become the yardstick. With this, as Schelsky aptly remarks, 'the demand for sexual ethics and sexual education is virtually given up completely'.[96]

Thus boundaries hitherto considered unassailable are now being attacked. Some years ago bills were brought before the parliaments of two European states making marriage between people of the same sex or marriage among more than two people, the so-called 'large family', possible. The bills of the parliamentary minorities were not enacted; nevertheless, they demonstrate just how far the discussion has gone and how far the erosion of traditional value-concepts has already advanced. Even the prohibition of incest, as the quotation from Haensch's book shows,[97] no longer goes uncontested. Jürgen Baumann, a professor in criminal law at the University of Tübingen, appeals for the annulment of this prohibition, affirming that there are no reasonable grounds for a father not to have sexual intercourse with his adult daughter.[98] Baumann is by no means alone in his demand. In 1977 at the annual congress of the Society for the Promotion of Social-Scientific Sex Research in Düsseldorf, Ostermeyer, a judge in family law from Bielefeld, stated: 'The prohibition against

94. *Sex in Society*, pp.13, 54.

95. Helmut Schelsky, *Soziologie der Sexualität*, p.111.

96. op. cit. p.53. According to the same logic shop-lifting ought to be accepted because so many people do it and because in all strata of society people have largely lost their inhibitions concerning this kind of theft.

97. cf. note 50, p.35.

98. 'Triebtäter – Menschen oder Unmenschen?' (Sex Criminals – Human Beings or Monsters?). A documentation by the German magazine *Stern* of a symposium that took place in 1969, published by Henri Nannen and Rudolf Wassermann, Hamburg, undated, p.25. But the incest taboo,

masturbation has been lifted, but the natural, physical and tender attraction between parents and children is still suppressed and is branded with the taboo of incest. Thus all sexuality is built up on a foundation that is in ruins. Without the removal of the taboo against incest sexual development will always be hampered by disturbances.' The sex educator Ernst Bornemann called for 'a society in which sexuality is no longer "taught" but can be practised naturally by the parents with their children from birth onwards'. For 'the more the parents allow their children sexual freedom and joy in discovery, the fewer neuroses and aggressions they develop as adults'. [99]

The justification given for this call for uninhibited sexual behaviour is that traditional sexual morality is an instrument of bourgeois domination and its sanctions produce aggression. Wilhelm Reich had already seen in 'sexual morality' and in 'religious mysticism' the 'inner powers' which hold man in a condition of 'bondage and self-subjugation'. [100] A causal relationship is seen between the authoritarian society and the prohibition of sexual activity for children and young people. Thus an important means for educating someone to be 'an emancipated personality' is the encouragement of free sexual activity in childhood and youth: 'The sexual drive should not be suppressed but should be lived out to the full. Thus even small children are encouraged to masturbate, and adolescents in the age of puberty are encouraged to have sexual intercourse with different partners.' [101] Gamm asks that even in schools, rooms be provided in which 'the pupils of both sexes can spend time without being checked up on and in which they are able to enjoy erotic communication'. [102] Sex education in schools should by no means be limited to the general description of the biological facts of sex but should include the use of vulgar expressions and treat all sexual deviations as alternatives. This is the view of two education-alists at the University of Hamburg, Horst Scarbath and Friedrich Koch, as reported in an interview with the magazine *Der Spiegel*, [103] during which Koch declared that part of the teacher's task was not 'to condemn homosexuality but to show it to be a form of sexual behaviour on the same level as heterosexual behaviour'. [104] The change in opinion has taken place

which forbids sexual intercourse between close blood relations, is based not only on moral and social but also on biological reasons. Detailed investigations in Czechoslovakia, England and the USA have shown that half the children produced by father–daughter and brother–sister relationships are mentally handicapped. In addition there is a grave risk of deformities occurring.

99. *Rhein-Neckar-Zeitung* of 28.12.1977.
100. *Die sexuelle Revolution*, p.21. The book was published in English under the title *The Invasion of Compulsory Sex-Morality*, New York, Farraf, Strauss & Giroux, 1971. The quoted passage is taken from a German foreword which is not included in the English edition.
101. W. Brezinka, *Erziehung und Kulturrevolution*, p.175.
102. Quoted in W. Brezinka, op. cit., p.176.
103. Vol. 12/13/1978, pp.95ff.
104. The volume edited by Hans Jochen Gamm and Friedrich Koch, *Bilanz der Sexualpädagogik*

so rapidly: a form of behaviour that until recently was punishable as a criminal offence is now to be offered in schools today as an alternative of equal validity.[105]

Programmes for sex education in U.S. schools, especially in California, which are supported by the Public Health offices and other public institutions, demonstrate that these trends are not a specifically German phenomenon but a Western one. In the Californian programmes of sex education the physiological motive is not stressed as much as the psychological, sociological and ideological motives. The pupils' heads are crammed full, not with knowledge but rather with 'new values'. With the same zeal and missionary fervour that once inspired the Puritan preachers, the message of sexual liberation is now proclaimed. All variations of sexual behaviour are treated in detail. Pupils between thirteen and fourteen years old are given a course in masturbation.[106] In England the Paedophile Information Office is lobbying for toleration of paedophilia and reduction of the legal age of consent for sexual intercourse to four years because they claim that such activity with an adult is 'a rewarding and natural part of a child's development'.[107] Similarly in Germany a 'Society for Paedophilia' is demanding that Paragraph 176 of the German Penal Code, which makes

(Balance-Sheet of Sex Education), Frankfurt 1977, provides a general view of the whole topic from the point of view of progressive pedagogy; see also H. J. Gamm, *Kritische Schule. Eine Streitschrift für die Emanzipation von Lehrern und Schülern* (Critical School. A Pamphlet for the Emancipation of Teachers and Pupils), Munich 1970; Bent H. Claësson, 'Sexualinformation für Jugendliche', Frankfurt, 6th edn, 1979, a sex-education pamphlet in vulgar jargon which explains that 'our attitude towards sexual forms of behaviour, like what we think is worth eating, is based mainly on opinions and prejudices that are conditioned by our culture. Just as we consider it correct to satisfy our hunger it should also be the right of every person to satisfy his sex-drive – even when the satisfaction sometimes occurs in forms that we find hard to comprehend both emotionally and rationally' (p.136). Deviant forms of sex, such as group sex, homosexuality, incest and sodomy are acknowledged and represented as equally valid forms of sex. The only exception is sexual activity with the use of violence.

105. Since April 1979 homosexuals or lesbians living in a relationship similar to marriage can have 'family reductions' on all public transport in the Netherlands (*Süddeutsche Zeitung* of 23.12.1978). The result of a survey carried out by the Allensbach Institute for Opinion Research, 'Morality 78', shows how quickly the change in practice follows upon the change in views. Whereas in 1963 90% of the women interviewed considered marriage necessary, only 42% thought the same in 1978. 70% (1963 : 31%) of the women had had sexual intercourse before their 18th birthday. Among the 13- to 15-year-olds 22% of the boys and 12% of the girls had already had sexual experience. In 1963 it was only 8% and 3% respectively. The comment of the Allensbach directress Elisabeth Noelle-Neumann was: 'This is a sexual revolution' (*Süddeutsche Zeitung* of 24–5.5.1978). A representative inquiry conducted in 1981 by the German Federal Ministry for Family Affairs showed that 82% of all girls and 73% of all boys between the ages of 14 and 17 have already experienced sexual intercourse (*Süddeutsche Zeitung* of 10.7.1981). In other industrial countries the situation is likely to be the same. According to an investigation by the American Congress, one fifth of 13- and 14-year-old American youth had already had sexual intercourse. In more than half of all illegitimate births, the mothers were juveniles (*Süddeutsche Zeitung* of 27.4.1979).

106. On the whole topic see Jacqueline Kasun, 'Turning Children into Sex Experts', in *The Public Interest*, No.55, 1980, pp.3–14, and, by the same author, 'More on the New Sex Education', op. cit., No. 58, 1980, pp.129–37.

107. *Süddeutsche Zeitung* of 19.3.1981.

sexual relations with children under fourteen years a punishable offence, be abolished. Even in Freud's works[108] one can find an insight, confirmed by child psychology, that sexual activity makes the child impossible to educate and that when natural feelings of modesty are destroyed, there is a loss of inhibitions in all other areas, leading to brutality and lack of respect for the personalities of other people. Today, however, this realization is cast to the winds.

An eloquent advocate of the permissive society who has taken an extreme position in his emancipatory drive for freedom is the philosopher Arno Plack.[109] In an impressive literary style he argues that human aggression is not an innate form of behaviour but is acquired when basic drives are frustrated. Man can attain to true fulfilment when his sexuality is no longer suppressed, when he is permitted to live out his spontaneous urges, and when our culture no longer makes such high moral demands on people but integrates the vital basic drives. This thesis can only be understood against the background of a totally materialistic, hedonistic, pansexual concept of man as presented by the popularized theory of 'libido'. According to Plack the root of all evil is the 'society which suppresses the basic drives'. In his opinion, 'It is impossible for a person to be contented, peaceable and at the same time sexually dissatisfied. To demand humility, love of one's fellow man and renunciation of the basic drives from the one and the same person is to demand too much of him, both of his morals and of his nerves.'[110] Man's only chance lies in his reconciling himself 'with his vital urges' and freeing himself from the 'compulsion to follow taboos which are hostile to his drives'.[111]

We can already see today that total emancipation from traditional rules of behaviour has not brought what its prophets had hoped for, namely freedom, but rather its opposite: a new form of slavery. Not happiness, as Nietzsche expected, but horror lies 'beyond good and evil'. The much-praised abolition of sexual taboos by the acceptance of pre-marital, extra-marital and deviant forms of sex, as well as by the view that marriage is simply a form of communal living on the same level as other forms, and the advancing tendency towards promiscuity, have not led to greater freedom[112] but created new frustrations and neuroses. The apparent gain in freedom which sexual liberation produced has changed abruptly into a loss of freedom, into the obligation to be sexually permissive. In our society, social convention now demands sexual success from everybody. Only someone who is sexually successful is considered to be fully developed. The

108. *Three Essays on the Theory of Sexuality*, pp.57–8.
109. *Die Gesellschaft und das Böse. Eine Kritik der herrschenden Moral*, Munich 1967.
110. *Die Gesellschaft und das Böse*, p.347. Cf. p.367.
111. Arno Plack, *Plädoyer für die Abschaffung des Strafrechts*, p.211.
112. This has also been observed by the psychoanalyst Erich Fromm, *To Have or to Be?* p.80.

achievement-orientated way of thinking is applied to this area too, and in its wake comes the fear of impotence. Schelsky describes how this profound mechanism works: 'When sexual potency and orgasm become the conventional norm, a generally accepted standard is created and simultaneously fear and anxiety are put into the mind of the individual that he might fail to live up to this standard. Fear of impotence and anxiety have thus become a widespread phenomenon of modern society. The "liberating" abolition of conventional modesty by means of sexual frankness only leads conversely to a new social convention in which the obligation to have orgasmic experience is imposed on the individual.'[113] The image of unlimited freedom is revealed as a chimera: 'Thus the girl who today indulges in petting, or even in free love, may be actuated by a spirit just as conventional as were her aunts or great-aunts who treated young men with the utmost formality.'[114]

Not even a hint of what Plack expects from the complete liberation of the basic drives, i.e. the gradual reduction of aggressiveness, can be seen. Some at least of the desired success should be visible by now; our society should have become just a little bit more peaceful and happy since the so-called 'sex-wave' in the course of a few years shattered and largely abolished the norms which had been regarded as absolutely valid for centuries. But lo and behold, the opposite is the case. In the meantime the simultaneous increase in aggressiveness has become an extensive research field for social scientists. Hans Schaefer aptly observes: 'The idea that the suppression of sexuality provokes aggression is a hypothesis for which there is absolutely no proof; history even proves it to be completely wrong. Not for centuries have sexual mores been so loose as they are today. Sexual morality was also at a low ebb after the Reformation and during the Enlightenment. It would be hard to outdo the atrocities of aggression that happened and are still happening in these sexually "enlightened" periods.'[115] Sweden's and Denmark's repression-free societies have also been unable to reduce the frequency of sexual neurosis and sex crimes. The complete liberation of sexuality is just as damaging as total restraint. 'Total freedom', says Schaefer, 'contains an element of total social destruction'.[116]

And otherwise, general permissiveness according to the Terentian motto *Homo sum; humani nil a me alienum puto* is the catch-word of our society. Personal action is determined by one's own will as long as direct social harm is not evident. The new humane attitude tends towards abso-

---

113. *Soziologie der Sexualität*, p.112.
114. Esther Harding, *The Way of all Women*, p.195.
115. 'Die Sexualität und die Medizin', p.725.
116. op. cit.

lute tolerance; it 'aims at the approval of absolutely everything that people dream up . . . Every peculiarity of human behaviour should now be able to claim public legitimation and moral approval.'[117] Our society 'respects qualities of every kind – except the spiritual ones: these are even contraband. This society demands that we show unlimited patience towards every kind of foolishness, buffoonery, absurdity and dullness; personal qualities should beg forgiveness or else be kept hidden.'[118] Tolerance, once a humane principle, has become an absolute duty: the obligation to compromise and to tolerate. The 'permissive society' not only permits everything, it also practically demands that everyone should allow everyone else to do whatever he wants. The moral indifference of society towards 'deviant behaviour' is a result of this. The concept of guilt is to be eliminated from the law: 'The "so-called Evil" has long been interpreted out of existence anthropologically, psychologically and sociologically, and thus it is actually no longer punishable.'[119] Every form of moral disapproval is publicly proscribed. Terms which contain negative moral judgements have been eliminated from German law and replaced by concepts that are neutral.[120] A hundred years after Friedrich Nietzsche's 'campaign against morality',[121] morality is lying in its death throes. It is not merely that the content of the traditional moral code has been undermined and has lost its general binding force, but that the moral code itself is no longer considered self-evident. It has been banished into the realm of private morals and even there is felt by many to be a kind of stupidity. Even the word 'moral' is gradually disappearing from the general vocabulary. Denounced as an instrument of social repression, it is now nothing more than a name for 'concepts which people uphold but which actually run counter to their real needs'.[122] When people speak of morality

---

117. Friedrich Tenbruck, 'Ethos und Religion in einer zukünftigen Gesellschaft', p.37.

118. Arthur Schopenhauer, *Counsels and Maxims*, V, 9.

119. H. Schelsky, *Die Arbeit tun die anderen*, p.379.

120. For instance, the term 'Unzucht' (fornication) in the 13th paragraph of the German penal code, because it represents a religious and moral value judgement, was replaced by 'sexuelle Handlung' (sexual behaviour). The terms 'Landstreicher' and 'Stadtstreicher' (vagabond, vagrant) are avoided because of their disparaging and discriminating connotation and are replaced by the neutral term 'Nichtseßhafter' (person of no fixed abode), a term which could also be applied to a nomadic Somalian shepherd. In general sociology tends to replace terms which imply a definite reproach by social terms that are neutral and abstract. One no longer says 'alcoholic', 'beggar', or 'criminal', but speaks of 'fringe groups', the 'underprivileged', the 'stigmatized', the 'socially discriminated', the 'socially discredited', etc. Schelsky points out that sociology has provided no other group with such a rich vocabulary (*Die Arbeit tun die anderen*, p.432).

121. *Ecce Homo*, p.91. According to Nietzsche morality is 'a useful error' (*The Will to Power*, No.402), a 'capital crime against life' (*The Will to Power*, No.251), 'anti-nature' (*Twilight of the Idols*, p.42), 'the great original sin of reason' (*Twilight of the Idols*, pp.47 – 8), 'the Circe of philosophers' (*The Dawn of Day*, Author's Preface, 3) and virtue is 'an honourable form of stupidity' (*The Will to Power*, No.320).

122. Dietrich Haensch, *Repressive Familienpolitik*, p.166.

it is almost always with an ironic undertone[123] (in terms such as 'peck-sniffery' or 'moralizer') or in the enlightened emancipatory sense (the 'prevailing morality'). 'Morality has lost its good conscience', writes Tenbruck, 'but without evil there is no good, without moral disapproval there are no ethics.'[124] The feeling for what is right, and firm moral concepts are, according to the animal behaviourist Konrad Lorenz, 'as indispensable for the interaction of our social behaviour patterns as the thyroid is for our hormones'.[125] In a statement that is valid for all time Aristotle defined the man without morals, without virtues and without law and justice: 'Man, when perfected, is the best of animals; but if he be isolated from law and justice he is the worst of all. Injustice is all the graver when it is armed injustice; and man is furnished from birth with arms (such as, for instance, language) which are intended to serve the purposes of moral prudence and virtue, but which may be used in preference for opposite ends. That is why, if he be without virtue, he is a most unholy and savage being, and worse than all others in the indulgence of lust and gluttony.'[126]

The Innocence Mania

A trend accompanying the general permissiveness of our society is revealed in the altered attitude to crime and to individual responsibility. When the Christian concept of man disappeared so too did belief in personal responsibility. In a famous play, Georg Büchner[127] expresses poetically the conviction that the individual acts under an unshakeable compulsion and has no freedom of choice: 'Who spoke that "must", who? What is it in us that whores, lies, steals, and murders? We're puppets drawn by unknown

---

123. Of course, there is a fusty, narrow-minded virtue which consists of superficial propriety and moral self-satisfaction and is but a caricature of true virtue. It is indeed difficult to bear paragons of such a stamp. Heinrich Heine, weary of the obvious virtue of the Biedermeier, wrote: 'Oh, daß ich große Laster säh,/Verbrechen, blutig kolossal – /Nur diese satte Tugend nicht,/Und zahlungsfähige Moral!' (Oh, that I might see great depravity, Crimes, bloody and terrific, But not this smug virtue, And complacent morality.) (Romances, 'Anno 1829', in *The Poetical Works of Heinrich Heine*, Vol. II, p.7.) If Heinrich Heine were to return to us today, his verses would probably, in the face of our reality, stick in his throat. The belief held by the philosophers of the Enlightenment (Diderot, d'Holbach), that the materialistic principle was a stronger basis for ethics than the religious principle of the 'transcendental soul' ever could be, has been conclusively refuted by the historical developments since that time. Feydeau and Labiche wrote bitter caricatures of the double standard of the bourgeoisie. Their comedies show that morality in the middle classes during the *fin de siècle* was to a large extent just a façade. People were expected to preserve the appearance of a morality to which they no longer felt obliged. Since then morality has evaporated in the atmosphere of a materialistic and atheistic ideology. As Alfons Auer notes with regard to morality's present crisis, 'the emancipation *of* the ethical' which occurred at the beginning of modern times was followed by the 'emancipation *from* the ethical' (*Autonome Moral und christlicher Glaube*, p.11).
124. Friedrich Tenbruck, 'Ethos und Religion in einer zukünftigen Gesellschaft', p.36.
125. *Civilized Man's Eight Deadly Sins*, p.52.
126. *The Politics of Aristotle*, Book I, 1253ª26.
127. 1813–37.

powers on wire; nothing, nothing in ourselves.'[128] Nietzsche called the concept of free will 'the most infamous of all the arts of the theologian' and Christianity because of its affirmation of man's responsibility 'a hangman's metaphysics'.[129]

Over the last few decades there has been an endless dispute about free will and human responsibility, especially in the sphere of penal law. Free will, responsibility and guilt are rejected as absurd.[130] The subject of research of the modern social sciences is man, and 'yet they have lost sight of man'.[131] Orientated towards a materialistic concept[132] of man they see him as a being determined by his drives and the restraints imposed upon him by society: man is not free to act independently: 'Man is described as a being that either only reacts to impulses (the behavioural model) or works off his drives (the psychodynamic model).'[133]

Arno Plack calls the teaching of indeterminism 'an egocentric theory which prescribes that man be a little god who can choose between good and evil in like manner'.[134] The idea of free will as 'the basis of decent bourgeois behaviour' seems to him 'a vain over-estimation of a person's subjective adaptation, following the uniform drilling of early childhood and conditioned by the ever-present compulsion to conform to social demands for more achievement and more consumption'.[135] Man, as the plaything of his own drives and compulsions from outside, as 'the transformer of blind causal powers which pass through him',[136] is consequently unable to decide between good and evil in an exercise of free will. The basis of this viewpoint is the 'Theory of Psychoanalysis' which holds that conscious actions are directed from depths of which the individual is

---

128. *Danton's Death*, Act II, Scene v.

129. *Twilight of the Idols*, p.53, No.7.

130. See Karl Menninger, *Strafe – ein Verbrechen?* (Punishment – a Crime?), Munich 1970; Manfred Danner, 'Die Bestimmtheit des Willens' (The Determination of the Will), special issue of the Kriminologische Schriftenreihe der Deutschen Kriminologischen Gesellschaft, from *Kriminologische Wegzeichen*, Husum 1977; Hellmut Groos, *Willensfreiheit oder Schicksal* (Free Will or Fate?), Munich 1939; B. F. Skinner, *Beyond Freedom and Dignity*, radically denies guilt, responsibility and the existence of objective values.

131. Wilhelm Revers, 'Die szientistische Einäugigkeit des modernen Realitätsbewußtseins', in O. Schatz (ed), *Hoffnung in der Überlebenskrise?*, p.198.

132. The 'new' concept of man is based on the discovery that man, on the pathway to higher development, has developed from animal forebears. The spiritual nature of man, his rational soul, which in the last analysis constitutes his being, is 'to a large extent seen as a mere "superstructure" over man's nature. This is considered to be determined by the basic drives, and therefore the soul has no independent meaning and is given no importance of its own.' (Anton Griffel, *Der Mensch – Wesen ohne Verantwortung?*, p.14. The author treats this whole question in detail.)

133. Viktor Frankl, 'Die Sinnfrage in der Psychotherapie', p.320. Frankl reproaches the social sciences with still not having come close to the real *Humanum*: 'They are not humane, but homuncular.'

134. *Plädoyer für die Abschaffung des Strafrechts*, p.210.

135. op. cit., p.208.

136. Reinhard Maurach, *Deutsches Strafrecht, Allgemeiner Teil*, p.359.

unconscious. It follows that he cannot be blamed for his actions and thus there can be no guilt, only failure; every act, both for the one who commits it and for the one who suffers from it, is an act of fate, just something that befalls him like the common cold or the plague. The findings of depth psychology have led to a moral exoneration of the individual: 'The evidence that man is influenced in his impulses by "socialization", i.e. by education, environment, economic conditions etc., leads him, overestimating this idea, to the irrational belief[137] that he has an excuse for behaviour that is directed against moral, lawful or political standards, and thus he demands that "the circumstances" be altered, i.e. the condition of the family, the schools, the teaching institutions and administration.'[138]

As a result, when man is not a responsible being acting under the firm command of a *thou shalt*, but a creature determined by natural and social forces and automatisms, deviation from the norm seems to be a kind of social sickness or a reflection of the prevailing socio-economic conditions, for which the perpetrator is only partly responsible, if at all: 'The principle of personal responsibility and the basic penal principle of guilt and atonement cannot be upheld, when the "deed", whatever it may be, is essentially the result of social factors unfavourable to the person. The person as "guilty party" cannot be made accountable for the deed but needs "resocialization", i.e. an alteration of the social circumstances which determine him.'[139]

In the meantime the popular opinion that crime is determined exclusively by social forces and is nothing but a reflection of social conditions has become a dogma. The current formula of the good individual and the bad society is not limited to academic discussion; as a highly welcome excuse it has penetrated the general consciousness and is thus in itself a factor that leads to crime. Viktor Frankl, professor at the University of Vienna, points out that this 'deductionism' persuades the individual that 'he is the victim of circumstances' and thus provides the criminal with an alibi. 'Now the responsibility can be shifted on to psychodynamic mechanisms or conditioning processes.'[140]

From this it is not far to depth psychology and Mechler's view that the criminal is a 'scapegoat on to which society projects and works out its own feelings of guilt'. The 'powerless and defenceless addressee of the aggressions which have been bottled up through the denial of the basic drives' stands for every individual and thus draws upon himself the punishment which 'every individual believes he himself has earned'.[141] When one

137. The author means 'belief' in the context of 'social salvation' which has replaced the 'salvation of the soul' of the dying traditional religion (cf. the discussion on pp.10ff.).
138. H. Schelsky, *Die Arbeit tun die anderen*, p.382.
139. H. Schelsky, op. cit., p.379.
140. 'Die Sinnfrage in der Therapie', p.330.

punishes delinquents one is vicariously attacking the hated and repressed asocial or unsocial traits within oneself. This psychological theory thereby insinuates that everybody has the desire to steal, deceive, rob, burn and rape, and maintains that the renunciation of such acts leads directly to aggression against the person who dares to fulfil his drives. Thus Plack sees in the penal code a 'mad system'[142] based on 'moral prejudices', the 'outgrowth of a society that has developed through aggression'.[143] Similarly he sees 'active hatred towards one's fellow men' at work in a society of 'vitally frustrated people who have to express their annoyance at their own renunciation either in direct aggression that is socially harmful or in the aggressive act of punishment'.[144] Plack then demands the abolition of all kinds of penal law.[145] Mauz states the same postulate: 'Criminal justice is class justice . . . Even in the classless society the class of the righteous judges over the class of the unrighteous . . . If class justice is to be abolished then criminal justice must be abolished.'[146] His alternative to the abolished penal code, namely 'total solidarity',[147] shows his remoteness from reality. Mauz believes: 'It only requires that we give up judging over others, that we decide with them, for them, and thus for ourselves as well, to strive to find solutions'[148] – empty catchphrases!

Such views are by no means restricted to academic theorizing but have already found expression in the demands of a practising judge: Hellmuth Ostermeyer, a judge in Bielefeld, considers punishment to be nothing but 'the revenge of society', and 'counter-aggression against the crime; in its nature it is not different from the crime itself, but pits violence against violence. The cause, the extent and the form of the punishment are different from the crime, but for the subconscious – and this is the main thing – they are one and the same, two similar items on two pages of the same account . . . It is the punishment which turns behavioural maladjustment into criminality, and imprisonment produces the hardest form of criminality, for it is the hardest reaction.' In this context Ostermeyer also speaks of 'so-called morality'. Like Plack he demands the abolition of punishment, the closing of prisons and the treatment of convicts in freedom. It is 'a reaction without blame, without declaring the culprit a criminal, without moral condemnation or stigmatization'.[149] He believes

141. 'Der Verbrecher als Sündenbock der Gesellschaft', p.1.
142. *Plädoyer für die Abschaffung des Strafrechts*, Foreword.
143. op. cit., p.19.
144. op. cit., p.23.
145. See also Max Stirner, *The Ego and His Own*, pp.238ff.
146. *Das Spiel von Schuld und Sühne*, p.132.
147. op. cit., pp.133, 286.
148. op. cit., p.7.
149. The offender is no longer judged from a moral point of view. Even serious criminal acts are no hindrance to receiving public honours and awards. In January 1980 the Senator for Culture in Bremen awarded the prize donated by the Free Hanseatic City of Bremen to encourage young authors and

that 'as the prisons disappear, so will gradually the criminals'. [150] 'Cure' instead of punish is the motto.

This is the ultimate consequence of a misunderstanding of the concept of equality: all men are equal, the good and the bad. No moral differences are acknowledged between men any more because a moral evaluation no longer occurs. This kind of thinking has grave consequences, both for the person who believes in these conclusions, and for the society which treats him accordingly. If structures, namely society and the environment, are the sole causes of socially harmful or even criminal behaviour, then it is no wonder that people who confess to being guilty as the result of their own mistakes, inadequacies and failures are becoming more of a rarity. The inability to see and acknowledge guilt, a kind of innocence mania, is on the increase. When a person is persuaded that his deed is only a behavioural maladjustment determined by the social influences of the environment and therefore morally of little consequence, and when he is told that he was unable to act otherwise, then he is deprived of the last things that might motivate him to act in future according to the behavioural norms: a guilty conscience, insight into his guilt and remorse. But these concepts are not spared by the modern enlighteners either. Nietzsche called the guilty conscience 'a sickness', [151] and this statement of Plack's cannot be outdone for its negative attitude to morality: 'This is the utmost humiliation for a human being: by means of an education hostile to the basic instincts or by manifest brainwashing he is made to have a feeling of sin or of guilt, although from a vital point of view (i.e. opposed to an anti-sensual morality) or even in relation to other cultures, he is in the right.' [152] Anyone who still feels guilty or remorseful is sick and in need of therapy.

This form of thinking, which will have enormous social consequences to an extent that cannot as yet be foreseen, is to be found among teachers, social workers, jurists and even theologians. It is widespread among psychiatric and psychological experts. Recently, however, the psychiatrist Viktor Frankl pointed out that the psychological concept of aggression in the Freudian sense or even the biological concept of Konrad Lorenz's com-

---

worth DM 5.000 to a writer who supports the terrorists and who had been sentenced to 15 years in prison for attempting to murder two policemen. The book for which the prize was awarded describes among other things how to set fire to the house of a judge or public prosecutor. Whereas in the past it was considered a stigma to have been in prison, criminals try nowadays to make capital out of their crimes: discharged prisoners go from door to door clutching their discharge papers, or wander through the streets wearing sandwich boards with the announcement: 'I don't want to steal', a statement which in reality means: If you don't give me anything, I'll go and get what I want.

150. *Kanal 22. Information des Lübecker Arbeitskreises Resozialisierungshilfe* (Channel 22. Information of the Lübeck Work Group for Aid in Resocialization), Vol. 4, No. 1, 1976, pp.21–5. Cf. also his book *Die bestrafte-Gesellschaft. Ursachen und Folgen eines falschen Rechts* (The Punished Society. Causes and Consequences of a Legal System that is Wrong), Munich, Vienna 1976.
151. *The Geneaology of Morals*, XIX.
152. *Plädoyer für die Abschaffung des Strafrechts*, p.214.

parative behavioural research cannot be applied to the emotional and instinctive life of man, since this expresses intention: 'Whatever the
biological or psychological causes of the aggression may be, on the human
level I let them (in Hegel's sense) develop into something quite different:
on the human level I *hate*! And in contrast to aggression hate is directed
towards something that I hate. Hate and love are human phenomena,
because they are intentional.' According to Frankl the human
phenomenon is not 'aggression' but 'hatred', and man 'will not stop
hating if he is persuaded that he is ruled by mechanisms and impulses.
This fatalism is not aware that whenever I am aggressive it is not the
mechanism and impulses that are in me and that may exist in my id, but it
is I who hates, and there is no excuse for that, only responsibility'.[153]

Secular Substitutes for Values

The fruits of the decay of the value-system are now manifest. The idea that
man has duties as well as rights, and that he owes a debt to society, has
vanished. 'The emphasis is now on one's "rights" – on what society owes
you. But there can never be rights without duties.'[154] The growing habit of
continually making claims, a form of behaviour 'that allows almost no
scope for political activity', is intensified by the fact that 'responsible
persons in politics, economics and science conform to the general trends for
opportunistic reasons'.[155] Human warmth and the readiness to help one
another are disappearing more and more. Selflessness no longer has any
value. It is not just that people are no longer encouraged to cultivate this
virtue; the virtue itself is ridiculed, although people cannot live together
successfully without it. Altruism is one of the greatest behavioural faults of
our time according to Ayn Rand, who forcefully argues that people should
strive for their own goals and live out their emotions without regard for
others.[156] Duty and discipline are rejected in favour of spontaneity and
emotion. A large number of so-called intellectuals, who live very well on
the surplus produced by others, condemn those very virtues to which, in
the final analysis, they owe their comfort and well-being: a sense of order,
diligence, efficiency, a sense of duty. But a society cannot exist without a
certain measure of discipline and a sense of duty, least of all a society like
ours which is so highly technical and thus more susceptible to disorders.
Taylor rightly points out that even the most dedicated drop-out can
scarcely want the surgeon who is removing his appendix not to carefully
count the clamps, nor will he want the mechanic who is doing the oil

153. 'Das existentielle Vakuum', p.92.
154. Taylor, *How to Avoid the Future*, p.99.
155. Reiner Schmidt, 'Der geforderte Staat', in *Neue Juristische Wochenschrift*, 1980, p.161.
156. Quoted in Taylor, *How to Avoid the Future*, p.100.

change on his car to forget to screw the cap back on tightly. There is a striking contradiction in the thinking of those who turn their backs on the 'achievement-society' and refuse their loyalty and co-operation, at the same time as they are maintained by this very society. Similarly, those who revile and reject the principle of performance morally condemn a system from which they themselves are reaping the benefits and which 'gives them moral authority together with good living and a high income'.[157] This contradiction does not disconcert them at all.

At the top of the hierarchy of secular 'values', after the demand for unlimited freedom comes the quadriga of doubt, criticism, protest and conflict in place of all the values which alone guarantee the cohesion and functioning of society. This 'gang of four', these modern 'cardinal virtues',[158] are increasingly replacing the old ones. Doubt[159] and criticize everything, protest[160] continually, and become conflict-conscious – that is the slogan.

Now it cannot be denied that doubt and criticism are indispensable and have a stabilizing influence in communal living and in a flourishing community. But these negative positions become dangerous when they are no longer integrated into the structure of values and then attain such an overpowering emphasis as to replace all those values which restrain and cultivate man. They then become the vehicle of unbridled aggressiveness. Social cohesion cannot be established exclusively on doubt, criticism, and protest.

Conflict is also inherent in human communal life, and even the best of all possible social orders, even the 'Kingdom of God on earth' – as far as this concept is imagined as something to be realized on this earth and is not naively misunderstood – will not rid the world of conflict between people. There will always be conflicts. Even the most peaceful of societies will not attain the peaceful tranquillity of the churchyard. But such a society will put at our disposal means by which we can deal with conflicts most effectively; it will stop the vicious circle of violence and guarantee a

---

157. H. Schelsky, *Die Arbeit tun die anderen*, p.252.
158. Cf. p.217 n.102 on the classical cardinal virtues.
159. Helmut Schelsky notes sarcastically that the self-assured motto *query everything* is 'one of the most valuable confirmations of one's own self-confidence. There is actually nothing which has not been "queried". Today there are whole institutions and associations simply for the task of continually "querying". Yet they have nothing more to offer on these questions than an upheaval of opinions and permanent reflection on them, called "dialogue".' (*Die Arbeit tun die anderen*, p.124; cf. also p.407.)
160. The education programme of emancipation is one that teaches protest. According to the guidelines put out by the Ministry of Education of one of the German states, young people 'should be able to either acknowledge or reject, independently and on their own responsibility, the present valid laws of our state'. That is, as Schelsky aptly remarks, 'as formulated in the best emancipatory style, the education of teaching people to break the law and revolt when they are convinced they are in the right'. (*Die Arbeit tun die anderen*, p.409.)

peaceful solution to conflicts. Johan Galtung was not so wrong in seeing conflict as the 'salt of life' and the 'great giver of energy'. He points out that 'we feel most alive just when we are confronted with a conflict that really challenges us and when we gradually succeed in mastering this conflict'.[161] However, when social conflict is greeted as a 'form of living'[162] and is given a decisive role as the generator of progress towards a humane society, when conflict is sought or artificially created and enacted in order to reveal the 'social contradictions' and to 'bring latent conflicts out into the open',[163] when rifts are created between people, rifts that would never have developed without agitation from outside, when existing conflicts are not only revealed but intensified, when conflict is taught by a form of education that denounces every form of rule, suspects social co-operation, defends the deliberate raising of conflict, and trains young people to distrust and rebel, when revolt is taught and practised instead of the mastering of conflicts, then aggression, polarization and destruction are inevitable.[164] Hans Heigert has satirized the new commandments in the following way: 'You must not conform! You must find yourself by first offering resistance; always speak your mind and express your interests. Don't let anyone persuade you of anything; be mistrustful, especially towards those who rule in your home, school and state. Expose your social environment, see through the manipulation, have the courage to confront structures and institutions, break through the taboos, always find the reality behind the accepted standard, unmask the interests of the others and analyze your role in society. So, provoke, refuse, fulfil yourself!' In his opinion 'those who educate their youth in such a way must not be surprised if at the end the opposite of freedom emerges, namely a fanaticism that is always linked with the readiness to put oneself totally at the disposal of others, in other words to subjugate oneself'.[165] There is a

161. *Strukturelle Gewalt*, p.129. Goethe also believed that 'in the course of life, the outer and the inner remain in incessant conflict, and that one must therefore daily arm himself to maintain the ever-renewed struggle'. (Letter to Thomas Carlyle of 14 March 1828, in *Correspondence between Goethe and Carlyle*, p.77.)
162. J. Galtung, *Strukturelle Gewalt*, p.129.
163. On the whole subject see W. Brezinka, *Erziehung und Kulturrevolution*, pp.59, 70, 117ff.
164. Under the misleading title of 'critical peace education' an 'education towards aggression' is expressly demanded, the aim of which is to 'develop didactic models for the use of violence which is to be collectively controlled and kept within democratic rules' (Eberhard Rauch and Wolfgang Anzinger, *Wörterbuch kritischer Erziehung* (Dictionary of Critical Education) quoted in W. Brezinka, op. cit., p.118). Advocates of conflict-orientated behaviour can also be found among the theologians. Cf. Hans-Eckehard Bahr, 'Konfliktorientierung und Versöhnungsziel. Instrumentelle Protestgewalt bei emanzipativem Ziel?' (Conflict Orientation and the Goal of Reconciliation), in *Zeitschrift für evangelische Ethik* (Journal for Protestant Ethics), January 1975, No. 1, pp.59ff. See also H. J. Krymansky, *Soziologie des Konflikts* (The Sociology of Conflict), Reinbek 1971; H. Schelsky, *Die Arbeit tun die anderen*, pp.394–8, p.307.
165. 'Das bedrohte Pfingsten' (The Threatened Pentecost), *Süddeutsche Zeitung*, Pentecost 1973. Cf. Hans Heigert, *Jugend ohne Normen? Eine Generation auf der Suche* (Youth without Standards? A Generation in Search of Something), Düsseldorf 1978; R. Oltmann, *Du hast keine Chance, aber nütze*

daily increase in the number of those who, growing up in a climate marked by the lack of religious orientation and not learning to be selfless, to be willing to sacrifice, to have a sense of duty and to be able to adapt, are taught hopeless scepticism, mistrust and the constant readiness to cause conflict. Thus they reject society, which is highly developed in technology, but all the more susceptible to disorders, and want to 'drop out'. They do not want to be 'oil, but sand in the machinery of society'.[166] Herbert Marcuse's sermon on the 'Great Refusal' of the 'achievement society', the defamation of performance and the denunciation of the demand for performance made by 'our social and economic system as the characteristic form of modern inhumanity'[167] has not gone unheard. A society of *rien ne va plus* casts a sinister shadow before it.

The moral decline of our society is apparent in all areas. Over forty years ago Shoghi Effendi described the signs of it as a result of the dethronement of religion: 'The recrudescence of religious intolerance, of racial animosity, and of patriotic arrogance; the increasing evidences of selfishness, of suspicion, of fear and of fraud; the spread of terrorism, of lawlessness, of drunkenness and of crime; the unquenchable thirst for, and the feverish pursuit after, earthly vanities, riches and pleasures; the weakening of family solidarity; the laxity in parental control; the lapse into luxurious indulgence; the irresponsible attitude towards marriage and the consequent rising tide of divorce; the degeneracy of art and music, the infection of literature, and the corruption of the press; the extension of the influence and activities of those "prophets of decadence" who advocate companionate marriage, who preach the philosophy of nudism, who call modesty an intellectual fiction, who refuse to regard the procreation of children as the sacred and primary purpose of marriage, who denounce religion as an opiate of the people, who would, if given free rein, lead back the human race to barbarism, chaos, and ultimate extinction – these appear as the outstanding characteristics of a decadent society, a society that must either be reborn or perish.'[168]

---

sie. Eine Jugend steigt aus (You have no chance, but use it. Young People Drop Out), Reinbek 1981; K. Angst, 'Jugendprotest und Krise der politischen Kultur', in *Neue Züricher Zeitung*, 3.9.1980; W. Hollstein, *Die Gegengesellschaft. Alternative Lebensformen* (The Counter Society. Alternative Ways of Life), Reinbek 1981; 'Jugend und Gesellschaft. Chronischer Konflikt – neue Verbindlichkeiten?', *Bergedorfer Gesprächskreis zu Fragen der freien industriellen Gesellschaft*, Protokoll No. 63, 1979; 'Was bleibt noch vom staatsbürgerlichen Grundkonsens? Jugendprotest, Wertwandel, Krise der politischen Kultur', *Bergedorfer Gesprächskreis*, Protokoll No. 70, 1981; J. Gehret (ed), *Gegenkultur heute. Die Alternativbewegung von Woodstock bis Tunix*, Amsterdam 1979.

166. Rolf Schwendter, *Theorie der Subkultur*, p.10.

167. H. Schelsky, *Die Arbeit tun die anderen*, pp.244ff. On the whole subject see Helmut Schoeck, *Ist Leistung unanständig?* (Is Performance Indecent?), Osnabrück 1971; Johannes Gross, 'Fußnoten zur Leistungsgesellschaft' (Footnotes on the Achievement Society), *Frankfurter Allgemeine Zeitung* of 25.5.1972.

168. 'The Unfoldment of World Civilization', in *The World Order of Bahá'u'lláh*, pp.187–8; see also Shoghi Effendi, *The Promised Day is Come*, p.43.

Today these features, recognized at that time with astonishing clarity, have been intensified and consolidated in a society that is in the process of disintegration. The barbarization of our lives and the decay of our culture[169] are considerably advanced. A counterculture[170] has established itself in which 'dishonesty, irrationality, prejudice, intolerance, incivility, violence and destruction appear as prime values, while honesty, reason, impartiality, tolerance, manners, care, effort and creation are denigrated and made anti-values', writes Taylor. He notes further: 'such a complete reversal is unprecedented in the history of Western culture'.[171] The extent to which public spirit and morality are vanishing is shown by the state's need to govern according to an ever-growing body of regulations. It is compelled to intervene more and more in the affairs of its peoples, creating more rules, ordinances and prohibitions, whereas in the past the sense of moral good and public spirit was ingrained in society so that the citizen knew without any external directive how he should behave. The flood of laws which now becomes necessary because of the lack of consensus is one of the reasons why the administrative machine has become so inflated, why democracy is suffocating under the pressure of bureaucracy and people are becoming increasingly disillusioned with the state. The fact that lack of morality cannot be compensated by law-making was postulated long ago by Lao Tse: 'The more display there is of legislation, the more thieves and robbers there are.'[172]

The moral condition of our society is demonstrated by the increase in lying. Of course, lying is as old as human history: 'All men are liars', said the psalmist,[173] and St. Augustine devoted a whole book to lying.[174] Man tends to misuse language in order to conceal rather than reveal thoughts.[175] But lying has never taken possession of man as overpoweringly as in our times. The extent to which lying pervades our private, social and political life is shown in a recent study by Sissela Bok, a teacher at Harvard University.[176] For a long time the Machiavellian principle that permits lying for the attainment of political goals has determined political practice in East and West in war as in peace. Talleyrand remarked: 'When the integrity of a politician is emphasized too much, people doubt his

169. Cf. Heinz Friedrich, *Kulturkatastrophe. Nachruf auf das Abendland*.

170. Taylor, *How to Avoid the Future*, pp.94ff; Daniel Bell, *The Cultural Contradictions of Capitalism*, pp.72ff, 143 – 4; on the whole subject: Rolf Schwendter, *Theorie der Subkultur*, Frankfurt 1980; David Martin, 'Christianity, Civic Religion and Free Counter-Cultures', in *The Dilemmas of Contemporary Religion*, pp.1– 19.

171. *How to Avoid the Future*, p.99.

172. *The Tao Teh King*, LVII.

173. Ps.116:11.

174. *De mendacio*.

175. From Talleyrand comes the famous saying: 'La parole a été donnée à l'homme pour déguiser sa pensée', quoted in G. Büchmann, *Geflügelte Worte*, p.650.

176. *Lying. Moral Choice in Public and Private Life*, New York 1978.

abilities.' It is an everyday thing in politics for official declarations to be revealed as false and for news reports that have been formally denied to be revealed as correct. It is also common for election promises to be retracted immediately after the election has been won.[177] All this reinforces the widely spread attitude that it is not necessary to be so careful with the truth. This tendency towards dishonesty leads people to lose trust in each other and to mistrust political leaders and institutions. But in a society which is based on dishonesty, deception and mistrust instead of truthfulness, honesty and trust, feelings of insecurity and fear gain ground.[178]

The culture of today is bloodless. In its death agony it is calling for a new breath of life. But instead of new aesthetic values or a new spirituality, there are only the forces of putrefaction and decomposition at work. Symptoms of cultural decadence are: the increasing disintegration of all social mores; the exhibition of ugliness[179] and dirtiness which surround us on all sides; the 'shabby look', the neglect of clothing, hair and social manners; the spread of vulgarity and the language of the gutter,[180] in which even academics carry out their disputes; the power of conviction attributed to faecal terms, i.e. the use of vulgar, sexual, pornographic or obscene words by young academics, obviously to 'create the supposed class identification of the students with the working-class';[181] the use of words related to anal or genital functions which modern writers and playwrights can scarcely do without today. In a society without taboos, nothing is shocking any longer. Delicate hints will no longer do; the gross is required.

177. Bismarck once remarked: 'There is never so much lying as before the elections and after the hunt.'

178. On truthfulness cf. p.210 n.30, also Rúhíyyih Rabbani, *Prescription for Living*, pp.46ff.

179. Punks and skin-heads, working-class subcultures which appeared in the seventies among the young people of English slums, are spreading terror and disgust in German cities too. Wearing the horror-look – close-cropped, brightly-coloured hair; ugly, demonic make-up; dog chains as necklaces; safety pins in pierced ears; clothing deliberately torn – juveniles outrage the public and tear riotously through the streets. With provocative vulgarity of speech and gesture, as well as with physical violence, they parade their contempt of society. Their motto is 'for nothing – against everything!' This new, anti-Establishment, protest wave expresses itself musically through punk-rock, whose shrill, aggressive tones are interpreted as the 'jungle cries' of a generation without a future. In the meanwhile smart businessmen have discovered this gutter trend and realized how this nihilistic lifestyle can be turned to profit. As the latest fashion gimmicks, they are offering clothing with holes at six hundred dollars a time, necklaces of razor blades or hypodermic needles, and earrings made of contraceptive pill wrappings or safety pins.

180. Praised by Herbert Marcuse as 'methodical subversion of the linguistic universe of the Establishment'. He wrote: 'The familiar "obscenities" in the language of the black and white radicals must be seen in this context of a methodical subversion of the linguistic universe of the Establishment . . . The methodical use of "obscenities" in the political language of the radicals is the elemental act of giving a new name to men and things, obliterating the false and hypocritical name which the re-named figures proudly bear in and for the system. And if the renaming invokes the sexual sphere, it falls in line with the great design of the desublimation of culture, which, to the radicals, is a vital aspect of liberation.' (*An Essay on Liberation*, p.35.)

181. Helmut Schelsky, *Die Arbeit tun die anderen*, p.334.

The theatre,[182] the film and the novel have burnt themselves out. They resort more and more to 'expressions of shock and to the exploration of extreme situations', to the 'tedious revelling in pornography and kinky sex'.[183] The aesthetics of shock and sensationalism prevail. The absurd, the glorification of the base, violence, cruelty and sexual perversion predominate; homosexuality, transvestism and sodomy are freely depicted. At the same time scenes of violence and cruelty in films are not 'meant to effect catharsis', but seek 'instead to shock, to maul, to sicken'.[184] Madness[185] is the main theme of the novels of the sixties; insanity, not normality 'has become the touchstone of reality'.[186] Jean Genet,[187] for instance, sentenced after many previous convictions to life imprisonment and pardoned after the intercession of Jean-Paul Sartre because of the works he wrote in prison, transfigures the morally and sexually abnormal man with ecstatic imagery and perverts the moral order into its very opposite. The world of thieves, rapists and murderers is in his eyes the only honest world, fantasies about cannibalism are 'the deepest truth about human desires'.[188] 'Perfectionist of evil', 'Creator of a negative theology', 'demiurge of a counterworld of crime' were among the names thus given to him. In the sensitivity of these writers Daniel Bell sees 'an apocalyptic tremor – like the swallows before a storm – that seems to warn of some impending holocaust'.[189]

Man experiences himself and behaves to a large extent according to the image he has of himself and of the society he lives in, and these images are now largely determined by books and films. Brezinka takes stock of our modern 'cultural business': 'The animal instincts, egoism, primitive behaviour and violence, arrogant individualism, sentimental self-pity, opposition to all kinds of authority, the mockery of all virtues, hostility towards society and culture, predominate in it. The manifestation of evil,

---

182. The theatre is one of those intellectual forces which accurately reflect the times. Today it is far from being the 'moral institution' which Schiller demanded it should be. The German theatre has become the place where the works of world literature are alienated and falsified, where everything to do with values and ideals is ridiculed and scoffed at, where the moral code is debunked and dashed to pieces. In his evaluation of German theatre during the period 1967–80, Georg Hensel (*Das Theater der siebziger Jahre*, Stuttgart 1980) comes to depressing conclusions. He describes the vanity of narcissistic directors who purvey a morbid aestheticism and who regard the portrayal of whatever is sick, perverse or ruined as the highest manifestation of art.

183. Daniel Bell, *The Cultural Contradictions of Capitalism*, pp.108, 144.

184. ibid., p.122.

185. *Wahnsinn, das ganze Leben ist Wahnsinn* (Madness, Life is Madness) is the title of a German film that came out in 1980.

186. D. Bell, op. cit., pp.137ff.

187. *The Thief's Journal*, London 1973; *Our Lady of the Flowers*, New York 1963, is a hymn to homosexuality and a song in praise of murder.

188. D. Bell, op. cit., p.139.

189. D. Bell, op. cit., p.137. There are other features which are undoubtedly part of the 'apocalyptic tremor', for example, films such as *Earthquake* and *Apocalypse Now* or the American phenomenon of 'survivalists', who, armed for survival, withdraw to woods and wildernesses.

the diseased and the ugly form a central theme. It is the world of madness, of crime, of sexual perversity, of total lovelessness, of cruelty, of despair and of suicide. It is a world without beauty, without order, without dignity and without love. The extremely negative experiences of the outsiders of society, the hate-filled fantasies of the failures, and the delusions of the insane are offered to our contemporaries as distorted images for the interpretation of man's nature. The basest is raised to the norm, the noble is negated and striving towards lofty ideals is made fun of. Anyone who is continually exposed to these professions of pessimism and nihilism through the leading literature of today (which is highly critical of our culture), or through philosophy, theatre, film and the visual arts and who does not get to know an alternative finally falls into this spiritual condition himself.'[190] When nothing is holy any more, when every taboo must be broken and every boundary crossed, then quite automatically the tendency to overcome the barrier between 'play-acting' and reality appears. Then 'the craving for violence, first in the theatre and then in the street demonstrations, becomes a necessary psychological drug, a form of addiction'.[191] In view of this situation, Pope John Paul II in Munich, November 1980, put the following question to politicians and artists: 'Is it not possible that the nihilism reflected in the various forms of present-day art could encourage people to find pleasure in things evil, in destruction, in decline and could it not lead to cynicism and contempt for human welfare?'

Escapism

The 'existential vacuum' in which we live leads to a feeling that 'nothing has meaning' and this in turn leads to neuroses and addictions.[192] And so it is not surprising that many people are dropping out and taking flight from a society that has no ideals to offer and transmits neither genuine values nor a sense of meaning. They may well prefer an unsteady, parasitic life without commitment as hippies,[193] vagabonds or vagrants,[194] to life in society; they may seek in nostalgic yearning the simple life; they may try the alternative forms of communal living in the city or the country in the hope of finding themselves, escaping from the practical realities of life[195] in order to find security and warmth in a collective; they may flee into

190. *Erziehung und Kulturrevolution*, pp.19–20.
191. D. Bell, *The Cultural Contradictions of Capitalism*, p.143.
192. Cf. pp.77ff.
193. The appearance of a mass hippy-drug-rock culture 'undermines the social structure' (Bell, op. cit., p.54). On parasitism see Gerd-Klaus Kaltenbrunner, *Die Schmarotzer kommen. Parasitismus als· Lebensform* (Parasitism as a Way of Life), Freiburg 1982.
194. In the Federal Republic of Germany their number is judged to be about 100,000. 40% of them are under the age of thirty (*Süddeutsche Zeitung* of 4.8.1981 and 31.8.1982).
195. Literature: Rosabeth Moss Kanter, (ed), *Communes – Creating and Managing the Collective Life*, New York 1973; Jerome Judson, *Families of Eden*, London 1975; Swami Satyanda, *Ganz ent-*

drugs or alcohol, or finally even commit suicide. What they all have in common is an attitude of radical refusal: they resist every kind of social coercion, curse technical progress and ridicule the bourgeois principle that peace and order should prevail in life.

In a society which has lost its spiritual bearings, which offers only an abundance of often superfluous consumer goods and amusements of the most trivial kind instead of a purpose in life and ideals, the craving grows for new sensations and more sophisticated thrills. Thus young people especially are seeking refuge in pharmaceutically fabricated worlds of fancy. The drug wave,[196] promoted by cynical international profiteers who have nothing but contempt for their fellow men, has ruined the health and emotional life of thousands of young people in the Federal Republic of Germany[197] and threatens to become a national emergency. Drugs, regarded as harmless and extolled in circles of the subculture who demand that they be placed freely at everyone's disposal,[198] came on the scene with the sex and pornography wave; they are the expression of an absolute demand for individual self-realization which regards duty, discipline and civic sense as outdated petit-bourgeois ideas.[199]

No less an evil is the spread of alcoholism. Everything points to

spannt im Hier und Jetzt (Total Relaxation in the Here-and-now), Reinbek 1979; Dieter Korczak, *Neue Formen des Zusammenlebens* (New Ways of Living Together), Frankfurt 1979; Gudrun Cyprian, *Sozialisation in Wohngemeinschaften* (Socialization in Communes), Stuttgart 1978; Claudia Mast, *Aufbruch ins Paradies? Die Alternativbewegung und ihre Fragen an die Gesellschaft* (Setting out for Paradise? The Alternative Movement and the Question it asks Society), Osnabrück 1980; W. Hollstein, *Die Gegengesellschaft, Alternative Lebensformen* (The Counter Society, Alternative Ways of Life), Reinbek 1981; M. Haller (ed), *Aussteigen oder rebellieren. Jugendliche gegen Staat und Gesellschaft* (Drop Out or Rebel. Youth against State and Society), Reinbek 1981.

196. Arthur Kreuzer, *Jugend – Rauschdrogen – Kriminalität* (Youth – Intoxicating Drugs – Criminality) Wiesbaden 1978; 'Abdul-Missagh A. Ghidirian, 'The Dilemma of Drug Abuse', in: World Order, Spring/Summer 1981, p.31–46.

197. The number of drug addicts in the Federal Republic of Germany has now reached about 80,000. 623 people died in 1979 of drug abuse. According to a report by the General Audit Office of the American Congress, approximately 453,000 U.S. citizens take heroin daily. Almost 10 million have already taken cocaine, 43 million marijuana. According to this report citizens of all social strata and professions are involved in the million dollar illegal drug racket in the U.S.A.: doctors, lawyers, tax consultants, businessmen, people in show business, workers, employees, schoolchildren (*Süddeutsche Zeitung* of 9.11.1979). According to figures of the U.S. Drug Enforcement Administration (DEA) the extent of illegal drug-dealing is estimated at 100 billion dollars annually (*Süddeutsche Zeitung* of 9.9.1981).

198. The demand for the release of the drug cannabis (hashish, marijuana) in particular is becoming louder, although well-established findings reveal that this is the drug that heroin users first start out with (Karl Ludwig Täschner, *Das Cannabisproblem. Die Kontroverse um Haschisch und Marihuana aus medizinisch-soziologischer Sicht* (The Cannabis Problem, The Controversy on Hashish and Marijuana from Medical and Sociological Viewpoint), Wiesbaden 1979, with comprehensive references; Wilhelm Feuerlein (ed), *Bestandsaufnahme zum Haschischproblem* (Cannabis Today. Taking Stock of the Hashish Problem), Wiesbaden, Akademische Verlagsgesellschaft, 1980.)

199. An example of the liberal and permissive attitude in Europe: in 1977 Radio Hilversum, a state broadcasting station, announced every Saturday the price per gram for hashish on the Amsterdam drug market in order to 'reveal the true market situation' (*Wirtschaftswoche*, No.8 of 18.2.1977, p.108).

alcoholism developing into the century's largest problem for social medicine. In 1979, thirty-nine thousand million German marks (about ten thousand million pounds sterling) were squandered on drinks in the Federal Republic; this is equivalent to 635 marks (£165) per inhabitant. [200] According to newspaper reports 37% of the adults in Germany are 'heavy drinkers', [201] 1.5 to 2 million are alcoholics, 150,000 of them being young people in the age range fourteen to twenty-five years. The number of those endangered by alcohol is estimated to be between three and four million. The number of addicted drinkers who can no longer hold a job has tripled during the last ten years. In other Western and Eastern European countries [202] and in the USA there are similar alarming tendencies.

The most striking indicator of people's increasing inability to find some meaning in their lives is the fact that, in a society of plenty, in the midst of the welfare state, the second most frequent cause of death is suicide. The number of those who commit suicide is particularly high in those industrial countries which have a high degree of social security. Thus in the Federal Republic of Germany 13,000 people take their own lives every year, almost as many as die in traffic accidents. [203] In addition there are approximately 200,000 attempted suicides every year. In Switzerland the number of suicides is higher than the number of those who die in traffic accidents. [204] In Japan the suicide rate among young people up to eighteen years of age increased in 1978 by 11%. Sociologists hold responsible the hectic changes in the structure of society. The dissolution of traditional close family ties leads to a feeling of isolation and hostility towards others. [205]

In contrast to this the suicide rate in underdeveloped countries where poverty and want prevail is, contrary to all expectations, relatively low, because there are still systems there which require commitment and impart a sense of meaning – another proof that not every action that one commits is socially determined. Viktor Frankl remarks aptly: 'If a person finds a sense of meaning, then he is also willing to suffer if it should be necessary. But on the other hand, if he sees no meaning in life, then he will not value it, even though outwardly he may be doing well. It is then possible that he

200. *Süddeutsche Zeitung* of 30.10.1980.

201. *Stuttgarter Zeitung* of 26.7.1977; *Süddeutsche Zeitung* of 19.9.1977 and 15.7.1980.

202. For decades alcoholism was described in the Soviet Union as 'a relic of the bourgeois past' that would soon die out just like prostitution and criminality, until it turned out that today the Soviet citizen drinks three times as much as his forefathers did in the time of the Tsars (*Rhein-Neckar-Zeitung* of 13.3.1980; compare also David Martin, 'Marxism: Functional Equivalent of Religion', in *The Dilemmas of Contemporary Religion*, p.83). At the 26th Party Congress of the Soviet Communist Party in February 1981, the Party Secretary lamented that the 'new man' was not yet in sight. He denounced the prevailing egoism and, more emphatically, the alcoholism that has become so widespread (*Süddeutsche Zeitung* of 25.2.1981).

203. According to the numbers available to the German government the number of suicides in the Federal Republic in 1977 amounted to 14,000.

204. *Rhein-Neckar-Zeitung* of 17.4.1976.

205. *Rhein-Neckar-Zeitung* of 28.3.1979.

will throw his life away despite prosperity and abundance.'[206]

The Crime Boom

Another characteristic of modern life is the rapid increase in behaviour damaging to society and the escalation in criminality over the last twenty-five years. To be sure, this fact is occasionally contested with the argument that the alleged increase in criminality is a reflection of improved efficiency on the part of the police in discovering and solving crimes and that criminal offences are given greater publicity by the mass media.[207] Actually there is a decrease everywhere in the number of cases solved. In addition, the explosive increase in crime is reflected in the constant growth of penal institutions and statistics relating to them, which cannot keep up with the development.[208] Taylor (1975) reports that the incidence of arson has increased by ten times in the USA and by thirteen times in the United Kingdom since 1950.[209] The most alarming aspect of this trend is that the number of children and juveniles represented in these statistics is extraordinarily high.[210] The catastrophic wave of juvenile delinquency in African countries is reported in the *Revue International de Criminologie et de Police Technique*.[211] The influence of Western civilization in Africa has had disastrous consequences: villages are emptying; towns are growing rapidly; many youths leave their parental homes to loaf aimlessly about in towns where they have no work and where they resort to crime or fall victim to drug addiction and homosexuality. The breakdown of marriage and the family is on the increase in urban areas, with the result that more and more youth are left to their own devices and tempted into crime.

At the first European Police Youth Conference in Aachen in October 1977 it was announced that the number of persons suspected of a crime had increased from 1963 to 1976 by 77% for youth (aged 18 to 21); among children who had not attained the age of criminal discretion the number had increased by 104%, and for juveniles (aged 14 to 18) the increase was 132%. Offences involving property and violence were mainly involved. Every third man of twenty-five in the Federal Republic of Germany has already been convicted of some offence or crime.[212] In 1980 the German

---

206. 'Die Sinnfrage in der Psychotherapie', p.317.

207. Cf. Taylor, *How to Avoid the Future*, p.92, who deals with this argument in detail.

208. For example, the number of criminal cases occurring each year in the Federal State of Baden-Württemberg more than doubled in the period 1970–79 (1970: 88,166; 1979: 182,280). The number of judges and public prosecutors increased by 10% during the same period.

209. *How to Avoid the Future*, p.93.

210. Literature: Wolfgang Salewski and Peter Lanz, *Die neue Gewalt und wie man ihr begegnet* (The New Violence and How to Encounter it), Droemer & Knaur, 1978; Arman Mergen, 'Kinderkriminalität' (Criminality among Children), in *Kriminalistik*, Vol.9, 1979, pp.399ff.

211. No.2, April–June 1980, Geneva.

212. *Süddeutsche Zeitung* of 24.10.1977.

Federal Republic reached a new record in crime: 3.8 million registered offenders – 380,000 (= 8%) more than in the previous year.

These tendencies are world-wide, and the highly developed industrial countries are particularly affected. In 1978, 60,900 male and female teachers in the USA were so badly beaten by their pupils that they required hospital treatment.[213] Even in Japan the violent behaviour of schoolchildren against their teachers has become overnight, so to speak, a social menace, to which the daily newspaper *Asahi Shimbum* devoted a series of articles in 1980.

Whereas 3,424 juvenile delinquents were arrested in New York in 1950, the figure reached 26,153 in 1975.[214] Between 1978 and 1979 the number of crimes of violence resulting in death rose by 10% and those of rape by 13%. In 1979 in the USA a theft occurred every 4.6 seconds, a break-in every 10 seconds, a rape every 7 minutes and every 24 minutes an American was murdered.[215] An investigation by the New York Health Authority revealed that the most frequent cause of death for male inhabitants of that city between 15 and 44 years of age is not accident or illness but murder. Mathematicians of the Massachusetts Institute of Technology have calculated that every child in New York grows up with a risk factor of 1 to 65 of being murdered one day.[216] In a noteworthy speech in New Orleans in September 1981, President Reagan described crime in the USA as an 'epidemic', against which the American judiciary were powerless. According to Reagan, the system for administering justice had collapsed. It had failed in its most important function, namely, 'the protection of the innocent and the punishment of the guilty'.[217] Crime and the fear of it are gradually paralysing American society and beginning to overshadow all other problems.

Paris now outranks Marseilles, London, Hamburg and Chicago as far as the increase in crime is concerned – 64% to 1979 since 1972. Every year 9,000 robberies, over 400,000 burglaries, 160 murders, about 35,000 automobile thefts and about 100,000 thefts are reported there. Only 38% of the cases are solved. A large number of crimes are not even reported to the police.[218]

The Communist countries have not been spared either from the escalation of crime. Both the Eastern European countries and the People's Republic of China are faced with a great increase in criminality. Hooliganism, acts of violence, hold-ups and pillaging have reached such an

---

213. *Heidelberger Tageblatt* of 6.3.1979.
214. *Süddeutsche Zeitung* of 5.4.1979.
215. *Rhein-Neckar-Zeitung* of 23.10.1980.
216. *Süddeutsche Zeitung* of 31.3.1980.
217. *Süddeutsche Zeitung* of 30.9.1981.
218. *Frankfurter Allgemeine Zeitung* of 19.11.1979.

extent in China's big cities that according to the mayor of Shanghai public order is 'seriously disrupted'. In the Peking People's Daily (*Jen-min jih-pao*) of 23 June 1981 complaints were loudly voiced about the rapidly growing crime rate, particularly with regard to the increase in serious crime such as bomb attacks, arson, murder and robbery, as well as rape which is often committed by gangs and ends with the death of the victim. In this article, an appeal was made to the public to help in the fight against crime. Public executions, intended as a deterrent, have been carried out.[219]

Usually social factors are held largely responsible for crimes. It is striking that a country with such a high degree of social security as Sweden should be afflicted with a wave of violence directed against the schools. After the 'Year of the Child' (1979) the Swedish Minister for Education proclaimed 1980 as the 'Year of the Campaign against Violence in Schools' to counteract the increasing brutalization of the schools. School reforms introduced in the name of freedom have obviously failed because the pupils did not know what to do with this new freedom: 'The materialistic, affluent society has paid for its financial wealth with the price of poverty in human relationships. Standards, guidelines and even instructions were thrown overboard, but not replaced – unless one accepts the promiscuity at the schools as an expression of the search for security.'[220]

A perfect example in this context is shoplifting. Since the introduction of self-service stores, shoplifting has increased to such an extent that gradually the increased economic efficiency is being neutralized. In the Federal Republic of Germany in 1963 the inclination to serve oneself without paying led to the conviction of 43,325 shoplifters; in 1977 it was approximately 200,000, and in 1978 almost 300,000.[221] At the same time it is rightly assumed that only 1% of all offenders are caught. The damage to the economy every year amounts to thousands of millions of marks. The causes of this epidemic lie in the lowering of the thresholds of inhibition and in the decline of personal conscience. They can scarcely be attributed to the class system, as is shown by the fact that all strata of society are represented in a typical cross-section of shoplifters, and the lower classes are by no means represented more often than the others. This is an indication of a change in individual consciousness and in the attitude of society as a whole. It is also expressed in the fact that shoplifting was almost declared exempt from punishment and classified as a summary offence during the recent reform of the penal code.[222] In the other European countries the situation is no better.[223]

219. *Süddeutsche Zeitung* of 26.9.1979, 23.6.1981 and 26.6.1981.
220. *Rhein-Neckar-Zeitung* of 8.2.1980.
221. *Süddeutsche Zeitung* of 17.7.1979.
222. Taylor tells of a Belgian judge who acquitted eighteen shoplifters with the argument that shoplifting is unavoidable because the situation leads to temptation (*How to Avoid the Future*, p.91).
223. Cf. Taylor, op. cit., p.90ff; on the whole subject see Karl-Heinz Kirchner, *Macht Klauen Spaß?*

This development has compelled the state to multiply its stock of criminal prosecution authorities – the police and the judiciary – and has led it almost to the limits of its efficiency. Because one cannot increase the number of staff employees and build prisons *ad infinitum* the state has coped with the situation in a different way, i.e. by 'de-criminalizing' the penal code, in other words by cancelling numerous penal provisions or redefining crimes as minor offences, and by replacing the prison sentence to a large extent by fines. And still the prisons are jam-packed. As a result of this modern mass criminality the 'principle of legality'[224] is undermined more and more by the 'principle of expediency': small crimes which are committed by many people, such as shoplifting, are usually no longer punished by criminal law[225] because the capacity of the judiciary, despite the increase in personnel, is exhausted. Thus justice surrenders to injustice. But if the state cannot fulfil its fundamental purpose, the protection of the interests of its citizens, then the cultural achievement of the material solution of conflicts by objective institutions is gradually destroyed and we get what we least desire – self-justice[226] and the law of the jungle.

Two limitations can be clearly observed: on the one hand that the capacity of society to cope with criminal acts is not endless, on the other hand that penal sanctions are powerless against the deeper causes of an increase in crime that has reached epidemic proportions. They can only provide a remedy as long as criminal offences are the exception in the life of society and as long as society itself is intact. But what is the ultimate reason for this development? Why has our society lost so much of its immunity to this provocation? Criminologists, sociologists and psychologists today are looking for the causes of this development, but only a small part of the answer is to be found where they are looking.

Terror and Violence – Stigmata of our Time

Probably nothing shows the decline of traditional ethics and the sickness of our society as clearly as the new dimension of evil with which we are confronted today: the brutalization of our world by the increase in violence. 'Just as high temperature warns us that all is not well in the body, so violence is an indication that something is wrong in society.'[227] It confronts us in the rapidly increasing readiness to settle conflicts with violence.

Now, violence is as old as humanity. What is new is its impact within

(Is Filching Fun?), Stuttgart 1977.

224. i.e. the duty of the public prosecutor to prosecute every violation of the criminal code (Paragraph 152, II, German Code of Criminal Procedure).

225. Cf. Paragraphs 153, 153a of the German Code of Criminal Procedure.

226. The department stores are now demanding that thieves who are caught repay rewards given for their capture.

227. Taylor, *How to Avoid the Future*, p.31.

highly technological societies, the constant presentation of it in the media, and its presence in our daily lives. Friedrich Hacker in his bestseller on violence[228] described its nature and the brutalization of the modern world. Violence, 'as infectious as cholera', owes its 'virulence to its semblance of justification, which makes it epidemical . . . Violence is simple, alternatives to violence are complicated . . . The opposite to complexity is aggressive simplification.'[229] Hacker shows how much violence has become part of our lives: 'The most horrifying dimension of modern brutalization is not that individual and collective violence flares up more frequently (mostly after it has been deliberately stirred up and fomented) but that it is becoming more and more common and customary. Violence has become an everyday, natural trivial event, a banal trifle . . . We are already so insensible that it needs a significant escalation of violence or especially dramatic acts of brutality to rouse us up out of our dull indifference, which supposedly derives from our feeling of helplessness.'[230]

People use violence for various reasons. Violence for the sake of violence is expressed in the hooliganism of the rocker gangs, in vandalism,[231] and in senseless destruction. Even here the use of violence finds advocates who support it from a sociological point of view. Vandalism, they tell us, is 'an indication not of social malaise but of moral health', 'an expression of high spirits', 'creative delinquency'.[232]

Criminals are using violence more and more to pursue their goals. The number of bank robberies in the Federal Republic of Germany has increased from 15 in 1953 to 632 in 1981.[233] In 1976 a robbery was committed every half-hour. Is it a coincidence that, in an affluent society characterized by ideologies that praise consumption, possession and growth,[234] the short cut to property by means of violence appears so en-

---

228. *Aggression*, Reinbek 1973.
229. op. cit., pp.13ff.
230. op. cit., p.17.
231. Of the approximately 111,000 telephone booths in the whole of the Federal Republic of Germany, 60,108 were wilfully destroyed in 1979. The damage amounted to DM 10.1 million, an increase of 11% compared to 1978 (*Süddeutsche Zeitung* of 10.5.1980). On the whole subject cf. Uwe Füllgrawe, 'Die psychologische und soziologische Analyse des Vandalismus' (The Psychological and Sociological Analysis of Vandalism), in *Kriminalistik. Zeitschrift für die gesamte kriminalistische Wissenschaft und Praxis*, February 1978, pp.56–61.
232. Quoted in Taylor, *How to Avoid the Future*, pp.77ff.
233. This is not counting 435 armed robberies of trucks transporting money (Statistics from the German Federal Office of Criminal Investigation).
234. Nothing reveals more clearly the attitude that judges a person not by what he *is* but by what he *has* than the advertising slogan 'You are something when you have something'. The inversion of this statement is also a mirror of the prevailing attitude in our society which sees the real essence of being in having: 'That if one *has* nothing, one *is* nothing' (E. Fromm, *To Have or To Be?* p.15). Affluence gave birth to *Homo consumens*, who wants to have, consume and amuse himself with more and more and who scarcely knows love of his neighbour or service to the common weal. Daniel Bell points out that nothing has destroyed the virtues of fulfilling one's duty and service to the common weal, has pushed the Protestant ethic out of bourgeois society and has contributed so much to the development of

ticing? The form of violence which is the most cynical and which reveals the most contempt for human life confronts us in kidnapping, taking hostages and airplane hijackings, where criminals can count on the inhibitions of people with morals who do not want others to die. This moral blackmail of the most despicable kind, unknown – at least in Europe – until the 1960s, has now become an everyday occurrence. International gangsters, who do not even shrink from sending severed parts of the hostage's body to those being blackmailed as proof of the seriousness of their intentions, are now building up a whole kidnapping and blackmailing industry. This enormous challenge to humanity is very likely an indirect result of the widely practised legitimation of violence for the pursuit of political goals and purposes.

The ultimate political goals, such is the opinion of not a few, justify the use of violence, if it is expedient and the goal cannot be achieved in any other way. The justification of violence by intellectuals of the extreme left, such as Frantz Fanon (*The Damned of this Earth*),[235] Jean-Paul Sartre (*The Dirty Hands*)[236] and Herbert Marcuse, and which was readily taken up by others despite its irrational aspects, has many forms: for instance, the differentiation between reactionary (reprehensible) and revolutionary (recommended) violence, or the concept of 'counter-violence'. Here the state's monopoly on violence, which guarantees the effectiveness of its laws, is disputed and, by means of a dialectic trick, a self-defence situation is constructed, which then makes illegal violence an (apparently) legal 'counter-violence'.[237] One claims the right to defend oneself against the so-called 'institutionalized' or 'structural' violence of the state against the individual. The word 'violence' is used differently from normal usage, for instance, when authorities waste one's time; credit institutions represent violence against housekeeping; advanced professional training is violence against the workers, who are trained so that business will become more profitable; examination regulations, prescribed study programmes, giving marks are the 'violence' of the 'privileged professors'.[238]

Violence against the state is the means 'of showing that one is still alive and of preserving the dignity of man'. The peace researcher Johan Galtung defines it this way: 'Violence exists when people are influenced in such a way that their actual somatic and spiritual realization is less than their

---

hedonism as has the invention of the hire purchase and immediate loan system. Thus our society is no longer characterized by needs, but by desires, and desires 'are psychological, not biological, and are by their nature unlimited' (*The Cultural Contradictions of Capitalism*, p.22).

235. Paris, *Présence Africaine*, 1963.
236. *No Exit and Three Other Plays*, New York, Vintage Books, 1956.
237. Cf. H. Schelsky, *Die Arbeit tun die anderen*, pp.328, 391.
238. H. Schelsky, op. cit., p.328; Wolfgang Brüggemann, 'Didaktische Reflexionen zur politischen Sprache' (Didactic Reflection on Political Language), in Zeitschrift *Gesellschaft, Staat, Erziehung* (Society, State, Education), August 1972, p.222.

potential realization.'[239] The consumer society imposes structural violence because it diminishes man's scope for action. It is also structural violence when one million husbands keep one million wives in ignorance. Then the thesis is: 'Personal violence is necessary to eliminate structural violence.'[240] Seen from this angle, damage to property is then 'a blow against the bourgeois in ourselves, an act of liberation from hitherto existent fetters, an-act of communication'.[241] 'Thus peace will come to earth', writes Friedrich Tenbruck, 'when we can fully realize ourselves as physical and spiritual beings. And when we are unable to do so, then it is because of structural violence . . . He who does not want to react to "structural violence" with "counter-violence" is excluded from the general levy. He who does not see in the state "the organized lack of peace" is outlawed. And thus revolution, both in its non-violent and (only too often) its violent form, becomes the shibboleth of peace research.'[242]

It is indisputable that there is such a thing as illegitimate structural violence. The Nazi state's legislation concerning the Jews was structural violence, which oppressed and finally annihilated millions. The apartheid laws of South Africa, which injure the human dignity of the coloured population and condemn a large part of the population to serfdom, can be described as 'structural violence'. However, it is the demagogic extension of this concept which makes it unusable and dangerous. The concept of violence is an example of Herbert Marcuse's demand for systematic reform of the vocabulary, his 'linguistic therapy'.[243]

Common to all these concepts of the legitimation of violence is the opinion that the use of violence is only a question of expediency and tactics. Just how much this seed has sprouted is shown by the most recent opinion polls (1982) in the Federal Republic of Germany: only 63% of the people reject violence, which means that over one-third of the population accepts violence as a means of settling political differences. It is not my intention nor is it necessary in this context to discuss the manifold forms of political terrorism in the world.[244] In my country[245] itself a large group of quite intelligent young people answer the question as to whether our lives are after all not worth living with a clear 'No!' and with destructive and self-destructive hatred. These people do not come from another planet; they are part of our society, a 'society of notoriously unhappy people: lonely, anxious, depressed, destructive, dependent'.[246] We have produced

239. *Strukturelle Gewalt*, p.9.
240. ibid., p.29.
241. ibid., p.138.
242. 'Friede durch Friedensforschung? Ein Heilsglaube unserer Zeit', in *Frankfurter Allgemeine Zeitung* of 22.12.1973.
243. *An Essay on Liberation*, p.8.
244. See Taylor, *How to Avoid the Future*, p.35–70.
245. i.e. Germany.
246. Erich Fromm, *To Have or To Be?* p.5.

them, just as we presently are also producing a horde of maladjusted children[247] and people who are psychologically sick;[248] just as we have already produced death on our roads. These people with their disgust for the world are but symptomatic of the fundamental illness of mankind. The repressive or therapeutic treatment of these symptoms, necessary as it is, is only a palliative. It will not cure the illness which creates these symptoms. The whole discussion of the causes of terrorism does not reach the real depths. Besides a plethora of conditions[249] the most basic reason for this

247. The president of the German *Association for the Protection of Children* declared on the occasion of World Health Day in 1977 that approximately 25% of all children had serious maladjustments and every third child felt lonely, neglected or unhappy. According to Nitsch the reason for this is over-indulgence of the children with material goods but emotional neglect of them, one of the results of our affluent society. But 'emotional hunger' cannot be satisfied by affluence (*Rhein-Neckar-Zeitung* of 14.4.1977). On the whole subject see Ekkehard Kloehn, *Verhaltensstörungen eine Kinderkrankheit? Ursachen, Symptome, Therapien* (Maladjustment a Children's Disease? Causes, Symptoms, Therapies), Gütersloh 1977. More and more young people are suffering from psychological disturbances. According to data from experts 15% of all the students at universities in the Federal Republic of Germany need psychotherapeutic help (*Rhein-Neckar-Zeitung* of 3.8.1978).

248. A full-scale 'psychoboom' is taking place. A steadily growing number of people are seeking refuge in psychotherapeutic theories and methods, drifting from one form of therapy to another, unaware that this psychotherapy is becoming less a means of healing than a prosthesis, a lasting compensation for defects and fears.

249. Terrorism: the syndrome of a disorganized, morally corrupt society which can no longer be understood in its functions and compulsions. In such a society people who are lost and disorientated, who long for salvation and are driven to perverted self-presentation, who are blind to the realization that crimes degrade the purpose, want to realize the exalted ideas of liberating mankind and making mankind happy by the destructive means of hatred, envy, the desire to destroy and lust for power. The book *Wiederkehr der Wölfe* (Return of the Wolves) edited by Gerd-Klaus Kaltenbrunner and published by the Herder-Bücherei-Initiative in 1978 informs the reader on the causes of terrorism; see also Manfred Funke (ed), 'Terrorismus, Ursachen und Folgen – eine Herausforderung für die politische Bildung' (Terrorism, Roots and Consequences – A Challenge for Political Education), in *Materialien zur politischen Bildung*, Vol. I, 1978; Heiner Geißler (ed), *Der Weg in die Gewalt – Geist und gesellschaftliche Ursachen des Terrorismus und seine Folgen* (The Road to Violence – The Spirit and Social Causes of Terrorism and its Consequences), Munich 1978; Hans Schwind (ed), *Ursachen des Terrorismus in der Bundesrepublik Deutschland* (Causes of Terrorism in the Federal Republic of Germany), Berlin 1978; Hermann Glaser, *Jugend zwischen Aggression und Apathie. Diagnose der Terrorismus-Diskussion* (Youth between Aggression and Apathy. Diagnosis of the Discussion on Terrorism), Karlsruhe 1980; Wanda von Baeyer-Katte, Dieter Claessens, Hubert Feger, Friedhelm Neidhardt, *Gruppenprozesse. Analysen zum Terrorismus*, herausgegeben vom Bundesinnenministerium (Investigations on Terrorism, ed. by the Federal Ministry of Interior), Opladen 1982; M. Funke (ed), '*Terrorismus. Untersuchungen zur Strategie und Struktur revolutionärer Gewaltpolitik*' (Terrorism – Investigations on the Structure and Strategy of the Revolutionary Politics of Violence), *Bundeszentrale für politische Bildung*, Vol. 123, Bonn 1977; W. Laqeur, *Terrorismus* (Terrorism), Kronberg 1977; Iring Fetscher, *Terrorismus und Reaktion* (Terrorism and Reaction), Cologne, Frankfurt 1977. The following were described as factors that favour the development of terrorism: 'The total criticism of the system' which has bred hatred of the state and its representatives (Hattich, in: Geißler, p.199); the crisis in the legitimation of democracy (Lübbe, in: Geißler, p.96); the 'blurring of the concept of violence'; the 'unchaining of the postulate of democracy' and the 'loss of reality' in certain areas of social scientific and social philosophical journalism (Kielmannsegg, in: Geißler p.72); the rigorous undermining of the authority of all educators and the socialization deficits that are determined thereby (Hofstetter, in: Geißler, p.163); 'mad utopias' (de Boor, in: Schwind, p.125).

phenomenon is the disintegration of our order of values and the existential vacuum in which the majority of people live today – the loss of value and meaning. Terrorism has its roots in the crisis in morality, in the question of how to distinguish justice from injustice, and right from wrong; and the crisis in morality is, in the last analysis, the crisis in the belief in God. When the discussion that has just begun arrives at this understanding,[250] it will then be realized that the problem is easier to recognize than to solve. It cannot be solved by social means: a new morality cannot be decreed by the state and no amount of persuasion can raise the old morality from the dead. A society cannot impart a sense of meaning in life when people themselves have lost[251] this very sense of meaning.

Looking back in history we find that there has always been assassination and even examples of genocide, such as that committed against the American Indians during four centuries. Violence, cruelty, racial and national hatred have always been. And yet the present situation has new features: 'Never has injustice, never have crimes occurred on such a large scale as in our mass society', writes Erich Fechner.[252] Violence and terror are the stigmata of our times as manifested in the bloody crimes of two world wars, in the mass murders of many revolutions, in genocide on an industrial scale,[253] in the concentration camps or in the jungle areas rich in raw materials, or in the reintroduction of torture[254] in not a few countries.

---

250. Which is occasionally the case, e.g. Ernst Topitsch, 'Der Weg in die Gewalt' (The Road to Violence), *Frankfurter Rundschau* of 10.12.1977; Cardinal Josef Ratzinger in his New Year's sermon in the Liebfrauendom in Munich, 1977 (*Süddeutsche Zeitung* of 2.1.1978). The Jewish thinker Schalom ben Chorin also sees the cause of terrorism in the spiritual vacuum of modern man: 'When there is no sound basis for the existence of man, the gravitational law of the vacuum makes itself felt. The abyss draws one downward into the unreal . . . Meaninglessness creates meaninglessness. In the despairing search for a sense of meaning in life extremists are driven to meaningless activity which readily turns into criminal activity.' (*Terroristen über uns*, p.10.)

251. Hans Heigert writes on the inability of our society to impart values that are binding: 'A result of the freedom from values and meaning, which as it were has been turned into a dogma of liberality, is that many people experience a loss of values and meaning. With this the generations have lost the ability to communicate. The older people no longer understand the youth and can no longer follow their morality, and the young people are only slightly interested in the experience and advice of the older people. Thus everything is reduced to bare rules for coping with daily problems, and law degenerates into a vehicle of more or less economic usefulness or "social harmfulness". The result is progressive disintegration which continually creates new doubts (and despair) about traditional values and about the possibility of mastering the future. (*Süddeutsche Zeitung* of 16.10.1976.)

252. 'Zukunft ohne Ethik?' p.75.

253. Beginning with the murder of two million Armenians in World War I, the civilized world of our century has been guilty of more genocide than the world committed from times of antiquity up to the present century: the holocaust of the Jews by Hitler, the mass murder of kulaks and Crimean Tartars, the acts of destruction against the Kurds, Ibos, Bihari and the Indian tribes of Brazil, and the repetition of the holocaust in Kampuchea, where half of an entire people have been annihilated. The cultural revolution in China cost hundreds of thousands of people their lives, while tens of thousands committed suicide.

254. On the occasion of its twentieth anniversary, the organization *Amnesty International* said that torture, murder and kidnapping have assumed 'epidemic proportions' (*Süddeutsche Zeitung* of 30–31.5.1981).

Protected by the anachronistic concept of state sovereignty, tyrants are permitted to murder without the community of nations intervening.

Violence, which is the result of a long chain of social events and has come upon us 'like some psychic Black Death',[255] will lead to the collapse of everyday life if it cannot be checked. Crime, violence and hatred constitute a sure path into the abyss. It is hardly probable that mankind will be able to master this problem in a short time. Violence is the result of resentment, despair and the desire to destroy. None of the social factors which are partly responsible for hatred and brutalization, such as slums, unemployment and broken homes, is being corrected. And the value system, the 'Archimedian Point'[256] is shattered, the determining cultural traditions are running dry. Thus there is every good reason to believe that the pathological phenomena of today's society will not improve in future but will get worse – 'a world dimmed by the steadily-dying-out light of religion'.[257]

The End of our Civilization?

What Alfred Weber once called the 'fourth man': amoral, without faith, intellectualized, mechanized, no longer a human being, but an inhuman being, an 'un-man',[258] is no longer a vision of the future, but as Jean Gebser stresses, 'a hard fact of our times'.[259] The writer Klaus Mehnert has summed up his most conspicuous 'values' and features in a negative catalogue: radicalism, anarchism and nihilism, utopianism and vandalism, arrogance and intolerance, vagabondage and libertinage, amorality and criminality, aversion to work, and drug addiction.[260] *Homo sapiens*, the pride of creation, has turned into *homo brutalis*, the unchained beast without inhibitions:[261] 'Where there is no vision, the people perish.'[262]

Secular value-substitutes have not made our world friendlier or better, and they will not bring about heaven on earth. They lead to the psychosocial poisoning of our communal living, the propagation of the friend-or-foe pattern, and the degeneration of communication into defamation. We must agree with Norbert Elias 'that we have lost our orientation in our own world, that the collection of concepts and categories we were brought up

255. Taylor, *How to Avoid the Future*, p.85.
256. An imaginary fixed point outside the earth, conceived by Archimedes in his statement: 'Give me a point where I can stand and I shall move the earth.'
257. Shoghi Effendi, *The Advent of Divine Justice*, p.39.
258. See footnote 86.
259. *In der Bewährung*, p.111 with further references.
260. *Twilight of the Young*, p.285.
261. Friedrich Hacker, *Aggression*, p.17.
262. Prov. 29:18.

with no longer corresponds to contemporary society'.[263] Can we then be surprised at the loss of authority experienced by the state institutions, at the growing instability of our social order, or at the rottenness of our culture? Can we be surprised that, in a world that has lost its spiritual bearings, insecurity, fear and hopelessness[264] are epidemic and people are looking towards the future with concern?

We are forced to ask ourselves uneasily whether we have not manoeuvred ourselves into a dead end. The existential fear of modern man reveals his loss of inner equilibrium and orientation,[265] his insensibility, his lack of love and security, his self-alienation. The decline in the number of births[266] in the leading industrial countries, the refusal to produce issue, is an expression of a basic crisis in human trust: the will to continue living has been broken. Our highly lauded civilization,[267] science, and progress cannot satisfy the fundamental needs of man. Behind the glossy façade[268] is a void.

Many are hoping for a 'change of wind' and console themselves with the hope that this emptiness may only be a passing phenomenon in the incessant surging movement of history. Many are homesick for the past. 'Nostalgia' has become a vogue word. 'The decline', writes Gustav Sievert, a philosopher from Aachen, 'has already been laid in every corner-stone. Everybody today knows this, feels and senses it. Fear is constantly

263. Speech made when the Adorno Prize was awarded in Frankfurt (*Frankfurter Allgemeine Zeitung* of 4.10.1977). F. v. Cube states the 'fundamental problems' of free democracy: 'As values have been made relative, there is no binding legitimation and people are uncertain how to behave.' (*Das Parlament*, Supplement of 16.6.1979, p.18.)

264. Even the protagonists of positive utopias are increasingly realizing that they have today failed. The French philosopher Michel Foucault complains: 'For the first time in the world since perhaps the October Revolution of 1917, or even the great European revolutionary movements of 1848, there is not one single chink through which the light of hope can shine. There is no point of orientation any more. There is not one single revolutionary movement, let alone a single socialist country . . . which we can refer to in order to be able to say: That's the way to do it! We are thrown back to 1830, i.e.: We must begin again.' (Quoted by Ulrich Greiner, 'Der Untergang der Titanic' (The Sinking of the Titanic), in *Frankfurter Allgemeine Zeitung* of 19.10.1978.)

265. 'Recently even sociologists have been on the look-out for moral patterns of behaviour, because they have noticed that it demands too much of people when they are required to give up completely the normative institutionalization of anthropological necessities.' (Alfons Auer, *Autonome Moral und christlicher Glaube*, pp. 11–12.)

266. 38% of marriages in the Federal Republic of Germany are without offspring; 26% have only one child. In Germany more money is spent annually on feeding dogs and cats than providing food for babies.

267. Heinz Friedrich describes how, through mass media and traffic on a global scale, the whole of mankind is being subjected to the contagious influence of a 'civilization that is genuinely European, insipidly Americanized and diseased with nihilism'. Thus, even the remotest corners of the planet are being drawn into the 'whirlpool of civilized decadence' (*Kulturkatastrophe*, p.279).

268. 'Abdu'l-Bahá writes: 'A superficial culture, unsupported by a cultivated morality, is as "a confused medley of dreams" (Qur'án 12:44, 21:5), and external lustre without inner perfection is "like a vapour in the desert which the thirsty dreameth to be water" (Qur'án 24:39). For results which would win the good pleasure of God and secure the peace and well-being of man, could never be fully achieved in a merely external civilization.' (*The Secret of Divine Civilization*, pp.60–61.)

breathing down our necks. Our century will go down in history as the century of fear.'[269]

Times of upheaval were always times of confusion, of collapse, of decadence, lawlessness, insecurity and fear. There are distinct parallels to our present situation in the decline of antiquity, the fall of Ancient Rome, both in its causes and in the reactions of those who experienced it. Some of the symptoms of the collapse of the Roman empire which have often been described are: drift from the land to the cities and the growth of an urban proletariat; an adverse balance of trade, constantly-rising inflation and increased burden of taxation; the tendency to provoke conflict and the use of violence; the decline in public safety through the appearance of armed bands and, as a result of this, the formation of private surveillance firms; the increase of corruption; the wide dispersion of protest literature and political lampoons; a rule of terror; the rulers courting the favour of the masses; the decline of artistic and technical performance; the great number of suicides; the proliferation of occult cults and every kind of superstition.[270] The spiritual cause of these symptoms of decline was the death struggle of the Greek and Roman religion[271] and the dying out of the old virtues. The Emperor Augustus, who tried to preserve and restore the old Roman piety and way of life through enactment of strict legislation against luxury and vice and by a rigorous marriage law (*lex Julia*), was unable to arrest the advancing decline in morality and the downfall of society. Vice became socially acceptable and licentious living was raised to the level of a principle. Seneca wrote: 'Noble ladies reckon their years, not by the number of consuls, but by the number of their husbands.'[272] Lawlessness spread everywhere, and even the disturbing of university lectures is not, since Augustine describes it, an invention of our times.[273] Those who experienced the collapse of the ancient world were also filled with horror and despair. 'The whole world groaned at the fall of Rome', wrote Augustine, and St. Jerome wrote from his monastery in Bethlehem that 'the human race' was affected by the downfall of Rome: 'My tongue cleaves to the roof of my mouth and sobs choke my words to think of it.'[274]

269. Quoted by Heribert Heinrichs, in *Die Zeit* of 29.11.1974. In 1844, one hundred years before the atom bomb, Soren Kierkegaard described the coming 'Age of Fear' in his work *The Concept of Fear*.
270. See Taylor, *How to Avoid the Future*, pp.105ff.
271. Cf. pp.111ff. for parallels in religious history.
272. De beneficiis III, 16, 2 and 3, in *Moral Essays*, p.155.
273. Augustine, who was a teacher of rhetoric at the time, left his teaching position in Carthage in 383 because of the prevailing conditions. He complained about the 'most uncivil and unruly licentiousness amongst the scholars', who, 'in insolent manner, rush in upon that man's school, where their own master professed not', and he writes: 'They break in audaciously, and almost with Bedlam looks, disturb all order which any master hath propounded for the good of his scholars. Divers outrages do they commit, with a wonderful stupidness, deserving soundly to be punished by the laws, were not custom a defendress of them.' (*Confessions*, Book V, VIII.)
274. Quoted in Radhakrishnan, *Recovery of Faith*, p.1.

And yet the gigantic changes of the past can scarcely be compared with those which the world is experiencing today: our highly technical civilization is much more susceptible to disturbances than the cultures of the past; and for the first time the upheaval is world-wide and the whole of mankind is affected by it. The Indian religious philosopher Sarvapalli Radhakrishnan describes our situation and the alternatives as follows: 'The contemporary situation is pregnant with great possibilities, immense dangers or immeasurable rewards. It may be the end or a new beginning. The human race may end by destroying itself or its spiritual vitality may revive and a new age may dawn when this earth will become a real home for humanity.'[275]

275. ibid. p.3.

3. Religion and Science – Harmony or Incompatibility?

The symptoms of the cultural crisis described in the previous chapter may be traced back without difficulty to what Friedrich Nietzsche called 'nihilism' or the loss of purpose: 'The aim is lacking; "Why?" finds no answer'; we have lost the highest and generally recognized values. Nietzsche regarded these two features of nihilism as the consequences of the 'death of God' and the dying out of religion.

All religions attempt to provide an answer to questions concerning aims and values: What is man? What is the purpose of his existence? To which goal is he striving? Are there objective values according to which man should live? What are they? The answer to the question of man's origin, nature and destiny was always an essential element of religion. The teachings of all religions claim that man has both his origin and his destiny in God. He has been created for eternal life, perfection and free choice; he is the citizen of two worlds, the one immanent, the other transcendent. The teaching concerning the individual's responsibility for his own life is as much a component of all revealed religions as the catalogue of virtues which prescribe how his life is to be lived.

Is science able to supply an answer concerning the nature of man and the purpose of his existence? Can it fill the gap left as a result of the abdication of transcendence?

The Question of Purpose

Those who give a positive answer to this question have overestimated science and failed to recognize its inherent limitations.[1] The question of

1. The natural scientist Hans Schaefer points out that science occupies an unduly high status in our

the origin, purpose and final destiny of human life is not of merely academic or theoretical interest but plays a vital role in certain decisions of life. It is a question which eludes empirical knowledge or experimental investigation, as does the question concerning the existence of God. At this point scientific knowledge reaches a boundary which it cannot overstep. The question of purpose therefore lies outside the field of competence of science. Whenever science does claim the right to answer this question, it is guilty of the same presumptuousness which the Church showed at the beginning of the modern age when it opposed the discoveries of science. For instance, science oversteps its boundaries when it offers a description of man as a 'machine' or a 'naked ape',[2] as a casualty of nature, 'product of chance' or 'a gypsy' who 'lives on the boundary of an alien world', whose duties and destiny have not 'been written down',[3] as an 'evolutionary misfit' or a 'biological freak'.[4] Equally science trespasses outside its borders when it claims that human existence is without purpose and asserts, as do Skinner and Monod, that this is a scientifically proven fact.[5] In giving an answer to this question, science sees in man nothing other than mere biological existence. It reduces the concepts of purpose and value to 'defence mechanisms' or 'reaction formations', and dismisses the human capacity for culture as the functioning of a useful mechanism in the struggle for existence. Viewed from this standpoint, man is an animal whose nature it is to develop history, language, art and religion, while culture as a whole is simply a special manifestation of evolution. What a pitiful way to describe such phenomena as Plato, Goethe, Shakespeare, Bach, Mozart, Michelangelo, Kant and the many other geniuses of human history, not counting the founders of the great religions!

To the question whether life has a purpose, philosophy also gives a negative answer. It is well-known that modern existentialism supports the theory that life is absurd. '*Une passion inutile*'[6] is Jean-Paul Sartre's definition of man: '*Il est absurde que nous soyions nés, il est absurde que nous mourions.*'[7] Thus a person's life is essentially the realization of a plan

---

society and he emphasizes 'that, no matter how important it may be, it is incapable by itself of determining our future' ('Der Mensch und das Ende seiner Menschlichkeit', p.166).

2. B. F. Skinner, *Beyond Freedom and Dignity*, pp.191ff.; Desmond Morris, *The Naked Ape; a Zoologist's Study of the Human Animal*, New York, Dell Publishing, 1967.

3. Jacques Monod, *Chance and Necessity*, pp.160, 167.

4. Arthur Koestler, *Janus*, pp.5, 100.

5. At an international symposium Viktor Frankl quoted from one of the more recent textbooks a definition of man which is tailored to the behaviouristic psychology of the Watson-Skinner school. According to this definition, man is nothing 'but a complex biochemical mechanism powered by a combustion system which energizes computers with prodigious storage facilities for retaining encoded information' (A. Koestler and J. R. Smythies, *Beyond Reductionism*, p.403).

6. 'L'homme est une passion inutile.' (*L'être et le néant*, p.708.)

7. ibid., p.631.

or design which he has chosen for himself. But man cannot live in a vacuum; he cannot bear this condition of purposelessness: 'The loss of meaning . . . creates a set of incomprehensions which people cannot stand and which prompt, urgently, their search for new meanings, lest all that remain be a sense of nihilism or the void.'[8] 'Existential vacuum' and 'existential frustration' lead to a way of life which is empty. To describe this human condition Viktor Frankl has coined the term *'Sinnlosigkeitsgefühl'* (feeling of purposelessness). He regards it as having superseded Alfred Adler's concept of the inferiority complex, and it is a term which is also well-known in communist countries. According to Frankl, the *Sinnlosigkeitsgefühl* is the 'neurosis of our times' and the reason for the diversified landscape of present-day psychopathology.[9] In the existential vacuum in which we live, aggressive impulses begin to rankle, the sexual drive begins to play a more prominent – though more isolated – role and addictive tendencies begin to appear.[10] There are many theories which try to explain the increase in crime. The same crimes are sometimes labelled 'crimes of poverty' and at other times 'crimes of affluence'. It is rare for anyone to entertain the idea that; along with many other factors, the deepest cause might lie in man's transcendental homelessness. If there is no God and no transcendental sanction, why should people act virtuously? If our existence is without meaning and we create our own design for living, if earthly jurisdiction is identical with the 'Last Judgement', then the motivation to avoid whatever is forbidden is very weak and there is a strong temptation to live not according to the Decalogue but according to the 'Eleventh Commandment': 'Thou shalt not get caught!'[11]

The Question of Values

We arrive at the same result when we consider values. Notions of value are of an axiomatic nature; no logical proof of their correctness can be supplied. Therefore neither reason nor science are adequate tools for providing standards of value or defining aims. Science is not competent to deal with moral issues. It cannot derive a watertight system of ethics. Ethical norms cannot be simulated in a computer. How a human being should behave in order to live a fulfilled and self-determined life cannot be defined in scien-

8. Daniel Bell, *The Cultural Contradictions of Capitalism*, p.146.
9. 'Das existentielle Vakuum', p.88.
10. ibid. pp.91 and 93. For the whole work see also Viktor Frankl, 'Die Sinnfrage in der Psychotherapie', pp.309ff.
11. 'The legal code and the police are not sufficient in all cases; there are offences, the discovery of which is too difficult; some, indeed, where punishment is a precarious matter; where, in short, we are left without public protection. Moreover, the civil law can at most enforce justice, not loving-kindness and beneficence; because, of course, there are qualities as regards which everyone would like to play the passive, and no one the active, part.' (Arthur Schopenhauer, *The Basis of Morality*, ch.II, p.135.)

tific terms. Certainly science is able to suggest methods for the realization of predetermined social aims, but it is unable to prescribe in any absolute way what these aims should be. An objective investigation of truth is possible only in the natural, causally-explainable world, in the realm of being and necessity, not in those areas pertaining to obligations, standards and cultural values.

Only to a very imperfect degree is reason able to distinguish between good and evil. What is right and what is wrong is not as easy to recognize as 'flies in a milk-pot'.[12] Dostoevsky decisively rejected the claim made by reason and science to autonomy or to moral and political authority. He considered that reason and science 'have, from the beginning of time, played a secondary and subordinate part in the life of nations' and believed that 'reason has never had the power to define good and evil, or even to distinguish between good and evil, even approximately; on the contrary, it has always mixed them up in a disgraceful and pitiful way; science has only ever supplied answers which are as crude as fist blows'.[13] As long as there existed in society a *communis opinio* with respect to central values, it was possible to maintain, as did Goethe, that 'A good man in his dark groping labour will always find the right in his own way'.[14] But in the pluralism of values now prevailing, we see more and more how divided are opinions on right and wrong. What seems to one as being reasonable and proper can appear to another as sheer folly. Examples of erroneously applied reason (individual as well as collective) in the sphere of morality are numerous, from racial prejudice to the sanctioning of violence and terror[15] as a means of securing personal or political objectives: 'To appoint "reason" as ruler of the earth is tantamount to abandoning everything to caprice.'[16] In the sphere of morality, reason has need of a final and absolute standard.[17] Religion alone is able to supply this standard.[18]

---

12. François Rabelais's very apt comparison reads: 'If the iniquity of men were as easily seene in categoricall judgement, as we can discerne flies in a milk-pot, the worlds four oxen had not beene so eaten up with Rats' (Gargantua and Pantagruel, Vol. I, chapter XII).

13. *The Possessed*, Night, p.230.

14. *Faust* I, Prologue in Heaven.

15. Marion Gräfin Dönhoff writes: 'It was only when all metaphysical ideas had been thrown overboard that the way was opened for totalitarian power, and for absolute terror to become a reality.' ('Leben ohne Glauben', in *Die Zeit* of 21.12.1979.)

16. Georges Sorel, quoted in Schelsky, *Die Arbeit tun die anderen*, p.106. Arthur Koestler refuses to name *homo sapiens* a 'reasonable being – for if he were, he would not have made such a bloody mess of his history' (*Janus*, p.5).

17. Christian theology is presently confused even about this principle which theologians themselves have been teaching for centuries. Furthermore, Catholic moral theology claims rationality and autonomy in morals and has thus secularized itself. This point will be followed up later (p.124ff).

18. Even Arthur Schopenhauer realized that 'the concept of ought, in other words the imperative form of Ethics, is valid only in theological morals, outside of which it loses all sense and meaning'. The 'Categorical Imperative' (Kant), and 'Human Dignity', as basic principles for moral legislation, were

Even if reason were able to distinguish between good and evil, it would be quite incapable of investing the good with inner authority, of making it morally obligatory. This obligatory character, however, is an indispensable component of any ethical system. A pluralism of non-obligatory values with regard to important aspects of life leads inevitably to a breakdown of the system. A non-obligatory, pluralistic ethic is a 'Lichtenberg knife'[19] without a handle or a blade.

Religion – the Origin of Purpose and Value

Normative ethics has always had its basis in religion. Religion alone is able to create 'a system of transcendental values and ideals into which the central values of society can be fitted. It builds up a hierarchy of values, declares some of them to be absolute and universal, while others are relative and particular. It sanctions, negates, differentiates and lays down priorities. It translates values into standards of behaviour, passes them on by education to the younger generation and keeps them alive in the consciousness of society.'[20] Torn loose from their metaphysical moorings these values lose their characteristic of faith and commonsense to the point where they are no longer 'believed', but instead critically questioned and negated. In the long run, moral standards can only be upheld if they have this character of faith: one must believe in them. Indeed, religion alone is able to invest man's central values with an inner authority and to urge him to comply with the standards which are derived from it. Pribilla aptly expresses it as follows: 'Without God, morality is cut adrift: the last moorings are gone', and goes on to ask: 'Why should man shy away from barriers which he or his kind have erected? Even culture, humanity and communal welfare pale into insignificance if, without a ray of eternal hope, happiness and life have to be sacrificed for them.'[21]

The scientist Hans Schaefer also believes that: 'If there is no religious doctrine deriving from a transcendental frame of reference, then moral conduct, without which no society is stable, is devoid of any obligatory foundation. Science is basically restricted to a cognitive sphere, which

---

described by Schopenhauer as 'empty phrases', 'cobwebs and the soap-bubbles of the Schools', principles 'on which experience pours contempt at every step, and of which no one, outside the lecture rooms, knows anything, or has ever had the least notion'. He considered Kant's basis for an ethical system, his categorical imperative, to be a philosophical error, an 'inadmissible assumption, and merely theological Morals in disguise' (*The Basis of Morality*, Part III, pp.133, 148, 149).

19. Georg Christoph Lichtenberg (1742–99), professor of physics at the University of Göttingen, famous for his aphorisms.

20. Erich Kellner, *Experiment eines kritischen Christentums*, p.7.

21. Messer and Pribilla, *Katholisches und modernes Denken*, p.95. Regarding the question whether a humane ethic without belief in God is at all possible, the reader is also referred to Ernst Feil, 'Grundwerte und Naturrecht' (Basic Values and Natural Law), in *Stimmen der Zeit* Freiburg, Herder Verlag, No.10, 1977, pp.651ff.

means that science can oblige people to focus their intellectual faculties on truth, but is unable of itself to provide a basis for action which is generally acceptable and therefore obligatory. Without such binding moral principles, a "humane" world cannot be realized. Even humanism represents a specific attitude towards human dignity and the duty of brotherly love, but one which needs religious support if it is to be an acceptable and binding foundation for action.'[22]

A similar conclusion about the incompetence of science in the field of norms and values was reached by Max Horkheimer, the founder of the 'Critical Theory'; 'There is no logical, compelling reason why I should not hate, provided it is not to my disadvantage in society. All attempts to base morality on worldly intelligence instead of seeing it in relation to the hereafter – a tendency which not even Kant always resisted – are built upon illusions. In the final analysis, everything pertaining to morality may be logically traced back to theology.'[23] Horkheimer also came to the realization, which he expressed in challenging terms, that politics based on morality was inconceivable in the absence of 'theism'.

The question whether man possesses an innate sense of justice was put to 'Abdu'l-Bahá. He answered in the negative and went on to say that man was dependent on divine revelation: 'if we ponder the lessons of history it will become evident that this very sense of honour and dignity is itself one of the bounties deriving from the instructions of the Prophets of God. We also observe in infants the signs of aggression and lawlessness, and that if a child is deprived of a teacher's instructions his undesirable qualities increase from one moment to the next. It is therefore clear that the emergence of this natural sense of human dignity and honour is the result of education. Secondly, even if We grant for the sake of the argument that instinctive intelligence and an innate moral quality would prevent wrongdoing, it is obvious that individuals so characterized are as rare as the philosopher's stone . . . Universal benefits derive from the grace of the Divine religions, for they lead their true followers to sincerity of intent, to high purpose, to purity and spotless honour, to surpassing kindness and compassion, to the keeping of their covenants when they have covenanted, to concern for the rights of others, to liberality, to justice in every aspect of life, to humanity and philanthropy, to valour and to unflagging efforts in the service of mankind. It is religion, to sum up, which produces all human virtues, and it is these virtues which are the bright candles of civilization.'[24]

Religious value-systems lie shattered. The pluralistic society is the reality

---

22. In *Experiment eines kritischen Christentums*, p.3.
23. *Die Sehnsucht nach dem ganz Anderen*, pp.60ff.
24. *The Secret of Divine Civilization*, pp.97–8. On the genealogy of moral virtues see ch.12, p.222.

of the present day. Everything pertaining to a religious world view or to moral principles has become a personal and private matter. The only thing on which people mutually agree is that they do not agree. To the question about what is good and what is evil, what is allowed and what is not allowed, there are no longer any unified answers. Hans Schaefer asks 'whether a stable society can be built upon the foundation of this pluralism of ultimate aims; whether a remnant, however small, of common convictions is still not essential . . . for providing the motivation necessary for socially stable behaviour'.[25] Indeed, a pluralism of non-obligatory values is far from being a firm foundation for a stable society:[26] the stability of society is in reality based upon mutual agreement among its members regarding its goals and the means permitted for attaining those goals. The weaker the *consensus omnium* is, the more unstable and vulnerable society will be.[27] A culture which no longer possesses a minimum of common values, but instead can only offer a multiplicity of non-obligatory opinions on basic questions of life, is certain to decline.

In this pluralism of values, Radhakrishnan too sees signs of cultural disintegration: 'Our values are blurred, our thought is confused and our aims are wavering. In the life of the spirit which is the vital secret of all civilization, which intellect may foster and develop but cannot create or even keep alive, we are uprooted. When the roots are destroyed, a tree may continue to live and even seem to flourish for a time, but its days are numbered.'[28] The modern sociology of religion shows how axioms, norms and principles only stabilize society if they have a transcendent foundation. The loss of transcendence destabilizes society, plunging it into crises and threats to its very survival. As Romano Guardini prophesied, the future will 'bring a frightful yet salutary preciseness' illuminating the relationship between religion, culture and the social order: 'As the benefits of Revelation disappear even more from the coming world, man will truly learn what it means to be cut off from Revelation.'[29] Day by day it will become increasingly apparent from what substance present-day man continues to draw his resources. 'Slowly the truth is dawning on us', writes Marion Gräfin Dönhoff, 'that a society without taboos and a binding system of values cannot function creatively, nor indeed continue to exist. For cen-

25. *Leib, Geist, Gesellschaft*, p.208.

26. Roegele also holds this opinion, 'Freiheit und Bindung in der gesellschaftlichen Kommunikation', p.196.

27. A politician sees it in the following way: 'A society in which there is no longer any mutual agreement over basic principles and values is heading for anarchy – unless it hands all questions of opinion, consent and decision over to a state which exercises absolute control, to an authoritarian state, to a dictatorship.' (Federal Chancellor Helmut Schmidt in a speech held in the Catholic Academy in Hamburg on 23rd May 1976, quoted from the *Süddeutsche Zeitung* of 26th May 1976.)

28. *Recovery of Faith*, pp.36–7.

29. *The End of the Modern World*, p.123.

turies, until the beginning of what is called modernism, this insight was self-evident and unquestioned.'[30]

The conclusion to be drawn from all this is that an obligatory ethic and a sense of purpose are essential to man. He can neither exist in a vacuum of purposelessness nor in an atmosphere in which values have been weakened to an unprincipled relativism. Because science is neither able to fill the vacuum of purposelessness nor set up absolute ethical standards, it follows that religion cannot be displaced by science. Both the individual and society depend upon religion because it alone is able to satisfy man's fundamental need for a compelling and comprehensive explanation of existence; because it alone is able to show man how to live; because it alone is able to offer him moral guidance and comfort in the face of unrelieved suffering.

The Correlation between Religion and Science

Religion and science are not opposed to one another; they are to be regarded not as alternatives but as correlates. The scientist Max Planck expressed it thus: 'The one does not exclude the other; rather they are complementary and mutually interacting. Man needs science as a tool of perception; he needs religion as a guide to action . . . Just as knowledge and ability cannot be replaced by philosophical speculation, so too the proper attitude to moral questions. cannot be derived purely from intellectual reasoning.'[31] He emphasizes that 'ethical questions . . . lie quite outside its [science's] field of competence'.[32] At the level where the two meet stands the question about the existence and nature of a supreme power which rules over the world. Here too Max Planck finds no contradiction. Science recognizes 'first, that a universal order exists which is independent of man, and secondly, that the essential nature of this order can never be directly known, but only indirectly grasped or surmised. In this respect, religion makes use of its own characteristic symbols, while the exact sciences rely on measurements which are based upon sense impressions. Our desire for knowledge impels us to look for a unified *Weltanschauung*. Thus there is nothing to prevent us from uniting these two powers in one; the universal order of science and the God of religion, two all-pervading and yet mysterious forces, may be identified with one another.'[33] For religion, God is the starting-point of all thinking: for science, God is the conclusion to which all thinking leads. In Max Planck's words: 'For the one He is the foundation: for the other He is the crowning superstructure of every scientific *Weltanschauung*.'[34]

30. 'Leben ohne Glauben', in *Die Zeit* of 21.12.1979.
31. *Religion und Naturwissenschaft*, p.31.
32. ibid., pp.30–31.
33. ibid., pp.28ff.
34. ibid., p.30.

Of course, in this connection one must distinguish between belief and superstition. Religion is the recognition of the Absolute, known as God, which is beyond all that is relative, conditional and human. Superstition, on the other hand, is the acknowledgement of absolute authority which is vested in something relative, such as material objects, a human personality, a human organization or a human idea. [35] Even revealed religion can in the course of time, as a result of false historical development, degenerate partly into superstition. This happens, for example, whenever religion assimilates heterogeneous elements foreign to its nature, or whenever it claims to have authority in the sphere of empirical knowledge.

Knowledge has its limits and needs to be perfected by that quality of faith which draws its strength from divine revelation. On the other hand, reason defines the limits of religious faith. This does not mean that faith can be explained by reason – fundamental religious truths lie beyond rational explanation. But anything which contradicts reason should not be believed. This is a negation of the fatal dictum: *Credo quia absurdum.* [36] For enlightenment, man requires both the light of reason and the light of faith. 'Abdu'l-Bahá compares human consciousness to a bird, which needs the two wings of science and religion to be able to fly. If mankind tries to fly only with the 'wing' of religion, then it falls, as in the Middle Ages, into a state of superstition. [37] If it tries to raise itself with the 'wing' of science alone, then it plunges into the condition which exists at the present time: materialism and nihilism, namely the conviction 'that nothing has any value, that no standards are binding, that no purpose exists, that there is nothing worth living or dying for, that everything is futile'. [38] 'Abdu'l-Bahá affirms that there is no conflict between religion and science 'for truth is one. When religion, shorn of its superstitions, traditions, and unintelligent dogmas, shows its conformity with science, then will there be a great unifying, cleansing force in the world which will sweep before it all wars, disagreements, discords and struggles – and then will mankind be united in the power of the Love of God.' [39]

35. Personality cults, party cults; absolute dedication to secular salvationary promises; blind belief in the notions of nation, race, class, science and progress; the rampant, pseudo-religious cults of the present-day – these are the modern forms which superstition has assumed. Meanwhile the ancient forms have by no means ceased to exist.
36. Tertullian, *De Carne Christi*, V.
37. 'But the religion which does not walk hand in hand with science is itself in the darkness of superstition and ignorance.' ('Abdu'l-Bahá, *Paris Talks*, p.144.)
38. Brezinka, *Erziehung und Kulturrevolution*, p.46.
39. For more details see 'Abdu'l-Bahá, *Paris Talks*, p.146. In this connection the reader is also referred to Hans Küng, *Existiert Gott? – Antwort auf die Gottesfrage*, who deals with the whole of Western philosophy and all arguments against the existence of God. Sigrid Hunke, in *Glauben und Wissen. Die Einheit europäischer Religion und Naturwissenschaft* (Belief and Knowledge. The Unity of European Religion and Science), Düsseldorf, Vienna 1979, also deals with the disastrous hiatus between religion and science.

4. God is not Dead

A Change of Wind?

The realization that religion is necessary and indispensable both to the individual and to society, the social order and culture, does not provide an answer to the question how the world-wide lack of faith, the loss of religious meaning and the vacuum resulting from the self-demolition of Christian theology are to be overcome.

Another aspect must also be considered. There is the danger that all the spiritual and material foundations of human civilization will be destroyed and that humanity itself will be wiped out. If this danger is to be banished, mankind has only one choice: the development of a completely new consciousness of the solidarity and brotherly commitment of all men, a consciousness that integrates all peoples and nations into a unified whole, that overcomes all antagonisms and is capable of effective action. In the face of this goal, which cannot be achieved by diplomacy and politics alone, does not mankind need a uniform standard, a new social morality, a great unifying idea? Are the great religions – isolated as they are from one another, encumbered with the claims of being in sole possession of the truth, and burdened with many historical encrustations – capable at all of producing such an idea? Where are these religions to get their integrating force from? Where are they to find the unity they themselves lack?

The first signs are now visible that there is a certain change from a purely materialistic to a transcendental way of thinking. The conviction is increasing that there is some inner and deeper meaning of our existence than just being and consuming. Some are turning back to religious values, are searching anew for a binding system of ethics and for a new religious commitment as the absolutely necessary requirement for a sound ethos. There is a great desire to get away from this confusion concerning meaning, values and goals, to escape this existential vacuum and the oppressive feeling of senselessness; there is a new search for meaning, [1] a great longing for a purpose in life that is based on faith, for a supra-rational spirituality, for commitment to one's fellow men in a community of like-minded souls, for tasks which go beyond self-interest, and for possibilities of identification. People feel cold in the rational coolness of modern society. They long for harmony, a means of orientation and a meaning in life, for 'security and support in situations of need and suffering'. [2] Who could have foreseen the 'isolation and estrangement that have come upon man, who has exchanged the security of religious certitude for secularized emancipation and autonomous striving for unrestricted progress, overburdening abundance and unlimited power?' [3]

Now that salvation by means of drugs, the chemical Pentecost experience, has turned out to be a chimera, meditation is suddenly *en vogue*. New movements, some of them very peculiar and often devoted to very worldly purposes, spring up, cause a new feeling of satiety concerning religion and often disappear again just as quickly as they appeared. [4] Erich Fromm remarked on this phenomenon: 'Today, millions of people in America and Europe try to find contact with tradition and with teachers who can show them the way. But to a large extent the doctrines and teachers are either fraudulent, or vitiated by the spirit of public relations ballyhoo, or mixed up with the financial and prestige interests of the respective gurus. Some people may genuinely benefit from such methods in spite of the shame, others will apply them without any serious intention of inner change.' [5] Another characteristic of these movements is that most of their adepts are concerned only with their own salvation and with looking after their souls; they have little or no interest in social problems, in helping to form this world or in the future of mankind.

Ansgar Paus finds on the whole a 'new burst of desire for a life "lived in the spirit"' which goes beyond the diversity and variety of the many religions and which is by no means to be found only in religious revival movements. 'The person who is searching for meaning longs for a "place" where he can meet the ultimate source of meaning in the world, and, spiritually affected, can acknowledge a final binding claim on his actions.' [6]

---

1. About the situation in the United States see Marilyn Ferguson, *The Aquarian Conspiracy*, pp.363–76.

2. Helmut Schelsky, *Die Arbeit tun die anderen*, p.204.

3. Marion Gräfin Dönhoff, 'Leben ohne Glauben'.

4. Cf. p.111.

5. *To Have or to Be?*, pp.75–6. Manfred Müller-Küppers and Friedrich Specht, in *Neue Jugend-'religionen'* (New Youth 'Religions'), Göttingen, Zürich 1979, discuss this topic; see also C. Evers, *Kulte des Irrationalen* (Cults of the Irrational), Hamburg 1976; *Dokumentation über die Auswirkungen der Jugendreligionen auf Jugendliche in Einzelfällen* (Documentation on the effects of the Youth Religions on Juveniles in individual Cases), edited by the Parents' Initiative Work Group, Bonn 1978.

6. *Suche nach Sinn – Suche nach Gott*, Foreword, p.8.

This search for transcendental commitment takes place outside institutionalized religion. Two representatives of the church write: 'This search is far removed from a return to Christian tradition; it is articulated simply as a question that is still to be answered. Between this unsolved question and the Christian answer yawns an abyss.'[7]

Religion Rediscovered

The many indications of a change towards a new religiousness which, it seems, are even to be found where the prevailing ideology of the state condemns the people to live without religion, are accompanied by a new phenomenon: while unbelief is spreading and taking hold of the masses, scientists and scholars of international rank and reputation who reflect on the causes of our miserable situation and the future of mankind have rediscovered religion. They have gained a new understanding of religion, not of its essence, but of its social and cultural function. Now that the consequences of the lack of religion are visible to the far-seeing, the 'frightful yet salutary preciseness' prophesied by Romano Guardini[8] is dawning.

Today the Polish philosopher Leszek Kolakowski, who comes from Marxism and teaches now from All Souls College, Oxford, realizes that absolute humanism, the 'complete freedom of man to create all meaning and significance, the lack of every kind of limitation in the determination of one's self', which once appeared to him especially attractive in Marxist philosophy, is 'especially dangerous'. He admits: 'Today I can see the dangers of an anthropocentric autonomist *Weltanschauung* much more clearly. I do not believe that men will ever be able or that it would be even desirable for them to be in the position to get rid of religion as a source of meaning and as an authority that imparts meaning.'[9]

Psychologists and sociologists wonder whether modern industrial society needs a new belief. Erich Fromm, the Nestor of North American psychoanalysis, and the Harvard sociologist Daniel Bell see very clearly that mankind has no future unless it acquires a new religious consciousness. Bell says bluntly that a society without religion is incapable of survival. In his opinion religion is something that is as universal among men as language;[10] it is 'a constitutive part of man's consciousness', the 'primor-

---

7. Gotthold Hild and Helmut Aichelin, 'Staat–Kirche–Gesellschaft', p.10. Concerning the 'overwhelming scepticism about organized religion, even among churchgoers' in the United States see Marilyn Ferguson, *The Aquarian Conspiracy*, pp.368ff. Describing the new spirituality, Marilyn Ferguson emphasizes that its adherents prefer 'direct experience . . . "excursion" to an inner world whose vision then infuses all of life to any form of organized religion', that these adherents are concerned in 'direct communion with the ultimate reality' (*The Aquarian Conspiracy*, pp.367, 371).

8. *The End of the Modern World*, p.123; cf. p.83.

9. In an interview with the Catholic Journal *Herderkorrespondenz*, No.10, October 1977, p.503.

10. *The Cultural Contradictions of Capitalism*, p.166.

dial need' both of the individual and of society.[11] Quoting Max Scheler, Bell contests that there is such a thing as a human being 'without belief': 'Every finite spirit believes either in God or in idols'[12] – an attitude which is also shared by the historian Arnold Toynbee: 'Since man cannot live without a religion of some kind or other, the recession of Christianity in the West has been followed there by the rise of substitute religions in the shape of the post-Christian ideologies – Nationalism, Individualism, and Communism.' These new forms of worship, which have invaded the 'spiritual vacuum left by the recession of traditional religion' and, starting in the West, have spread across the whole world, are 'forms of Man's worship of his own power'.[13] It is the worship of the 'three false Gods'[14] which has replaced the worship of God.

Bell observes that religion provides security for a culture in two essential ways: by guarding the portals against the demoniacal and by providing continuity with the past.[15] Religion offers protection against the anarchic impulses of man and provides the atavistic roots of life. As the authority of religion declined, the culture took up contact with the demoniacal, surrendering to 'the shambles of appetite and self-interest and the destruction of the moral circle which engirds mankind'.[16]

Bell refers to Rousseau's statement that every society is held together either by force – the army, militia and police – or by moral laws. In religion he sees the form of consciousness which is orientated towards ultimate values as the basis of a common moral order.[17] Bell realizes that the erosion of traditional values has led to hedonism, a way of life devoted to consumption, luxury and satisfaction of the basic drives. This way of life is threatening to destroy our world because it leads to the disappearance of *civitas*, 'that spontaneous willingness to obey the law, to respect the rights of others, to forego the temptations of private enrichment, at the expense of the public weal'.[18]

11. ibid. p.169.

12. ibid. p.169. Hans Küng writes: 'Men have always believed in some kind of "God", if not in the true God then in some kind of idol' ('Nine Theories on Religion and Science', a lecture given at the Academy of Social Sciences in Peking and quoted in *Die Zeit* of 19.10.1979). In this context Bahá'u'lláh has revealed the following: 'Arise, O people, and, by the power of God's might, resolve to gain the victory over your own selves, that haply the whole earth may be freed and sanctified from its servitude to the gods of its idle fancies – gods that have inflicted such loss upon, and are responsible for the misery of, their wretched worshippers. These idols form the obstacle that impeded man in his efforts to advance in the path of perfection.' (*Gleanings* 43:3.)

13. *Change and Habit*, pp.169–71.

14. Shoghi Effendi, *The Promised Day is Come*, p.117, names the three: nationalism, racialism, and communism.

15. *The Cultural Contradictions of Capitalism*, p.157.

16. Daniel Bell, op. cit., p.171.

17. ibid. p.154.

18. ibid. p.245. Bell refers to the Arab thinker Ibn Chaldun (1331–1406) who described the rise

The decisive factor in our secular world, in the culture of modern times, is, according to Bell,[19] the break with the past. Only the present moment counts; tradition is eliminated. This attitude leads directly to nihilism, for 'lacking a past or a future, there is only a void'.[20] Thus Bell sees his only hope in the fact that 'despite the shambles of modern culture . . . some religious answer surely will be forthcoming',[21] although he knows that belief 'cannot be called into being by fiat'.[22]

Erich Fromm comes from another direction. He is influenced by Freud and Marx and is certainly what one calls an atheist. Nevertheless, he is searching for a new religious consciousness. Fromm sees the signs of the times and realizes that this world will fall into fragments unless there is a fundamental change in our relationships and a radical change in our way of thinking. He too sees hedonism (in a way of life and an economic order based on egoism, selfishness and greed), the desire for worldly goods, the illusion that material values are eternal, and the 'having' mentality, as comprising the basic evil that has brought the world to the verge of a catastrophe. Man's true possessions consist of what he *is*, not what he *has*. In Fromm's eyes these two forms of existence are battling for the soul of mankind: the mode of *having*, which is concentrated on material possessions, on greed, power and aggression, causing avarice, envy and violence; and the mode of *being* which is based on love, the readiness to share, and creative activity. He sees this form of existence, the form of being, 'pre-formed' in the teachings of the great founders of the religions, Moses, Jesus, Buddha – 'the great masters', as he called them – and he does not hesitate to include Meister Eckhart, Karl Marx, Sigmund Freud and Albert Schweitzer in the list. Religious consciousness means, as Fromm rightly sees it, the overcoming of selfishness, of greed, of egoism, of desire for fame and power and every form of self-centredness and egocentric thinking[23] through the ethos of being: love and solidarity.

Fromm is fascinated by the fundamental religious concept of detachment: someone who is exclusively orientated towards possession is 'a neurotic, mentally sick person', and a society in which this character structure predominates, a socio-economic system like our Western industrial

---

and fall of cultures and discovered that with a hedonistic form of life society declines within three generations, because 'in the hedonistic life, there is a loss of will and fortitude'. What is worse, men 'lose the ability to share and sacrifice. There then follows, says Chaldun, the loss of '*aṣabiyyah*, that sense of solidarity which makes men feel as brothers to one another, that 'group feeling which means affection and willingness to fight and die for each other' (*The Cultural Contradictions of Capitalism*, p.83).

19. ibid. pp.99ff, 132.
20. ibid. pp.28–9.
21. ibid. p.169.
22. ibid. p.244.
23. *To Have or to Be?*, pp.7–8, 19, 65, 123–4.

society that moulds these characteristics, is similarly to be described as 'sick'.[24] Greed, according to Fromm, leads to the destruction of nature and to endless class struggles: 'Greed and peace preclude each other[25] . . . Peace as a state of lasting harmonious relations between nations is only possible when the having structure is replaced by the being structure'.[26] Thus the only alternatives for men are: 'Either a radical change of their character or the perpetuity of war', which in reality is 'mutual suicide'.[27]

Fromm sees that the mere survival of mankind depends on a radical transformation, a fundamental change in basic human values and attitudes, on the practice of a new system of ethics and an altered attitude towards nature: 'For the first time in history the physical survival of the human race depends on a radical change of the human heart',[28] which must be accompanied by drastic economic and social changes. The demand for an ethical change is the 'rational consequence of economic analysis'.[29] Fromm also sees the need for a new man.[30]

But how can this change be brought about? Fromm knows that without the 'impelling force of a strong motivation', the goal, the new man and the new society, cannot be achieved, and he is on the look-out for a new vision: 'Our only hope lies in the energizing attraction of a new vision.'[31] He sees that the necessary energy for such an extensive change comes from 'religious impulses', that a 'new object of devotion' must take 'the place of the present one',[32] that in order to survive, such an 'object of devotion'[33] and a new religious group attitude are needed: 'For we are what we are devoted to, and what we are devoted to is what motivates our conduct.'[34] Fromm expects the new man to develop out of a 'new nontheistic, noninstitutionalized *religiosity*'.[35]

A New Vision?

Were the farewell from religion to be a final one, the consequences for the survival of mankind would be disastrous. If, contrary to prevailing opinion today, religion still has a future, there are two possibilities: either the old

---

24. ibid. pp.18, 84.
25. ibid. p.6.
26. ibid. p.114.
27. ibid.
28. ibid. p.10.
29. ibid. p.164.
30. Fromm considers the expectation that once the new society is established it 'will quasi-automatically produce the new human being' to be as illusory as the contrary belief that a truly humane society can only be established when man has changed (op. cit., p.134). His opinion corresponds to the view of the Bahá'ís (compare pp.139–42).
31. *To Have or to Be?*, p.201.
32. ibid. p.133.
33. ibid. p.137.
34. ibid. pp.135–6.
35. ibid. p.202.

religions have the renewing power to break out of the rigid forms of their orthodoxy and escape the process of dissolving into humanism, the power to go back to their simple fundamental truths and overcome the scepticism of men caused largely by the religions themselves; or something new is coming. The ardent followers of the traditional religions have not given up the belief that their religions still possess the vital force to encounter the enormous challenge of unbelief – even Daniel Bell hopes for a revival of the old religions – although some of them realize that the 'firewood' will never again become a 'forest', 'for where there is no longer any possibility of anything new happening, there hope also comes to an end'.[36]

The other possibility is usually not considered, namely that in our times an upheaval is taking place similar to that which took place as the world of antiquity declined and Christianity dawned. It seems to be unreal, not worthy of discussion, that in our epoch a new breakthrough of transcendence could occur. And yet today many who reflect on our times feel that 'something decisive is happening', that we are at the 'turn of an age'.[37] Hans Schaefer is awaiting a 'new Moses'[38] and the Roman Catholic theologian Thomas Sartory in a remarkable radio talk[39] on the topic: 'The Turn of the Age? The Hope of a Coming Saviour in the Religions', pointed out that all religions expect a promised one who, at the time of the end, is to renew the world, cause a radical change in humanity, and, after a time of chaos and confusion, bring about a new age of peace and justice: 'Is it possible that we are in the middle of a change of epochal dimensions? Is perhaps what we are experiencing and suffering not just the result of human mistakes, errors and false attitudes but something like the birth pangs of a new era? . . . The apocalyptic writings have always compared the distress and afflictions of upheaval with the pains of a woman in labour.' Sartory refers to the fact that according to the age-old teachings of astrology concerning the Cosmic Ages we are now in the transition from the Age of Pisces into the Age of Aquarius,[40] and he sees enough indications that speak for a profound change of the times: 'The old is tumbling down, but the new that is coming just will not become clear in its contours. Is the reason', he asks, 'because it is so gigantic in its dimensions, so unfamiliar and different, that we cannot get a proper view of it, just as someone at the foot of an enormous mountain cannot get a proper picture of it?'

36. Jürgen Moltmann, *Theology of Hope*, pp.92, 93.

37. Jean Gebser, *In der Bewährung*, p.143.

38. 'Thus a new Moses must give us the tablets of such laws, and as we may dimly foresee, this Moses will not be a scientist himself.' ('Der Mensch und das Ende seiner Menschlichkeit', p.166.)

39. In 'Südwestfunk', on 5.1.1975.

40. Cf. Alfons Rosenberg, *Durchbruch zur Zukunft* (Breakthrough into the Future), Bietigheim, Turm-Verlag, undated.

Religion Renewed: God has Spoken

The Bahá'ís believe that God is not dead, that at the same time as the old religions were consuming their life-force and the philosophers and theologians were declaring God to be dead, the living God spoke to mankind through Bahá'u'lláh.

The nineteenth century is not only the century of science and the destruction of faith; it is also the century of manifold religious yearnings, messianic hopes, the eager expectation of the time of the end, and the century of the new beginning. In the first decades adventist movements, aflame with the anticipation of the return of the Lord, arose in Europe and the USA. Pietists from Württemberg emigrated to Palestine, settled on the slopes of Mount Carmel and awaited the coming of the Lord.[41] William Miller, the founder of the group later called the 'Seventh Day Adventists' had even calculated a time for the expected coming from the prophecies of the Old and New Testaments: 21 March 1844, and then later, 22 October 1844. The disappointment and resignation were great when Christ did not appear on the clouds in the visible heavens, as they had expected.[42]

41. The houses they built with inscriptions such as 'Der Herr ist nahe' (the Lord is nigh) can still be seen today in Haifa on the slopes of Carmel not far from the spot where Bahá'u'lláh pitched his tent.

42. The history of the expectation of the time of the end, which comprises quite a large part of the New Testament, shows that the history of man's salvation has run a singularly interesting course. Early Christianity lived in the expectation that the Lord would soon return, and believed that the world would soon end. In the course of the early centuries, especially after the change brought about by Constantine, the expected event was delayed more and more to a remote period in the future. However, over the centuries apocalyptic speculations and the belief that the world would end in the immediate future blazed up again and again. Joachim von Fiore (1130–1202) expanded them into a system of historical-allegorical interpretation, related the year 1260 (= 42 months = 3½ times, cf. Rev. 11:2; 11:9; 12:6; 12:14; 13:5) to the Christian calendar and prophesied it as the time when a Messianic figure would bring the 'everlasting gospel' (Rev. 14:6). The concepts of the renewal of religion and progressive revelation can be found in his writings. ('Abdu'l-Bahá in *Some Answered Questions*, chapters 11 and 13, relates the number 1260 to the Islámic calendar; cf. also Howard Garey, '1260 A.D. or A.H.? Case of the Mistaken Date', in *World Order*, A Bahá'í Magazine, Wilmette, Illinois, Fall 1972.)

In the eighteenth and nineteenth centuries at the same time as Christianity was increasingly losing its power to influence culture, expectations of the return, as described above, revived again stronger than ever before, not, however, in the church, but in certain Christian groups. In the church the expectation of the time of the end, the hope that Christ would return, has long been lost. She wears no 'wedding garment' (Matt. 22:11). The cock on the church tower, the symbol of watchfulness (cf. Matt. 25:1ff.; 24:43; 2 Pet. 3:10; Rev. 16:15), is no longer awaiting the Lord. A meeting of the World Council of Churches held in Evanston, USA in 1954 under the title 'Christ – the Hope' could not agree on whether a return of Christ can be expected. Although there are texts in the Bible that justify these elemental yearnings, it has been a long time since theology has considered them a topic of study. Thus they have drifted into the different sects, leading their own particular existence in movements such as the Seventh Day Adventists, Jehovah's Witnesses, and numerous splinter groups. With their literal interpretations of the Holy Writings and their resultant expectation of a miraculous event these groups have blocked their own view completely. (cf. Kurt Hutten, who gives a detailed treatment of the adventist groups from a Protestant point of view in his book *Seher, Grübler, Enthusiasten* pp.9–14.)

At the same time as the adventist movements there arose the atheistic 'religion of salvation' founded in philosophy, a secular Messianic movement which has taken up the Biblical promises, the expectation

But the Christians are not the only ones who are hoping for the return of the Lord and the transformation of the world. All the religions, even the religions of the American Indians,[43] know of an 'end', a saviour who comes at the time of the end, and the Golden Age of mankind. Although there are differences in the concepts and images used, these expectations are astonishingly similar: time is coming to an end. After a long period of decline, destruction and chaos, a world saviour will bring about the turning-point, introduce a new age and renew the world. In Hinduism, Vishnu is incarnated to men in a new form throughout the different ages in order to restore order in the world.[44] The doctrine of the *avatars*, the 'coming down' of God, culminates in the expectation of the tenth avatar, Kalkin. This messenger of God will appear at the end of the Kali period (according to Brahman tradition riding on a white horse)[45] and will renew the world. Buddhism also has its eschatology. According to Buddhist teachings the age of Gautama Buddha will be followed by that of Buddha Maitreya, who will inaugurate a new era of active neighbourly love.[46]

The concept of a herald[47] who precedes the world saviour is also quite common, and thus many religions expect a twin constellation to bring salvation: Judaism awaits the Messiah ben Joseph before the Messiah ben David, the Zoroastrian religion awaits the Ushídar-Má who will precede the Sháh Bahrám. And Islám, which of all religions has probably the most pronounced eschatology, expects two messengers: the Sunnis await the Mahdi

of the time of the end including the transformation of all things and which promises to fulfil all that religion left unfulfilled: the liberation of man and the harmony of all things. Under the influence of social doctrines of salvation, theology, in which for a long time the Messianic idea had had no place, is now experiencing the world today 'in expectation of a divine transformation'. Jürgen Moltmann was the first to re-discover the central significance of the eschatological aspects of Jesus's message for theology. In his eyes Christianity is the 'religion of expectation'. Eschatology is for him 'the universal horizon of all theology as such' (*Theology of Hope*, p.137; Jürgen Moltmann, 'Die Zukunft als neues Paradigma der Transzendenz' (The Future as a New Paradigm of Transcendence), in *Internationale Dialog-Zeitschrift*, 2, 1969, pp.2ff). The founder of the Bahá'í Faith, who claims to fulfil the promises of all religions, appeared about the same time as the adventist expectations were reaching their peak and the secular substitute religions were being formulated. In this singular concurrence the Bahá'ís see divine providence at work: a path becomes visible 'where none suspected it' (Martin Buber, *For the Sake of Heaven*, p.xiii), and the Messiah appeared like a 'thief in the night' (Matt. 24:43; 1 Thess. 5:2; 1 Pet. 4:15; Rev. 3:3; 16:15).

43. William Willoya and Vinson Brown, *Warriors of the Rainbow. Strange and Prophetic Dreams of the Indian Peoples*, Healdsburg, Calif., Naturegraph, 1962.

44. In the Bhagavadgita is written: 'Whenever there is a decline of righteousness and rise of unrighteousness, then I send forth Myself . . . For the protection of the good, for the destruction of the wicked and for the establishment of righteousness, I come into being from age to age.' (IV, 7 and 8.)

45. An amazing parallel to the Apocalypse of St. John, where the beginning of the new Era, the millennium, is marked by the return of Christ on a white steed (19:11).

46. See Jamshed Fozdar, *Buddha Maitrya-Amitabha has Appeared*, New Delhi 1976.

47. The announcement by a herald is a religious archetype. Cf. Luke 1:26ff and the function of John the Baptist in Christianity. In Islám there were four men who appeared one after the other to announce Muhammad's coming to the people. Rúz-bih (later known as Salmán) was the servant of each one after the other , and was then sent by the last to Hijáz, where he attained the presence of Muhammad. (cf. Bahá'u'lláh, *Kitáb-i-Íqán*, p.65. See also H. M. Balyuzi, *Muhammad and the Course of Islám*, pp.51, 55–6, 94, 201, 222, on the part played by Salmán al-Fársí in Islám.)

and the return of Jesus Christ;[48] and the Shí'ah expect the Qá'im and the Qayyúm (Imám Husayn).

These Messianic expectations[49] in the nineteenth century were not only rampant in Christianity but also in Judaism and Islám. At the end of the eighteenth century Shaykh-Ahmad-i-Ahsá'í founded an adventist reform movement that caused quite a stir in Iraq and Persia. Its main teaching was that the time was ripe for the 'Great Announcement' promised by the Prophet Muhammad,[50] for the 'Hour', the 'Day of Judgement' and for the immediate appearance of the Qá'im awaited by Shí'ah Islám. On the fifth day of Jamádíyu'l-Avval, 1260,[51] in the city of Shíráz in Southern Persia a twenty-five-year-old merchant by the name of 'Alí Muhammad, a Siyyid, a descendant of the Prophet, declared himself to a follower of Shaykh Ahmad as the awaited herald of the Promised One, as the Qá'im. This event marked the birth of the Bahá'í Revelation.

'Alí Muhammad, who assumed the spiritual name of the 'Báb', meaning the 'Gate', quickly found many ardent followers, but he also attracted the relentless opposition of the orthodox Shí'ah clergy and, at their instigation, that of the state authorities. Over 20,000 martyrs died in the bloody persecutions that followed, and the Báb was publicly executed in 1850 in a barrack square in Tabríz.

The central figure of the Bahá'í Faith is Bahá'u'lláh (1817–92)[52] who was banished to Baghdád in 1852 because he was a follower of the Báb. There he became the spiritual centre of the new Faith and on the eve of his banishment to Constantinople in 1863[53] he revealed himself to his followers as the Promised One of all religions. On the request of the Persian Government Bahá'u'lláh was banished again to Adrianople[54] and from there to the Turkish penal colony of 'Akká in the Holy Land in 1868;

48. The Messianic Messengers of God are not mentioned in the Qur'án, but are the subject of numerous traditions (hadíth). There are numerous proofs concerning the return of Christ and that He will judge mankind according to the law of the Sharí'ah. According to Muslim, Abu Huraira reported that the messenger of Allah said: 'By Him in Whose hand is my life, the son of Mary (may peace be upon him) will soon descend among you as a just judge.' (*Kitáb al-Imán*, chapter LXXII, ed. by 'Abdu'l Hamíd Siddiqui.)

49. For information on this see William Sears, *Thief in the Night*, Oxford, George Ronald, 6th RP 1973; Nigg, Walter, *Das ewige Reich. Geschichte einer Hoffnung* (The Eternal Kingdom. History of a Hope), 2nd edn, Zürich 1954; Guiness, H. Grattan, *The Approaching End of the Age Viewed in the Light of History, Prophecy and Science*, New York, A.C. Armstrong, 1881; Hans Meyer, *Geschichte der abendländischen Weltanschauung* (History of the Western View of Life), Würzburg 1947, Vol. 2, p.150.

50. Cf. Qur'án 78:2.

51. The year 1260 in the Moslem calendar corresponds to 1844 in the Christian calendar. The date corresponds to 23rd May, 1844.

52. A spiritual title. The Arabic word means 'Glory of God'. The name given Bahá'u'lláh at birth was Mírzá Husayn 'Alí Núrí. His father was a Vazír at the court of Fath-'Alí Sháh.

53. Bahá'u'lláh was accompanied by an escort of guards on horseback on the journey from Baghdád to Constantinople. He himself rode 'a red roan stallion of the finest breed' (Shoghi Effendi, *God Passes By*, p.155). See this chapter, note 45.

54. Adrianople is the present-day Edirne in Turkey.

thus he spent forty years in prison or in exile. In a number of letters ('tablets') Bahá'u'lláh addressed Himself to the crowned heads, religious and secular, of East and West: Napoleon III, Kaiser Wilhelm I, Kaiser Franz Joseph, Queen Victoria, Tsar Alexander II, Násiri'd-Dín S͟háh, Sulṭán 'Abdu'l-'Azíz, Pope Pius IX, and called upon them to recognize his message. In challenging and unequivocal words He proclaimed that the promised day had come: 'Say, by the righteousness of God! The All-Merciful is come invested with power and sovereignty. Through His potency the foundations of religions have quaked and the Nightingale of Utterance hath warbled its melody upon the highest branch of true understanding. Verily, He who was hidden in the knowledge of God and is mentioned in the Holy Scriptures hath appeared. Say, this is the Day when the Speaker on Sinai hath mounted the throne of Revelation and the people have stood before the Lord of the worlds. This is the Day wherein the earth hath told out her tidings and hath laid bare her treasures; when the Sun hath shed its radiance and the Moons have diffused their light, and the Heavens have revealed their stars, and the Hour its signs, and the Resurrection its dreadful majesty; when the pens have unloosed their outpourings and the spirits have laid bare their mysteries. Blessed is the man who recognizeth Him and attaineth His presence, and woe betide such as deny Him and turn aside from Him.'[55]

Bahá'u'lláh called upon the sovereigns to follow the principles of his teachings in their politics, to reduce their armaments and to establish world peace. He revealed his task of giving the world new life, of reforming its order under divine guidance and of leading the whole of mankind on the path of spiritual progress. He saw the purpose of his mission as the bringing together of humanity in an all-encompassing order in a spirit of harmony, peace and unity. The means of achieving this goal would be the unification of mankind in the all-embracing Faith which he revealed and in obedience to his counsels. Bahá'u'lláh warned the peoples about the divine judgement which was at hand and of the misery which would come upon mankind, but this divine punishment was to be, according to Bahá'u'lláh, at the same time a purification of the human race. Through it humanity would be welded together into an organic, indivisible and world-wide community to whom he promised a radiant future, the coming of the 'Most Great Peace'. In a large number of writings that have been handed on to us he announced to mankind God's will for a new age. He died in 1892 at Bahjí near 'Akká, where after mitigation of his imprisonment he had spent the latter years of his life.

He appointed his eldest son, 'Abdu'l-Bahá, to succeed him as the spiritual head of the Faith and as the authoritative interpreter of his

---

55. Is͟hráqát, *Tablets*, p.107. Extensive quotations from Tablets to the rulers are to be found in *The Proclamation of Bahá'u'lláh to the Kings and Leaders of the World*, Haifa 1967.

writings. 'Abdu'l-Bahá was released from captivity by the Young Turks' Revolution which overthrew the Ottoman Government in 1908 and then had the freedom and opportunity to travel to Egypt, Europe and the USA where he acquainted many with the Bahá'í religion. Innumerable contemporary publications testify to the deep respect accorded him in public by churches, universities and renowned personalities. He died in Haifa in 1921, leaving in his Will and Testament a charter for the future development of the Bahá'í Faith under the guidance of Shoghi Effendi, whom He appointed Guardian of the Faith, and of the Universal House of Justice. Authority to interpret the revelation was vested in the Guardian, while authority in the legislative and administrative realms had been given to the Universal House of Justice by Bahá'u'lláh himself. In 1963, one hundred years after Bahá'u'lláh's declaration, the Universal House of Justice was elected for the first time by representatives of the whole Bahá'í world, and is the supreme administrative body of the Bahá'í Faith, deriving its powers from the express command of Bahá'u'lláh and endowed by him with binding authority. This body has its seat on Mount Carmel in Israel, where the main holy places of the Bahá'í Faith are also to be found.

The Bahá'í Faith has spread to almost every country of the world. Apart from Persia, the land of its birth, most of its followers are to be found in South America, Africa, India and South-East Asia. Today (1980) there are Bahá'ís in more than 106,000 places in the world. There are over 25,500 communities and 131 National Spiritual Assemblies. Bahá'í communities are growing in the farthest corner of the earth.[56]

The Quickener of the World: Bahá'u'lláh

The prophets of atheism and the prophet of the living God were contemporaries.[57] Karl Marx, who proclaimed the religion of revolution, the

56. On the history of the Bahá'í Faith see Shoghi Effendi, *God Passes By*, Wilmette, 5th edn, 1965; Nabíl-i-A'zam, *The Dawn-Breakers. Nabil's Narrative of the Early Days of the Bahá'í Revelation*, translated and edited by Shoghi Effendi, Wilmette 1932; H. M. Balyuzi, *The Báb*, Oxford 1973; *Bahá'u'lláh. The King of Glory*, Oxford 1980; 'Abdu'l-Bahá, London 1971; 'Abdu'l-Bahá, *A Traveler's Narrative*, translated by E. G. Browne, Cambridge 1891, rev.edn Wilmette 1980. On the teachings of the Bahá'í Faith see J. E. Esslemont, *Bahá'u'lláh and the New Era*, London 1923, 4th rev.edn 1974; John Huddleston, *The Earth is but One Country*, London 1976; John Ferraby, *All Things Made New*, London 1975; Huschmand Sabet, *The Heavens are Cleft Asunder*, Oxford 1975; Rudolf Jockel, *Die Lehren der Bahá'í-Religion* (The Teachings of the Bahá'í Faith), Tübingen 1952. Critical works: Gerhard Rosenkranz, *Die Bahá'í*, Stuttgart 1949; F. Vahman, in TRE, Theologische Realenzyklopädie, Berlin, New York, Walter de Gruyter, Vol.V, 1979, pp.115–32; Encyclopaedia Britannica, 15th edn, Chicago 1974. See also *The Bahá'í World, An International Record*, Bahá'í World Centre, Vol.XVII, 1982.

57. The Báb was born in 1819, Bahá'u'lláh in 1817, Karl Marx in 1818 and Ludwig Feuerbach in 1804. *The Essence of Christianity*, in which Feuerbach criticizes religion, appeared in 1841; Marx wrote his early critical works on religion in 1843 and 1844 in Paris. The *Communist Manifesto* appeared in 1848, the same year in which the Bábí religion, after the Conference in Badasht, cut its ties with Islám, declaring the abrogation of the Law of Sharí'ah.

religion of social salvation, and who gave new dimensions to the political Messianism that had developed in the eighteenth century, did not want to present a new interpretation of the world; he wanted to change it.[58] And he has changed it: half of mankind is already being ruled by maxims that are based on his writings.[59] Although communism is no longer a unified monolithic bloc but has developed into many and sometimes antagonistic forms, it is nevertheless the political aim of many peoples and the secular creed of a large part of the younger generation. Countless numbers of people hope to find a means of orientation for a humane world in Marxist theories. It remains to be seen whether his teachings are the remedy for curing the world of its ills.

Has Bahá'u'lláh changed the world? The answer to this is: the change is on the way. A revolution is taking place quietly. Bahá'ís believe that the unrest which erupted in the nineteenth century and the changes the world has undergone since have their ultimate spiritual cause in the fact that there has been a new revelation: 'The world's equilibrium hath been upset through the vibrating influence of this most great, this new World Order. Mankind's ordered life hath been revolutionized through the agency of this unique, this wondrous System – the like of which mortal eyes have never witnessed.'[60]

Like earlier prophets Bahá'u'lláh appeared as *Bashír wa Nadhír*[61] proclaiming a joyous message and bringing a warning. Like Noah[62] he warned mankind that God's divine judgement was about to be implemented and he prophesied the far-reaching changes that were to be expected: the condition of unbelief and the breakdown of the old order as its consequence.[63] As the proclaimer of a new gospel he promised the spiritual renewal and the unification of mankind, the construction of a new world order, the like of which had never been seen before, and therewith the beginning of the time when God's Kingdom on earth would be established: 'This is the Day that God hath ordained to be a blessing unto the righteousness, a retribution for the wicked, a bounty for the faithful and a fury of His wrath for the faithless and the froward.'[64]

Bahá'u'lláh wrote that atheism would become a world-wide phenome-

---

58. 'The philosophers have only interpreted the world in various ways; the point is to change it.' (11th thesis on Feuerbach, *The German Ideology*, p.653.)

59. Leszek Kolakowski says, however: 'The present Marxism neither interprets the world nor changes it: it is merely a repertoire of slogans serving to organize various interests, most of them completely remote from those with which Marxism originally identified itself . . . The self-deification of mankind, to which Marxism gave philosophical expression, has ended in the same way as all such attempts, whether individual or collective: it has revealed itself as the farcical aspect of human bondage'. (*Main Currents of Marxism*, Vol.III, p.530.)

60. Bahá'u'lláh, Kitáb-i-Aqdas, *Synopsis*, No. 21, p.27 (= *Gleanings* 70:1).

61. 'Verily we have sent thee with the truth; a bearer of good tidings and a warner.' (Qur'án 35:22.)

62. Matt. 24:37.

63. Cf. the comments on pp.145ff.

64. Bahá'u'lláh, Ishráqát, *Tablets*, p.103.

non and that every attempt to breathe new life into the old religions would fail: 'In this day the tastes of men have changed, and their power of perception hath altered. The contrary winds of the world, and its colours, have provoked a cold, and deprived man's nostrils of the sweet savours of Revelation [65] . . . The face of the world hath altered. The way of God and the religion of God have ceased to be of any worth in the eyes of men [66] . . . The vitality of men's belief in God is dying out in every land; nothing short of His wholesome medicine can ever restore it. The corrosion of ungodliness is eating into the vitals of human society; what else but the Elixir of His potent Revelation can cleanse and revive it?' [67] According to Bahá'u'lláh religion is the fundamental basis of the order of the world, and thus the decline of religion will also cause the order of the state to decline: 'Religion is, verily, the chief instrument for the establishment of order in the world, and of tranquillity amongst its peoples. The weakening of the pillars of religion hath strengthened the foolish, and emboldened them, and made them more arrogant. Verily I say: The greater the decline of religion, the more grievous the waywardness of the ungodly. This cannot but lead in the end to chaos and confusion. Hear Me, O men of insight, and be warned, ye who are endued with discernment [68] . . . Soon will the present-day order be rolled up, and a new one spread out in its stead.' [69]

The decline and the upheaval are inevitable and necessary, because they make place for the new: 'Neither do men put a new wine into old bottles.' [70] Man is not shaper of events in the stormy process of change which afflicts the peoples today and is preparing them for the coming of the 'Most Great Justice'. However, consciously or unconsciously, he is helping to introduce, as part of the divine plan of salvation, 'the Golden Age of a long-divided, a long-afflicted humanity' by means which 'He alone can bring about'. [71]

The remedy that God has given mankind through Bahá'u'lláh, his teachings and his commandments, his world-renewing spirit, first has an effect on those who have gathered around him. The changing and healing of the world by the new Word of God needs time. Nietzsche's impressive words, 'lightning and thunder need time, the light of the stars needs time, deeds need time, even after they are done, to be seen and heard', [72] can be applied in particular to the advent of the great revealed religions. Their power to shape the world needs time to be recognized by man. Bahá'u'lláh

65. Quoted by Shoghi Effendi, *The Promised Day is Come*, p.119.
66. Quoted by Shoghi Effendi, op. cit., p.117.
67. *Gleanings* 99.
68. *Epistle to the Son of the Wolf*, p.28. See also Kalimát-i-Firdawsíyyih, Second Leaf, *Tablets*, pp.63–4.
69. *Gleanings* 4:2.
70. Matt. 9:17.
71. Shoghi Effendi, *The Promised Day is Come*, p.120.
72. *The Joyful Wisdom*, No. 125.

revealed the following concerning the power that has come into the world and is effective in his revelation: 'The universe is pregnant with these manifold bounties, awaiting the hour when the effects of its unseen gifts will be made manifest in this world[73] . . . The whole earth is now in a state of pregnancy. The day is approaching when it will have yielded its noblest fruits, when from it will have sprung forth the loftiest trees, the most enchanting blossoms, the most heavenly blessings . . . The onrushing winds of the grace of God have passed over all things. Every creature hath been endowed with all the potentialities it can carry.'[74] And 'Abdu'l-Bahá wrote on the forthcoming renewal of the world: 'The Call of God, when raised, breathed a new life into the body of mankind, and infused a new spirit into the whole creation. It is for this reason that the world hath been moved to its depths, and the hearts and consciences of men been quickened. Erelong the evidences of this regeneration will be revealed, and the fast asleep will be awakened[75] . . . Whatsoever is latent in the innermost of this holy cycle shall gradually appear and be made manifest, for now is but the beginning of its growth and the dayspring of the revelation of its signs.'[76]

When the world begins to take the *skandalon* (scandal) seriously and realizes that the allegedly dead God has spoken to mankind through Bahá'u'lláh, it will then be obvious that this is the most outstanding event in history: the turn of the age, the gateway to the Kingdom of God on earth as promised by Christ.

73. *Kitáb-i-Íqán*, p.60.
74. Quoted by Shoghi Effendi, 'The Unfoldment of World Civilization', in *The World Order of Bahá'u'lláh*, p.169.
75. ibid. p.169.
76. 'The Dispensation of Bahá'u'lláh', op. cit., p.111.

5. Divine Revelation in History

Who is God?

The Bahá'ís believe that this world is more than the result of coincidence or of blind forces, that man is more than nature's 'lucky strike', that our life has a meaning and a goal, and that there is another reality beyond the reality of our own world, one that transcends immanent existence.

For the Bahá'ís, God is the Absolute, the first cause and the final goal. He is by no means a mere idea (Kant), or a 'useful fiction' (Vaihinger). The Bahá'ís believe in an almighty Creator of 'heaven' and 'earth' Who created man in his own image; they believe in an unbegotten cause of all existence, in a single God, as is expressed in the prayer revealed by Bahá'u'lláh: 'Magnified be Thy Name, O Lord my God! Thou art He Whom all things worship and Who worshippeth no one, Who is the Lord of all things and is the vassal of none, Who knoweth all things and is known of none. Thou didst wish to make Thyself known unto men; therefore, Thou didst, through a word of Thy mouth, bring creation into being and fashion the universe. There is none other God except Thee, the Fashioner, the Creator, the Almighty, the Most Powerful.'[1] The verse: 'No one on earth, O my Lord, can withstand Thy power, and none in all the kingdom of Thy names is able to frustrate Thy purpose',[2] bears witness to the omnipotence of God.

The word 'God' represents the first cause and the actual reason for all existence; it denotes that reality beyond our world by which the world of being as we experience it is ruled and maintained. A Bahá'í is not misled by the fact that the concepts of God and religion and its teachings have often been used for very ungodly, selfish motives and repeatedly misused

---

1. *Prayers and Meditations*, No. 4.
2. Bahá'u'lláh, *Prayers and Meditations*, No. 13.

to justify existing social and economic differences which were considered sacred because they were apparently given by nature and willed by God. A Bahá'í is not confused by the fact that – especially in Christian thought – conditions on earth were often considered unreal, transitory and unessential, that responsibility for this world was neglected because only one thing seemed important: the salvation of the soul, in need of redemption from its sinfulness.

To evaluate a phenomenon when it has reached a stage of degeneration and decadence is prejudice and can only lead to erroneous conclusions.[3] There are people who go through the history of the church with a waste-bin in their hands, picking up all the rubbish which has accumulated there: forced baptism, *autodafé*, the wars of the Crusades, the persecution of the Jews, witch hunts, the Massacre of St. Bartholomew's Eve and the Te Deum which followed it, and much more. These dreadful deeds were indeed committed and they have blackened the annals of the Christian religion. 'Christianity – two thousand years of error!' stated a renowned theologian in a conversation with the author.

This is not the way the Bahá'ís see it. Christianity cannot be dismissed as a dismal chronicle of atrocities. There is far far more to it than that. For almost two thousand years Christianity has enlightened countless human beings and given their lives a goal, a meaning and a mainstay. The innumerable works of active Christian charity which no historian has recorded, the devotion, the selfless acts of mercy which were carried out in the name of Christ, and the evidence of a brilliant culture cannot be outweighed by the disastrous misdeeds of misdirected fanatics. Religious history very clearly shows not only that the religions – including Christianity – legitimized the prevailing order of things, the nobility and the bourgeoisie; but that they also in their very essence provided the revolutionary élan for renewal and change. Daniel Bell, referring to Max Weber, emphasizes that religion, 'at crucial junctures of history, is sometimes the most revolutionary of all forces. When traditions and institutions become rigidified and oppressive, or when the discordance of voices and the babble of contradictory beliefs become intolerable, men look for new answers . . . In these circumstances, we look for new prophets. Prophecy breaks down ritualistic conservatism when it has lost all meaning, and prophecy provides a new gestalt when there have been too many meanings.'[4]

The misuse of a thing does not disprove the thing itself; the misuse of the concept of God and of religion does not reduce to absurdity that which

3. This can also be said of Tilman Moser's vicious reckoning with the belief in God (*Gottesvergiftung* (God's Poison), Frankfurt 1976). The kind of religion in which his neurotically disturbed, hate-ridden relationship towards God developed was a caricature, and this is what he is now fighting against.
4. *The Cultural Contradictions of Capitalism*, p.169.

we call God, 'the One Power which animates and dominates all things'.[5] God is transcendental, beyond our comprehension and imaginative power. Therefore belief in God cannot be proved rationally,[6] because – as we have known since Kant – the central concepts of metaphysics such as 'God, free will and immortality'[7] are not subjects of epistemological inquiry. The existence or non-existence of metaphysical concepts is a matter which cannot be decided by rational means. Similarly all speculation about the essence of God, such as the concepts of the Incarnation[8] and the Trinity in Christian theology, is vain and doomed to failure. Bahá'u'lláh proclaims the absolute transcendence of God: 'The conceptions of the devoutest of mystics, the attainments of the most accomplished amongst men, the highest praise which human tongue or pen can render are all the product of man's finite mind and are conditioned by its limitations. Ten thousand Prophets, each a Moses, are thunderstruck upon the Sinai of their search at His forbidding voice, "Thou shalt never behold Me!"; whilst a myriad Messengers, each as great as Jesus, stand dismayed upon their heavenly thrones by the interdiction, "Mine Essence thou shalt never apprehend!". From time immemorial He hath been veiled in the ineffable sanctity of His exalted Self, and will everlastingly continue to be wrapt in the impenetrable mystery of His unknowable Essence. Every attempt to attain to an understanding of His inaccessible Reality hath ended in complete bewilderment, and every effort to approach His exalted Self and envisage His Essence hath resulted in hopelessness and failure.'[9]

God is a mystery[10] that cannot be understood; He cannot be subjected to our thought processes, our perception, our concrete knowledge. He is beyond our empirical rational understanding; man has to decide for God without rational proof. The only faculty that can recognize him is the human heart, 'the seat of the All-Merciful and the throne wherein abideth the splendour of His revelation'.[11] The heart is 'the recipient of the light of God and the seat of the revelation of the All-Merciful'.[12] Bahá'u'lláh quotes the Islámic tradition: 'Earth and heaven cannot contain Me; what

5. Bahá'u'lláh, *The Hidden Words. Words of Wisdom and Communes*, p.61.
6. Equally, the opposite, atheism, cannot be proved rationally. In any case it is more difficult to prove the non-existence of a thing than to prove its existence. The only tenable position for the non-believer is that of agnosticism, which rejects the question as impossible to answer.
7. Immanuel Kant, *Critique of Pure Reason*, Introduction, III.
8. 'Know thou of a certainty that the Unseen can in no wise incarnate His Essence and reveal it unto men. He is, and hath ever been, immensely exalted beyond all that can either be recounted or perceived.' (Bahá'u'lláh, *Gleanings* 20.)
9. *Gleanings* 26:3, cf. also *Gleanings* 148.
10. 'Man is My mystery, and I am his mystery' (a saying of Muḥammad's from the oral traditions (ḥadíth), quoted by Bahá'u'lláh, *Gleanings* 90:1).
11. Bahá'u'lláh, *Gleanings* 93:3. For a thorough examination of the question of the recognition of God see 'Abdu'l-Bahá, Letter to Dr. Forel, in *Auguste Forel and the Bahá'í Faith*, pp.15ff.
12. Bahá'u'lláh, *Gleanings* 93:5. In this sense Paul speaks of man as being the 'temple of God' in which the 'spirit of God' dwells (I Cor. 3:16; II Cor. 6:16), and St. Augustine says God is *'interior intimo meo'* (*Confessions* III, 6).

can alone contain Me is the heart of him that believeth in Me, and is faithful to My Cause', and says at the same time that 'it is the waywardness of the heart that removeth it far from God, and condemneth it to remoteness from Him'.[13] The Qur'ánic verse: 'And we are closer to him than his neck-vein'[14] is also directed to the heart that 'hath strayed from His path, hath shut out itself from His glory, and is stained with the defilement of earthly desires'.[15] Similarly Bahá'u'lláh says: 'Consider, moreover, how frequently doth man become forgetful of his own self, whilst God remaineth, through His all-encompassing knowledge, aware of His creature, and continueth to shed upon him the manifest radiance of His glory. It is evident, therefore, that, in such circumstances, He is closer to him than his own self.'[16] When called upon in prayer God is ever 'ready to answer':[17] 'Thou disappointest no one who hath sought Thee, nor dost Thou keep back from Thee any one who hath desired Thee.'[18]

Man can comprehend only the attributes of God. His *essence* will always be hidden from man, as Bahá'u'lláh teaches: 'The way is barred, and all seeking rejected.'[19] Thus God is 'the Hidden'.[20] But at the same time He is also 'the Seen', for He reveals Himself to mankind through His revelation, as religious history testifies.

The Nature of Manifestation

Bahá'ís do not proclaim a God that has no relationship to the world or to history, a God that created the world and then delivered it to the forces of chance. They believe in a God who has an active part in history and acts upon this world. The Creator of mankind is the Lord of history who manifests Himself in His revelations and through them has made a covenant with humanity. From time immemorial, through His chosen prophets and messengers, He has announced His will to the peoples of the earth and sent them His guidance: 'And to every people have we sent an apostle saying: "Worship God and turn away from Taghout".'[21] He has thereby decreed 'the knowledge of these sanctified Beings to be identical with the knowledge of His own Self'.[22] The recognition of God can only be

---

13. *Gleanings* 93:5.
14. 50:17
15. Bahá'u'lláh, *Gleanings* 93:3.
16. *Gleanings* 93:6.
17. Bahá'u'lláh, *Prayers and Meditations*, No.154.
18. Bahá'u'lláh, *Prayers and Meditations*, No.156.
19. A saying of the Imám 'Alí, quoted by Bahá'u'lláh, in *Kitáb-i-Íqán*, p.141.
20. 'He is the first and the last; the Seen and the Hidden; and He knoweth all things!' (Qur'án 57:3.) The concept of the hidden God (*Deus absconditus*) is also known in Judaism and Christianity: 'Verily thou art a God that hideth thyself.' (Isa. 45:15.)
21. Qur'án 16:38. Taghout (Ṭághút) was an Arabian idol. A. J. Arberry translates: 'Serve you God and eschew idols.'
22. Bahá'u'lláh, *Gleanings* 21.

achieved through the Manifestation.[23] Bahá'u'lláh says clearly and unequivocally that recognition of God without the Manifestation, for instance in the sense of *Unio mystica*, is not possible: 'He Who is everlastingly hidden from the eyes of men can never be known except through His Manifestation, and His Manifestation can adduce no greater proof of the truth of His Mission than the proof of His own Person.'[24] The Manifestations are 'the representative and mouthpiece of God' on earth,[25] the 'Gems of Detachment', the 'embodiments of wisdom',[26] the 'channels of God's all-pervasive grace',[27] the 'Day Stars of His divine guidance',[28] 'His Voice';[29] they are the mediators between God and mankind: 'These sanctified Mirrors, these Day Springs of ancient glory, are, one and all, the Exponents on earth of Him Who is the central Orb of the universe, its Essence and ultimate Purpose. From Him proceed their knowledge and power; from Him is derived their sovereignty. The beauty of their countenance is but a reflection of His image, and their revelation a sign of His deathless glory. They are the Treasuries of Divine knowledge, and the Repositories of celestial wisdom. Through them is transmitted a grace that is infinite, and by them is revealed the Light that can never fade.'[30] Just as the unfiltered light of the sun dazzles the eye so much that it must turn away from its fiery profusion, man cannot look directly into the light of God; it can only be withstood when reflected in the 'mirror' of the Manifestation. It is in these divine Manifestations that man encounters God: 'Whoso recognizeth them hath recognized God. Whoso hearkeneth to their call, hath hearkened to the Voice of God, and whoso testifieth to the truth of their Revelation, hath testified to the truth of God Himself. Whoso turneth away from them, hath turned away from God, and whoso disbelieveth in them, hath disbelieved in God. Every one of them is the Way of God that connecteth this world with the realms above, and the Standard of His Truth unto every one in the kingdoms of earth and heaven.'[31]

All the messengers of God have appeared among men in order to 'safeguard the interests and promote the unity of the human race, and to foster the spirit of love and fellowship amongst men'[32] and 'to carry forward an ever-advancing civilization'.[33] God's revelations, the history of

---

23. The term 'prophet' is ambiguous. The Qur'án uses the term *rasúl*, which means messenger; Bahá'u'lláh uses the term *zuhúr*, which means manifestation.
24. Bahá'u'lláh, *Gleanings* 20.
25. Bahá'u'lláh, *Gleanings* 28:2.
26. Bahá'u'lláh, *Gleanings* 81.
27. Bahá'u'lláh, *Gleanings* 27:4.
28. Bahá'u'lláh, *Gleanings* 21.
29. Bahá'u'lláh, *Gleanings* 21.
30. Bahá'u'lláh, *Gleanings* 19:3.
31. Bahá'u'lláh, *Gleanings* 21.
32. Bahá'u'lláh, *Gleanings* 110:1.
33. Bahá'u'lláh, *Gleanings* 109:2.

religious salvation, form the driving force of history, and the goal of religious history and of religion itself is twofold: first, the divine education of the human race[34] with the goal of an ever richer development of man's innate mental, spiritual and moral potentialities and his development into a spiritual being according to the plan of creation; secondly, the structuring of this world according to the divine will and the development of an ever-advancing culture on this planet: 'God's purpose in sending His Prophets unto men is twofold. The first is to liberate the children of men from the darkness of ignorance, and guide them to the light of true understanding. The second is to ensure the peace and tranquillity of mankind, and provide all the means by which they can be established.'[35] The divine messengers, the central figures of the religions, are the necessary mediators between God and man; they are the perfect mirrors of God's bounties and attributes. God is manifest in them. It is in this sense and not in the sense of ontological identity that Bahá'ís understand the words of Christ: 'I am the way, the truth, and the life; no man cometh unto the Father, but by me.'[36] 'He that hath seen me hath seen the Father';[37] 'I and my Father are one.'[38]

Whereas to this day the church has referred to these texts as proof of the exclusive claim of Christianity to absolute truth and a judgement on the non-Christian religions, Bahá'u'lláh's allegory,[39] according to which man can only recognize God in the mirror of the Manifestation, opens up a new hermeneutical dimension for these words of Jesus. These verses deny the possibility of direct knowledge of God and confirm the necessity of a mediator. That no one can come 'unto the father' but through Jesus is a statement that the Bahá'í can affirm with all his heart, for he who turns away from one of the Manifestations has, according to Bahá'u'lláh, rejected them all: 'Whoso maketh the slightest possible difference between their persons, their words, their messages, their acts and manners, hath indeed disbelieved in God, hath repudiated His signs, and betrayed the Cause of His Messengers.'[40]

---

34. In 1780 Gotthold Ephraim Lessing published a work entitled *The Education of the Human Race*, in which he developed the idea of progressive divine revelation, based on the teachings of Joachim von Fiore (cf. p.93 note 42). He was awaiting a new era, in which the Torah and the Gospels, as promised in the Revelation of St. John (14:6) would be superseded by an 'Everlasting Gospel', an era of reason and of the self-fulfilment of man, thus at the same time the fulfilment of the Christian Revelation (see Karl Löwith, *Meaning in History*, p.208). However, the work ends with the theory of the transmigration of souls, a view not subscribed to by the Bahá'ís. See p.195.
35. Bahá'u'lláh, *Gleanings* 34:5.
36. John 14:6.
37. John 14:9.
38. John 10:30.
39. cf. *Kitáb-i-Íqán*, p.99.
40. *Gleanings* 24.

The Unity of the Manifestations

The belief of the Bahá'ís is thus based on strict monotheism and, in addition, on two fundamental principles. The first is that there is no essential difference between these divine messengers. Even before, in the Qur'án, it was proclaimed: 'Say ye: "We believe in God, and that which hath been sent down to us, and that which hath been sent down to Abraham and Ismael and Isaac and Jacob and the tribes: and that which hath been given to Moses and to Jesus, and that which was given to the prophets from their Lord. No difference do we make between any of them."''[41] 'Our command was but one word.'[42] And Bahá'u'lláh confirms this: 'There is no distinction whatsoever among the Bearers of My Message.'[43] Abraham, Moses, Krishna, Buddha, Zoroaster, Christ and Muḥammad – all came with the same mission: 'to bring the light of love and truth into a darkened world',[44] to enlighten mankind, to quicken men's hearts and to educate them to piety, forbearance, honesty, mercifulness, brotherliness, love, justice and submission to the will of God. They are all 'tabernacles of holiness', the 'primal Mirrors which reflect the light of unfading glory'; they are but 'expressions of Him Who is the Invisible of the Invisibles'. All the prophets of God are 'without exception, the bearers of His names, and the embodiments of His attributes. They only differ in the intensity of their revelation, and the comparative potency of their light.'[45] We find a similar statement in the Qur'án: 'Some of the apostles we have endowed more highly than others.'[46]

The second principle is the claim, which is certainly a provocative one for modern man, that today, just as all religions have become questionable, God has fulfilled His promise and has once again spoken to mankind through Bahá'u'lláh.

The Manifestation as Skandalon

To modern man the very claim seems a shocking, unreasonable assertion, sheer presumption. Like the Gospels in former times it is a 'stumbling block' for those who still believe and 'foolishness'[47] for those who no longer believe. Today opinions on this claim diverge just as widely as they did upon the appearance of the preceding divine messengers. In their teachings, all the founders of the great religions of the world departed from tradition. They all consummated the inevitable break with the obso-

41. 2:130.
42. 54:50.
43. Bahá'u'lláh, *Gleanings* 34:3.
44. 'Abdu'l-Bahá, *Paris Talks*, ch. 52, p.171.
45. Bahá'u'lláh, *Kitáb-i-Íqán*, pp.103, 104.
46. 2:254.
47. Cf. I Cor. 1:23.

lete, worn-out forms and institutions in order to protect the remaining substance of the religion and to adapt it creatively to the needs and requirements of the particular age. But this break with outmoded tradition always took place against the will of men. None of the messengers of the Almighty was joyfully welcomed. Many examples throughout religious history bear witness that whenever 'the true Light, which lighteth every man'[48] shone in the darkness, the people loved darkness more than light.[49] Whenever the messenger came into the world, the world did not recognize him; whenever he came to claim his own, his own people did not receive him.[50] None of the divine messengers appeared without encountering rejection, derision, conflict and turmoil, violence and indignation from the people.[51] The Qur'án is full of complaints about the hardened hearts of men: 'O! the misery that rests upon my servants! No apostle cometh to them but they laugh him to scorn.'[52] 'Each nation schemed against their apostle to lay violent hold on him, and disputed with vain words to refute the truth.'[53] 'So oft then as an apostle cometh to you with that which your souls desire not, swell ye with pride, and treat some as impostors, and slay others?'[54] 'Hearts have they with which they understand not, and eyes have they with which they see not, and ears have they with which they hearken not. They are like the brutes: Yea, they go more astray.'[55]

Both the Báb and Bahá'u'lláh had to drink deeply of the cup of persecution and sorrow because they brought truth to men, and men, as in former ages, 'thrust their fingers into their ears':[56] 'Though encompassed with a myriad griefs and afflictions, We have, with mighty confidence, summoned the peoples of the earth to the Day Spring of Glory[57] . . . Tribulation is a horizon unto My Revelation[58] . . . We have made abasement the garment of glory, and affliction the adornment of thy temple, O Pride of the Worlds[59] . . . Verily God hath made adversity as a morning dew upon His green pasture, and a wick for His lamp which lighteth earth and heaven.'[60] In the Kitáb-i-Íqán Bahá'u'lláh revealed the following about the rejection which the new revelation always met at

48. John 1:9.
49. John 3:19.
50. John 1:10–12.
51. Martin Luther judged the situation correctly when he said: 'If Christ were to walk about once more in human form and preach, people would crucify Him once again' (Table Talks, IV, 4387).
52. 36:29.
53. 40:5.
54. 2:81.
55. 7:178.
56. Qur'án 2:18.
57. Bahá'u'lláh, *Gleanings* 163:6.
58. Bahá'u'lláh, *Gleanings* 17:6.
59. Bahá'u'lláh, *Qad-Ihtaraqa'l-Mukhlisún. The Fire Tablet.*
60. Bahá'u'lláh, *Epistle to the Son of the Wolf*, p.17.

the hands of men: 'And whensoever the portals of grace did open, and the clouds of divine bounty did rain upon mankind, and the light of the Unseen did shine above the horizon of celestial might, they all denied Him, and turned away from His face – the face of God Himself.'[61] In the same book Bahá'u'lláh states that the religious leaders are responsible for this attitude because they held the people back from the path of God: 'Leaders of religion, in every age, have hindered their people from attaining the shores of eternal salvation, inasmuch as they held the reins of authority in their mighty grasp. Some for the lust of leadership, others through want of knowledge and understanding, have been the cause of the deprivation of the people. By their sanction and authority, every Prophet of God hath drunk from the chalice of sacrifice, and winged His flight unto the heights of glory.'[62]

But Bahá'u'lláh's claim is a challenge, both for those members of religions who still believe, and for the modern agnostic. The obvious objection is: anyone could make such a claim! How is it possible amidst the irritating clamour of rival claims to discover where truth lies and where falsehood?

61. p.4.
62. *Kitáb-i-Íqán*, p.15.

6. What is Truth?

Even as the sun, bright hath He shined, but Alas, He hath come
to the town of the blind!

Jalálu'd-Dín Rúmí (1207 – 1273, Mathnaví)

Pontius Pilate's question[1] is posed whenever a claim to truth is made, and in every age man has had to decide whether he would accept the message of God, reject it, or meet it with indifference. All the religions agree that this decision which man is required to make is of decisive relevance for his spiritual life. Belief is necessary for salvation.[2] The prophet Muḥammad compares the obdurate unbelievers with the dead in their graves: 'And the blind and the seeing are not alike; neither darkness and light; nor the shade and the hot wind; nor are the living and the dead the same thing! God indeed shall make whom He will to hearken, but thou shalt not make those who are in their graves to hearken.'[3]

The Profusion of Salvation Offers

Now the recognition of truth has always been most difficult in the early period of the revealed religions. It is precisely at such times of upheaval

1. John 18:38.
2. Mark 16:16; John 3:17–18; Luke 12:8; Matt. 10:32; Qur'án 57:7; 48:28.
3. Qur'án 35:20–21. The same metaphor is used in the Qur'án 6:122, in Matt. 8:22: 'Follow me; and let the dead bury their dead'; see also John 8:52; Bahá'u'lláh revealed: 'Well is it with the man of discernment who hath recognized and perceived the Truth, and the one possessed of a hearing ear who hath hearkened unto His sweet Voice, and the hand that hath received His Book with such resolve as is born of God . . . And woe betide him who hath rejected the grace of God and His bounty, and hath denied His tender mercy and authority; such a man is indeed reckoned with those who have throughout eternity repudiated the testimony of God and His proof.' (Tajallíyát, Tablets, pp.47–8.) 'Be thou assured in thyself that verily, he who turns away from this Beauty hath also turned away from the Messengers of the Past and showeth pride towards God from all eternity to all eternity.' (Tablet of Ahmad.) 'Attainment unto the Divine Presence can be realized solely by attaining His presence.' (Tajallíyát, 1st Tajallí, Tablets, p.50.) See also Bahá'u'lláh, Kitáb-i-Íqán, pp.119ff; cf. the discussion on pp.195ff.

that a profusion of offers of salvation appear, confusing the observer and making it difficult for him to judge. Facts that are irrelevant to the search for truth can also cloud one's judgement: a community that is still relatively small in numbers is usually not taken seriously.[4] And yet the truth of an idea is independent of the size of its following. Popularity is not a criterion of truth.[5] Even if I were the only person in the world to believe in the truth it would still be the truth. And yet the opinion that anything 'small' is of little value is one which prevails in the realm of religion more than anywhere else. But a mere glimpse at religious history would show that when the great revealed religions came into existence there was only a 'little flock',[6] a point of crystallization, which, like the seed that becomes a tree, eventually grew to become a great people of God. But this is overlooked if one expects the truth to become visible in a concrete way and to manifest itself in convincing greatness. In addition there is the possible prospect of being a member of a minority group, of being regarded as an outsider and finally of suffering inconveniences or even persecution. For many that is reason enough to not even take the first step of seriously examining the Cause of God. Thus the dynamic force of this community and the transforming power of the new Word of God remains concealed from them. However, once the 'critical mass' has been reached, a trend has become recognizable and the obscurity of the Cause of God has been overcome; then the rate of its growth accelerates at an unanticipated speed.

The history of Christianity demonstrates this very clearly. Even before the birth of Christ and in the first centuries afterwards there was a large number of religious movements and cults, some with a high standard of ethics and a considerable intellectual standard with a large and widely spread following; the rivalry of claims to truth was great. Shoghi Effendi writes of the 'great variety of popular cults, of fashionable and evasive philosophies which flourished in the opening centuries of the Christian Era, and which attempted to absorb and pervert the state religion of the Roman people': 'The pagan worshippers who constituted, at that time, the

---

4. Small religious communities are often carelessly described as 'sects' without regard for their own understanding of themselves and without taking into account their socio-religious structure. Over the last twenty years noted theologians and scholars such as Gerhard Rosenkranz, Helmuth von Glasenapp, Alessandro Bausani and others have shown that the Bahá'í Faith is not an Islámic sect. See also my book *The Light Shineth in Darkness*, pp.55ff, and the literature quoted there. In the *Enciclopedia Cattolica* published by the Vatican, A. Bausani calls the Bahá'í Faith a 'new religion'. F. Vahman ("Bahá'ísmus" in *TRE, Theologische Realenzyklopädie*, Vol. V 1/2, pp.131ff) describes the Bahá'í Faith as the 'most recent revealed religion' and classes it among the World Religions. On the whole subject: Udo Schaefer, *Sekte oder Offenbarungsreligion? Zur religionswissenschaftlichen Einordnung des Bahá'í-Glaubens*, Hofheim-Langenhain 1982.

5. The Mithras cult, Marcionism and Manichaeism had at times more followers than the Christian Church.

6. Luke 12:32.

bulk of the population of the Western Roman Empire, found themselves surrounded, and in certain instances menaced, by the prevailing sect of the Neo-Platonists, by the followers of nature religion, by Gnostic philosophers, by Philonism, Mithraism, the adherents of the Alexandrian cult, and a multitude of kindred sects and beliefs, in much the same way as the defenders of the Christian Faith, the preponderating religion of the Western world, are realizing, in the first century of the Bahá'í Era, how their influence is being undermined by a flood of conflicting beliefs, practices and tendencies which their own bankruptcy had helped to create.'[7] The question as to why Jesus should be 'the way, the truth and the life'[8] and not one of the rival teachers of salvation was just as provoking for the people of that time as is the question for the people of today concerning the truth of Bahá'u'lláh's claim. History has spoken its judgement. Only the Gospel had the world-conquering, transforming power to create new men and lay the basis of a splendid culture. The explanation for today's confusing variety of forms of religious expression, which shows clear parallels to the variety at the end of the antique age, lies now as then in the decline and powerlessness of the existing forms of religion. Shoghi Effendi remarks on this point: 'So marked a decline in the strength and cohesion of the elements constituting Christian society has led, in its turn, as we might well anticipate, to the emergence of an increasing number of obscure cults, of strange and new worships, of ineffective philosophies, whose sophisticated doctrines have intensified the confusion of a troubled age. In their tenets and pursuits they may be said to reflect and bear witness to the revolt, the discontent, and the confused aspirations of the disillusioned masses that have deserted the cause of the Christian churches and seceded from their membership.'[9]

The sociologist Daniel Bell comes to the same verdict: 'Where religions fail, cults appear. This situation is the reverse of early Christian history, when the new coherent religion competed with the multiple cults and drove them out because it had the superior strength of a theology and an organization. But when theology erodes and organization crumbles, when the institutional framework of religion begins to break up, the search for a direct experience which people can feel to be religious facilitates the rise of cults.'[10]

7. 'The Unfoldment of World Civilization', in *The World Order of Bahá'u'lláh*, pp.184-5.
8. John 14:6.
9. 'The Unfoldment of World Civilization', in *The World Order of Bahá'u'lláh*, p.184.
10. *The Cultural Contradictions of Capitalism*, p.168. Of course one could ask if the Bahá'í Faith is not one of these 'cults'. Its religious-sociological structures and the recognition accorded it even by its Christian critics (Rosenkranz, Hutten) provide a clearly negative answer. None of the features named by Bell as typical of 'cults' can be found in the Bahá'í Faith: 'A cult differs from a formal religion in

The future will show which claim to truth has God's world-conquering power behind it. The Bahá'ís are confident that during the growth of their religion the rate at which the new teachings will be recognized and accepted will be governed by the 'critical mass' principle. Bahá'u'lláh promises: 'When the victory arriveth, every man shall profess himself as believer and shall hasten to the shelter of God's Faith. Happy are they who in the days of world-encompassing trials have stood fast in the Cause and refused to swerve from its truth.'[11]

The New: 'Small' and 'Different'

There is another factor to be considered. In comparison with other religions the Bahá'í Faith is very young. It is only one hundred and thirty-nine years old.[12] This fact may be overlooked by those who only read the introductory brochures, which are generally simple, but of course fragmentary, descriptions. The reader who misses intellectual brilliance[13] and the aura of the historical and time-honoured, is then inclined to doubt the importance of this phenomenon *sub specie aeternitatis*.

Today the Bahá'ís tend not to put the emphasis on theological reflection at all, but on the proclamation of the message of Bahá'u'lláh, the spreading of the faith and the concrete realization of the personal and social structure envisaged. Thus it is also necessary to make the holy texts available to everybody.[14] Intellectual confrontation with the revealed word, the rational, historically philological, scientifically systematic, apologetic presentation of the content of the revelation has always been the

---

many significant ways. It is in the nature of a cult to claim some esoteric knowledge which had been submerged . . . for a long time but has now suddenly been illuminated . . . There are communal rites which often permit or spur an individual to act out impulses that had hitherto been repressed. In the cult, one feels as though one were exploring novel or hitherto tabooed modes of conduct. What defines a cult, therefore, is its implicit emphasis on magic rather than theology, on the personal tie to a guru or to the group, rather than to an institution or a creed. Its hunger is a hunger for ritual, and myth.' (op. cit.) A prominent characteristic of pseudo-religious cults is that the new adepts of these obscure communities break off all their former connections. All ties to the home, the family, profession and friends must be given up and replaced by commitment to the living leader of the particular community – the most disastrous requirement apart from practices that come near to brain-washing. Events in Guyana in 1980 have shown how people in their longing for faith can be misused by unscrupulous money-makers. (See p.87 n.5 for more literature.)

11. *Gleanings* 150.

12. The Bahá'ís have their own calendar known as the 'Badí calendar'. The new calendar begins with the spring equinox of A.D. 1844 (= A.H. 1260). The year is divided into 19 months, each of which has 19 days with four or five intercalary days at the end of the 18th month (the recurring numbers, 9 and 19, have a mystical significance).

13. The message of Bahá'u'lláh is addressed to all mankind, not just to the well-educated.

14. The difficult task of translating the extensive original writings from Arabic or Persian into English or the existent English translations into the different languages of the earth is a truly Herculean task, consuming much time and effort.

work of later generations.[15]

In addition, what often irritates the reserved, sceptical observer of a phenomenon with such an exceptional claim is the language of the holy writings. Bahá'u'lláh's language is different in style and expression from all the other writings of revelation.[16] Written in the literary language of late Islámic culture,[17] the revelatory writings are indeed 'unusual for our Western literary tradition'.[18] Rich in metaphor and profound symbolism, often mystical with occasional references to earlier revelatory writings, in particular to Qur'ánic verses and Islámic traditions (ḥadíth), containing concepts, ideas and references to institutions that mean little or nothing to the uninitiated Westerner, the language of Bahá'u'lláh at first seems strange, queer, flowery, typically oriental, and unsuitable for the Westerner. This judgement is very subjective, however. We forget that the language of our times, which we take as our yardstick, is characterized by the scientific, technical and economic development of the last hundred years; it is sober, rational, functional, and poor in emotional values, far removed from the language of Adalbert Stifter and Johann Wolfgang v. Goethe, of Charles Dickens and Alfred Tennyson.

Not long ago a translation of the Bible – admittedly a controversial one – into everyday colloquial German was produced to comply with the changed language of today.[19] Actually our language today has become impoverished: 'Modern vocabulary is purely rational, with no reference other than its self-contained mathematical formulae . . . The poverty of emotive language in our time reflects the impoverishment of a life without litany or ritual.'[20] Therefore we should not take our modern ideas and feelings about language as the measure of all things. We should also remember that all religions have come from the East – *ex oriente lux*! – and the texts of the Holy Writings, the Bible, and the many Hebrew names seemed just as strange to the Germanic, Celtic and Slavic

15. In Christianity this began in the second and third centuries (Tertullian, Clemens of Alexandria, Origen), reaching its first high point with St. Augustine in the fifth century and achieving its highest phase of scholastic perfection with the great systematician of the Middle Ages, St. Thomas Aquinas (1225–74). In Islám systematic theology began with the Mu'tazila in the second and third centuries A.H. Ash'arí (d. A.D. 935) was the actual founder of Islámic dogmatics (Kalám) which in the sixth century A.H. culminated in the works of the greatest Islámic theologian, Al-Ghazálí (d. A.D. 1111).

16. Cf. my discussion of the language of the Qur'án in *The Light Shineth in Darkness*, pp.139ff.

17. Just as the Christian writings assumed the form of late Judaism.

18. Alessandro Bausani, *Originalliteratur der Bahá'í Religion* (Original Literature of the Bahá'í Religion), p.5. Regarding the style of Bahá'u'lláh's language, see also Adib Taherzadeh, *The Revelation of Bahá'u'lláh*, Vol.I, pp.21–3, 42ff.

19. In order to bridge the gap between religion and daily life, Swiss, Austrian and German Bible publishers have been preparing St. Luke's Gospel in the form of a comic strip, in the style of Tarzan, Batman, Asterix, etc. This series on Jesus of Nazareth – in which Jesus is referred to as 'Jeschi' – appeared on the German book market at Christmas 1980.

20. Daniel Bell, *The Cultural Contradictions of Capitalism*, pp.86, 98.

peoples who accepted Christianity as do the texts of Bahá'u'lláh to modern Western man. Here, as with all new ideas, a certain degree of unprejudiced acceptance is called for. He who has become familiar with the new Word of God discovers in it a wealth, an abundance and a power that he would not miss for anything in the world.

The Principle of Distinction

It would be foolish to maintain that the recognition of the revelation is an easy matter. The question can indeed be asked why God has arranged things in such a way that, as Goethe realized, truth is not 'near our hands' and 'gentle, dear, and good'.[21] The recognition of truth is, on the contrary, associated with a series of requirements which demand quite a bit from man. Nietzsche blasphemously complained that this God did not speak clearly, making Zarathustra say that God was like a priest: 'He was equivocal. He was also indistinct. How he raged at us, this wrath-snorter, because we understood him badly! But why did he not speak more clearly?'[22] And elsewhere: 'The worst thing is: he seems incapable of making himself clearly understood: is he himself vague about what he means?'[23]

The answer is that God has given every human being the ability 'to know his Creator and to attain His Presence[24] . . . Had he not been endowed with such a capacity, how could he be called to account for his failure?'[25] If it were the will of God, then the whole of mankind would immediately recognize the truth of His revelation: 'Had thy Lord pleased he would have made mankind of one religion.'[26] Bahá'u'lláh states why it is not so: 'His purpose, however, is to enable the pure in spirit and the detached in heart to ascend, by virtue of their own innate powers, unto the shores of the Most Great Ocean, that thereby they who seek the Beauty of the All-Glorious may be distinguished and separated from the wayward and perverse.'[27] This 'principle of separation and distinction' is also the reason why the prophets of God 'when they appeared amongst men' have

---

21. The quotation in full: 'Why dwells Truth in far-off lands,/Or hides in deep abysses mewed?/None at the right time understands!/If only then men understood,/Broad Truth were also near our hands,/And Truth were gentle, dear, and good./(*West-Eastern Divan, VI. Book of Maxims*, XXVIII.)

22. *Thus Spake Zarathustra*, Book IV, 'Out of Service', p.291.

23. *Beyond Good and Evil*, No.53.

24. Bahá'u'lláh, *Gleanings* 29:1.

25. Bahá'u'lláh, *Gleanings* 75:1. It has already been explained that the recognition of God is identical with the recognition of the Manifestation. (cf. pp.104ff. and the quotations cited there; cf. also Bahá'u'lláh, *Gleanings* 155:1.)

26. Qur'án 11:120; cf. also Bahá'u'lláh, *Gleanings* 29:2. The Báb revealed in the Qayyúmu'l-Asmá': 'Should it be Our wish, it is in Our power to compel, through the agency of but one letter of Our Revelation, the world and all that is therein to recognize, in less than the twinkling of an eye, the truth of Our Cause.' (Chapter 87, *Selections*, p.68.)

27. *Gleanings* 29:2.

always 'been destitute of all earthly dominion and shorn of the means of worldly ascendancy.'[28] Bahá'u'lláh explains this principle, which was effective in all the religious dispensations of the past, with great clarity: 'Were the Eternal Essence to manifest all that is latent within Him, were He to shine in the plenitude of His glory, none would be found to question His power or repudiate His truth. Nay, all created things would be so dazzled and thunderstruck by the evidences of His light as to be reduced to utter nothingness. How, then, can the godly be differentiated under such circumstances from the froward?'[29]

In the *Kitáb-i-Íqán* Bahá'u'lláh explains that because of this principle of distinction the divine Manifestations, 'the Doves of Eternity speak a two-fold language. One language, the outward language, is devoid of allusions, is unconcealed and unveiled; that it may be a guiding lamp and a beaconing light whereby wayfarers may attain the heights of holiness, and seekers may advance into the realm of eternal reunion. Such are the unveiled traditions and the evident verses already mentioned. The other language is veiled and concealed, so that whatever lieth hidden in the heart of the malevolent may be made manifest and their innermost being be disclosed. Thus hath Ṣádiq, son of Muḥammad,[30] spoken: "God verily will test them and sift them." This is the divine standard, this is the Touchstone of God, wherewith He proveth His servants.'[31] The veil which separates man from the recognition of truth is nothing but his own self. Thus Bahá'u'lláh advises: 'Tear asunder, in My Name, the veils that have grievously blinded your vision, and, through the power born of your belief in the unity of God, scatter the idols of vain imitation . . . Suffer not yourselves to be wrapt in the dense veils of your selfish desires, inasmuch as I have perfected in every one of you My creation, so that the excellence of My handiwork may be fully revealed unto men.'[32] The faith of a man can be determined by no one but himself: 'If, in the Day when all the peoples of the earth will be gathered together, any man should, whilst standing in the presence of God, be asked: "Wherefore hast thou disbelieved in My Beauty and turned away from My Self", and if such a man should reply and say: "Inasmuch as all men have erred, and none hath been found willing to turn his face to the Truth, I, too, following their example, have grievously failed to recognize the Beauty of the Eternal", such a plea will, assuredly, be rejected. For the faith of no man can be conditioned by any

---

28. *Gleanings* 29:3.
29. *Gleanings* 29:3.
30. It is not the Prophet Muḥammad, whose four sons all died in early infancy, that is meant here, but Ja'far as-Ṣádiq, the sixth Imám of the Shí'ah, the son of the fifth Imám Muḥammad al-Báqir (A.H. 57–114). Cf. H. M. Balyuzi, *Muḥammad and the Course of Islám*, p.211.
31. pp.254–5. See also pp.53 and 82.
32. *Gleanings* 75:1.

one except himself.'[33] The following verses apply to those who fulfil the prerequisites for the recognition of truth: 'The signs of God shine as manifest and resplendent as the sun amidst the works of His creatures[34] . . . The portals of grace are wide open before the face of all men.'[35]

Prerequisites

What now are these prerequisites? It has always been the case that before one finds truth, one must first seek it. The search for truth can only be carried out by oneself; nothing in the world of the spirit can be achieved without effort. The divine kingdom is no *Schlaraffenland*;[36] it must be earned. In the Qur'án is written: 'And whoso maketh efforts for us, in our ways will we guide them',[37] and in the Gospels is said: 'Because strait is the gate, and narrow is the way, which leadeth unto life, and few there be that find it.'[38] In his mystical work *The Seven Valleys* Bahá'u'lláh describes the path of the soul on its way towards the recognition of God and quotes an Arabic proverb: 'Whoso seeketh out a thing with zeal shall find it', and continues: 'Labour is needed, if we are to seek Him; ardour is needed, if we are to drink of the honey of reunion with Him.'[39]

Patience is also necessary when one is striving to recognize truth: 'The first is the valley of search. The steed of this Valley is patience; without patience the wayfarer on this journey will reach nowhere and attain no goal.'[40]

And finally the *conditio sine qua non* when men search for truth: intellectual humility, an open mind, and the readiness 'to incline their ears unto the divine Melody'[41] and then to accept the truth even if it is quite different from what one has previously imagined and believed.[42]

33. Bahá'u'lláh, *Gleanings* 75:1.
34. Bahá'u'lláh, *Gleanings* 75:3.
35. Bahá'u'lláh, *Gleanings* 126:3.
36. *Schlaraffenland*: Wonderland. A fairy-tale land of milk and honey where roast chickens fly into the mouths of the indolent and hot dogs grow on fences. Idleness is the highest virtue and diligence the worst vice. The laziest in the land is king. The stories of *Schlaraffenland* go back to myths of a lost paradise.
37. 29:69.
38. Matt. 7:14.
39. 'The Valley of Search', p.7.
40. Bahá'u'lláh, *The Seven Valleys*, p.5.
41. Bahá'u'lláh, *Kitáb-i-Íqán*, p.164.
42. St. Augustine also laid the Bible aside in disappointment when he first read it before he then joined Manichaeism. The reasons which he gave in his *Confessions* (III, 5) are revealing: 'I resolved thereupon to bend my studies towards the Holy Scriptures, that I might see what they were. But behold, I espy something in them not revealed to the proud, not discovered unto children, humble in style, sublime in operation, and wholly veiled over in mysteries; and I was not so fitted at that time, as to pierce into the sense, or stoop my neck to its coming. For when I attentively read these Scriptures, I

Two false attitudes, which are diametrically opposed to each other, must be avoided like Scylla and Charybdis: the one is the kind of scepticism that prevails in Europe, and the other is uncritical enthusiasm. In his profound mistrust the sceptic has already formed his verdict before occupying himself with the matter. His efforts are directed solely towards satisfying his intellectual curiosity and confirming his doubts. The enthusiast is quite different. He approaches the matter uncritically, and there is no objective reflection to follow his early enthusiasm. Faith acquired in this way lacks a solid foundation; it wants depth. Such faith is one-sided, being anchored only in the emotions but not in thought as well; thus it is easily shattered.

Purity of Heart

Whoever encounters the light of truth with a sceptical, prejudiced mind set in the religious traditions of the past and their conventional interpretation, whoever is guided by his self-made concept of the world, whoever is crammed with ideas of his own which he has come to cherish so much that he is unwilling to correct them, for him truth will remain hidden behind the veil of his 'idle fancies and vain imaginations'.[43] Only he who purifies 'his heart . . . from the obscuring dust of all acquired knowledge' can become a seeker of truth:[44] 'He must so cleanse his heart that no remnant of either love or hate may linger therein, lest that love blindly incline him to error, or that hate repel him away from the truth.'[45] This is the purity of heart referred to by Jesus when He said: 'Blessed are the pure in heart: for they shall see God',[46] and 'every one that is of the truth heareth my voice'.[47] Bahá'u'lláh assures us that God 'hath endowed every soul with the capacity to recognize the signs of God'[48] and that no sincere seeker is ever turned back by God: 'No man that seeketh Us will We ever disappoint, neither shall he that hath set his face towards Us be denied access unto Our court.'[49] Bahá'u'lláh compares his revelation to 'an ocean in whose depths are concealed innumerable pearls of great price, of surpassing lustre' and he assures us: 'This most great, this fathomless and

---

thought not then so oft them as I now speak; but they seemed to me far unworthy to be compared to the stateliness of the Ciceronian eloquence. For my swelling pride soared above the temper of their style, nor was my sharp wit able to pierce into their sense. And yet such are thy Scriptures as grew up together with thy little ones. But I much disdained to be held a little one; and big swollen with pride, I took myself to be some great man.'

43. Bahá'u'lláh, *Gleanings* 100:9.
44. Bahá'u'lláh, *Kitáb-i-Íqán*, p.192.
45. ibid.
46. Matt. 5:8.
47. John 18:37.
48. *Gleanings* 52:2.
49. *Gleanings* 126:3.

surging Ocean is near, astonishingly near, unto you. Behold it is closer to you than your life-vein! Swift as the twinkling of an eye ye can, if ye but wish it, reach and partake of this imperishable favour, this God-given grace.'[50] To the true seeker who rends the obscuring veils of preconceived ideas, the light of divine truth will appear as manifest 'as the sun in its noon-tide glory'.[51] Of those who have attained the goal of their search it is said: 'No veil hideth or obscureth the verities on which their Faith is established.'[52]

This discernment excels by far a purely intellectual understanding. It is bestowed upon the seeker in his encounter with this message of truth and light.[53] Both are necessary for the seeker: rational reflection, and the experience itself. The words of Jesus apply to this point: 'My doctrine is not mine, but his that sent me. If any man will do his will, he shall know of the doctrine, whether it be of God, or whether I speak of myself.'[54] 'But he that doeth truth cometh to the light, that his deeds may be made manifest, that they are wrought in God.'[55]

The Touchstone

Jesus also stated the criterion for distinguishing between the true and the false prophets: 'Ye shall know them by their fruits.'[56] For Bahá'u'lláh too the touchstone of the truth of his claim is the vivifying and renewing effect that emanates from his words: 'The proof of the sun is the light thereof, which shineth and envelopeth all things. The evidence of the shower is the bounty thereof, which reneweth and investeth the world with the mantle of life. Yea, the blind can perceive naught from the sun except its heat, and the arid soil hath no share of the showers of mercy.'[57] With regard to the revival of religion and the transformation of the world Bahá'u'lláh says: 'The Word of God, alone, can claim the distinction of being endowed with the capacity required for so great and far-reaching a change.'[58]

Anyone who observes with an unbiased mind what is beginning to take

---

50. *Gleanings* 153:5.
51. *Gleanings* 52:1.
52. Bahá'u'lláh, *Gleanings* 126:2.
53. In an interview with the Catholic *Herder Korrespondenz* (Vol. 10, October 1977, pp.501ff), Leszek Kolakowski strongly emphasized that religious experience 'does not occur in the same way' as rational knowledge. Meaning, as it is found in religion, differs in its constitution from meaning as represented in the realm of science or in everyday life. Meaning in religion is constituted in a certain context, in rites, in prayer and in the religious experience.'
54. John 7:16–17.
55. John 3:21.
56. Matt. 7:16.
57. Bahá'u'lláh, *Kitáb-i-Íqán*, p.209.
58. *Gleanings* 99.

shape on a small scale – namely, the unity of mankind in the Bahá'í
community, in which men of all races, nations and religions come together
in concord, will perhaps be able to comprehend the integrating and
transforming power which stems from Bahá'u'lláh. It is the profound experience of the Bahá'ís that God, who is said to be dead, is alive and that
He has fulfilled the promise He made to the prophets by speaking to
mankind through Bahá'u'lláh.

7. The Unity of the Religions

Progressive Revelation

According to the Bahá'í teachings the history of mankind proceeds in great periods, in universal cycles, which for their part are divided again into ages: the aeons. The universal cycle of the last six thousand years began with Adam. According to the teachings of the Bahá'í Faith (and of Islám too) he was a prophet, a Manifestation, and before him there were other divine messengers of whom nothing has been handed down to us. Within the period that began with Adam the religions of mankind that we know today came into being. The Qur'án reports that God sent messengers to all peoples and that He made known His will and His truth through them. Noah, Abraham, Moses, Krishna, Buddha, Zoroaster, Christ and Muḥammad were the central figures of the Adamic cycle. Every single one of these Manifestations introduced a new aeon within which their teachings and commandments were the ultimate moral standard both for the individual and for the society of the particular culture. Thus history has a *telos*. It is not to be seen as a circle, an endless recurrence of becoming and passing away. But it is not linear either as Christianity often sees it, moving from a point at the beginning to a point at the end. The recurrence of the same events always takes place on a higher plane; the course of world history resembles a spiral.

From this vantage point another central article of Bahá'í faith is clearly seen: besides the unity of God, there is another unity, namely, the transcendental unity of all religions. All the religions of mankind are included in the history of religious salvation; all have their origin in God and are but different reflections of the same truth. Despite the variety in their appearance and expression, in language and terminology, in metaphors and laws, they have a common basis: the unchanging central core of God's religion.

The pivot of the teachings of Bahá'u'lláh is the belief in a progressive, cyclically recurring divine revelation.[1] God did not manifest Himself in a human temple once and for all in the past, but in cyclic intervals: 'God hath sent down His Messengers to succeed to Moses and Jesus, and He will continue to do so till "the end that hath no end"; so that His grace may, from the heaven of Divine bounty, be continually vouchsafed to mankind.'[2]

This idea is familiar to Hinduism and Buddhism and is connected with the concept of the *avatara* (coming down). Christianity already sees the beginning of the salvation of man in the prophets of the Old Covenant. Islám has formulated the concept of progressive revelation most clearly. The chain of the successive divine messengers is, as it were, the *basso ostinato* of the Qur'án.[3] Thus previous development has always been confirmed, but in all the religions people claim that their own religion is final, its manifestation unique and its message unsurpassable. For the Christians the Jewish prophets attain their final perfection in Jesus Christ; for the Muslims Muḥammad represents the end of all revelation and the Qur'án is God's final message to mankind.[4]

Bahá'u'lláh has firmly rejected the claim 'that all Revelation is ended, that the portals of Divine mercy are closed, that from the day-springs of eternal holiness no sun shall rise again . . . and that out of the Tabernacle of ancient glory the Messengers of God have ceased to be made manifest',[5] and has promised that the 'portals of mercy' will be opened whenever it so pleases God. Thus Bahá'u'lláh does not represent the final stage in the history of the salvation of man. God will continue in the future to send His messengers to mankind 'to summon all mankind to truthfulness and sincerity, to piety and trustworthiness, to resignation and submissiveness to

---

1. This is quite different in quality to what Christian theologians understand by the term 'progressive revelation' (Richard Rothe, Ernst Troeltsch), namely: 'that the impulse of the Christian spirit in the history of the West links up again and again with the spirit of the modern age and produces progressively better views of the world and of life . . . that the revelation becomes progressive in the progress of the human spirit, or that the progress of the human spirit can be interpreted as the self-movement of absolute Spirit.' (Jürgen Moltmann, *Theology of Hope*, pp.225, 226.) According to the teachings of Bahá'u'lláh divine revelation is 'progressive' in the sense that new outpourings of the divine spirit occur in recurring cycles when God speaks to mankind through a Manifestation.

2. Súriy-i-Ṣabr, quoted by Shoghi Effendi, 'The Dispensation of Bahá'u'lláh', in *The World Order of Bahá'u'lláh*, p.116. The same truth has been revealed by the Báb in His Persian Bayán IV, 12 (*Selections* pp.105–106).

3. Abu'l A'lá Mawdúdí, *Towards Understanding Islam*, pp.37–41.

4. This conclusion is drawn from the Qur'án text 33:40, where Muhammad is given the title 'seal of the prophets'. Cf. Mawdúdí pp.57ff, and my treatment of the subject in *The Light Shineth in Darkness*, p.125, n.452. The Bahá'ís regard Muhammad as the last prophet of the prophetic age: 'When God sent forth His Prophet Muhammad, on that day the termination of the prophetic cycle was foreordained in the knowledge of God.' (Báb, *Selections*, p.161.) With Bahá'u'lláh, the 'Most Great Announcement' (Qur'án 78:2, *Gleanings* 141:5), a new universal cycle has begun: the cycle of fulfilment.

5. *Kitáb-i-Íqán*, p.137.

the Will of God, to forbearance and kindliness, to uprightness and wisdom' and 'to array every man with the mantle of a saintly character, and to adorn him with the ornament of holy and goodly deeds'.[6] The Báb also upheld this fundamental and eternal principle: 'The process of rise and setting of the Sun of Truth will thus indefinitely continue – a process that hath had no beginning and will have no end.'[7]

Thus religion is not static but dynamic. The progressive development of the human race is dependent on the progressive divine revelation. The birth of each revealed religion is actually as the 'tide of Fortune'.[8] What is the reason for this dynamic process? What are the arguments in favour of the recurrence in cycles and against the uniqueness and exclusiveness of the revelation?

First, there is the concept of impulse. For the Bahá'í, religion is more than just a system of teachings, commandments, prohibitions, rites and customs. In its essence it is a living, active, mutating force. With each revelation a new force is released into the world, a force which is able to transform and integrate. On each occasion it caused the appearance of a new kind of man, a new order and a new culture. Bahá'u'lláh says of the transforming power inherent in the Word of God: 'Every word that proceedeth out of the mouth of God is endowed with such potency as can instil new life into every human frame . . . Every single letter proceeding out of the mouth of God is indeed a mother letter, and every word uttered by Him Who is the Well Spring of Divine Revelation is a mother word, and His Tablet a Mother Tablet.'[9] 'The Word of God is the king of words and its pervasive influence is incalculable. . . The Word is the master key for the whole world, inasmuch as through its potency the doors of the hearts of men, which in reality are the doors of heaven, are unlocked.'[10]

Every revelation gives mankind a new impulse. But because this impulse is always used up in the course of history, because religion, like all living things, is also subject to time's process of deterioration, a new outpouring of the spirit and a renewal of the religion of God is necessary from age to age.

Another reason for the cyclic recurrence of the divine revelation is that man's receptivity and spiritual comprehension differ from age to age. The prophets of God encountered very different cultural and social conditions, which they then had to mould into shape. Mankind as a whole is in a constant state of development; conditions on earth are constantly changing. The divine revelation takes this into account: 'Know of a certainty that in

---

6. Bahá'u'lláh, *Gleanings* 137:4.
7. Persian Bayán IV, 12 (*Selections*, p.106.)
8. 'Sternstunden der Menschheit.' This concept is from Stefan Zweig (1881–1942), who gave this title to a volume of essays published in 1927.
9. Bahá'u'lláh, *Gleanings* 74.
10. Lawḥ-i-Maqṣúd, *Tablets*, p.173.

every Dispensation the light of Divine Revelation hath been vouchsafed unto men in direct proportion to their spiritual capacity. Consider the sun. How feeble its rays the moment it appeareth above the horizon. How gradually its warmth and potency increase as it approacheth its zenith, enabling meanwhile all created things to adapt themselves to the growing intensity of its light. How steadily it declineth until it reacheth its setting point. Were it, all of a sudden, to manifest the energies latent within it, it would, no doubt, cause injury to all created things . . . In like manner, if the Sun of Truth were suddenly to reveal, at the earliest stages of its manifestation, the full measure of the potencies which the providence of the Almighty hath bestowed upon it, the earth of human understanding would waste away and be consumed; for men's hearts would neither sustain the intensity of its revelation, nor be able to mirror forth the radiance of its light. Dismayed and overpowered, they would cease to exist[11] . . . As the body of man needeth a garment to clothe it, so the body of mankind must needs be adorned with the mantle of justice and wisdom. Its robe is the Revelation vouchsafed unto it by God. Whenever this robe hath fulfilled its purpose, the Almighty will assuredly renew it. For every age requireth a fresh measure of the light of God. Every Divine Revelation hath been sent down in a manner that befitted the circumstances of the age in which it hath appeared.'[12]

Divine Reformation

A further reason for the need of religion to be renewed is given by the centrifugal developments to which all religions throughout their long history have been subjected. Through error, misunderstandings, their own additions and their struggles for power, men have darkened the original light of faith, thereby bringing about the many encrustations and deformations which have consumed the force of God's religion. To a certain degree this is a natural process. All that lives, and this includes religion, has a springtime, a time of maturity, of harvest, and a winter-time; during the winter-time of religion, it becomes barren, a lifeless adherence to the letter, and suppresses man's spiritual life. Attempts by man to reform religion are doomed to fail in the long run. The fundamental renewal, radical in the true sense of the word, can only come from God. The history of religion shows that God has spoken to men precisely at times when they have reached the nadir of their degradation and cultural decadence. Moses came to Israel when it was languishing under the Pharaohs' yoke. Christ appeared at a time when the Jewish Faith had lost its power and had become rigid, and the culture of antiquity was in its death throes.

---

11. Bahá'u'lláh, *Gleanings* 38.
12. Bahá'u'lláh, *Gleanings* 34:7. The Báb revealed: 'Indeed no religion shall We ever inaugurate unless it be renewed in the days to come.' (*Selections*, p.159.)

Muḥammad came to a people who lived in barbaric ignorance at the lowest level of culture and into a world in which the former religions had strayed far away from their origins and nearly lost their identity. The Báb addressed himself to a people who had irretrievably lost their former grandeur and who found themselves in a state of hopeless decadence. Bahá'u'lláh came to a humanity which was approaching the most critical phase of its long history.

'Abdu'l-Bahá writes on the subject of the renewal of God's religion: 'God leaves not His children comfortless, but, when the darkness of winter overshadows them, then again He sends His Messengers, the Prophets, with a renewal of the blessed spring. The Sun of Truth appears again on the horizon of the world shining into the eyes of those who sleep, awaking them to behold the glory of a new dawn. Then again will the tree of humanity blossom and bring forth the fruit of righteousness for the healing of the nations.' [13]

This knowledge leads immediately to the realization that all religions are divine in their origin, and consequently there are no religions which contradict or exclude each other, but only one indivisible divine religion which is renewed periodically and according to the requirements of the age, in cycles of about a thousand years: 'Our command was but one word.' [14] It is therefore hardly surprising if many of Bahá'u'lláh's teachings are to be found in former religions either expressly or in an embryonic form. [15] As 'Abdu'l-Bahá says, the Bahá'í Faith is 'not a new path to immortality' but 'the ancient path cleared of the debris of strife and misunderstandings and is again made a clear path to the sincere seeker, that he may enter therein in assurance, and find that the word of God is one word, though the speakers were many'. [16] On account of this transcendent unity of all religions, [17] Bahá'u'lláh exhorted His people to associate with followers of

13. *Paris Talks*, ch. 7, p.32.

14. Qur'án 54:50. In the Qayyúmu'l-Asmá' the Báb appeals to the peoples of the West: 'Become as true brethren in the one and indivisible religion of God, free from distinction.' (Ch. 46, *Selections*, p.56.)

15. See also pp.226ff.

16. Quoted in *Principles of the Bahá'í Faith*. A pamphlet, New York, Bahá'í Publishing Committee, undated.

17. This concept of the unity of the religions is not so un-Christian as Karl Barth has so implacably stated (*Church Dogmatics*, I, 2, pp.325ff). St. Augustine wrote: 'What we now call the Christian religion already existed among the Ancients and has always been present since the beginning of the human race until Christ appeared in the flesh, from which time the true religion, which was already existent, began to be called the Christian religion.' (*Retractationes* I, 13.) The following prayer was written by Nicolaus Cusanus (1401–64), a cardinal and theologian of the Catholic church: 'Thou art He, O God, who is sought in the different religions in different ways and is named with different names, for Thou remainest as Thou art, incomprehensible to all and ineffable. Be Thou gracious and reveal Thy countenance . . . If Thou wouldst be so gracious, then the sword, envious hatred, and all evil will cease and all will realize that there is but one religion in the variety of the religious customs (*Una religio in rituum varietate*).' (*De pace seu concordia fidei*, 1453, quoted in Friedrich Heiler, *Einheit und Zusammenarbeit der Religionen*, p.16.)

all religions in a spirit of loving-kindness and to make religion the cause of harmony and peace, not of discord and strife, of hatred and division.[18]

The second conclusion is that we cannot perceive the essence of religion or its power of achievement if we examine the traditional great religions in their present form. They have achieved much, but have reached the end of their road; they were the foundation of great cultures and for thousands of years they were the guiding-star of millions of people in their everyday life and activities. But they have also accumulated large amounts of historical ballast. They have moved a long way from their origin and are burdened with their followers' misdeeds and cravings for power. They do not present an attractive picture today, least of all to young people, who no longer see in these religions the 'salt of the earth'[19] but rather the 'opium of the people'. And one is easily inclined to pass judgement on religion as a whole, and to see in it an anachronism of past times, long since overcome, like the belief in demons in former times or the witch-hunts in the Middle Ages. But a withered plant does not give us the faintest idea of its appearance when it was mature and blossoming. In reality, the religions are the 'light of the world'[20] and, according to Bahá'u'lláh's teachings, the foundation of human culture. They are as necessary for mankind as sunlight is for the plant. Without divine revelation there would be neither progress nor culture on earth: 'Were this revelation to be withdrawn, all would perish.'[21]

---

18. Cf. *Gleanings* 43:8; in *Epistle to the Son of the Wolf* He warns: 'Religious fanaticism and hatred are a world-devouring fire, whose violence none can quench. The Hand of Divine power can, alone, deliver mankind from this desolating affliction . . . Consort with all men, O people of Bahá, in a spirit of friendliness and fellowship.' (pp.14, 15.) Cf. also the Ishráqát, 9th Ishráq, *Tablets*, pp.129ff.

19. Matt. 5:13.

20. Matt. 5:14.

21. Bahá'u'lláh, *Gleanings* 93:14.

8. The New Society

The Horizontal Dimension

An important difference between the Bahá'í understanding of faith and the traditional Christian view, particularly in Protestant thought, is to be found in the value given to this world and this life, and in the relevance of religion for society. Christianity considered itself over the centuries as a signpost showing the way for the salvation of the individual. Only the hereafter had significance; this life on earth was considered unreal and unessential.[1] Martin Luther dismissed state and society from the realm of God's sovereignty with his teaching of the two kingdoms and his differentiation between law and gospel, between the kingdom of God and the secular kingdom. For him the whole of religion was reduced to one question: How can man acquire a merciful God?[2] Only the vertical dimension of religion was seen; the horizontal was forgotten. During the last few decades this kind of belief has been almost turned into its opposite – as described at the beginning – as a result of the influence of sociological and Marxist thought on Catholic and Protestant theology.[3]

The Bahá'í sees religion as a total power that orders, embraces and lays

---

1. Referring to statements made by the Fathers of the Church Lactantius, Ambrose and Augustine, who calls life in the flesh 'an uninterrupted illness' (Serm. ad. pop.) and to Pascal, Feuerbach the critic of religion writes: 'Nature, the world, has no value, no interest for Christians. The Christian thinks only of himself, and the salvation of his soul.' (*The Essence of Christianity*, p.282.) 'The practical end and object of Christians is solely heaven, i.e. the realized salvation of the soul.' (ibid. p.283.)

2. Feuerbach (pp.160–61) quotes a statement of Luther which shows the latter's lack of interest in this life: 'Wherefore a Christian man should rather be advised to bear sickness with patience, yea, even to desire that death should come, – the sooner the better. For, as St. Cyprian says, nothing is more for the advantage of a Christian, than soon to die. But we rather listen to the pagan Juvenal, when he says: "*Orandum est, ut sit mens sana in corpore sano.*"'

3. Cf. pp.16ff.

claim to all aspects of our existence. Religion is not limited to the individual and his relationship with God. It also has a social component, which is just as valid as the element of personal salvation: society too must be redeemed, liberated from its deformations and obsolete moribund structures. For, on his own, without reference to the transcendent realities, values and examples that form the essence of religion, man is unable to solve the great social contradictions and create a just order in which the individual can develop freely in accordance with his true interests and destiny. This means that the process of secularization of society and state comes to an end and an opposite process is put into motion, the aim of which is to bring the whole of mankind under the law of God and to establish a universal order in which, as promised by the prophets, God Himself rules His people.

Thus the secular society created by the Enlightenment, from which all religious faith has been banished, must be left behind. Likewise its counterpart, the 'autonomous individual', devoid of belief, wholly self-determining and responsible only to himself (apart from the institutions of the state) must be replaced by the 'new man'.[4] Replacing the secular society, in which religion is exclusively a private matter, necessarily excludes the restoration of clerical privilege or any degeneration into the conditions which characterized the Dark Ages. For there will exist no form of priesthood, and therewith no class distinction between priest and layman. In the new world order, the theocratic element will be subsumed into democratically structured institutions.[5]

Society's Need for Salvation

A society is not able to exist for a long period of time without certain ultimate values, without a framework with absolute limits to provide orientation. There must be fundamental agreement on the basic questions of man's life and the final goals according to which society is organized, if society is not to lose its cohesion and gradually dissolve into the components of its various hostile interest groups.

This applies even more to the highly differentiated mass society. W. Brezinka describes the living conditions and the uncertainty of orientation to which people within this society are exposed: 'The increase in population, industrialization, the growth of bureaucracy, the alienation from nature, the extreme specialization in the professions, the mobility of modern man, the trend towards the cities, the falling away from religion, the increase in knowledge, the incessant flood of stimuli, and many other factors have contributed to make the situation enormously complicated

4. See pp.206ff.
5. See ch. 13 on the theocratic idea.

and difficult to comprehend. Most people have only a limited field of action open to them, both in their private and their professional lives, and
what they experience there is not sufficient to help them acquire an
understanding of the social and cultural conditions on which they are
dependent.'[6] Helmut Schelsky also speaks of the constantly increasing
'complexity, entanglement and abstraction of social relationships in vast
modern societies with their inundation of information, their unlimited
freedom to criticize and the obtrusiveness of every kind of subjectivity'.[7]
Technical civilization with its highly specialized division of labour is suc-
cumbing more and more to 'material and social relationships that are
anonymous and remotely controlled. The individual is no longer able to
understand . . . this anonymous system of relationships in the world of
work; individual rationality is no longer equal to the complexity of the
modern world and is rejected by its own creation.'[8] Life in society is thus
far too complex for anyone to be able to gain 'insight into the conditions of
social existence'.[9] In view of this Schelsky, referring to Friedrich Tenbruck,
speaks of the 'limited rationality' of man and the 'arrogance of reason'
which lies at the basis of the planning of the *whole* society'.[10] Thus the
idea that man is able to perceive 'society in its totality', comprehend 'the
connections between . . . social conditions and the structure of man's consciousness', 'pierce through all the veils and ideologies' and understand
how 'the single component is imparted by the whole',[11] a notion which
lies at the basis of the belief that society can be rationally planned as a con-
trollable process,[12] is, as Brezinka aptly states, 'an unrealistic over-
estimation of the power of reason'.[13] The belief that man can understand
social processes in their entirety and that he has the ability to 'act
autonomously' and practise 'self-determination by reason' without any
kind of commitment to authority is 'an illusion' which amounts to the
presumptuous claim of 'wanting to be like God both in knowledge and in

6. *Erziehung und Kulturrevolution*, p.12.
7. *Die Arbeit tun die anderen*, p.116; cf. also p.110.
8. ibid. p.195.
9. Klaus Mollenhauer, *Erziehung und Emanzipation* (Education and Emancipation), quoted in
Brezinka, op. cit., p.114.
10. 'One of the hardest lumps for modern man's pride to swallow is the fact that the world which
he himself created imposes upon him the insight into his fundamentally "limited rationality".'
(Tenbruck, quoted by Helmut Schelsky, *Die Arbeit tun die anderen*, p.195.)
11. Franz Heinisch, *Politische Bildung – Integration oder Emanzipation?* (Political Education
– Integration or Emancipation?), quoted by W. Brezinka, p.114.
12. This goes back to Auguste Comte (1798–1857), the founder of sociology. He was convinced that
all processes, whether of the body or of the mind, were subject to inalterable laws. The sociology conceived by him and called 'social physics' was to calculate and rule the processes in society, just as physics
rules the processes of inanimate matter and makes them technically useful. This was to make it possible
to plan accurately the social life of the future in advance and to ensure the path to a progress never seen
before (*Discours sur l'esprit positif*, 1844).
13. *Erziehung und Kulturrevolution*, p.115.

the freedom to act'.[14] Karl Steinbuch has described in great detail man's inadequacy to absorb information.[15] He sees that the consciousness of man cannot keep up with the complexity of this world, that the more we know about our world, the more our inability to understand it comprehensively[16] becomes apparent, that we only 'know in part'[17] and stay that way, and that 'the disproportion between the complexity of our world and our inadequate consciousness becomes more and more flagrant'.[18] Thus the social planners run aground, 'not on the intrigues of hostile reactionaries, but on reality', because in their limited understanding of the world they have not realized 'that the world is more complicated than our consciousness is capable of comprehending'.[19] According to Steinbuch the most important insight of our time is that since reason is limited, one must also act according to experiences that cannot be traced back to cause and effect'.[20]

Political economists, sociologists and social thinkers are gradually though reluctantly realizing that the problems of society are more complex than they assumed, and that experience alone, without an orientating aid for human behaviour and existential questions, 'is no longer a sure guide to the complex, technical problems of a modern society':[21] 'The system of social relations is so complex and differentiated and experiences are so specialized, complicated, or incomprehensible, that it is difficult to find common symbols to relate one experience to another.'[22]

The orientating structure which gives meaning to society, which points out the goal and indicates the way, which supplies the basis of a common moral order that holds society together, stabilizes and integrates it, is religion: 'To say, then, that "God is dead" is, in effect, to say that the social bonds have snapped and that society is dead.'[23] Gradually the

---

14. W. Brezinka, op. cit., p.115. Cf. pp.155ff. on the role of religion as a comprehensive social system of orientation.
15. *Maßlos informiert*, pp.156ff.
16. ibid. pp.161, 204.
17. I Cor. 13:9.
18. *Maßlos informiert*, p.272.
19. ibid. p.190.
20. ibid.
21. Daniel Bell, *The Cultural Contradictions of Capitalism*, pp.251, 202.
22. Daniel Bell, op. cit., p.95. Hermann Krings, a philosopher from Munich, also realizes that reason is not inherent in progress, that rationality, which directs scientific and technological progress, is incapable of checking itself or giving itself its own rational orientation, and that a 'higher reason', which is not subject to the laws of progress, is necessary. The sociologist Niklas Luhmann sees that our advanced industrial society is disintegrating increasingly into partial systems which are acting more and more unilaterally and that there is no centre any more in which a common meaning, a common form of reason, could be preserved or developed. Thus Luhmann doubts whether in the future it will be possible to stabilize society as a whole (according to Malte Buschbeck, 'Was ersetzt uns den Fortschrittsglauben? Vom therapeutischen Nutzen der Apokalypse für die säkulare Gesellschaft', *Süddeutsche Zeitung* of 14–15.6.1980, reporting the Spring 1980 convention of the *Civitas* society).
23. Daniel Bell, op. cit., p.155.

realization is dawning on political scientists that the oft stated and deplored 'ungovernability' of the Western industrial states is connected with the destruction of 'transcendence as part of the political framework', that 'the state as the embodiment of a moral order subsists on religion', and that religion 'in its function as a producer of values cannot be dispensed with': 'Democracy is, as a noted American scientist (Samuel H. Beer) stated, a "remarkably empty doctrine". Democracy lives spiritually on the remnants of values that existed prior to our modern times; it no longer contains within itself any new ideas that are binding. A state that thinks it can leave religious.concepts behind it as one-sided ideologies becomes more and more devoid of meaning and susceptible to attack and decay.'[24]

According to the teachings of Bahá'u'lláh both the individual and the whole of humanity need enlightenment and guidance by the divine Manifestations. Without this divine guidance neither man as an individual nor human society is capable of existing. The Manifestation is, as it were, a physician, who in His perfect wisdom, makes the diagnosis and prescribes the remedy for mankind: 'The Prophets of God should be regarded as physicians whose task is to foster the well-being of the world and its peoples, that, through the spirit of oneness, they may heal the sickness of a divided humanity. To none is given the right to question their words or disparage their conduct, for they are the only ones who can claim to have understood the patient and to have correctly diagnosed its ailments. No man, however acute his perception, can ever hope to reach the heights which the wisdom and understanding of the Divine Physician have attained[25] . . . The All-Knowing Physician hath His finger on the pulse of mankind. He perceiveth the disease, and prescribeth, in His unerring wisdom, the remedy. Every age hath its own problem, and every soul its particular aspiration. The remedy the world needeth in its present-day afflictions can never be the same as that which a subsequent age may require.'[26] The fact that the body of mankind has been granted no relief, let alone healing, that 'its sickness waxed more severe'[27] is due to the fact that the true physician is prevented 'from administering the remedy, whilst unskilled practitioners are regarded with favour, and are accorded full freedom to act'[28] and that the patient – mankind – 'fell under the treatment of ignorant physicians, who gave full rein to their personal desires, and have erred grievously'.[29]

24. Reiner Schmidt, 'Der geforderte Staat', p.161.
25. Bahá'u'lláh, *Gleanings* 34:6.
26. ibid. 106:1.
27. ibid. 120:1.
28. ibid. 16:3.
29. ibid. 120:1.

Religion – the Foundation of Social Order

According to the Bahá'í teachings, religion is both the foundation of order and the power which rules and stabilizes society. Bahá'u'lláh has often stressed the outstanding and indispensable function of religion for society, law and order: 'Religion is, verily, the chief instrument for the establishment of order in the world, and of tranquillity amongst its peoples [30] . . . religion is a radiant light and an impregnable stronghold for the protection and welfare of the peoples of the world, for the fear of God impelleth man to hold fast to that which is good, and shun all evil. Should the lamp of religion be obscured, chaos and confusion will ensue, and the lights of fairness and justice, of tranquillity and peace cease to shine.' [31]

The insight that religion is the glue which holds society together is in no way new but it has been forgotten. Francis Bacon already knew that 'religion being the chief Band of human society, it is a happy thing, when it self, is well contained within the true Band of Unity' [32] and Jacob Burckhardt writes that 'religion is the chief bond in human society for it is the only satisfactory guardian of that moral condition which holds society together'. [33] But when the support and basis of our culture and our order, religion, is shaken, because the faith of contemporary man is dwindling, and when the tradition of living one's faith is broken off because the values imparted by the religion on which our cultures have grown up are no longer accepted as binding, are no longer 'believed in', but instead are critically questioned and denied, then we need not be surprised by the rapidly advancing moral decadence of our society, the disintegration of our cultures and the wave of violence, terrorism and lawlessness that is afflicting the nations.

The World Order of Bahá'u'lláh

Bahá'u'lláh has renewed the values of morality, [34] has filled them with new meaning and spirit, has supplied them with a new force of commitment and thereby laid the foundation for a new man and a new culture. When the barbarians destroyed the Roman Empire, an intact Christian understanding of the world was waiting for them. Thus out of the ruins of Rome a new culture arose. Whereas our old world is falling into pieces, the Bahá'ís are working on the construction of a new order and a new society that will be the pattern and example for the coming world order.

---

30. *Epistle to the Son of the Wolf*, p.28.
31. Ishráqát, 1st Ishráq, *Tablets*, p.125; cf. also Shoghi Effendi, *The World Order of Bahá'u'lláh*, pp.186–7.
32. *Essays*: 'Of Unity in Religion', p.6.
33. *Reflections on History*, p.93.
34. See pp.209ff.

Bahá'u'lláh has laid the keystone of this new order in which all peoples, united by their common belief in God and His revelation, will live together in peace and justice. He has come to establish the promised Kingdom of God on earth.[35] This kingdom is neither a supernatural supraterrestrial place nor a metaphor for the abode of the deceased, but it is a kingdom on this planet. It is none other than the realization of the unity of mankind and of world peace, the 'Most Great Peace', as Bahá'u'lláh called it, the creation of an all-embracing and just order, in which every human being can live in security and fulfil himself in conformity with God's law, a kingdom in which God Himself rules His people.

The Unity of Mankind

The basic problem with the human race is, so Bahá'u'lláh says, its disunity and discord, the hatred and the prejudices which separate men from one another. All the ills that afflict mankind today are only symptoms of this disease: 'Behold the disturbances which, for many a long year, have afflicted the earth, and the perturbation that hath seized its peoples. It hath either been ravaged by war, or tormented by sudden and unforeseen calamities. Though the world is encompassed with misery and distress, yet no man hath paused to reflect what the cause or source of that may be. Whenever the True Counsellor[36] uttered a word in admonishment, lo, they all denounced Him as a mover of mischief and rejected His claim. How bewildering, how confusing is such behaviour! No two men can be found who may be said to be outwardly and inwardly united. The evidences of discord and malice are apparent everywhere, though all were made for harmony and union.'[37]

The remedy which Bahá'u'lláh, the divine physician, has prescribed for mankind is its unity: 'That which the Lord hath ordained as the sovereign

---

35. Jesus's statement: 'For, behold, the kingdom of God is within you' (Luke 17:21) is not a contradiction of the expectation of a kingdom of God in this world. The statement is timeless since it describes a condition of the heart, and those who have not first founded the kingdom of God within themselves are not able to establish it as an order on earth. A redeemed order cannot be created and maintained by unredeemed people. But the statement of Jesus also pertains to a particular time in history, in the sense that the time for the coming of the Kingdom of God as promised by the prophets of the old covenant (Isa. 2:1-4; 9; 11; 62:1-2; Zech. 14:9-16) had not come with the Christian Revelation. Islám brought to redeemed man a piece of the redeemed society in the theocratic order it established. A theocratic world order has only become possible in our time now that the world has become smaller through technology and the peoples have moved closer to one another. From the point of view of religious history it is no coincidence that Bahá'u'lláh has appeared just as this development was beginning. The kingdom of God on earth as an immanent kingdom of peace appearing at the time of the end is also familiar to Christian thought, although the inclination to see this kingdom not as real and political but exclusively as a metaphysical reality prevails. See also pp.139ff.
36. the divine Manifestation.
37. Bahá'u'lláh, *Gleanings* 112.

remedy and mightiest instrument for the healing of all the world is the
union of all its peoples in one universal Cause, one common Faith[38] . . .
The well-being of mankind, its peace and security, are unattainable unless
and until its unity is firmly established.'[39] Men alone cannot achieve this
integration of all peoples and races nor overcome all the separating barriers
unaided. It can only be achieved with the help of God: 'This unity can
never be achieved so long as the counsels which the Pen of the Most High
hath revealed are suffered to pass unheeded.'[40] To this day, however, we
find 'most people take the opposite point of view: they look upon unity as
an ultimate, almost unattainable goal and concentrate first on remedying
all the other ills of mankind. If they did but know it, these other ills are
but various symptoms and side effects of the basic disease – disunity.'[41]

Religion – the Cause of Unity?

Nothing has such an integrating effect as the bond of a common faith. The
history of religion shows that all religions had this unifying power. It is the
essence of religion. Christianity united such highly civilized peoples as the
Greeks and Romans with the barbarian peoples of the North, Germanic
tribes, Slavs and Celts – not politically, for the time was not ripe for such
a unity or for the abolition of war[42] – but by directing their thinking
towards central values and common religious teachings and thus created
the Christian culture of the West. Islám is probably the most outstanding
example of the unifying power which emanates from God's religion. Even
during his lifetime the prophet Muḥammad united the warring tribes of
Arabia, who were constantly feuding with one another, and subjected
them to his discipline. Within two centuries Islám created an empire that
extended from the Pyrenees to the Ganges, in which God's law was the absolute guideline, and in which the peoples, though different ethnically,
racially and in their religious traditions, were united by the bond of the
new Faith. Thus God's religion laid the foundations of a culture that lasted
for centuries. Today it is time to establish the *Civitas maxima*. Bahá'u'lláh
has come to lead all mankind to unity and to found a world community
that embraces all peoples: 'Today, this servant has assuredly come to vivify
the world and to bring into unity all who are on the face of the earth. That
which God willeth shall come to pass and thou shalt see the earth even as

38. ibid. 120:3.
39. ibid. 131:2.
40. ibid. 131:2. Today the unity of mankind is being treated more and more in studies by the
Ecumenical Council of Churches. See Geiko Müller-Fahrenholz (ed), *Einheit in der Welt von heute*
(Unity in the World of Today) with numerous contributions, Frankfurt 1978.
41. The Universal House of Justice, in *Wellspring of Guidance*, p.131.
42. Cf. Matt. 10:34.

the 'Abhá Paradise.'[43]

An objection which seems obvious must be discussed here, namely the fact that religious history can also be quoted to prove the exact opposite, i.e. that religions lead to the separation of men, the separation into 'believers' and 'unbelievers'. This disintegrating effect of religion results from the uncompromising and hostile claims to finality and exclusiveness with which these religions are burdened.[44] Traditional Christianity has been the most implacable on this point,[45] even though the early harshness has been overcome. Today it admits that the non-Christian religions contain certain partial truths, but nevertheless still maintains that the fullness of truth is to be found only in Jesus Christ.

The disintegration which the religions and confessions have caused arises from historical developments that took a wrong turn; it is contrary to the true nature of religion. This shows again that a particular substance can be a remedy, but if used wrongly, that same substance can also be a poison. Bahá'u'lláh warns: 'The purpose of religion as revealed from the heaven of God's holy Will is to establish unity and concord amongst the peoples of the world; make it not the cause of dissension and strife',[46] and 'Abdu'l-Bahá said: 'Religion should unite all hearts and cause wars and disputes to vanish from the face of the earth, give birth to spirituality, and bring life and light to each heart. If religion becomes a cause of dislike, hatred and division, it were better to be without it, and to withdraw from such a religion would be a truly religious act. For it is clear that the purpose of a remedy is to cure; but if the remedy should only aggravate the complaint it had better be left alone . . . All the holy prophets were as doctors to the soul; they gave prescriptions for the healing of mankind; thus any remedy that causes disease does not come from the great and supreme Physician.'[47]

One can scarcely quote history to refute the objection that the Bahá'í Faith is not immune either to such developments, since the Bahá'í Faith is still in an early period of its development. Nevertheless, despite many attempts to split it, it has still kept its unity. In marked contrast to earlier revealed religions, the Bahá'í Faith is supported by an abundant collection of authenticated original writings by the Manifestation, by the copious documentation from the hands of the divinely chosen, authoritative interpreters of the revealed word – 'Abdu'l-Bahá and Shoghi Effendi – and by an administrative order, which Bahá'u'lláh established for His community. The Bahá'ís believe that these measures form a certain

43. Bahá'u'lláh, Lawh-i-Ra'ís, quoted by J. E. Esslemont, *Bahá'u'lláh and the New Era*, p.147.
44. Cf. Arnold Toynbee, *Change and Habit*, pp.166ff.
45. Karl Barth in his Church Dogmatics states that the Christian religion is the 'religion of truth' and the non-Christian religions are the 'religions of error' (I,2, p.344).
46. Ishráqát, 9th Ishráq, *Tablets*, p.129.
47. *Paris Talks*, ch.40, p.130.

bulwark against the elements that previously led to religious division with all its attendant consequences: disputes about the revealed teachings and the proper order of the community. Furthermore, the Bahá'ís strongly believe in the promise of Bahá'u'lláh that this is a 'day' that will not be followed by 'night': 'The Hand of Omnipotence hath established His Revelation upon an unassailable, an enduring foundation. Storms of human strife are powerless to undermine its basis, nor will men's fanciful theories succeed in damaging its structure.'[48]

Unity in Diversity

The unity which Bahá'u'lláh calls for is not uniformity. It is not the mechanical unity of the robot or of rigid organization,[49] but organic unity. It is the unity of the flower garden, the beauty of which is revealed in its very diversity: 'Behold a beautiful garden full of flowers, shrubs, and trees. Each flower has a different charm, a peculiar beauty, its own delicious perfume and beautiful colour . . . So it is with humanity. It is made up of many races, and its peoples are of different colour, white, black, yellow, brown and red – but they all come from the same God, and all are servants to Him.'[50]

This unity in diversity is not mere theory, but real living practice. It is also shown in the increased interest and special attention given to minorities; 'Abdu'l-Bahá recommended that the Bahá'ís take special care of them.[51] Their cultural identity is to be acknowledged and preserved; their self-assurance is to be strengthened. This is not possible so long as still widely-spread cultural and racial prejudices are not overcome. He who takes seriously these words of Bahá'u'lláh 'Ye are the fruits of one tree, and the leaves of one branch',[52] has no reason to be overly proud of his own race: 'O children of men! Know ye not why We created you all from the same dust? That no one should exalt himself over the other.'[53] No one race is qualitatively superior to another. People are only different in the stage of their development: 'Some are like children who are ignorant, and must be educated until they arrive at maturity. Some are like the sick and must be treated with tenderness and care.'[54]

48. Quoted by Shoghi Effendi, 'The Dispensation of Bahá'u'lláh', in *The World Order of Bahá'u'lláh*, p.109.
49. Cf. Hermann Grossmann, *Umbruch zur Einheit*, pp.19ff.
50. 'Abdu'l-Bahá, *Paris Talks*, ch.15, p.52.
51. *The Promulgation of Universal Peace*, quoted in H. M. Balyuzi, *'Abdu'l-Bahá*, pp.179, 182, 228, 326–9; addressing the American Bahá'ís, 'Abdu'l-Bahá mentioned in particular the Indians and Eskimos (*Tablets of the Divine Plan*, pp.28, 32–3; see also Balyuzi, op. cit., p.424). He compared the original inhabitants of America to the Arabs before the coming of Muḥammad. Just as the Arabs were transfigured by Muḥammad's teachings, so too were the aboriginal Americans being transformed by the newest revelation and were beginning even then to reflect its light, illumining all regions. (ibid.)
52. *Gleanings* 132:3.
53. Bahá'u'lláh, *The Hidden Words*, Arabic No. 68.
54. 'Abdu'l-Bahá, *Paris Talks*, ch. 42, p.138.

Dies Irae

The promise that there will be 'one fold and one shepherd'[55] is to be fulfilled. However, the near future of mankind is, as Bahá'u'lláh has prophesied, painfully dark: 'How long will humanity persist in its way-wardness? How long will injustice continue? How long is chaos and confusion to reign amongst men? How long will discord agitate the face of society? The winds of despair are, alas, blowing from every direction, and the strife that divideth and afflicteth the human race is daily increasing[56] . . . Oh, the misery that resteth upon you, ye that are far astray! . . . Soon shall the blasts of His chastisement beat upon you, and the dust of hell enshroud you[57] . . . O ye peoples of the world! Know verily that an unforeseen calamity is following you and that grievous retribution awaiteth you. Think not the deeds ye have committed have been blotted from My sight.'[58]

Our present situation is, as described at the beginning,[59] characterized by advancing lawlessness, the increase of injustice and the omnipresence of evil. Bahá'u'lláh clearly predicted this condition, which was described in the Gospels as a sign of the time of the end:[60] 'The light of Justice is dimmed, and the sun of Equity veiled from sight. The robber occupieth the seat of the protector and guard, and the position of the faithful is seized by the traitor[61] . . . Justice is in this day bewailing its plight, and Equity groaneth beneath the yoke of oppression. The thick clouds of tyranny have darkened the face of the earth, and enveloped its peoples[62] . . . In these days truthfulness and sincerity are sorely afflicted in the clutches of falsehood, and justice is tormented by the scourge of injustice. The smoke of corruption hath enveloped the whole world.'[63] In the Lawḥ-i-Dunyá Bahá'u'lláh revealed: 'At present no day passes without the fire of a fresh tyranny blazing fiercely, or the sword of a new aggression being unsheathed . . . The world is in great turmoil, and the minds of its people are in a state of utter confusion.'[64] And in Qad-Iḥtaraqu'l-Mukhliṣún: 'The infidels have arisen in tyranny on every hand . . . Coldness hath gripped all mankind . . . Calamity hath reached its height . . . Anguish hath befallen the peoples of the earth . . . The

55. John 10:16.
56. *Gleanings* 110.
57. Bahá'u'lláh, *Gleanings* 103:4,5.
58. Bahá'u'lláh, *The Hidden Words*, Persian No. 63.
59. Cf. pp.64ff.
60. Matt. 24:12; II Tim. 3:1–5. The following is revealed in the Qur'án with reference to the depravity of the world: 'But true shall be the word which hath gone forth from me – I will surely fill hell with Djinn and men together.' (32:13.)
61. Ishráqát, *Tablets*, pp.124–5.
62. Lawḥ-i-Dunyá, *Tablets*, p.84 (= *Gleanings* 43:2).
63. Ṭarázát, 5th Ṭaráz, *Tablets*, p.39.
64. Lawḥ-i-Dunyá, *Tablets*, pp.90, 94.

agonies of death have laid hold on all men . . . The lamps of truth and
purity, of loyalty and honour have been put out . . . The universe is
darkened with the dust of sin.'[65]

Concerning the approaching catastrophe, Bahá'u'lláh has revealed: 'The
world is in travail, and its agitation waxeth day by day. Its face is turned
towards waywardness and unbelief. Such shall be its plight, that to disclose
it now would not be meet and seemly. Its perversity will long continue.
And when the appointed hour is come, there shall suddenly appear that
which shall cause the limbs of mankind to quake. Then, and only then,
will the Divine Standard be unfurled, and the Nightingale of Paradise
warble its melody.'[66] Bahá'u'lláh, who also prophesied the discovery of
atomic power and its destructive effects,[67] speaks in this passage of a
general deterioration of all forms of sovereignty and of a world-embracing
calamity that will precede the rise of the Cause of God: 'After a time all the
governments on earth will change. Oppression[68] will envelop the world.
And following a universal convulsion,[69] the sun of justice will rise from the
horizon of the unseen realm.'[70] 'Abdu'l-Bahá also predicted that there
would come a time when unbelief and, in its wake, anarchy and chaos
would prevail because man is not created to exercise unrestricted freedom.
In 1904 he wrote: 'Know this, that hardships and misfortunes shall increase day by day, and the people shall be distressed. The doors of joy and
happiness shall be closed on all sides. Terrible wars shall happen. Disappointment and the frustration of hopes shall surround the people from
every direction until they are obliged to turn to God.'[71]

Nonetheless, the Bahá'ís are by no means pessimists, for Bahá'u'lláh has

65. Known as 'The Fire Tablet'.
66. Bahá'u'lláh, *Gleanings* 61.
67. 'An infernal engine hath been devised, and hath proved so cruel a weapon of destruction that its
like none hath ever witnessed or heard. The purging of such deeply-rooted and overwhelming corrup-
tions cannot be effected unless the peoples of the world unite in pursuit of one common aim and
embrace one universal faith. Incline your ears unto the Call of this Wronged One . . . Strange and
astonishing things exist in the earth but they are hidden from the minds and the understanding of
men. These things are capable of changing the whole atmosphere of the earth and their contamination
would prove lethal.' (Kalimát-i-Firdawsíyyih, *Tablets*, p.69.)
68. In this context Bahá'u'lláh warns: 'O oppressors on earth! Withdraw your hands from tyranny,
for I have pledged Myself not to forgive any man's injustice.' (*The Hidden Words*, Persian No.64.)
69. Isaiah prophesied on this Last Judgement: 'Behold, the Lord maketh the earth empty, and
maketh it waste, and turneth it upside down, and scattereth abroad the inhabitants thereof (24:1) . . .
The land shall be utterly emptied, and utterly spoiled: for the Lord hath spoken this word. The earth
mourneth and fadeth away, the world languisheth and fadeth away . . . The earth also is defiled under
the inhabitants thereof; because they have transgressed the laws, changed the ordinance, broken the
everlasting covenant. Therefore hath the curse devoured the earth, and they that dwell therein are
desolate: therefore the inhabitants of the earth are burned, and few men left (24:3–6) . . . And the
foundations of the earth do shake. The earth is utterly broken down, the earth is clean dissolved, the
earth is moved exceedingly. The earth shall reel to and fro like a drunkard, and shall be removed like a
cottage; and the transgression thereof shall be heavy upon it' (24:18–20).
70. Quoted by Shoghi Effendi, *The Promised Day is Come*, p.121.
71. Quoted by J. E. Esslemont, *Bahá'u'lláh and the New Era*, p.227. On this whole subject see also
Robert F. Riggs, *The Apocalypse Unsealed*, New York, Philosophical Library, 1981.

also promised that 'Through the movement of Our Pen of glory We have, at the bidding of the omnipotent Ordainer, breathed a new life into every human frame, and instilled into every word a fresh potency. All created things proclaim the evidences of this world-wide regeneration. This is the most great, the most joyful tidings imparted by the Pen of this Wronged One to mankind. Wherefore fear ye, O My well-beloved ones?[72] . . . Let not the happenings of the world sadden you. I swear by God! The sea of joy yearneth to attain your presence, for every good thing hath been created for you, and will, according to the needs of the times, be revealed unto you.'[73]

The Kingdom of God

Bahá'ís are thus convinced that 'the darkness and the coldness which fill this vale of misery and woe'[74] will pass away, and that mankind, in the course of a great general regeneration, is approaching a radiant future, a future to which Bahá'u'lláh refers in these words: 'This is the Day whereon the unseen world crieth out: "Great is thy blessedness, O earth, for thou hast been made the foot-stool of thy God, and been chosen as the seat of His mighty throne!"'[75]

Being a Bahá'í, then, does not imply selfish endeavour, with an eye always on the next world, and with personal salvation one's first concern; rather it calls for a full participation in this earthly life and zealous cooperation in the establishment of this kingdom of peace as envisioned by the prophets.

This kingdom will not come upon mankind, as some Christian fundamentalists, who interpret the Bible literally,[76] expect. Nor will it be secured as many socialists imagine, through destruction of the old social structures in revolutionary civil wars, and by trying to build a new society free from contradictions in which man, no longer suppressed or exploited, can fulfil himself and will spontaneously become 'good'.[77] We cannot

---

72. Lawḥ-i-Dunyá, *Tablets*, p.83 (= *Gleanings* 43:2).
73. Quoted by Shoghi Effendi, *The Advent of Divine Justice*, p.69.
74. Bertolt Brecht, *The Threepenny Opera*, Act III, scene 3, p.288.
75. *Gleanings* 14:6.
76. i.e. the Jehovah's Witnesses.
77. The Marxist concept of man underlying this attitude originates in the anthropological theories of the Enlightenment. It can be traced back to Rousseau and is basically the conviction that uncorrupted human nature is good, that it is spoiled by pernicious social conditions, and that personal potential is virtually unlimited. Marxism blames man's degeneration on the institution of private property, while the 'New Left' identifies the living conditions in contemporary capitalistic industrial society as responsible. These are held to cause the 'deformation of men' and the 'crippling of his psyche': 'People could be guided towards good, social virtues could be developed in them, the attitude of neighbourly love could offer basic support for all, if the social conditions permitted.' (Hans Jochen Gamm, quoted by Brezinka, *Erziehung und Kulturrevolution*, p.107; see Bertolt Brecht's 'Ballad of the Good Man' on

expect God's cosmic interference in our order of existence with the consequent transformation of human nature, which would then no longer be capable of evil. And Leo Tolstoy's belief that solely the resolute adherence to the commandment of love, and the whole-hearted observation of the exhortations of the Sermon on the Mount will bring about the peace and happiness of mankind is just as unrealistic as the expectation that the kingdom of peace will come from the 'barrel of a gun' (Mao Zedong).

Peace and justice on earth cannot be bombed into being. They will not be the fruit of hatred.[78] 'The harvest of force', says 'Abdu'l-Bahá, 'is turmoil and the ruin of the social order.'[79] The lofty goal of a society of free men, in which the freedom and self-determination of man can be realized, is corrupted by the means used to achieve that goal. Is there anything in history to justify the hope that revolutionary processes would of themselves lead to good? If fear, envy and hatred are the motivation for social progress, instead of public spirit, civic sense and the all-embracing love for mankind, then the question must be asked: when in history did hatred cause good? Can anything good result when inhuman barbaric means are declared permissible and necessary for achieving the desired goal, when the goal of a morality valid for all is postponed to some time in the far future, when morality is nevertheless used immediately to condemn the conduct of one's opponent but for the justification of one's own conduct an interim morality[80] is declared necessary?

p.230 note 187). Once the capitalistic social order is abolished in favour of a 'domination-free' or 'socialist' order, man will overcome his society-imposed self-alienation and his original goodness will appear once again. The new man will emerge as product of the new classless society. Positive ethical orientation will not be required.

As yet there has been no historical example to justify this expectation, which Nietzsche mocked as 'nonsensical optimism concerning the "good man", who is waiting to appear from behind the scenes if only one would abolish the old "order" and set all the "natural drives" free' (*The Will to Power*, No. 755, p.398). Nowadays one does in fact find even orthodox Marxists grappling with ethical questions. The experience of living in the socialist states has initiated a discussion of values that would have been unthinkable earlier. After painful experiences the People's Republic of China has drawn some conclusions: in a large-scale propaganda campaign, the central organ of the Chinese Communist Party, the *Jen-min jih-pao* (the Peking People's Daily) on the 6th of April 1981 tried to compensate for the devastation of ethical norms which the Cultural Revolution had brought in its wake. It is the '"inner and outer civilized man" that is now being propagandized – in other words, the image of a courteous, clean, truth- and order-loving, selfless, industrious, helpful, self-sacrificing Chinese, who cultivates decency in behaviour and language, and is of a cheerful disposition. These are nothing other than those virtues which were despised and banished during the Cultural Revolution. An "All-Chinese Association for Ethics" is supposed to ensure the dissemination of the new (= old) morality.' (*Frankfurter Allgemeine Zeitung* of 7.4.1981; see ch.12 for Bahá'u'lláh's concept of man.)

78. In a speech held on the occasion of the awarding of the Peace Prize of the German Book Trade in 1977 ('Education to Hatred – Education to Dignity') Leszek Kolakowski made clear that, whatever the circumstances, there is no right to hate. 'Every right becomes wrong as soon as it tries to fortify itself with hatred; likewise, it is self-destructive to harness hatred for the cause of justice.' (*Süddeutsche Zeitung* of 17.10.1977.)

79. *Selections*, No. 79.

80. Such as the Nazi slogan: 'Good is that which helps the people' or the slogan of the Left: 'Good is that which brings us closer to the goal of history.'

One of the most fateful attitudes of contemporary thought is the naive belief that all political and social problems could and should be solved immediately, i.e. the optimistic belief 'that there is a ready-made, immediate answer to all problems and misfortunes, and that only the malevolence of enemies stands in the way of its being instantly applied'.[81] No virtue is so rare in our society as patience. For this reason our society has been called the *instant society*. But as Georg Christoph Lichtenberg[82] rightly remarks: 'Wanting to do everything at once destroys everything at once.' The idea that the social problems of mankind and all other problems could be solved quickly and immediately, that the conflict-free society could be established if people only decided unreservedly to destroy completely all the present structures, is just as naive and unrealistic as the chiliastic expectation that with the second coming of Christ everything will be changed at once. Peace and justice will be the fruit of the spiritual rebirth of mankind, a complete change in the consciousness of the new man, a new order and a laborious process of construction.[83]

Striving to walk the path of virtue and to lead a life orientated towards the norms of Christian ethics and pleasing to God is not sufficient to save mankind from its torments and troubles. For this striving, even in those few places where it still exists today, is becoming intolerably restricted by men's superstitions and prejudices and by the constraints of a sick society. How can the commandment to love one's neighbour overcome the basic illness of mankind, its division and disunity, when to this day that commandment – and the events in Northern Ireland, South Africa, and Lebanon are sad examples – is still confined to 'neighbour' in the literal sense of the word, i.e. to the member of the same race, the same colour, the same nation, the same confession, and mankind is not seen as one? Has this commandment ever prevented unjust social structures from being formed? Is it not precisely in 'God's own land', puritanical America, where the pilgrim fathers wanted to build a Christian state directed by the precepts of the Sermon on the Mount, that the gap between rich and poor, black and white, is most unbearable and gives rise to confrontations reminiscent of civil war? A child born in the slums of Harlem or Calcutta sees not the light of this world but its gloom. What chance does he stand of leading a virtuous life when poverty, hunger, dirt and crime surround him from early childhood and when he lacks the barest necessities for his material and spiritual development? One has to agree with the sociologist Iring Fetscher: 'A social order which forces all those living in it to be con-

---

81. Leszek Kolakowski, *Main Currents of Marxism*, Vol. III, p.530.
82. (1742–99), Professor of Physic at the University of Göttingen, famous for his aphorisms (*The Lichtenberg Reader: Selected Writings*. Translated, edited and introduced by Franz H. Mautner & Henry Hatfield, Boston, Beacon Press, 1959).
83. This is a reference to what Bahá'u'lláh calls the 'Most Great Peace' (cf. pp.142ff).

stantly on their guard against all the others and to fight for their share in the goods of life changes the individuals into beasts of prey and turns their human hands into claws.'[84] Unless all prejudices are overcome, as Bahá'u'lláh so urgently commands, and the great social contradictions are solved, mankind will not find peace, nor will the individual be able to fulfil his exalted destiny.

On the other hand even the best of all imaginable social orders will not cause man, who is completely orientated towards this worldly life with his consciousness limited to collective and political aspects, his thinking restricted to argumentative thought, no longer aware of the personal problems of his existence, to win back again his 'natural goodness'. Unless man has an elevated goal and is answerable to a power superior to the institutions of society, even such a social order will not cause him to control his selfishness, master his aggressions, overcome his baser instincts, ennoble his character and be more than a mere wolf among wolves.[85] The 'new man' cannot come into existence without personal effort; he does not come free of charge. He can only be the result of a spiritual rebirth, the total transformation of his thinking, believing and acting.

Bahá'ís believe that two processes – the elements of a single historical dialectic process already taking place – will bring about mankind's golden age: first the transformation of man, his spiritual rebirth through God's creative word that transforms all;[86] secondly, the transformation of society, structurally in accordance with the divine will proclaimed by Bahá'u'lláh, culturally by the establishment of a world-wide commonwealth, in which all men can live in peace; the world order of Bahá'u'lláh.

The Most Great Peace

On the political level there are two distinct processes. One is the political unification of peoples by international treaty, the establishment of a world federation of nations evolving into a majestic global commonwealth, wherein 'war as simply a continuation of political intercourse, with the addition of other means'[87] will be forbidden and forgotten. Mankind as a whole, though as 'yet unconscious of His[88] Revelation and yet unwillingly enforcing the general principles which He has enunciated',[89] nonetheless carries forward this constructive process. Its motivating power will be the external conditions which leave men no choice but to transcend their

---

84. 'Der Tod im Lichte des Marxismus' in Paus, *Grenzerfahrung Tod*, p.308.

85. The English philosopher Thomas Hobbes (1588–1679) put forward the theory that man in his natural state behaves like a wolf towards his fellow-men: 'Homo homini lupus' (*Elementa philosophiae*, 'De Cive', Paris 1642).

86. Cf. pp.208ff.

87. Carl von Clausewitz, *On War*, p.605.

88. Bahá'u'lláh.

89. Shoghi Effendi, *The Promised Day is Come*, p.128.

ideological and political differences and to co-operate with one another. Through the violent transformation now shaking all peoples, barriers impeding world unification will be torn down, thereby 'forging humankind into a unified body in the fires of suffering and experience'.[90] Bahá'u'lláh entitled this 'world commonwealth, destined to emerge, sooner or later, out of the carnage, agony, and havoc of this great world convulsion'[91] as the 'Lesser Peace'. In His Tablet to Queen Victoria, Bahá'u'lláh addresses the rulers of the earth: 'Now that ye have refused the Most Great Peace, hold ye fast unto this, the Lesser Peace, that haply ye may in some degree better your own condition and that of your dependents. O rulers of the earth! Be reconciled among yourselves, that ye may need no more armaments save in a measure to safeguard your territories and dominions. Beware lest ye disregard the counsel of the All-Knowing, the Faithful. Be united, O kings of the earth, for thereby will the tempest of discord be stilled amongst you, and your people find rest, if ye be of them that comprehend. Should any one among you take up arms against another, rise ye all against him, for this is naught but manifest justice.'[92]

The second process is the spiritual transformation of the world, which will lead to harmony among the peoples, races, classes and religions. It is the establishment of the promised Kingdom of God on Earth, in which the strong and the weak, the rich and the poor, will have overcome their prejudices, their hatred and enmity and will live together in love and justice, as the prophets have promised: 'The wolf also shall dwell with the lamb, and the leopard shall lie down with the kid; and the calf and the young lion and the fatling together; and a little child shall lead them. And the cow and the bear shall feed; their young ones shall lie down together; and the lion shall eat straw like the ox. And the sucking child shall play on the hole of the asp, and the weaned child shall put his hand in the cockatrice's den[93] . . . and they shall beat their swords into plowshares, and their spears into pruninghooks: nations shall not lift up swords against nation, neither shall they learn war any more.'[94]

The 'Most Great Peace' is the appellation Bahá'u'lláh has given the fruition of this unprecedented spiritual metamorphosis which breathes new 'life into this unified body' of a politically united humanity, 'creating true unity and spirituality'.[95] The task 'of the Bahá'ís, who are labouring con-

90. The Universal House of Justice, in *Wellspring of Guidance*, p.133.

91. Shoghi Effendi, *The Promised Day is Come*, p.128.

92. *Gleanings* 119:3. See also Lawh-i-Maqṣúd, *Tablets*, p.165 (= *Gleanings* 117).

93. Isa. 11:6–8. The predatory animals here cited are metaphors for hostile peoples and races. Cf. 'Abdu'l-Bahá, *Some Answered Questions*, ch. 12, for an interpretation of the whole chapter.

94. Isa. 2:4.

95. The Universal House of Justice, in *Wellspring of Guidance*, p.134. There is a certain analogy to the concepts 'Lesser Peace' and 'Most Great Peace' in the concepts of 'negative peace' and 'positive peace' employed by scientists working in peace research. 'Negative peace' is descriptive of an absence

sciously, with detailed instructions and continuing Divine guidance, to erect the fabric of the Kingdom of God on earth, into which they call their fellowmen, thus conferring upon them eternal life',[96] is to be active agents of this process.

'All nations and kindreds', wrote 'Abdu'l-Bahá, '. . . will become a single nation. Religious and sectarian antagonism, the hostility of races and peoples, and differences among nations, will be eliminated. All men will adhere to one religion, will have one common faith, will be blended into one race, and become a single people. All will dwell in one common fatherland, which is the planet itself.'[97] The fruit of the unification and the spiritual rebirth of the human race will be a civilization 'with a fullness of life such as the world has never seen nor can as yet conceive. Then will the Everlasting Covenant be fulfilled in its completeness. Then will the promise enshrined in all the Books of God be redeemed.'[98]

of violence between states, the absence of lethal conflicts, the freedom from civil war, or co-existence, whereas 'positive peace' demands the harmonious order of societies within themselves and with each other, an order in which 'the individual interacts in the best possible way with others in his environment' (Galtung). However, the concepts of Most Great Peace and Lesser Peace touch upon a reality which goes far beyond all that Utopian peace researchers could imagine even in their boldest dreams.

96. The Universal House of Justice, in *Wellspring of Guidance*, p.134.
97. Quoted by Shoghi Effendi, *The Promised Day is Come*, p.121.
98. Shoghi Effendi, *The Promised Day is Come*, p.128.

9. The Bahá'ís in the Old Order of Things

Breakdown and Renewal

The apocalyptic events so emphatically announced by Bahá'u'lláh and to which we are now witnesses, the spiritual upheaval, the crisis besetting human culture, the increasingly obvious decomposition of our social order with all its consequences, the menace of imminent catastrophe and the real danger of our extinction as a species – these conditions have been described by philosophers, theologians and scientists for decades. Anyone who does not live merely from day to day, who examines himself and the world and who does not repress or reject the results of his thinking must be aware of this situation. The causal chain which Bahá'ís see here and the interpretation which they give this historically unparalleled upheaval has been described in earlier chapters: the popular desertion of religion led to the abandonment of meaning, to the disintegration of religious values, to nihilism, and so directly to the rejection of all authority, to 'crumbling, destruction, ruin and overthrow'[1] as Nietzsche so clearly foresaw, and to the end of the old order.

The Western democracies are in a permanent state of siege, both with regard to their legitimacy and to their accountability. Every state institution is exposed to social criticism which becomes ever more biting and pessimistic. Young people rebel against authority and the way in which we are being governed; they question and challenge our forms of government. And indeed, by the measures and methods of contemporary political

1. *The Joyful Wisdom*, No. 343.

systems the impending catastrophe cannot be averted.[2] Many see only one remedy – revolutionary violence. Others hope to find a remedy in reforms. But it is daily becoming clearer that notwithstanding all the reforms a confusion reigns and our problems and conflicts are well nigh insoluble. The old order cannot be changed by reform; our epoch is no longer the epoch of reforms. The sick body of mankind cannot be restored with palliatives, it requires a radical cure. Radical means 'from the root'.[3] Jean Gebser, who realizes that we are now at a decisive turning-point and that something completely new is coming, also refutes the possibility of recovery through reform: 'Indeed nothing can be achieved by reform; only with a positive attitude towards the [new] forces and their effect upon us, for which our new perceptions act as signposts, can anything constructive be achieved. Reform, that is resuscitation, is senseless when it becomes clear that a decisive new creation has begun and hence the "old" is destined for transformation. Obsolete and exhausted forms cannot be filled with new life.'[4]

Over a hundred years ago, when people believed that 'the glorious height we've reached at last'[5] when no one could imagine the extent of our present-day crisis, Bahá'u'lláh foretold the collapse of this old order: 'Soon will the present-day order be rolled up, and a new one spread out in its stead. Verily, thy Lord speaketh the truth, and is the Knower of things unseen[6] . . . By My Self! The day is approaching when We will have rolled up the world and all that is therein, and spread out a new order in its stead. He, verily, is powerful over all things.'[7] However, just as the Revelation of St. John promises not only decline and destruction but also a 'new heaven' and a 'new earth', Bahá'u'lláh foretells both the breakdown of the old social order and the rise of a new one. Transformation, not annihilation, is our destiny, and every transformation is 'both destructive and constructive'.[8]

The breakdown of the old is a painful and precarious process. But it is

2. This fact is increasingly gaining recognition: 'For a long time the peoples of the world have sensed the insecurity and helplessness of those who govern them.' People stare in confusion at the approaching disaster, 'from which there is no one to save them, nor indeed is there anyone to warn them about it. In the coming decades this uneasiness will increasingly break out in the form of protest and will finally lead to a global discharge. In the face of this dawning world revolution with its accompanying world anarchy, the governments of both the East and the West should not short-sightedly close their eyes, but should interpret the signs of the times as they really are – as signs portending a hurricane.' (Heinz Friedrich, *Kulturkatastrophe*, p.297.)

3. Lat. *radix*: root. It is only fairly recently that the word has acquired the emotional connotation of extremism.

4. *Abendländische Wandlung* p.166. The scientist and theologian Günther Altner argues vigorously that a mere correction of our course is not sufficient; since we are at a decisive turning point in history we need a 'complete change of direction' in order to survive. (At the convention of the society *Civitas* in spring 1980, quoted by Malte Buschbeck in *Süddeutsche Zeitung* of 14–15.6.1980.)

5. J. W. von Goethe, *Faust*, I, Night, Wagner.

6. *Gleanings* 4:2.

7. *Gleanings* 143:3.

8. Jean Gebser, *Abendländische Wandlung*, p.166.

necessary and cannot be stopped. It is as necessary as the cold winter wind which sweeps away dead leaves from the trees, making room for the tender spring buds already sprouting. 'Wo aber Gefahr ist, wächst das Rettende auch',[9] for this breakdown is only one side, the destructive aspect, of a world-shaking revolution. At the same time, a constructive movement is under way. A new spirit, a new world-view, a new value-system and new institutions – for the people of Bahá these do not belong to a vague and futuristic Utopia, they have concrete reality here and now.[10]

As the decline of the ancient world and the fall of the Roman Empire were paralleled by the appearance of a 'new race of men' and new values which became the basis of western Christian culture, so also is the new appearing in our day, although generally ignored or ridiculed by the worldly-wise.[11] This epochal transition is characterized by 'interference' in which two opposing processes collide: a new age of historical development has begun, while the age-old structures are gradually disintegrating. As Novalis has it: 'Does not the very best always begin with illness?'

The Task of the Bahá'ís

How do the Bahá'ís respond to this clarion call: 'Die and be new-born'?[12] Their position is clear. They do not subscribe to the maxim, 'What falleth, that shall one also push!'[13] It is not their task to tear down the outworn social order 'which parts this one mankind into hostile nations, into powerful and weak, privileged and outcast, rich and poor', which 'makes one man wretched through want, another through overflow'.[14] They are called upon not to demolish but to build. The radical cure mentioned earlier, the healing of the tree of mankind from the roots up, requires that the foundation of a stable society be laid anew. This foundation is a new Faith, capable of imbuing modern man with a new consciousness, a world consciousness, of endowing him with a new set of values, with new goals and new meaning and of illuminating the exit from his labyrinth of hopelessness. It is the responsibility of the Bahá'ís to lay this foundation through the proclamation of Bahá'u'lláh's message and by bringing the new social structures into existence. Thus the Bahá'ís are the 'real radicals' and the Bahá'í Faith is the most radical movement around.

9. 'But where danger threatens, that which saves from it also grows.' Friedrich Hölderlin, Hymns, 'Patmos', in *Poems and Fragments*, p.463.
10. Shoghi Effendi, *The Promised Day is Come*, p.16.
11. Here is a clear parallel to the beginning of the Christian era: during its first two centuries Christianity was regarded by cultivated Romans as a Jewish sect, and a 'pernicious superstition' (Tacitus, *The Annals*, Book XV, XLIV).
12. J. W. von Goethe, *West-Eastern Divan*, Book of the Singer, XVIII, 'Blessed Yearning': 'And while thou spurnest at the best;/Whose word is "Die and be new-born!"/Thou bidest but a cloudy guest/Upon an earth that knows not morn.'
13. Nietzsche, *Thus Spake Zarathustra*, 'Old and New Tables', Third book, 20.
14. Richard Wagner, *The Revolution* (1849) in *Richard Wagner's Prose Works*, Vol.VIII, p.237.

The Bahá'ís are not radical, however, in their methods – they are neither subversive nor violent. They do not act as fermenting agents in social decomposition; they are not 'revolutionaries' who barricade and bomb. They know that this swelling mass of over one hundred and fifty sovereign nations will burst open like a rotten fruit without their assistance, and that they are needed to construct the new world order based on the sovereignty of God.

Whence Party Politics?

Bahá'ís do not engage in partisan political activities. They carry out all obligations expected of a citizen, including voting in elections if required or if they so wish.[15] They do not affiliate themselves with any political party. Every political activity must be carried out within a system and with the methods of that system, and the present systems are corrupt and corrupting. Moreover, the Bahá'í Faith would lose its unifactory power if its believers were to become involved in political disputes, taking sides in a separatist or seditious manner, and to dissipate their efforts in working for contradictory and competing parties. Shoghi Effendi has convincingly demonstrated that the Faith of God suffers when believers enter 'the arena of party politics': 'We Bahá'ís are one the world over; we are seeking to build up a new World Order, divine in origin. How can we do this if every Bahá'í is a member of a different political party . . . Where is our unity then? . . . The best way for a Bahá'í to serve his country and the world is to work for the establishment of Bahá'u'lláh's World Order, which will gradually unite all men and do away with divisive political systems.'[16] This strict abstinence from party politics may be unexpected in a religion which is directed towards the transformation of this temporal world. To many this attitude may appear to be inconsistent and therefore weak or sick or ignorant, and often Bahá'ís are reproached for holding themselves back from facing the 'real problems' of the social ensemble and of fellow individuals and for passively watching the world hasten to the cliff's naked edge.

Is this reproach justified? The question is: what is 'reality'? What is the real world? For him who accepts as real only what can be physically perceived, what can be physically experienced or empirically verified, and for him for whom the true determinants of society are its socio-economic conditions, the political abstinence of the Bahá'ís often appears as a refusal to co-operate in the building up of a humane and just body-politic, as well as a cowardly indifference towards the evils of the present order. Bahá'ís affirm that the physically perceptible world is only a small portion of reality, and furthermore 'that the working of the material world is merely a reflec-

---

15. Bahá'í electors vote according to their personal conscience and receive no instructions from Bahá'í institutions. The same principles apply as in elections within the Bahá'í Community. See p.245.
16. Through his secretary, quoted in *Principles of Bahá'í Administration*, p.43.

tion of spiritual conditions and until the spiritual conditions can be changed there can be no lasting change for the better in material affairs'. [17] As a Bahá'í it would be a dangerous error to believe oneself better able to ease the burden of mankind and to battle more effectively against misery by meddling in partisan politics: 'What we Bahá'ís must face is the fact that society is disintegrating so rapidly that moral issues which were clear a half century ago are now hopelessly confused and, what is more, thoroughly mixed up with battling political interests. That is why the Bahá'ís must turn all their forces into the channel of building up the Bahá'í Cause and its administration. They can neither change nor help the world in any other way at present. If they become involved in the issues the governments of the world are struggling over, they will be lost. But if they build up the Bahá'í pattern they can offer it as a remedy when all else has failed.' [18]

In this context Bahá'ís assert that most of those who expect to save mankind by political programs and material modifications themselves 'have no clear concept of the sort of world they wish to build, nor how to go about building it. [19] Even those who are concerned to improve conditions are therefore reduced to combating every apparent evil that takes their attention. Willingness to fight against evils, whether in the form of conditions or embodied in evil men, has thus become for most people the touchstone by which they judge a person's moral worth. Bahá'ís, on the other hand, know the goal they are working towards and know what they must do, step by step, to attain it. Their whole energy is directed towards the building of the good, a good which has such a positive strength that in the face of it the multitude of evils – which are in essence negative – will fade away and be no more. To enter into the quixotic tournament of demolishing one by one the evils in the world is, to a Bahá'í, a vain waste of time and effort. His whole life is directed towards proclaiming the Message of Bahá'u'lláh, reviving the spiritual life of his fellow-men, uniting them in a divinely-created World Order, and then, as that Order grows in strength and influence, he will see the power of that Message transforming the whole of human society and progressively solving the problems and removing the injustices which have so long bedevilled the world.' [20]

The future of mankind is not just a problem for politicians and

---

17. The Universal House of Justice, letter dated 7th July, 1976 (unpublished).

18. Shoghi Effendi, through his secretary, quoted in *Wellspring of Guidance*, p.135.

19. Richard Shaull, an advocate of radical theology, warns against fashioning an idol of 'revolution': 'The overthrow of the old order will not automatically bring about a more just society.' ('Revolutionary Change in Theological Perception', in John C. Bennett, *Christian Social Ethics in a Changing World*, p.35.)

20. The Universal House of Justice, letter dated 7th July, 1976 (unpublished).

diplomats; it is mainly the problem of the generation of a new man and of a new social morality. Bahá'u'lláh clearly states that our political leaders are at a standstill, that they will not find the solution to our distress which worsens every day.[21] He declares that in its collective disease the world requires an 'all-knowing Physician' who 'hath His finger on the pulse of mankind' and who 'in His unerring wisdom' diagnoses the illness and prescribes the cure: 'We can well perceive how the whole human race is encompassed with great, with incalculable afflictions. We see it languishing on its bed of sickness, sore-tried and disillusioned. They that are intoxicated by self-conceit have interposed themselves between it and the Divine and infallible Physician. Witness how they have entangled all men, themselves included, in the mesh of their devices. They can neither discover the cause of the disease, nor have they any knowledge of the remedy. They have conceived the straight to be crooked, and have imagined their friend an enemy.'[22]

World salvation cannot be expected from political action alone. On the day after every successful revolution the old problems are still waiting to be solved. Without undergoing a spiritual rebirth mankind will not be restored to health. The task of the Bahá'ís is therefore entirely constructive; it is their duty to proclaim the glad-tidings, to deliver the divine balm to a sorely-stricken humanity, to quicken the hearts of men, to educate them and to unite the peoples of the world. It is in this light that Bahá'u'lláh's insistence upon obedience to government[23] can be understood. Rebellion and strife are destructive and exacerbate an evil condition. Bahá'u'lláh warns His people not to take part in the uproar and conflict possessing the rest of mankind: 'Address yourselves to the promotion of the well-being and tranquillity of the children of men. Bend your minds and wills to the education of the peoples and kindreds of the earth, that haply the dissensions that divide it may, through the power of the Most Great Name, be blotted out from its face, and all mankind become the upholders of one Order, and the inhabitants of one City. Illumine and hallow your hearts;

---

21. 'Humanity, whether viewed in the light of man's individual conduct or in the existing relationships between organized communities and nations, has, alas, strayed too far and suffered too great a decline to be redeemed through the unaided efforts of the best among its recognized rulers and statesmen – however disinterested their motives, however concerted their action, however unsparing in their zeal and devotion to its cause. No scheme which the calculations of the highest statesmanship may yet devise; no doctrine which the most distinguished exponents of economic theory may hope to advance; no principle which the most ardent of moralists may strive to inculcate, can provide, in the last resort, adequate foundations upon which the future of a distracted world can be built.' (Shoghi Effendi, 'The Goal of a New World Order' in *The World Order of Bahá'u'lláh*, pp.33–4).

22. *Gleanings* 106:1,2.

23. 'In every country where any of this people reside, they must behave towards the government of that country with loyalty, honesty and truthfulness.' (Bishárát, The fifth Glad-Tidings, *Tablets*, pp.22–3.) 'What mankind needeth in this day is obedience unto them that are in authority, and a faithful adherence to the cord of wisdom' (*Gleanings* 102); compare also 'Abdu'l-Bahá, *Selections*, No. 225, p.293.

let them not be profaned by the thorns of hate or the thistles of malice. Ye dwell in one world, and have been created through the operation of one Will. Blessed is he who mingleth with all men in a spirit of utmost kindliness and love.'[24]

Respect for the laws of the state and obedience to the government contribute to this constructive task. Chaos is even worse than the continuation of the present social order, and rebellion and sedition bring us closer to chaos, not to a just social order. In the truly equitable world commonwealth of the future, eager obedience to the law and to the government will be recognized as essential requisites for its stability, for without loyalty civilization will not flourish.

24. *Gleanings* 156.

10. Authority and Freedom

The Authority of the Manifestation

To embark on a life lived according to aims and values not imposed autonomously by man himself but imposed absolutely upon him, implies an attitude of mind which is no longer greatly valued today: obedience. After the abuse of this virtue in the past by both spiritual and temporal authorities, it is no wonder that it has been discredited. An anti-authoritarian outlook has bedevilled it and other religious values such as humility and self-denial, as the morality of exploitation.[1] Besides, obedience implies àuthority, and what authority is still recognized today, when everything is being called into question? Yet religion without obligations, without obedience, is unthinkable. Religion is the 'encounter with the sacred',[2] the purely absolute: 'The essence of religion is to testify unto that which the Lord hath revealed, and follow that which He hath ordained in His mighty Book.'[3] The word which the Manifestation proclaims is the Word of God. Therefore the divine Messenger speaks with the highest degree of authority. This authority must be carefully examined. If it is accepted, then all that the Manifestation says and does is 'absolute wisdom, and is in accordance with the reality. If some people do not understand the hidden secret of one of His commands and actions, they ought not to op-

---

1. The Catholic theologian Hubertus Halbfas points out that obedience was the basic behaviour of the Commandant of Auschwitz concentration camp and of other war criminals and draws the conclusion, in all seriousness, that a Christian who believes in the authority of God is a threat to democracy: 'The praying child is practising a belief in God which represents the complete embodiment of hierarchical sovereign authority. Praying can in itself thus bring about the internalization of structures which often encourage a whole life of unfree obedience and authoritative restrictions.' ('Gegen die Erziehung zum Gehorsam.') Halbfas is mistaken, because he does not distinguish between genuine and presumed authority.
2. The definition can be found in Rudolf Otto, *The Idea of the Holy*.
3. Bahá'u'lláh, Aṣl-i-Kullu'l-Khayr, *Tablets*, p.155.

pose it, for the supreme Manifestation does what He wishes.'[4]

The laws proclaimed by the divine Messenger are God's will and command and therefore the absolute infallible yardstick of all morality, no longer open to question. They are unfathomable to human intelligence, capable of rational justification, but in no need of it, for their origin bestows on them the character of faith and they apply primarily by virtue of their existence,[5] only secondarily by virtue of the power of conviction residing in them. As the Qur'án quite clearly says: 'God doth what He will[6]. . . He shall not be asked of his doings[7]. . . Whoso obeyeth the Apostle, in so doing obeyeth God.'[8]

The Sovereignty of God

Bahá'u'lláh has also explained this principle of the 'Most Great Infallibility'.[9] He refers to the two highest duties of man, obedience to which is necessary to salvation. One is the acceptance of the manifestation of God: 'The first duty prescribed by God for His servants is the recognition of Him Who is the Dayspring of His Revelation and the Fountain of His laws, Who representeth the Godhead in both the Kingdom of His Cause and the world of creation. Whoso achieveth this duty hath attained unto all good; and whoso is deprived thereof, hath gone astray, though he be the author of every righteous deed.'[10] The second duty is fulfilment of the divine law from inner devotion:[11] 'It behoveth every one who reacheth this most sublime station, this summit of transcendent glory, to observe every ordinance of Him Who is the Desire of the world. These twin duties are inseparable. Neither is acceptable without the other. Thus hath it been decreed by Him Who is the Source of Divine inspiration.'[12] And above all stands the Word which reveals the majesty of the divine law and the de-

---

4. 'Abdu'l-Bahá, *Some Answered Questions*, ch. 45, p.173. The same idea is found in the Qur'án: 'Yet haply you are averse from a thing, though it be good for you, and haply ye love a thing though it be bad for you: And God knoweth; but ye, ye know not'.(2:213.)

5. We must acknowledge with the Catholic theologian Alfons Auer that traditional moral norms 'are unhesitatingly set aside today unless they are convincingly justified', i.e. can be supported by rational arguments, and that every moral demand of concrete content soon leads 'with certainty into the bottleneck of the whole problem of substantiation' (*Autonome Moral und christlicher Glaube*, p.11). However, when he says that 'even authorities have no other means', he is falling prey to the error of failing to distinguish between human authorities (who need rational justification) and the divine authority of the Manifestation recognized in the act of faith. Auer is paying homage to the mentality of one-dimensional rationalism criticized above (p.33).

6. 2:254; 14:32; 22:14; 22:19.

7. 21:23.

8. 4:82.

9. See Kitáb-i-Aqdas (= *Gleanings* 155); Ishráqát, *Tablets*, pp.106–16.

10. Kitáb-i-Aqdas (*Synopsis*, No.1; = *Gleanings* 155:1).

11. A purely external, legalistic observance of the law is not enough: 'Walk in My statutes for love of Me.' (Bahá'u'lláh, *The Hidden Words*, Arabic 38 and *Gleanings* 155:4).

12. Kitáb-i-Aqdas (*Synopsis*, No.1; = *Gleanings* 155:1).

mand for unconditional obedience to it: 'Whenever My laws appear like the sun in the heaven of Mine utterance, they must be faithfully obeyed by all, though My decree be such as to cause the heaven of every religion to be cleft asunder. He doth what He pleaseth. He chooseth; and none may question His choice.' [13] 'Were He to decree as lawful the thing which from time immemorial had been forbidden, and forbid that which had, at all times, been regarded as lawful, to none is given the right to question His authority. Whoso will hesitate, though it be for less than a moment, should be regarded as a transgressor. Whoso hath not recognized this sublime and fundamental verity, and hath failed to attain this most exalted station, the winds of doubt will agitate him, and the sayings of the infidels will distract his soul. He that hath acknowledged this principle will be endowed with the most perfect constancy.' [14]

Revelation and Philosophy

These writings are of fundamental importance to an understanding of the Bahá'í faith. They compel one to realize that a partial acceptance of the revelation of Bahá'u'lláh is not possible, because as soon as parts of His message are rejected Bahá'u'lláh is put on the level of a fallible human being. There are people who wholeheartedly agree with the peace-loving, cosmopolitan, and humanitarian strivings of the Bahá'ís and with their goal, the unification of mankind. But they have their own ideas as to the way to achieve this goal and refuse to follow Bahá'u'lláh when His word does not suit them for some reason. They enthusiastically accept those parts of the word which 'accord with their inclinations and interests', rejecting those verses 'which are contrary to their selfish desires: "Believe ye then part of the Book, and deny part?"' [15] Shoghi Effendi has stated in unmistakable terms that such a selective attitude is not possible for a true believer: 'Allegiance to the Faith cannot be partial and half-hearted. Either we should accept the Cause without any qualification whatever, or cease

13. Kitáb-i-Aqdas (*Synopsis*, No.2; = *Gleanings* 155:6). Cf. also the Báb, The Persian Bayán 7:19, *Selections*, p.79.

14. Kitáb-i-Aqdas (*Synopsis*, No.18, pp.26–7; = *Gleanings* 37:2–3). On the Most Great Infallibility Bahá'u'lláh revealed in the Ishráqát: 'Indeed He is a Light which is not followed by darkness and a Truth not overtaken by error. Were He to pronounce water to be wine or heaven to be earth or light to be fire, He speaketh the truth and no doubt would there be about it; and unto no one is given the right to question His authority or to say why or wherefore. Whosoever raiseth objections will be numbered with the froward in the Book of God, the Lord of the worlds . . . Know thou for a certainty, that the Will of God is not limited by the standards of the people, and God doth not tread in their ways. Rather is it incumbent upon everyone to firmly adhere to God's straight path. Were He to pronounce the right to be the left or the south to be the north, He speaketh the truth and there is no doubt of it. Verily, He is to be praised in His acts and to be obeyed in His behests. He hath no associate in His judgement nor any helper in His sovereignty. He doeth whatsoever He willeth and ordaineth whatsoever He pleaseth.' (*Tablets*, pp.108–9.) On the absoluteness of divine law cf. also *Gleanings* 160:2–3.

15. Qur'án 2:79, quoted by Bahá'u'lláh, *Kitáb-i-Íqán*, p.169.

calling ourselves Bahá'ís. The new believers should be made to realize that it is not sufficient for them to accept some aspects of the teachings and reject those which cannot suit their mentality in order to become fully recognized and active followers of the Faith. In this way all sorts of misunderstandings will vanish and the organic unity of the Cause will be preserved.'[16] From a true believer is demanded 'unreserved acceptance of, and submission to, whatsoever has been revealed by their[17] Pen'.[18]

This is where religion differs from philosophy. However inspiring the teaching of a philosopher and however convincing his arguments, it is a fallible man who speaks, one with no greater authority than the convincing power of his words. Insofar as the laws of logic permit, I can adopt one part of his knowledge and reject another, for all human knowledge is a 'part'[19] and all philosophy is subject to the principle '*errare humanum est*'. The Word of God belongs to a different category. The revelation is a closed system of orientation, the doctrines, action programmes, principles and norms of which demand unalterable, ultimate authority. They are absolute, immune to criticism, unquestionable, authoritative and apodictic, yet both in content and in purpose they are humanitarian, in other words their aim is the progress and well-being of human life. Man must be guided by them in his thoughts, actions and feelings; they are the guidelines for social life.[20]

But might not the acceptance of prescribed organizational structures lead to a static concept of the world? Might not such a system lead to rigid adherence to views which become obsolete within a foreseeable period and are overtaken by social development, to the paralysis of thought, to spiritual death? Norbert Elias sees 'authority-mania', the 'search for spiritual crutches, for the books of past generations, for prescribed norms, principles which have simply to be interpreted as authoritative without any need for independent thought and observation', as a disease of the intellect[21] and considers that the theoretical and empirical media of social orientation, like every other scientific work, are in need of examination, revision or extension. He deplores any thinking incapable of taking in events which do not fit into the scheme of thought and principles accepted as authoritative: 'The courage to go on thinking has gone. This disease of

16. *Bahá'í Procedure*, p.18. See also Shoghi Effendi, in *Directives from the Guardian*, No.173.

17. i.e. the Báb, Bahá'u'lláh and 'Abdu'l-Bahá.

18. Shoghi Effendi, *Bahá'í Administration*, p.90.

19. I Cor. 13:9.

20. The materialistic philosophy of history cannot recognize, let alone accept as an insurmountable barrier, such constants, which are independent of historical practice and beyond the reach of human capability. Kolakowski comments 'that in the whole universe man cannot find a well so deep that when he leans over it he will not discover his own face at the bottom.' (*Traktat über die Sterblichkeit der Vernunft*, p.80.)

21. Speech on the occasion of the award of the Adorno Prize in Frankfurt (*Frankfurter Allgemeine Zeitung* of 4.10.1977).

belief in authority condemns man, in other words, to an epigonous existence for evermore.'[22]

If all thought, including religious, is human thought, that is to say philosophy, if there is no other category beyond the rational, then Elias is right. Then there can be no fixed areas immune to criticism; then the constant correction of theory by experience is indispensable to all recognition of truth. It is in fact the weakness of every ideology[23] that thought is bound up in a system of ideas based on the experience and knowledge of an earlier age and is permanently incapable of satisfying changing conditions and needs. At any point in philosophy where recourse to reason and experience has been cut off and a level of knowledge has been fixed once for all, independent thought, the independent search for truth, is over, the courage to go on thinking has been crushed.

The unassailable, infallible authority of the revealed word is based on the categorical difference between human knowledge and divine wisdom. Just as the 'secret' of man will forever evade the knowledge of psychology, however far advanced, so social life is complex and inscrutable to the point that no social science, however developed, will ever be capable of understanding and giving conclusive evidence of the structures which maintain the stability of a communal system, a state, the community of nations, over a lengthy period. Elias, who rightly complains that we have lost our direction in our own world, has resigned himself to the idea that it is bound to take many years of patient work 'in order to develop the social scientific models to such an extent that they can make a better contribution to ameliorating the increasing disorientation and insecurity of our social cosmos.'[24] But for reasons discussed at the beginning,[25] even this hope is unjustified. Whatever science can or cannot do, revealed religion provides man with the universal system of orientation; the divine manifestation 'in His unerring wisdom' provides 'the remedy',[26] which alone, unlike all human attempts at a solution, is capable of flexible survival down the centuries. The Book of God is not some spiritual crutch, paralysing thought, but a means of knowing those areas where man's rational knowledge comes to a boundary. That is why it calls for absolute obedience even when man does not recognize the profound wisdom contained in it.

Submission to the Will of God

Now every human being comes into contact with the Cause of God from different standpoints and different convictions and it often happens that

22. ibid.
23. Ideology in the sense of a closed philosophical system.
24. Speech on the occasion of the award of the Adorno Prize (see above, note 21).
25. Compare pp.77ff., 128ff.
26. Bahá'u'lláh, *Gleanings* 106:1.

the very thing which attracts and convinces one fills another with scepticism and reservations. There are prepared souls to whom the recognition of the truth comes naturally when they meet God's word; many people need years of search and thought until they tear aside the veil of their own ideas and 'recognize the signs of God'.[27] In each case, faith is a process of inner growth and it is necessary not to become obsessed with articles of faith which one cannot understand at first, and to be confident that one's knowledge and understanding will grow, provided one is always mindful of Bahá'u'lláh's exhortation to 'cleanse and purify his heart . . . from the obscuring dust of all acquired knowledge'[28] and regard 'the Book itself' as the 'unerring balance established amongst men'.[29]

The submission to the will of God required of the believer is the essence of religion. Muḥammad called the religion he founded *Islám* and *Islám* means submission to the will of God. A *Muslim* is a man who has submitted[30] to the will of God.[31] Man was created for this manner of existence, in which he finds his way to his true self. When St. Augustine said the human soul was *naturaliter christiana*, he was referring to this aspect of the human constitution, which actually finds its fulfilment only in turning towards God, not in complete autonomy. Nietzsche rightly perceived that 'the man of faith, the "believer" of any sort is necessarily a dependent man', that his conviction is 'his backbone'.[32] Consistent with his viewpoint but completely contrary to the religious image of man is his conclusion that all kinds of faith are 'an evidence of self-effacement, of self-estrangement' and 'slavery'. His theory is that 'men of convictions are prisoners', the need for faith is 'a need of weakness', not faith but scepticism is worthy of the higher man.[33] According to the Bahá'í teachings, man's real self-estrangement is his separation from God. Since man has been thus created, he is incapable of survival without this backbone of a conviction founded on faith and without the compass of a morality anchored in faith: 'A man who is without good faith – I do not know how he is to manage! How can a wagon without its yoke-bar for the ox, or a carriage without its collar-bar for the horses, be made to move?'[34] The man without faith loses direction and goes astray. This is the path taken by modern man.

Man's path to God, the path of salvation, always begins with knowledge

---

27. Bahá'u'lláh, *Gleanings* 52:2.
28. *Kitáb-i-Íqán*, p.192.
29. *Gleanings* 98:1.
30. According to the terminology of the Qur'án, the name *Muslim* does not apply solely to the followers of Muhammad and his revelation but in general to those who were devoted believers in one of God's revealed religions. Thus Abraham was called a *Muslim* (Qur'án 3:60).
31. Cf. Bahá'u'lláh, *Gleanings* 160:2–3.
32. *The Antichrist*, No.54.
33. ibid.
34. Confucius, *The Analects*, II, 22.

of oneself,[35] renunciation and abnegation, and leads via moral discipline to meditation and prayer. The believer is placed in a confrontation between his ego and God, between his selfish, earthly desires and the divine commandments. Bahá'ís are not enjoined to flee this life as ascetics, but to turn to God, to strive for an inner detachment from everything transitory and to subordinate their whole lives to their faith: 'O Son of Spirit! There is no peace for thee save by renouncing thyself and turning unto Me'[36] . . . 'Say: Deliver your souls, O people, from the bondage of self, and purify them from all attachment to anything besides Me.'[37]

At the outset we have instinctual, intractable, thoughtless, contradictory man, who through faith voluntarily relinquishes his unrestrained freedom and submits to the divine law, takes himself in hand, directs his life by the highest values and adopts the divine virtues and perfections. At the end of this self-knowledge and self-conquest, this morally educative process, we find the moral person, the 'new man', what the Torah and Gospels call the 'righteous',[38] the 'children of the Lord',[39] and Confucius 'the noble'. At the end there is also the reward of everlasting happiness: 'O My servants! Sorrow not if, in these days and on this earthly plane, things contrary to your wishes have been ordained and manifested by God, for days of blissful joy, of heavenly delight, are assuredly in store for you.'[40]

The fulfilment of God's commands demands constant vigilance and a lifelong striving for self-restraint, self-control and self-education. Observance of the divine prohibitions means the restriction of his own freedom of action. This is obvious: all forms of ethics set limits to one's freedom of action and every religion has done this.

Man and Freedom

It is no wonder that it was in his Book of Laws, Kitáb-i-Aqdas, that Bahá'u'lláh expressed his concept of the human desire for freedom. He leaves no doubt that freedom can exist only within the structure of laws: 'Regard men as a flock of sheep that need a shepherd for their protection. This, verily, is the truth, the certain truth. We approve of liberty in certain circumstances, and refuse to sanction it in others.'[41] The principle of moderation[42] so urgently recommended by Bahá'u'lláh applies equally to human freedom: 'It is incumbent upon them who are in authority to exer-

35. Compare Bahá'u'lláh, Ṭarázát, 1st Ṭaráz, *Tablets*, p.35; *Gleanings* 153:6; Aṣl-i-Kullu'l-Khayr, *Tablets*, p.156.
36. Bahá'u'lláh, *The Hidden Words*, Arabic 8.
37. Bahá'u'lláh, *Gleanings* 136:1.
38. Ps.5:12; Prov.4:18.
39. Deut.14:1; Matt.5:9; John 1:12; 1 John 5:2.
40. Bahá'u'lláh, *Gleanings* 153:9.
41. *Synopsis*, No.16 (= *Gleanings* 159:3).
42. More details on pp.217ff.

cise moderation in all things. Whatsoever passeth beyond the limits of moderation will cease to exert a beneficial influence. Consider for instance such things as liberty, civilization and the like. However much men of understanding may favourably regard them, they will, if carried to excess, exercise a pernicious influence upon men.' [43] Bahá'u'lláh sees the appetite for unlimited freedom as the expression of human 'pettiness': 'They ask for that which injureth them, and cast away the thing that profiteth them. They are, indeed, of those that are far astray.' [44] Those 'desiring liberty, and priding themselves therein' are 'in the depths of ignorance'. [45] Boundless freedom, in which autonomous man observes no limits other than those – not ultimately binding ones – which he sets himself, 'must, in the end, lead to sedition, whose flames none can quench . . . That which beseemeth man is submission unto such restraints as will protect him from his own ignorance, and guard him against the harm of the mischief-maker. Liberty causeth man to overstep the bounds of propriety, and to infringe on the dignity of his station.' [46]

The question of the freedom of man is one of humanity's fundamental problems. The answer given by Bahá'u'lláh fits his concept of man. [47] Bahá'u'lláh adheres to the idea of man created in God's image. Man is 'the noblest and most perfect of all created things', [48] 'the highest work of creation', 'the nearest to God of all creatures', [49] and 'is intended to become the recipient of the effulgences of divine attributes' [50] distinguished from animals by his reasoning mind, his capacity for knowledge and faith, he is 'the noblest and most perfect of all created things', [51] 'for in him are potentially revealed all the attributes and names of God to a degree that no other created being hath excelled or surpassed'. [52] Man is the ontological summit of the universe. In him evolution achieves self-awareness. Conse-

---

43. *Gleanings* 110. Of his epoch-making masterpiece, Montesquieu confessed: 'I have undertaken this work with no other view than to prove it; the spirit of moderation ought to be that of the legislator; political, like moral good, lying always between two extremes.' (*The Spirit of Laws*, (1748) Book XXIX, ch.1, 1.) When we survey our present political landscape we can observe that the crumbling of our order is possibly more manifest in the loss of this political wisdom, in the remarkable preference for extreme positions and extreme means for their realization, than in anything else. German history of the twentieth century is the clearest proof that the loss of the centre in politics leads to polarization and destruction. It is a fact reinforced by historical experience that excessive freedom is always transformed into despotism, an insight which Plato himself proclaimed: 'So from an extreme liberty one is likely to get . . . a reaction to an extreme of subjection . . . We expect tyranny to result from democracy, the most savage subjection from an excess of liberty.' (*The Republic*, Book VIII, 564.)
44. Kitáb-i-Aqdas (*Synopsis*, No.16, = *Gleanings* 159:1).
45. ibid. (= *Gleanings* 159:1).
46. ibid. (= *Gleanings* 159:2).
47. See also Schaefer, *The Light Shineth in Darkness*, pp.91–3.
48. Bahá'u'lláh, *Gleanings* 90:2.
49. 'Abdu'l-Bahá, *Paris Talks*, ch.5, p.24.
50. 'Abdu'l-Bahá, *The Promulgation of Universal Peace*, p.404.
51. Bahá'u'lláh, *Kitáb-i-Íqán*, pp.102–3.
52. Bahá'u'lláh, *Kitáb-i-Íqán*, p.101.

quently he is also responsible for its further progress.

But is this statement, which is almost equivalent to an apotheosis, not contradicted by historical experience? Is not man's history written in blood, is it not a series of never-ending acts of violence? Is this not why Hobbes called man a wolf?[53] Is historical experience not sufficient reason for the theory that man is evil and rotten to the core? Is not Schopenhauer right in his description of man's situation: 'But, in general . . . the world is in a very bad way. In savage countries they eat one another, in civilized countries they deceive one another; and that is what people call the way of the world! What are States and all the elaborate systems of political machinery, and the rule of force, whether in home or foreign affairs – what are they but barriers against the boundless iniquity of mankind? Does not all history show that whenever a king is firmly planted on the throne, and his people reach some degree of prosperity, he uses it to lead his army, like a band of robbers, against adjoining countries? Are not almost all wars ultimately undertaken for purposes of plunder?'[54]

Nevertheless, Bahá'u'lláh calls man 'God's mystery', but He also tells us in what his apparent inadequacy consists: 'Lack of a proper education hath, however, deprived him of that which he doth inherently possess.'[55] Bahá'u'lláh compares man to 'a mine rich in gems of inestimable value' and immediately adds: 'Education can, alone, cause it to reveal its treasures.'[56]

The Power of Education

The quotations above show the outstanding importance attached by Bahá'u'lláh to education. In no other religion is the idea of education given such fundamental importance. 'The primary, the most urgent requirement is the promotion of education', says 'Abdu'l-Bahá, for: 'The principal reason for the decline and fall of peoples is ignorance.'[57] The purpose of education is to overcome the ignorance of man.

The Bahá'í Faith believes in man's educability and need for education. In contrast to the dogma of the Church[58] man does not perceive the light of the world in a state of sin, with a corrupt nature and dull understanding. In *The Hidden Words* Bahá'u'lláh says: 'O Son of Spirit! I created thee rich, why dost thou bring thyself down to poverty? Noble I made thee, wherewith dost thou abase thyself?'[59] At birth man is morally an unwrit-

53. See p.142 n.85.
54. *Counsels and Maxims*, V, 29.
55. Bahá'u'lláh, *Gleanings* 122.
56. Bahá'u'lláh, *Gleanings* 122.
57. *The Secret of Divine Civilization*, p.109.
58. The dogma of original sin, that is the idea that a compulsion to sin came into the world through Adam, is as alien to the Bahá'í Faith as it is to Judaism, from whose Holy Book the allegory of the Fall stems (cf. Schaefer, *The Light Shineth in Darkness*, pp.90ff).
59. Arabic 13.

ten page. It is only education and environmental influences which 'give significance and distinction to character traits'.[60]

The Bahá'í doctrine in this respect is similar though not identical to the philosophy of the Enlightenment, which believed in the perfectability of man and the power of education. John Locke (1632–1704) called man at the beginning of his life a 'blank sheet of paper', inscribed only by the impressions reaching him from the exterior. He thought that nine out of ten men 'are what they are, good or evil, useful or not, by their education. It is that which makes the great difference in mankind.'[61] The whole of civilization is in fact the result of education.

In need of education as he may be,[62] man's capacity for education nevertheless has its limits. According to the Bahá'í doctrine human nature is not comparable with the wax which can be moulded in any way, take on any form allotted to it. Every man has his own essential nature which can be unfolded and developed for the highest benefit of himself and society. The mind and understanding of human beings differ in character and this difference cannot be ironed out by education. Nor should it be, for the variety of human beings constitute the manifold nature of the human race: 'A large body of scholars is of the opinion that variations among minds and differing degrees of perception are due to differences in education, training and culture. That is, they believe that minds are equal to begin with, but that training and education will result in mental variations and differing levels of intelligence, and that such variations are not an inherent component of the individuality but are the result of education: that no one hath any inborn superiority over another . . . The Manifestations of God are likewise in agreement with the view that education exerteth the strongest possible influence on humankind. They affirm, however, that differences in the level of intelligence are innate; and this fact is obvious, and not worth debating. For we see that children of the same age, the same country, the same race, indeed of the same family, and trained by the same individual, still are different as to the degree of their comprehension and intelligence. One will make rapid progress, one will receive instruction only gradually, one will remain at the lowest stage of all. For no matter how much you may polish a shell, it will not turn into a gleaming pearl, nor can you change a dull pebble into a gem whose pure rays will light the world. Never, through training and cultivation, will the colocynth[63] and the bitter tree[64] change into the Tree of Blessedness.[65] That is to say, education

60. Hermann Grossmann, *Umbruch zur Einheit*, p.48.
61. *Some Thoughts concerning Education*, p.6.
62. 'Man, if he is left without education, becomes bestial, and, moreover, if left under the rule of nature, becomes lower than an animal, whereas if he is educated he becomes an angel.' ('Abdu'l-Bahá, *Some Answered Questions*, ch.3, p.7.)
63. *Citrullus colocynthis*, an Asiatic vine, the dried fruit of which is used in the manufacture of a powerful laxative.
64. The Tree of *Zaqqúm*, compare Qur'án 37:60–65.

cannot alter the inner essence of man, but it doth exert tremendous influence, and with this power it can bring forth from the individual
whatever perfections and capacities are deposited within him.'[66] Thus the
teacher is like a gardener tending a variety of plants. Whereas one may love
bright sunlight another flourishes only in cool shade. Each must receive the
care which suits its nature.

This attitude differs considerably from the anthropological basic
assumption supported in much of the Anglo-Saxon (or Anglo-Saxon
oriented) psychology and educational theory, according to which all men
are equal,[67] and from the behaviourist assurance that any behaviour
desired can be learned, the result of which is the pedagogical optimism
which claims that in suitable surroundings anyone, no matter what his
gifts, inclinations and capacities, can be educated for any profession; that
everybody is potentially an Einstein or a Shakespeare. No regard is paid to
the fact that natural propensities set limits, that not every personality trait
is the result of learning and that talents are no more exclusively the result
of environment than they are the result of inheritance.

However, the educational outlook of the Bahá'í Faith differs most essentially from modernistic educational doctrines in that the goals of the latter
are of an exclusively reasonable, intellectual or cognitive nature. Man has
to be educated to rationality, sense and discrimination so that with the
help of his critical reason he will be capable of governing himself. A
positive goal indeed, if only *emancipatory pedagogics* did not mean
something different by 'coming of age' and 'sensibleness' from what is
usually understood by these words,[68] and if only education did not end
with these goals. Education is something essentially different from – *horribile dictu!* – 'going through the formal educational processes'.[69]

The fact that the development of man's intellectual capacities is an indispensable educational goal is obvious. Bahá'u'lláh says: 'First and
foremost among these favours, which the Almighty hath conferred upon
man, is the gift of understanding.'[70] The intelligence of the rational soul,
in which all men share, whether 'they be . . . believers or deniers' . . .
'can discover the realities of things, comprehend the peculiarities of beings, and penetrate the mysteries of existence. All sciences, knowledge,
arts, wonders, institutions, discoveries, and enterprises come from the exercised intelligence of the rational soul.'[71]

65. Compare Qur'án 24:35.
66. 'Abdu'l-Bahá, *Selections*, No.104.
67. The egalitarian claim that no person is worth more than another (e.g. Article 3 of the Federal
German constitution), as Brezinka rightly sees, becomes 'turned into a statement on being, which is in
contradiction to the results of scientific research' (*Erziehung und Kulturrevolution*, p.108).
68. For more details of the reinterpretation of concepts see pp.38ff.
69. Ulrich Oevermann, in *Bergedorfer Gesprächskreis*, *Protokoll* No.41.
70. *Gleanings* 95:1.
71. 'Abdu'l-Bahá, *Some Answered Questions*, ch. 58, p.217.

So it is this intelligence which must be developed. In Islám there was a constant insistence that man should acquire knowledge: 'Shall they who have knowledge and they who have it not, be treated alike?'[72] And Bahá'u'lláh proclaims: 'Knowledge is one of the wondrous gifts of God.'[73] 'Knowledge is as wings to man's life, and a ladder for his ascent. Its acquisition is incumbent upon everyone. The knowledge of such sciences, however, should be acquired as can profit the peoples of the earth, and not those which begin with words and end with words . . . In truth, knowledge is a veritable treasure for man.'[74]

No less important an educational goal than the development of understanding is character building, the creation of emotional commitments to prescribed values, symbols, maxims, spiritual signposts and ultimate goals, what 'Abdu'l-Bahá has called 'divine education': 'it consists in acquiring divine perfections, and this is true education; for in this state man becomes the focus of divine blessings, the manifestation of the words, "Let Us make man in Our image, and after Our likeness."'[75] Only this spiritual education awakens the spiritual capacities lying dormant in man and unfold his true being. Without this spiritual education man is 'like a mirror which, although clear, polished and brilliant, is still in need of light. Until a ray of the sun reflects upon it, it cannot discover the heavenly secrets.'[76] The progress of mankind is dependent on this spiritual education. To transmit 'what hath been revealed through the Pen of Glory'[77] is the beginning of all education, because character and conscience-formation take place in the first years of man's life: 'Schools must first train the children in the principles of religion, so that the Promise and the Threat recorded in the Books of God may prevent them from the things forbidden and adorn them with the mantle of the commandments.'[78] Nevertheless, here too Bahá'u'lláh recommends moderation and wisdom; 'but this in such a measure that it may not injure the children by resulting in ignorant fanaticism and bigotry.'[79] 'Abdu'l-Bahá stressed the fact that the moral education of man precedes his purely intellectual education: 'Training in morals and good conduct is far more important than book learning. A child that is cleanly, agreeable, of good character, well-behaved – even though he be ignorant – is preferable to a child that is rude, unwashed, ill-natured, and yet becoming deeply versed in all the sciences and arts. The reason for this is that the child who con-

72. Qur'án 39:12.
73. Tablet of Ṭarázát, 6th Ṭaráz, *Tablets*, p.39.
74. Tablet of Tajalliyyát, *Tablets*, pp.51–2.
75. 'Abdu'l-Bahá, *Some Answered Questions*, ch. 3, p.8.
76. 'Abdu'l-Bahá, *Some Answered Questions*, ch. 55, pp.208–9.
77. Bahá'u'lláh, quoted from Esslemont, p.144.
78. Kalimát-i-Firdawsíyyih, *Tablets*, p.68.
79. ibid.

ducts himself well, even though he be ignorant, is of benefit to others, while an ill-natured, ill-behaved child is corrupted and harmful to others, even though he be learned. If, however, the child be trained to be both learned and good, the result is light upon light.'[80]

Education must therefore be comprehensive, and in the Ishráqát Bahá'u'lláh expressly ordains that parents must bestow this comprehensive education and training on their children, both sons and daughters. He explains: 'He that bringeth up his son or the son of another, it is as though he hath brought up a son of Mine.'[81]

The overwhelming importance of education in the Bahá'í Faith simply demonstrates the facts that the prophets of God are seen as 'Divine Educators'[82] and the progressive revelation of God as 'the divine education of the human race',[83] and that the faithful are summoned to devote themselves to this work of education: 'They who are the people of God must, with fixed resolve and perfect confidence, keep their eyes directed towards the Day Spring of Glory, and be busied in whatever may be conducive to the betterment of the world and the education of its peoples . . . They who are the people of God have no ambition except to revive the world, to ennoble its life, and regenerate its peoples.'[84]

Through divine education, with the teachings and commandments of the manifestations, man is to be brought to true self-knowledge:[85] 'True

---

80. *Selections*, No.110.

81. Seventh Ishráq, *Tablets*, p.128. Cf. also Kitáb-i-Aqdas, *Synopsis*, No. 8, p.16. 'Abdu'l-Bahá expressed himself on many occasions on the inalienable obligation of parents to give their children the best possible education. One of the Tablets states: 'It is for this reason that, in this New Cycle, education and training are recorded in the Book of God as obligatory and not voluntary . . . O ye beloved of God and the maid-servants of the Merciful! Teaching and learning, according to the decisive texts of the Blessed Beauty (Bahá'u'lláh), is a duty. Whosoever is indifferent therein depriveth himself of the great bounty. Beware! beware! that ye fail not in this matter. Endeavour with heart, with life, to train your children, especially the daughters. No excuse is acceptable in this matter.' (*Bahá'í World Faith*, pp.398ff.) In matters of education daughters even have preference over sons. 'Abdu'l-Bahá explains why this is so: 'If it be considered through the eye of reality, the training and culture of daughters is more necessary than that of sons, for these girls will come to the station of motherhood and will mould the lives of the children. The first trainer of the child is the mother. The babe, like unto a green and tender branch, will grow according to the way it is trained. If the training be right, it will grow right, and if crooked, the growth likewise, and unto the end of life it will conduct itself accordingly. Hence, it is firmly established that an untrained and uneducated daughter, on becoming a mother, will be the prime factor in the deprivation, ignorance, negligence and the lack of training of many children.' (op. cit., p.399.) Praise, reasonable advice and, when necessary, admonition and criticism are intended to bring forth desirable qualities and mould good characters, but: 'It is not, however, permissible to strike a child, or vilify him, for the child's character will be totally perverted if he be subjected to blows or verbal abuse.' ('Abdu'l-Bahá, *Selections*, No.95.)

82. 'From the heaven of God's Will, and for the purpose of ennobling the world of being and of elevating the minds and souls of men, hath been sent down that which is the most effective instrument for the education of the whole human race.' (Bahá'u'lláh, *Gleanings* 43:6.)

83. Compare also p.106.

84. Bahá'u'lláh, *Gleanings* 126:1,2.

loss is for him whose days have been spent in utter ignorance of his self.'[86] Bahá'u'lláh demands 'that man should know his own self and recognize that which leadeth unto loftiness or lowliness, glory or abasement, wealth or poverty'.[87] According to Bahá'u'lláh there is an internal connection between the knowledge of God and the knowledge of self.[88] He confirms the Islámic tradition: 'Man is My mystery, and I am his mystery' and the pronouncement passed down from the Imám 'Alí: 'He hath known God who hath known himself', and refers[89] to the verses of the Qur'án: 'And also in your own selves: Will ye not then behold the signs of God?[90] . . . And be ye not like those who forget God, and whom He hath therefore caused to forget their proper selves.'[91]

Man is consequently not a fallen being who – as the pessimistic anthropology of the Church teaches us – gambled and lost his freedom against God in the Fall and has lived since then in utter corruption, his nature perverted and his reason completely clouded. In contrast to the optimistic image of man on which all forms of socialism are based, however, man is not programmed for good either, so that under the right social conditions happiness and peace become his lot 'free of charge'. Even in the best of all possible worlds these advantages would not be available if man lost the purpose of his life and failed to develop – through his own efforts and through the grace of God – into that for which he was created.

This purpose of life is, as the daily prayer has it, 'to know Thee and to worship Thee', by 'strict observance of whatsoever hath been sent down from the empyrean of the Divine Will',[92] to clothe man 'with the mantle of a saintly character, and to adorn him with the ornament of holy and goodly deeds'[93] and 'to carry forward an ever-advancing civilization'.[94] 'To act like the beasts of the field is unworthy of man.'[95] Man's position is dependent on the extent to which he fulfils this destiny: 'How lofty is the station which man, if he but choose to fulfil his high destiny, can attain! To what depths of degradation he can sink, depths which the meanest of creatures have never reached!'[96] Man can raise himself through the grace of God to become like the angels; he can sink to the lowest level of existence if he strays from the 'straight path':[97] 'Whosoever Thou exaltest is raised

85. This injunction to self-knowledge has been of special significance in all religions since time immemorial. 'Know thyself!' was inscribed over the Temple of Apollo at Delphi.
86. Aṣl-i-Kullu'l-Khayr, *Tablets*, p.156.
87. Tablet of Ṭarázát, 1st Ṭaráz, *Tablets*, p.35.
88. *Gleanings*, 153:6.
89. *Kitáb-i-Íqán*, p.101.
90. 51:21.
91. 59:19.
92. Bahá'u'lláh, *Gleanings* 2.
93. Bahá'u'lláh, *Gleanings* 137:4.
94. Bahá'u'lláh, *Gleanings* 109:2.
95. Bahá'u'lláh, ibid.
96. Bahá'u'lláh, *Gleanings* 101.
97. Cf.Bahá'u'lláh, *Gleanings* 82:5; 110; 114:1; 116:3; 128:2.

above the angles, and attaineth the station: "Verily, We uplifted him to a place on high!"; and whosoever Thou dost abase is made lower than dust, nay, less than nothing.'[98] So human nature is as capable of development as it is of degradation.

Evil and Suffering

This freedom, to which man was created, also contains the explanation of the evil, the chaotic, the blind destruction, the elements inimical to life which can no more be overlooked in this world than the good. 'Satan'[99] is not some independent power opposed to God, not a fundamental evil principle existing side by side with God, but a cypher for the base and

98. Bahá'u'lláh, *Epistle to the Son of the Wolf*, pp.9–10.

99. In traditional Catholic and Protestant theology Satanology has up to now played an indispensable role: 'Behind the Cross stands the Devil', according to a Spanish proverb. According to ecclesiastical doctrine Satan is a genuinely existing power with whom Christ is in constant struggle. Until the recent past every Low Mass was followed by the prayer: 'Holy Michael Archangel, defend us in the day of battle! Be our safeguard against the wickedness and snares of the devil . . . by the power of God thrust down to hell Satan and all wicked spirits, who wander through the world for the ruin of souls.' No litany is without its invocations against the 'crafts and assaults of the Devil', who is invoked three times in the Church's final service of the day, Compline, and mentioned in the service of Baptism, the celebration of the First Communion, the annual Feast of Easter and in many Catholic and Protestant hymns. There is a well-known story that Martin Luther threw an inkpot at Satan when he met him in person on the Wartburg. It is Satan's own temptation which makes us doubt the Satanology of the Church: 'La plus belle ruse du diable est de nous persuader qu'il n'existe pas', as Baudelaire says, and in *Das Goldene Katholikenbuch* by F. X. Wetzel (p.198), we read: 'There is no hell: so most professors say . . . so say the bons vivants over their venison and champagne.' 1953 saw the publication of Giovanni Papini's work about the Devil, *Il Diavolo* (The Devil, New York, Dutton, 1954). And even today, as the Aschaffenburg exorcists' trial in April 1978 disclosed, devils are still driven out according to the regulations laid down in the *Rituale Romanum* of 1614 for the grand exorcism.

Modern tendencies within the Catholic Church not to take the Devil seriously were resolutely opposed many times by Pope Paul VI, as when on 29 June 1972, when preaching in St. Peter's, he declared that the outstanding feature of the Church's situation today was that 'the smoke of Satan had entered the temple of God through a crack', and on 15 November 1972, when in an address to pilgrims he declared that the Devil was 'an active force, a living, spiritual being, destroyed and destroying, a terrible reality, mysterious and frightening'. To criticism of these statements the Franciscan Concetti responded on 17 December 1972 in the *Osservatore Romano* that without the Devil sin would no longer be a mystery, indeed the existence and activity of the Devil was one of the supporting pillars of Christianity, without which it would collapse. The autumn assembly of German bishops in September 1976 was also concerned with the Devil and attested his existence (cf. Herbert Haag, 'Rettet den Teufel!', in *Süddeutsche Zeitung* of 12–13.3.1977). This reveals the whole spectrum of the Christian faith today: while to the progressive, God is simply a metaphor for human love, the conservatives cling to the Devil.

To the Christian critics of the Bahá'í Faith the doctrine of the non-existence of the Devil has always been a main objection; for Kurt Hutten, for instance, who accuses it of disarming evil and sin (*Seher, Grübler, Enthusiasten*, p.314). By now, however, there is an increasing tendency in Protestant and Catholic theology to support positions which approach the Bahá'í teaching set out above on the Devil. Christianity takes leave of the Devil, as the title (*Abschied vom Teufel*) of a book by Herbert Haag published by Benziger, Einsiedeln, in 1969 tells us – a book which, admittedly, exposed him to doctrinal disciplinary proceedings (on the whole question, see also Wolfgang Beinert, 'Müssen Christen an den Teufel glauben?' (Must Christians believe in the Devil?) in *Stimmen der Zeit*, Vol. 102, No. 8, August 1977, pp.541–4; Herbert Haag, 'Vor dem Bösen Ratlos?' in *Zur Debatte*, themes discussed by the Catholic Academy of Bavaria, 1979, Issue 2).

worldly nature of man from which all evil comes, unless it is overcome by the life-giving spirit which is the source of all perfections. Evil and hence sin are rooted exclusively in the thoughts and deeds of man, who unless he deliberately turns to God falls short of his essential nature and a prey to evil. Evil is simply the absence of good, as darkness is the absence of light, ignorance the lack of knowledge, illness the lack of health, weakness the lack of strength, poverty the lack of riches. Therefore all evil can be overcome by the good as can darkness by light, because evil, like darkness, is essentially non-existent.[100] The question arises as to why the divine God, who can never want or approve evil, nevertheless allows it, why he does not prevent man from doing evil – and with it comes the question of suffering in the world. Insofar as people in our time think about religious questions at all, the suffering in the world is the subject which moves them most. The question constantly reiterated ever since Job, as to why God in his omniscience and infinite goodness should allow suffering, especially the suffering of the innocent[101] – the question of theodicy[102] – has become the chief objection to belief in God in our time, after Auschwitz, Hiroshima, Vietnam, the Gulag Archipelago, Kampuchea. 'Why do I suffer? That is the rock of atheism', as Büchner put it.[103] A God who remains silent when there is so much injustice and suffering in the world is unjust, cruel, sadistic, so the accusation runs,[104] and the theologian Dorothee Sölle declares: 'How one is to praise the God who governs everything so wonderfully, after Auschwitz, I do not know.'[105] In fact, the horrors of the extermination camps and the event of Hiroshima have confronted us with such a dimension of evil that the foundations of many people's faith have been rocked. But this question about the dark areas of the world and the goodness of God has not arisen only since Auschwitz. The whole of history is brimful of atrocities, and yet people in the past did not stray from their belief in God.

There is no philosophically and logically satisfactory solution to the

---

100. On the whole theme: 'Abdu'l-Bahá, *Some Answered Questions*, ch. 29, 57 and 74. It is surprising to find Thomas Aquinas expressing thoughts which remind one of this doctrine of the non-existence of the Devil: '*Relinquitur igitur quod nomine mali significetur quaedam absentia boni*' (*Summa theologica* I questio 48).

101. A passionate accusation against a creation in which children suffer, in Albert Camus, *The Plague*, Penguin Books, 1968, pp.174ff.

102. 'The vindication of God', so called by Leibniz in his book *Essai de théodicée sur la bonté de Dieu, la liberté de l'homme et l'origine du mal* (1720). Leibniz tried to approach the problem with the premise that the existing world was the best of all possible worlds and that the evil which nevertheless attached to it was in its totality the smallest possible quantity. For the question of theodicy from the Catholic standpoint cf. Hans Küng, *Gott und das Leid* (God and Suffering), Zürich, Einsiedeln, Köln 1967; and *Existiert Gott?* by the same author, pp.757–60.

103. *Danton's Death*, Act II, scene 5.

104. Moser, *Gottesvergiftung*, p.20. A critique of this: *Ist Gott grausam?* (Is God cruel?), an opinion on Tilman Moser's *Gottesvergiftung* published by Wolfgang Böhme, Evangelisches Verlagswerk, Stuttgart 1977.

105. Quoted from Fries, *Gott ist tot?*, p.79.

problem of theodicy, nor can there be one, since the essential nature of God has forever been inaccessible and inscrutable, impenetrable to human reason. The question as to why God allows evil, and with it, suffering, is a question about the actions of God and these cannot be judged according to human criteria: 'He shall not be asked of His doings.'[106] The absolute sovereignty of God sets an insurmountable barrier to human knowledge. Man would himself be like God if he knew or understood why God made creation thus and not otherwise.

Even if human wickedness and historical tragedy conspire against a final answer to the theodicy question, this does not mean that the question is shrouded in darkness.[107] It should be seen in the context of man's freedom. If God has created man as a free being, in contrast to animals which are bound by their instincts, the morally good deed must depend on freedom of choice, which leaves evil as a possibility. For any creature which was always prevented by divine intervention from acting when it decided against the norm imposed on it, would not be free. Man, according to the divine creative design, as Hans Küng puts it, is not intended to be 'God's plaything, but a free partner in the game'.[108] Evil and suffering are intimately linked with this freedom of man. Even temptation, the conflict in the human heart urging him to do evil instead of the good required, is founded in this freedom. And because man will constantly be faced with the choice between good and evil, evil will not disappear completely from the world even when God's Kingdom comes on earth, any more than will sorrow, grief and suffering.

Anyone who regards suffering as the 'rock of atheism' is deliberately overlooking the fact that it has always been man who has brought suffering on man in its most unbearable form, in its greatest darkness. Oppression and exploitation of large population groups, the barbaric wars, the extermination of entire peoples, the annihilation of people like insects by nuclear weapons of mass destruction, the destruction of whole civilizations, were crimes committed by human beings. No intervention from God would have been needed in order to avoid the sufferings thus created. God was not silent. He spoke to men through his prophets and messengers and told them of His teachings and commandments for a fulfilled life, worthy of man and acceptable to God. If people had listened and lived as He instructed, had turned away from evil, had practised love instead of hate, justice instead of oppression, most of the evil and most of the suffering

---

106. Qur'án 21:23.

107. It is worth noting Schopenhauer's view: 'If suffering is not the first and immediate object of our life, then our existence is the most inexpedient and inappropriate thing in the world. For it is absurd to assume that the infinite pain, which everywhere abounds in the world and springs from the want and misery essential to life, could be purposeless and purely accidental.' (*Parerga and Paralipomena*, Vol.II, p.291.)

108. *Existiert Gott?* p.713.

would be removed from the world. [109] The inhumanity of man, who is now in the process of making this 'blue planet', this oasis in the desert of the universe uninhabitable, his love of power, his hatred and envy are responsible for unspeakable suffering. Man cannot unload this guilt on to God. Fries rightly asks: 'Would it not be incomparably more appropriate to place man, not God, before the tribunal of history and to confront the question "Where are you, God?" with another: "Adam, where are you – what have you done?"' [110] It is in fact a reversal of the yardsticks, 'to attribute the good in the world to man, to glorify man, his freedom and his all-embracing and effective creativity, while ignoring evil and calamity, exempting himself from them, declaring himself "not competent", "not involved", "not guilty", as impotent, claiming that someone else – "God" – is responsible.' [111]

Anyone who believes he can cast aside the whole of religion and the theodicy question following Auschwitz is judging from the basis of a picture of the world in which suffering does not occur, in which it has no purpose and no task. The belief that suffering has its purpose in the divine order of salvation is, however, part of the common ground of all religions. It is undoubtedly man's duty to remove as much suffering as possible from the world through moral effort and the use of his reason, yet there will never be a world without suffering. Man, who was 'created weak', [112] will always fall into sin and will always cause his neighbour to suffer. Man will also always have to live with loss and disappointment, disease and death. Despite all the technical progress, there will always be natural catastrophes and other calamities. The experience of suffering is as it were immanent to human life. But suffering, which, according to those who believe that they can get rid of it by rational analysis and political struggle and by changing consciousness and structures, is simply a 'breakdown' or an 'industrial accident', has according to the Bahá'í teaching a rewarding, instructive and refining function in the order of creation. It is not purposeless, it is a trial sent by God to man for the growth of his soul. Shoghi Effendi emphasizes that: 'We should not . . . forget, that an essential characteristic of this world is hardship and tribulation and that it is by overcoming this that we achieve our moral and spiritual development. As the Master [113] says, sorrow

109. In this connection Bahá'u'lláh revealed: 'Say: Follow, O people, what hath been prescribed unto you in Our Tablets, and walk not after the imaginations which the sowers of mischief have devised, they that commit wickedness and impute it to God, the Most Holy, the All-Glorious, the Most Exalted.' (*Gleanings* 141:2.)
110. *Gott ist tot?* p.82.
111. Fries, op.cit. On the same subject, see also Albert Keller S. J., *Schmerz, Leid, Tod* (Pain, suffering, death), Kevelaer 1980.
112. Qur'án 4:32.
113. 'Abdu'l-Bahá.

is like furrows, the deeper they go, the more plentiful is the fruit we obtain.'[114]

So trials and tribulations are 'benefits from God, for which we should thank Him. Grief and sorrow do not come to us by chance, they are sent to us by the Divine Mercy for our own perfecting.'[115] That is why Bahá'u'lláh says: 'O Son of Man! For everything there is a sign. The sign of love is fortitude under My decree and patience under My trials . . . The true lover yearneth for tribulation even as doth the rebel for forgiveness and the sinful for mercy . . . If adversity befall thee not in My path, how canst thou walk in the ways of them that are content with My pleasure? If trials afflict thee not in thy longing to meet Me, how wilt thou attain the light in thy love for My beauty?'[116] People who do not suffer 'attain no perfection. The plant most pruned by the gardeners is that one which, when the summer comes, will have the most beautiful blossoms and the most abundant fruit.'[117] 'Were it not for tests, genuine gold could not be distinguished from the counterfeit. Were it not for tests, the courageous could not be known from the coward. Were it not for tests, the people of faithfulness could not be known from the people of selfishness. Were it not for tests, the intellects and faculties of the scholars in the great colleges would not be developed. Were it not for tests, the sparkling gems could not be known from worthless pebbles. Were it not for tests, the fisherman could not be distinguished from Annas and Caiaphas, who had great worldly dignity.'[118] So the profusion of suffering has its origins in the evil deeds of men, which God permits because he created man free. The suffering sent by God to man helps him to perfect himself, even if man often fails to recognize it: 'O Son of Man! My calamity is My providence, outwardly it is fire and vengeance, but inwardly it is light and mercy.'[119] That is why it is written in the Qur'án: 'Whatever good betideth thee is from God, and whatever betideth thee of evil is from thyself.'[120] And in the Fire Tablet Bahá'u'lláh revealed: 'Were it not for calamity, how would the sun of thy patience shine, O Light of the Worlds?'[121]

The painful upheavals currently being visited on the nations should also be seen in this light. The philosopher Karl Löwith comments: 'Men learn through suffering, and whom the Lord loveth he chasteneth. Thus Christianity was born in the death throes of a collapsing Hellenic society.'[122]

---

114. Through his secretary in *Living the Life*, p.11. The same idea can be found in Meister Eckhart: 'Suffering is the fastest ride to perfection'.
115. 'Abdu'l-Bahá, *Paris Talks*, ch. 14, p.50.
116. *The Hidden Words*, Arabic 48–50.
117. 'Abdu'l-Bahá, *Paris Talks*, ch. 14, p.51.
118. 'Abdu'l-Bahá, quoted from *The Divine Art of Living*, ch.12, p.91.
119. Bahá'u'lláh, *The Hidden Words*, Arabic 51.
120. Qur'án 4:81.
121. Qad Ihtaraqa'l-Mukhlisún.
122. *Meaning in History*, p.13.

Richard Shaull, a representative of the 'theology of revolution', is absolutely right when he says: 'The God who tears down old structures in order to create the conditions for a more human existence is himself in the midst of the struggle. His presence in the world and his pressure on the structures which stand in his way are the reason for the dynamics of this process.'[123] But the destruction of the old structures in the revolutionary process does not automatically mean the entrance of the 'good', neither peace on earth nor the 'new order', let alone the 'new man'. The painful upheavals now being visited on mankind are not only intended to tear down outmoded social structures but also at the same time, and more importantly, to change the obdurate hearts, refine them and turn them to God. Shoghi Effendi writes about this: 'This judgement of God, as viewed by those who have recognized Bahá'u'lláh as His Mouthpiece and His greatest Messenger on earth, is both a retributory calamity and an act of holy and supreme discipline. It is at once a visitation from God and a cleansing process for all mankind. Its fires punish the perversity of the human race, and weld its component parts into one organic, indivisible, world-embracing community[124] . . . The flames which His Divine justice have kindled cleanse an unregenerate humanity, and fuse its discordant, its warring elements as no other agency can cleanse or fuse them. It is not only a retributory and destructive fire, but a disciplinary and creative process, whose aim is the salvation, through unification, of the entire planet. Mysteriously, slowly, and resistlessly God accomplishes His design, though the sight that meets our eyes in this day be the spectacle of a world hopelessly entangled in its own meshes, utterly careless of the Voice which, for a century, has been calling it to God, and miserably subservient to the siren voices which are attempting to lure it into the vast abyss.'[125]

Bahá'u'lláh's Verdict on Hedonism

It can be deduced from this high destiny of man that the erotic Utopia of a life in 'luxe, calme et volupté', as Baudelaire[126] defined it, represents a total failure of existence. The immoderate desire for the satisfaction of urges and enjoyment of pleasure, the insatiable striving for material prosperity and luxury, the cult of the orgasm and the cult of Mammon, in which life is currently being generally exhausted, the widespread notion that life is not worth living until one has cast off all the compulsions of morality,[127] the irrational belief that our society would be happier, freer and healthier if man's impulses, emotions and drives were not suppressed

123. 'Revolution in theologischer Perspektive', in T. R. Rendtorff and H. E. Tödt, *Theologie der Revolution*, pp.117ff.
124. *The Promised Day is Come*, p.2.
125. op. cit., p.120.
126. *Les fleurs du mal*, XLIX: 'L'invitation au voyage.'
127. Aperçu of Edith Piaf: 'Morality is when you live in a way which makes living no fun.'

and deformed by a repressive morality, is a grave mistake. Man's loudly claimed right to govern himself, his emancipation from all standards and authorities, is the road to barbarism. Liberation from any prescribed standard will not produce what Karl Marx called the 'universally cultivated personality', but the rootless barbarian. If humanity were really to go ahead with the further dismantling of all institutionalized forms of behaviour and the liberation of all sexual relationships according to personal choice, then we would not have long to wait for the civilization of the rabbit hutch and if, as demanded, we were to do away with penal law, chaos would soon be absolute.

Like all Manifestations, Bahá'u'lláh points the way. Man was created not for incessant enjoyment and unrestrained self-indulgence, but in order 'to become the recipient of the effulgences of divine attributes'[128] and to act as the standard-bearer of 'an ever-advancing civilization'.[129] But man's true essence will not emerge and civilization is not possible unless the emphasis is placed on immaterial values, renunciation, self-denial, sacrifice and discipline: 'Discipline is necessary for the mobilization of psychic and physical energies for tasks outside the self, for the conquest and subordination of the self in order to conquer others.'[130]

Bahá'u'lláh has described and sharply condemned this hedonism, which implies a complete rejection of the common values of all religions and which is now characteristic of our Western world, increasingly embraced by the rich nations, while the poor lead a miserable existence and succumb to sheer poverty:[131] 'Greed hath made captive all mankind: Where are the embodiments of detachment, O Lord of the worlds? . . . The drunkenness of passion hath perverted most of mankind: Where are the daysprings of purity, O Desire of the worlds?'[132] Bahá'u'lláh points to the futility of the world and the transitory nature of earthly riches and counsels his people to acquire imperishable treasures: 'The world is continually proclaiming these words: Beware, I am evanescent, and so are all my outward appearances and colours. Take ye heed of the changes and chances contrived within me and be ye roused from your slumber.'[133] 'The world is but a show, vain and empty, a mere nothing, bearing the semblance of reality. Set not your

128. 'Abdu'l-Bahá, *The Promulgation of Universal Peace*, p.404.
129. Bahá'u'lláh, *Gleanings* 109:2.
130. Daniel Bell, *The Cultural Contradictions of Capitalism*, p.82. 'What is man, if his chief good and market of his time be but to sleep and feed? A beast, no more.' (Hamlet IV, 4.)
131. According to the Qur'án as well, those who know only the appearance of this world, 'but of the next life are . . . careless' (30:6) and concerned only with the increase of their worldly goods, will forfeit eternal life. Sura 102 runs: 'In the name of God, the Compassionate, the Merciful. The desire of increasing riches occupieth you, till ye come to the grave. Nay! but in the end ye shall know. Nay! once more, in the end ye shall know your folly. Nay! would that ye knew it with knowledge of certainty! Surely ye shall see hell-fire. Then shall ye surely see it with the eye of certainty; then shall ye on that day be taken to task concerning pleasures.'
132. Qad-Ihtaraqa'l-Mukhliṣún (The Fire Tablet).
133. *Tablets*, p.258.

affections upon it. Break not the bond that uniteth you with your Creator, and be not of those that have erred and strayed from His ways. Verily I say, the world is like the vapour in a desert, which the thirsty dreameth to be water and striveth after it with all his might, until when he cometh unto it, he findeth it to be mere illusion[134] . . . The generations that have gone on before you – whither are they fled? And those round whom in life circled the fairest and the loveliest of the land, where now are they? Profit by their example, O people, and be not of them that are gone astray. Others ere long will lay hands on what ye possess, and enter into your habitations. Incline your ears to My words, and be not numbered among the foolish. For every one of you his paramount duty is to choose for himself that on which no other may infringe and none usurp from him. Such a thing – and to this the Almighty is My witness – is the love of God, could ye but perceive it. Build ye for yourselves such houses as the rain and floods can never destroy, which shall protect you from the changes and chances of this life.'[135]

The shortness of life and the transitoriness of worldly goods is a subject often repeated in Bahá'u'lláh's writings. In the Kitáb-i-Aqdas he revealed: 'Rejoice not in the things ye possess; tonight they are yours, tomorrow others will possess them. Thus warneth you He Who is the All-Knowing, the All-Informed. Say: Can ye claim that what ye own is lasting or secure? Nay! By Myself, the All-Merciful. The days of your life flee away as a breath of wind, and all your pomp and glory shall be folded up as were the pomp and glory of those gone before you. Reflect, O people! What hath become of your bygone days, your lost centuries? Happy the days that have been consecrated to the remembrance of God, and blessed the hours which have been spent in praise of Him Who is the All-Wise. By My life! Neither the pomp of the mighty, nor the wealth of the rich, nor even the ascendancy of the ungodly will endure. All will perish, at a word from Him. He, verily, is the All-Powerful, the All-Compelling, the Almighty. What advantage is there in the earthly things which men possess? That which shall profit them, they have utterly neglected. Ere long, they will awake from their slumber, and find themselves unable to obtain that which hath escaped them in the days of their Lord, the Almighty, the All-Praised. Did they but know it, they would renounce their all, that their names may be mentioned before His throne. They, verily, are accounted among the dead.'[136]

These verses of Bahá'u'lláh should not be misconstrued as escapist otherworldliness. In the Tablet of Ṭarázát Bahá'u'lláh states unambiguously: 'Having attained the stage of fulfilment and reached his maturity, man

134. *Gleanings* 153:8.
135. Bahá'u'lláh, *Gleanings* 123:1–4; compare also 'Abdu'l-Bahá, *Selections*, No.1; Matt. 6:19–21.
136. *Synopsis*, No. 6, p.15 (= Gleanings 70:1).

standeth in need of wealth.'[137] Without a certain amount of material goods man cannot evolve freely in this world. But well-being is not luxury. In this context, too, Bahá'u'lláh counsels that the boundaries of moderation should not be transgressed. He warns against 'laying up riches' and acquiring 'the things that are of no benefit'. The distribution of wealth should be in such a form 'that none among them may either suffer want, or be pampered with luxuries. This is but manifest justice.'[138] Above all, prosperity is not an end in itself. Like poverty, it is transitory. Man should be aware of its relative nature: 'O Son of Man! Should prosperity befall thee, rejoice not, and should abasement come upon thee, grieve not, for both shall pass away and be no more.'[139] The only imperishable thing which man can acquire is his self, the structures of his own person. That is why Bahá'u'lláh says: 'O Son of Spirit! My first counsel is this: Possess a pure, kindly and radiant heart, that thine may be a sovereignty ancient, imperishable and everlasting.'[140] Those whose sole aim is the pursuit of pleasure receive a sharp reprimand: 'Alas! Alas! O lovers of worldly desire! Even as the swiftness of lightning ye have passed by the Beloved One, and have set your hearts on satanic fancies. Ye bow the knee before your vain imagining, and call it truth. Ye turn your eyes towards the thorn, and name it a flower. Not a pure breath have ye breathed, nor hath the breeze of detachment been wafted from the meadows of your hearts. Ye have cast to the winds the loving counsels of the Beloved and have effaced them utterly from the tablet of your hearts, and even as the beasts of the field, ye move and have your being within the pastures of desire and passion.'[141] There are many verses in which Bahá'u'lláh exhorts the faithful to curb and control the passions and desires – which by no means refers only to sexual ones. He castigates a life-style intent only on Mammon and sensuality, and those souls who have 'made a God of' their passions[142] and 'breathe nought but the breath of selfish desire and who lie imprisoned in the cage of their idle fancies': 'Like the bats of darkness, they lift not their heads from their couch except to pursue the transient things of the world, and find no rest by night except as they labour to advance the aims of their sordid life. Immersed in their selfish schemes, they are oblivious of the divine Decree. In the day-time they strive with all their soul after worldly benefits, and in the night-season their sole occupation is to gratify their carnal desires.'[143] There are countless warnings that desirousness may

---

137. 1st Taráz, *Tablets*, p.35. The verses of Bahá'u'lláh, *Gleanings* 128:4 and of the Báb, *Kitáb-i-Asmá'* 16:14 (*Selections*, p.149), show that it is not an ascetic flight from the world which is required; cf. also the explanations on pp.233ff.
138. Tablet to Sultán 'Abdu'l-'Azíz (= *Gleanings* 114:9).
139. Bahá'u'lláh, *The Hidden Words*, Arabic 52.
140. *The Hidden Words*, Arabic 1.
141. *The Hidden Words*, Persian 45.
142. Qur'án 45:22.
143. Bahá'u'lláh, *Kitáb-i-Íqán*, p.225.

estrange man from the purpose of his existence: 'God grant that your desires and unmortified passions may not hinder you from that which hath been ordained for you.'[144] 'Suffer not the habitation wherein dwelleth My undying love for thee to be destroyed through the tyranny of covetous desires . . . Obstruct not the luminous spring of thy soul with the thorns and brambles of vain and inordinate affections[145] . . . Deliver yourselves from your evil and corrupt affections[146] . . . How great, how very great, the gulf that separateth Us from them who, in this Day, are occupied with their evil passions, and have set their hopes on the things of the earth and its fleeting glory[147] . . . They that follow their lusts and corrupt inclinations, have erred and dissipated their efforts. They, indeed, are of the lost.'[148]

Bahá'u'lláh pities those who are content with what is 'like the vapour in a plain' and who are 'willing to forego the Ocean whose waters refresh, by virtue of the Will of God, the souls of men[149] . . . They drink of the tainted water, and know it not . . . They hasten forward to Hell Fire, and mistake it for light.'[150] One of Bahá'u'lláh's recurrent themes is the assurance that men would be delivered from their worldliness and turn to the divine commandments if only they knew the purpose for which they were created: 'Were the mysteries, that are known to none except God, to be unravelled, the whole of mankind would witness the evidences of perfect and consummate justice. With a certitude that none can question, all men would cleave to His commandments, and would scrupulously observe them. We, verily, have decreed in Our Book a goodly and bountiful reward to whosoever will turn away from wickedness and lead a chaste and godly life. He, in truth, is the Great Giver, the All-Bountiful.'[151]

Since modern man's hedonistic, materialistic way of life and the autonomy to which he aspires, together with the dismantling of traditional morality which has already taken place, are most clearly demonstrated in sexuality, we will look now at Bahá'u'lláh's sexual ethics, although it should already be quite clear from the previous passages what this implies: a retreat from 'emancipation' to control by means of standards. It is all the more essential to discuss these questions because, as chapter 12 describes, chastity[152] is one of Bahá'u'lláh's catalogue of virtues and none of the traditional virtues has been so corrupted, deformed and abused, none of the old virtues has become so alien to modern man or such an intolerable

144. Bahá'u'lláh, *Gleanings* 147:2.
145. Bahá'u'lláh, *Gleanings* 153:1.
146. Bahá'u'lláh, *Gleanings* 153:4.
147. Bahá'u'lláh, *Gleanings* 100:2.
148. Bahá'u'lláh, *Gleanings* 136:6; see also Kalimát-i-Firdawsíyyih, 9th Leaf, *Tablets*, p.70.
149. *Gleanings* 135:6.
150. *Gleanings* 17:4.
151. Bahá'u'lláh, *Gleanings* 59:5.
152. On this whole theme see also Rúḥíyyih Rabbaní, *Prescription for Living*, pp.61–72.

imposition as this virtue of chastity. Now almost gone from linguistic usage, it gives rise at best to an indulgent smile, if not to outright mockery or biting sarcasm. Nowadays many people regard unbridled sexuality as a part of self-realization and are convinced that to be chaste is to have a frustrated sex life.

This crude rejection of a value which was for centuries central to Christian morality is the result of its over-emphasis and exaggeration by the fanatical enemies of the body, headed by the Apostle Paul, who wrote: 'It is good for a man not to touch a woman' [153] and to whom marriage was no more than permissible fornication. [154] The fear of sex came into the Church through him and all later fanatics – Clement of Alexandria, who castrated himself, Cyprian, Tertullian of Carthage, Jerome, Ambrose and above all Augustine, who called for married couples to have joyless intercourse for the sake of reproduction. Deliberate celibacy and virginity were recognized by the Church as superior to marriage and from the third century on, the precept of charity has been pushed into the background by that of chastity, which became the quintessence of morality. [155] From then on, sin started below the belt.

This contempt for the body, identifying the sinful nature of man with his sensuality and glorifying life-long continence and virginity as first-class Christianity, had appalling historical consequences. [156] It put man at odds with himself and led to a state of affairs where, as Nietzsche judged: 'It is highly probable that for whole centuries Christians generated children with a bad conscience.' [157] The contraction of the natural basis in Christianity, the suspicion cast on the 'natural inclinations' and the defamation of Eros which has become the trauma of a whole civilization were the subject of emotional attack by Nietzsche[158] and criticism by Berdyayev,[159] even before Freud and his followers began to pillory ecclesiastical sexual mor-

---

153. I Cor. 7:1ff.

154. I Cor. 7:2–6.

155. Schaefer, *The Light Shineth in Darkness*, pp.73–5.

156. The bottled-up sensuality of the unmarried was terribly discharged in the witch-hunting which continued from the end of the Middle Ages until the Enlightenment in the eighteenth century in Europe and also raged through puritanical America in the seventeenth century. The worst caricature of chastity, Victorian prudery, led to such excrescences as the draping of table legs because they were supposed to arouse associations with male genitals.

157. *Human – All-too-Human*, Vol.I, No.141, p.144.

158. 'Christianity gave Eros poison to drink – he did not die of it, to be sure, but degenerated into vice.' (*Beyond Good and Evil*, No.168.)

159. He accused the Church of having condemned Christians to live in a state of inner disunity and in constant conflict with themselves. Man could not bear this merciless rigidity (according to Franz Arnold, 'Sinnlichkeit und Sexualität im Lichte von Theologie und Seelsorge' (Sensuality and sexuality in the light of theology and spiritual ministry), in *Beiträge zur Sexualforschung*, published by H. Bürger-Prinz and H. Giese, No. 1, 1952). Other literature: Herbert Preisker, 'Christentum und Ehe in den ersten drei Jahrhunderten', (Christianity and marriage in the first three centuries A.D.) in *Studien zur Geschichte der Theologie und der Kirchen*, published by Reinhold Seeberg, Berlin 1927; Walter Schubart, *Religion und Eros* (Religion and Eros), published by Friedrich Seifert, Munich 1941.

ality. And we can still trace the effects of the zealously exaggerated concept of chastity even today, in the dialectical reversal to the opposite extreme and in the emotive negation of the applicability of religion to sexuality.

Bahá'u'lláh's precept of chastity in no way implies a return to the anti-sexual tendencies which cast their shadow over Christianity for so long. As in Judaism and Islám,[160] so in the Bahá'í Faith chastity is not a denial of the natural inclinations of man, nor a defamation of his sexuality. For the goal is not to suppress the instincts but to discipline, channel, guide and religiously sublimate man's procreative power and capacity for love in order to elevate the personality into higher forms of love. The dependence of the human sexual drive, which by its very nature is chaotic like all other drives, on guidance and cultivation corresponds with the anthropological recognition that whereas animal sexuality operates and is triggered instinctively, the characteristic of human sexuality is a far-reaching reduction of instinct, an excessive sex drive and the fact that sensual lust can be detached from breeding purposes. Man possesses an excessive sex drive and manifests sexual behaviour which is not controlled by the safety valve of instinct as is the case with animals. These two together constitute a biological danger to human sexuality which has a propensity towards uncontrolled promiscuity. Man has escaped from the total compulsion of instincts. This means a gain in freedom but also the loss of the automatic security provided by the functionalism of the instincts. Nevertheless, his cultural opportunity is also to be found here: 'Since man has escaped from the compulsion of dependence on the environment and the rigidity of instinct, he can and must have control over his urges in conscious action . . . The

---

160. The Islámic traditional collection by Muslim (published and translated into English by 'Abdu'l Ḥamíd Ṣiddíqí, New Delhi, 1977–8) is an impressive explanation of how, despite the strictness of its sexual ethics, Islám recognizes the individual value of the vital sphere of man. The Kitáb al-Haid (Ch. CXIX–CXXVII) contained in this collection and the Kitáb al-Nikah (Ch. DLVI–DLXIII) clearly reveal how the faithful asked the prophet's advice on the ultimate details of intimate life, and received it. In the commentary on Ch. CXXIV of the Kitáb al-Haid, No. 512 states: 'It is one of the greatest contributions of Islam to human morality that it has illuminated the carnal desire of man with the glow of spirituality and religious piety. The idea behind ablution is that even sexual intercourse (a sensual act) should be performed with the decency of a spiritual life and not like beasts and animals.' In the commentary on Ch. DXXXIX, No. 1840 states: 'Islam does not believe in the absolute suppression of the sensual side of human nature. The conception of the saintly life in Islam is not, therefore, the extermination of all carnal impulses, but to control them and keep them within the proper limits. Islam does not make the life of an individual completely dark and dreary, devoid of all enjoyment of life, Islam encourages healthy enjoyments and one out of these is the satisfaction of the sexual desire. Islam does not associate the idea of sexual pleasure with that of sin and vice. Pleasure gives strength to the moral side of a man provided one does not transgress the limits of ethical codes.' Ch. DLV and DLVI state: 'This ḥadíth also shows how close did the Prophet's Companions (both men and women) feel towards his august personality and how frankly they looked to his help and guidance in all affairs of life. This ḥadíth is quite significant in the sense that it shows how Islam permeates and diffuses God-consciousness and piety even in those activities of life which are generally looked down upon by other religions as mundane activities of life. The sexual act is considered as an act much below the high level of religious piety or as one which undermines God-consciousness and makes man the slave of his base desires. Islam is opposed to such a view. There is nothing profane in Islam.'

cultural sublimation of sexual drives is certainly just as much one of the
original civilized achievements and existential requirements of man as tools
and speech, indeed there is nothing to contradict the idea that the primary
social form of all human behaviour can be seen in this regulation of man's
sexual and reproductive relations.'[161]

So in the Bahá'í Faith chastity does not mean joyless intercourse on
behalf of procreation, as recommended by St. Augustine, or actual renunciation of sexual activity, but the rigorous monopolization of all sexual relations by marriage, involving renunciation of pre-marital and extra-marital
intimacy. In spite of their strictness, which they share with all the moral
systems of the world religions, Bahá'u'lláh's sexual ethics are in no way
hostile to the senses, as is shown by the paramount position given to marriage by Bahá'u'lláh. Far from being 'permitted fornication', a *remedium
peccati* (Luther), it is a divinely ordained way of life: 'Enter into wedlock,
O people, that ye may bring forth one who will make mention of Me.'[162]
Bahá'u'lláh expressly forbade priestly celibacy.[163] In the Kalimát-i-
Firdawsíyyih Bahá'u'lláh revealed: 'O people of the earth! Living in seclusion or practising asceticism is not acceptable in the presence of God. It
behoveth them that are endued with insight and understanding to observe
that which will cause joy and radiance. Such practices as are sprung from
the loins of idle fancy or are begotten of the womb of superstition ill
beseem men of knowledge.'[164]

But Bahá'u'lláh condemns not only man's desire for the riches of this
world and the satisfaction of his lusts, but the whole life-style of modern
man. Since his life no longer has a goal or a purpose, because he is constantly fleeing from himself, man is constantly forced to invent fresh
distractions in order to escape from satiety and not die of boredom, and
these distractions are of the crudest and most tedious kind. Today's masses
still want bread and circuses – *'panem et circenses'*[165] just as they did in
Ancient Rome. The importance of show business and commercialized sport
(especially football and boxing)[166] in our society, the leisure and holiday
structure of today, mass tourism, the hollow chumminess of beer and wine
drinking or card-playing or at the pop gigs and discothèques, gossip col-
umns, comics and other ways of killing time are the expression of a completely non-spiritual, superficial life-style aimed at diversion,[167] which

---

161. Helmut Schelsky, *Soziologie der Sexualität*, p.12.
162. Bahá'u'lláh, Kitáb-i-Aqdas (*Synopsis*, No. 12, p.17).
163. *Epistle to the Son of the Wolf*, pp.49ff.; Bishárát, eighth Glad-Tidings, *Tablets*, p.24. See also
Qur'án 57:27.
164. Tenth leaf, *Tablets*, p.71.
165. Juvenal (A.D. 60–140), *Satires*, X, 81.
166. 'Les hommes s'occupent à suivre une balle et un lièvre; c'est le plaisir même des rois.' (B.
Pascal, *Pensées*, 76.)

keeps man from what is essential and stops him from doing what he should be doing: achieving self-knowledge and studying to perfect his personality, working for the well-being of his neighbour, of society and of humanity as a whole and seeking spiritual treasures. What a transformation it would be in men's lives if they would only begin to be guided by the verses of Bahá'u'lláh: 'Man's merit lieth in service and virtue and not in the pageantry of wealth and riches. Take heed that your words be purged from idle fancies and worldly desires and your deeds be cleansed from craftiness and suspicion. Dissipate not the wealth of your precious lives in the pursuit of evil and corrupt affection, nor let your endeavours be spent in promoting your personal interest. Be generous in your days of plenty, and be patient in the hour of loss. Adversity is followed by success and rejoicings follow woe. Guard against idleness and sloth, and cling unto that which profiteth mankind, whether young or old, whether high or low.'[168]

On Hostility to the Law

The disintegration of traditional values has led to a crisis of law. The self-estimation of the law as a constitutional structure of norms sanctioned by the State, oriented towards the idea of justice and binding on social co-existence, has been shattered. Not only because the Utopia of a society without law, authority and domination, anarchic socialism, is finding more and more supporters in a number of countries,[169] but to Marxist thinking as well, the law is simply a means of power and suppression by the ruling class, which will decline in the classless society, vanish altogether and give way to a mere 'administration of goods'. According to the Marxist doctrine of the 'withering away of the law', it is not only the contents but the form itself of the law which is destined to decline:[170] 'Justice is only the ideological reflection of the market with its *do ut des*, destined to disappear with the individualist market economy.'[171] The attitude of sociology

167. 'La seule chose qui nous console de nos misères est le divertissement, et cependant c'est la plus grande de nos misères. Car c'est cela qui nous empêche principalment de songer à nous, et qui nous fait perdre insensiblement. Sans cela, nous serions dans l'ennui, et cet ennui nous pousserait à chercher un moyen plus solide d'en sortir. Mais le divertissement nous amuse, et nous fait arriver insensiblement à la mort.' (B. Pascal, *Pensées*, 128.) This is even more true of our modern society 'in which people have no idea how to occupy themselves other than to keep themselves relatively happy by the means of affluence, which is a kind of gratifying substitute for real existence. At all costs, even if thereby the sense of purpose is annihilated, our society seeks distraction and escape. It is hysterically afraid of the passage of time and terrified by the thought of death.' (Heinz Friedrich, *Kulturkatastrophe*, pp.278–9.)
168. Lawḥ-i-Ḥikmat, *Tablets*, p.138.
169. The centres of our intellectual life, the European universities, have become breeding grounds for anarchistic machinations. The slogans smeared on walls appeal for sedition and resistance against the state and are the same from country to country; everywhere a blatant 'A' in a black circle is the international symbol of anarchy.
170. Gustav Radbruch, *Legal Philosophy*, p.122.
171. ibid.

too, and with it peace research, to the law is a critical one at the least. The law is interpreted predominantly in the sense of the political slogan 'the ruling law is the law of the rulers', in order to pillory and oppose the injustice of the existing legal order. 'Law and order', fine and desirable in itself, has been degraded into a political slogan. It is true that as guarantor of existing social structures, the law can help to preserve and petrify intolerable social conditions. But it is scarcely accepted any more that the law can at the same time be the 'universal means of non-violent social change'.[172]

It is clear that the bastions of the law crumbled long ago. With Martin Luther, Protestantism as a whole has had a peculiarly disturbed relationship to earthly law as the foundation and form of social life. For Luther the law is simply a 'makeshift', a 'temporal government'.[173] Law as exclusively a dimension of the temporal world is a consequence of the evangelical doctrine of justification – man achieves salvation *sola fide*. Justice has no place in the catalogue of virtues of Protestantism, as Luther's well-known saying shows: 'Lawyers are the enemies of Christ, as one says: "a lawyer, a bad Christian", for he lauds and praises the justice of works, as if they made one just and blessed before God.'[174] The low estimation of justice in Protestantism, the recourse to the freedom of Christians and the one-sided emphasis on love, the evangelical antinomian element was a rich breeding ground for the dissemination of anarchical ideas. From the proclamation of freedom from the law in the religious and theological field it is not far to scepticism towards the law and finally its rejection and defamation as the tool of social repression. In this connection Schelsky aptly remarks: 'The Christian rejection of the world is reproduced as a socio-religious[175] rejection of the existing political and legal order.'[176] In our secular codex of values the genuinely Christian values of love, mercy and pity have become blurred into the diffuse value of humanitarianism,[177] while the idea of justice continues to lead a shadowy existence as protest against the injustice of conditions.

This peculiar shift of emphasis in the value structure is a significant one, which shatters the very foundations of society. While 'the love of many shall wax cold',[178] the central value of justice has lost its place in the world

---

172. Helmut Schelsky, *Die Arbeit tun die anderen*, p.392.
173. *Temporal Authority: To what extent it should be obeyed* (1523).
174. *Table Talks*, 4, 4915.
175. In the sense of the comments on pp.10ff.
176. *Die Arbeit tun die anderen*, p.409.
177. As penal law, above all, shows (see details on p.183), Helmut Schelsky indicates that with the altered concept of man, the concept of 'humanity' has also changed: '"human" and "social" are increasingly becoming a conceptual unity and "humanity" is actually only practised now in social measures or front-line situations . . . It is always worthwhile to ask in a critical sense who at any time is *not* allowed to be made an object of humanity.' (*Die Arbeit tun die anderen*, p.381.)
178. According to Matt. 24:12, a sign of the end.

of order. Love has infiltrated the dwelling place of justice. Love has its rightful place in the life of the individual and in personal relationships,[179] but it is presently being misapplied in the sphere of social order.[180] Perhaps, having been unchained from its metaphysical anchor, nothing has so greatly shaken our order of values as this process.

Bahá'u'lláh has described this decline of the law: 'The light of Justice is dimmed, and the sun of Equity veiled from sight[181] . . . Justice is in this day bewailing its plight, and Equity groaneth beneath the yoke of oppression[182] . . . Equity is rarely to be found, and justice hath ceased to exist.'[183] 'In these days the tabernacle of justice hath fallen into the clutches of tyranny and oppression. Beseech ye the One true God . . . not to deprive mankind of the ocean of true understanding, for were men but to take heed they would readily appreciate that whatever hath streamed from and is set down by the Pen of Glory is even as the sun for the whole world and that therein lie the welfare, security and true interests of all men; otherwise the earth will be tormented by a fresh calamity every day and unprecedented commotions will break out.'[184]

Bahá'u'lláh's absolute repudiation of anarchical tendencies is demonstrated by the fact that in his catalogue of virtues justice takes first place: 'The best beloved of all things in My sight is Justice',[185] as he says in *The Hidden Words*. In another place Bahá'u'lláh stresses 'that equity is the most fundamental among human virtues[186] . . . The essence of all that We have revealed for thee is Justice.'[187]

The praises of justice abound everywhere in Bahá'u'lláh's writings: 'No light can compare with the light of justice. The establishment of order in the world and the tranquillity of the nations depend upon it.'[188] It serves the highest good of this earthly life, of unity and peace: 'The light of men is justice. Quench it not with the contrary winds of oppression and tyranny.

---

179. For a thorough and outstanding investigation of the relationship between love and justice, see Emil Brunner, *Justice and the Social Order*, ch. 15, pp.125–30, also my dissertation *Die Grundlagen der Verwaltungsordnung der Bahá'í*, pp.45–8.

180. Here is a particularly crude example. An offender who has been fined receives, as it might be in Frankfurt-am-Main, the necessary funds to pay the fine from the municipal social welfare office in order to avoid serving the term of imprisonment for failure to pay. The penalty exists only on paper. The State as it were punishes itself, moving the expiatory money from one pocket to the other.

181. Iṣhráqát, *Tablets*, pp.124–5.

182. Lawḥ-i-Dunyá, *Tablets*, p.84 (= *Gleanings* 43:2).

183. *Epistle to the Son of the Wolf*, p.131.

184. Lawḥ-i-Maqṣúd, *Tablets*, p.166.

185. Arabic No.2.

186. *Gleanings* 100:6. Schopenhauer also saw justice as 'the first and original cardinal virtue' (*The Basis of Morality*, Part III, ch. III, p.155; on the theme as a whole see also ch. VI, pp.176–97).

187. Aṣl-i-Kullu'l-Khayr, *Tablets*, p.157.

188. *Epistle to the Son of the Wolf*, pp.28–9.

189. Bahá'u'lláh, Kalimát-i-Firdawsíyyih, *Tablets*, p.67.

The purpose of justice is the appearance of unity among men.'[189] Because justice is the basis of peace it should also be the virtue of rulers: 'Take heed, O concourse of the rulers of the world! There is no force on earth that can equal in its conquering power the force of justice and wisdom . . . Blessed is the king who marcheth with the ensign of wisdom unfurled before him, and the battalions of justice massed in his rear. He verily is the ornament that adorneth the brow of peace and the countenance of security.'[190]

Bahá'u'lláh confirms the tenet *Iustitia fundamentum regnorum*: 'The Great Being saith: The structure of world stability and order hath been reared upon, and will continue to be sustained by, the twin pillars of reward and punishment . . . Justice hath a mighty force at its command. It is none other than reward and punishment for the deeds of men. By the power of this force the tabernacle of order is established throughout the world, causing the wicked to restrain their natures for fear of punishment.'[191] In the Bishárát it is revealed: 'That which traineth the world is Justice, for it is upheld by two pillars, reward and punishment. These two pillars are the sources of life to the world.'[192]

Bahá'u'lláh is making it clear that justice, the law, and not merciful love secularized into humanism is the foundation of social order. 'Abdu'l-Bahá has expressed this idea in more detail: 'The tent of existence is upheld upon the pillar of justice and not upon forgiveness. The continuance of mankind depends upon justice and not upon forgiveness . . . Then what Christ meant by forgiveness and pardon is not that, when nations attack you, burn your homes, plunder your goods . . . you should . . . allow them to perform all their cruelties and oppressions. No, the words of Christ refer to the conduct of two individuals towards one another: if one person assaults another, the injured one should forgive him. But the communities must protect the rights of man.'[193] 'Abdu'l-Bahá summons believers to mercy: 'Strive ye then with all your heart to treat compassionately all humankind',[194] but also shows where the limits of mercy lie: 'Kindness cannot be shown the tyrant, the deceiver, or the thief, because, far from awakening them to the error of their ways, it maketh them to continue in their perversity as before. No matter how much kindliness ye may expend upon the liar, he will but lie the more, for he believeth you to be deceived, while ye understand him but too well, and only remain silent out of your extreme compassion.'[195] It is apparent here that the Bahá'í ethic is not one

190. Bahá'u'lláh, *Gleanings* 112.
191. Lawh-i-Maqsúd, *Tablets* p.164 (= Gleanings 112).
192. The thirteenth Glad-Tidings, *Tablets*, p.27; compare also Ishráqát, the third and eighth Ishráq, *Tablets*, pp.126, 129; Kalimát-i-Firdawsíyyih, 6th Leaf, *Tablets*, p.66.
193. *Some Answered Questions*, ch. 77, pp.270–71.
194. Here too, as with all virtues, the principle of moderation applies. Mercy, when practised to excess, is sentimental and destructive to society (compare p.219).
195. *Selections*, No.138.

of 'idealistic enthusiasm', but an ethic which can be realized practically in this world, a guideline for daily conduct. 'Abdu'l-Bahá Himself, who also warns us elsewhere to act 'with caution and prudence',[196] 'treads the mystical way with practical feet'.[197]

Against the Abolition of the Penal Code

The statements above necessitate a comment on punishment by the State and the ideas and theories now prevalent on this subject.[198] In an intact society the penal law is the ultimate remedy in effecting the protection of legal property. It is the *ultima ratio*, punishing offences harmful to society when all other controlling structures are unable to prevent it. The penal law has to rely on systems of control outside the law, which guarantee social peace in important areas of life. These are, in the first place, religion; and corollary to this, the norms of morality; conscience; the family, as the most important social factor in socialization; and besides these the social environment, such as school, neighbourhood, community. This web of conduct regulators, when intact, as a rule protects a person from breaking the law and committing what in normal circumstances is generally shunned and redounds to his discredit: a criminal act.

These control mechanisms encompassing penal law no longer operate. Religion has lost its determining force and, as we said at the beginning, is losing more and more of its stabilizing effect on society. Following the disintegration of our value order, caused by this and the decline of morality, the remaining control systems on which penal law depends were dismantled in the modern industrial society: 'The growing urbanization and concomitant anonymization of our life and increasing mobility go hand in hand with an increasing loss in the significance of pre-emptive conduct regulators such as custom, usage, morality and naturally also religion. The far-reaching loss of function of the family as a socialization factor and instrument of primary control, above all, is estimated to be particularly distressing here.'[199] At the same time the need for social regulation is increasing, consequent upon the escalation in the numbers of conflicts. This gives penal law the function of a positive 'fire-fighting service'. It must take the place of the no longer operative extra-legal control systems and ensure social peace on its own, and it is not up to this demand. It is of

196. *Will and Testament*, p.25. Bahá'u'lláh counsels to act 'with tact and wisdom' (Lawḥ-i-Maqṣúd, *Tablets*, p.172). Compare also Matt. 10:16: 'Behold, I send you forth as sheep in the midst of wolves: be ye therefore wise as serpents, and harmless as doves.'

197. ''Abdu'l-Bahá's whole life contradicted this assumption that He was a visionary, an impractical idealist. When He addressed the student body at Leland Stanford University, He was introduced by its president, David Starr Jordan, in these words: "''Abdu'l-Bahá will surely unite the East and the West for He treads the mystical way with practical feet.'' ' (Howard C. Ives, *Portals to Freedom*, p.242.)

198. Compare pp.49–54.

199. Walter Hauptmann, 'Was lässt die Kriminologie vom Strafrecht über?', in *Kriminalistik, Zeitschrift für die gesamte Kriminalwissenschaft*, No. 1, 1980, p.22.

course well able to supplement social control, but certainly not to replace it: '*Quid leges sine moribus vanae proficiunt?*'[200] Because it is unable to fulfil this expectation many no longer see any sense in it and, as we have described, call for the complete removal of the whole system, without of course being able to offer an acceptable alternative. Thus the certain expectation that the world will continue to be humanized and that crime, as the fruit of still unresolved conditions, will die out with this growing humanization, the idea that the problem of criminality will solve itself with the removal of punishment and the dissolution of prisons,[201] is shown to be becoming more of an illusion from day to day. The epidemic rise in criminality over recent decades and the many and varied symptoms of the re-barbarization of society described earlier on,[202] show that the anarchic impulses of mankind are coming more and more unrestrainedly to the fore, thanks to the dismantling of the control mechanisms.

Besides this, the Western nations are displaying an increasing tendency towards gentleness, humanity, understanding and sympathy in their penal sanctions. The idea of re-socialization as the purpose of punishment is now overwhelmingly prevalent and has displaced all other purposes: atonement, compensation for guilt, deterrence. Even Catholic moral theology, bound for so many centuries to the idea of atonement and absolute penal goals – *punitur quia peccatum est* – is now in favour of a fundamental revision of the penal system. In place of guilt and atonement the principle of 'reconciliation' should be given first place.[203] More and more doubts are arising as to the purpose and justification of punishment. Hans-Joachim Schneider proposes replacement of the penal process by a 'process of compensation and mediation' in which judge, prosecuting and defending counsel, accused, victim and experts attempt to settle the dispute by agreement. In his opinion, treatment in freedom will be the normal reaction to criminality in the future: 'The age of penal law is coming to an end because – even in its modern form – it is unable to assist in the elimination of the personal and social disintegration from which criminality proceeds.'[204]

Yet it is the devastating experience of the 'progressive' penal system in Sweden which has shown that the widespread hopes for the re-socialization of offenders have not been fulfilled. Despite the most generous equipment of prisons, the most liberal leave regulations and unsupervised visits with the opportunity for sexual contact, recidivism has been high and crimi-

200. Horace, *Odes*.

201. Compare p.52.

202. Compare pp.57ff.

203. 'Punitive measures must increasingly be reduced in favour of measures of reconciliation.' (W. Molinsky at the International Congress of German Moral Theologians in Munich, 1979; quoted by the *Süddeutsche Zeitung* of 24.9.1979.)

204. 'Behandlung in Freiheit', in *Psychologie Heute*, 9 September 1978.

nality has grown enormously, instead of receding as expected. Whereas over the last twenty years Europe has been looking hopefully towards Sweden, which believed it had found the philosopher's stone in the area of criminology, today the disillusioned Swedes are looking 'over the fence, to the outside, to see what other countries do'.[205]

Because in our present social system punishment has lost all metaphysical reference, the idea of atonement has been banished from penal law. Even the purpose of deterrence is increasingly rejected as inhumane. The only penal purpose left is that of re-socialization, re-integration of the offender. Since it is becoming clearer and clearer that this may be possible for young and first-time wrongdoers, but not for men with an ingrained tendency towards criminality,[206] the entire system is rejected. In Sweden, for instance, the only alternative to imprisonment is treatment in freedom, protective custody, supervision of the culprit at liberty. But a fresh disappointment is already making itself felt here: the expected success has not materialized, for very obvious reasons.

Now no one will deny that there were great omissions in the past and that a great deal that is reasonable is being achieved today in the treatment of prisoners before and after their release, in order to re-integrate someone who has done wrong into society and to reduce the danger of recidivism. But when the idea of re-socialization is elevated to the rank of dogma and becomes a myth, when more and more demands are being made for the elimination of imprisonment for life, because in the case of 'life' there would be nothing to re-socialize, when in the course of a tearful understanding with the wrongdoer the victim is more or less forgotten,[207] when the prison sentence has to be reconciled as far as possible with life

205. Quoted by Rudolf Gerhard in *Frankfurter Allgemeine Zeitung* of 19.1.1980. The degree to which the concept of resocialization has been idealized without any regard for justice, so that the process of resocialization turns into a privilege for the offender, is shown in a rehabilitation programme for juvenile delinquents in Sweden. The Swedish authorities for remedial treatment organize adventure journeys to exotic places, for example trips through the Sahara to Ghana and Nigeria. The average, law-abiding, hard-working citizen would never be able to afford such holidays. The community of Västeras in central Sweden has arranged for a 16-year-old, drug-addicted schoolboy to spend two years on the Caribbean island of St. Vincent so that he could cure himself of his addiction. For this the community pays 15,000 Kronen per year, i.e. about 75,000 dollars for the two years. (*Süddeutsche Zeitung*, 12.3.1982.)

206. 'Abdu'l-Bahá points out the salient importance of the education of children: mothers should 'put forth every effort in this regard, for when the bough is green and tender it will grow in whatever way ye train it. Therefore is it incumbent upon the mothers to rear their little ones even as a gardener tendeth his young plants.' (*Selections*, No.95.) Rehabilitation of habitual adult criminals is like trying to straighten a crooked full-grown tree – a fruitless enterprise!

207. Compare the contribution in *Der Spiegel*, 1979, No. 42, pp.38–57, where a leading official of the Baden-Württemberg Ministry for the Interior is quoted: 'As soon as the murderer of a taxi driver has been arrested a social worker is sent to him to sort out his personal problems. But the murdered man's wife is left alone with her three children and her problems. No social worker is sent to help her with all the running around to the authorities or to deal with her financial troubles, which only start with the funeral expenses. The first thing *she* is likely to receive is the bill for transporting the corpse from the scene of the crime to the department of forensic medicine.' (pp.49–52.)

outside,[208] when the State deals more and more tenderly and benevolently with the law-breaker, one can scarcely wonder that the new barbarism is stirring with more and more violence, that the crime rate is increasing at greater speed, while on the other hand the call for bloody retribution grows louder, the 'gesunde Volksempfinden'[209] is aroused and cries out for the instant justice of the Vehm[210] Court, and for lynch law. Werner Ross rightly comments: 'Increasing humanity on the part of the State encourages increasing brutality in all those who are indifferent to the civic, Christian norm system.'[211] The State 'cannot deputize by taking upon itself the compassion of his fellow men with the wrongdoer. Its watchword is justice, that is assessment and settlement.'[212]

Bahá'u'lláh has left us in no doubt that punishment is one of the pillars of state order: 'The canopy of world order is upraised upon the two pillars of reward and punishment.'[213] Yet as an inevitable social sanction punishment is simply an external remedy, which is ultimately impotent against the deeper causes of criminality. In the Lawḥ-i-Dunyá Bahá'u'lláh revealed: 'In formulating the principles and laws a part hath been devoted to penalties which form an effective instrument for the security and protection of men. However, dread of the penalties maketh people desist only outwardly from committing vile and contemptible deeds, while that which guardeth and restraineth man both outwardly and inwardly hath been and still is the fear of God. It is man's true protector and his spiritual guardian.'[214]

In this connection 'Abdu'l-Bahá pointed out that harshness leads only to 'destruction of morals and perversion of characters' and the real solution is to be found only in the moral recovery of society. And this recovery is achieved by overcoming the 'ignorance', which 'is the cause of crimes' and the moral education of the masses, so that they do their best 'to acquire virtues, to gain good morals and to avoid vices, so that crimes may not occur.'[215] These utterances by 'Abdu'l-Bahá have little connection with the current endeavours to influence offenders by way of psychological treatment in order to re-integrate them into society. The psychological deformities which lead to criminal acts are character defects, not sicknesses vulnerable to therapy like 'flu or malaria. But character formation demands moral discipline and moral responsibility in relation to an omnipresent authority, which a society in which all that is metaphysical has been

---

208. See Paragraph 3, Strafvollzugsgesetz (Law on Treatment of Prisoners) of 16 March 1976.

209. During the Nazi regime even acts which offended the 'healthy instinct of the people' were made punishable, and thus the principle *nullum crimen, nulla poena sine lege* abrogated.

210. Medieval German court at which the guilty could be executed on the spot.

211. *Rhein-Neckar-Zeitung*, 20–21.5.1978.

212. Werner Ross, op. cit.

213. Ishráqát, 3rd Ishráq, *Tablets*, p.126.

214. *Tablets*, p.93.

215. *Some Answered Questions*, ch.77, pp.272,271.

swept aside cannot provide. 'Abdu'l-Bahá has referred in this connection to the difference between our current, materialistic civilization and the coming, divine civilization: 'Material civilization, through the power of punitive and retaliatory laws, restraineth the people from criminal acts; and notwithstanding this, while laws to retaliate against and punish a man are continually proliferating, as ye can see, no laws exist to reward him . . . Divine civilization, however, so traineth every member of society that no one, with the exception of a negligible few, will undertake to commit a crime. There is thus a great difference between the prevention of crime through measures that are violent and retaliatory, and so training the people, and enlightening them, and spiritualizing them, that without any fear of punishment or vengeance to come, they will shun all criminal acts. They will, indeed, look upon the very commission of a crime as a great disgrace and in itself the harshest of punishments. They will become enamoured of human perfections, and will consecrate their lives to whatever will bring light to the world and will further those qualities which are acceptable at the Holy Threshold of God.'[216] This is the sense of 'Abdu'l-Bahá's advice to think more 'of preventing crimes, rather than of rigorously punishing them.'[217] But it is proper at all times to find the right proportion between kindness and strictness. This, however, is a function of dispensing and compensating justice.[218]

Law, justice and order are accordingly the foundations of Bahá'u'lláh's kingdom of peace, of the 'Most Great Peace'. The coming kingdom of justice and peace is not the Utopia of an ungoverned society but a common system based on cogent legal norms and institutions exercising authority. A divinely founded commonwealth, indeed, in which the age-old conflict between freedom and order has found its optimal solution.[219]

---

216. *Selections*, No. 105.

217. *Some Answered Questions*, ch.77, p.272.

218. In the Islámic view the penalty imposed and served has a metaphysical, expiatory effect on the lawbreaker: 'But in this law of retaliation is your security for Life, O men of understanding!' as the Qur'án (2:175) has it; and in the collection of traditions by Tirmédhi, Nawádir'ul Usúl (Constantinople, undated, photomechanical impression by Dar Sadir Publ., Beirut, p.138) there is a hadíth by the Prophet Muhammad according to which God will not impose a second punishment on him who 'has committed a sin and been punished in this world' – a type of metaphysical *Ne bis in idem* principle which must of course be seen in the context of the penal provisions of the Qur'án, which being divine law, were the quintessence of justice. Only just punishment has the liberating effect.

The principle contained in this hadíth is confirmed by an utterance of 'Abdu'l-Bahá in which the expiatory character of punishment is quite clearly expressed: 'As to the question regarding the soul of a murderer, and what his punishment would be. The answer given was that the murderer must expiate his crime: that is, if they put the murderer to death, his death is his atonement for his crime, and following the death, God in his justice will impose no second penalty upon him, for divine justice would not allow this.' (*Selections*, No. 152.) The Kitáb-i-Aqdas gives life imprisonment as an alternative to capital punishment in the cases of murder and arson.

219. See also p.244. There are many Christian theologians who expect the Messianic Kingdom of God as a kingdom of absolute freedom from government like the Catholic Josef Blank (*Die Ethik Jesu*, p.176). However, this is a sentimental notion which does not take the Kingdom of God seriously as an

The Divine Law

Another word about the Bahá'í understanding of the law.[220] The constitutive defining principle of the Bahá'í Faith is that of the Covenant, familiar to us from the Old Testament.[221] The symbol of God's promises of salvation handed down over the centuries is the rainbow.[222] It is an ethereal image formed by the play of beams of light in drops of water, almost beyond the material, and hence a symbol of the divine stretching into the earthly world, not to be grasped by our hands, but visible to the human eye. The idea of the Covenant expresses the mutuality of the relationship between God and man. God loves 'the one that turneth towards him':[223] 'Love Me, that I may love thee. If thou lovest Me not, My love can in no wise reach thee.'[224] The belief, the recognition of God must be followed by the execution of the divine will manifested in the law: 'But believers and doers of good works, for them is mercy, and a great reward.'[225] Execution of the law without inner submission, good works without faith do not lead to redemption.[226] Faith without works is empty, for it is the 'essence of faith' to show an 'abundance of deeds'.[227]

Now as everyone knows, even the believing and God-fearing man often falls short of the demands of the law. He falls into sin and becomes guilty. But the redemptive power of the divine law cannot be reduced by this fact to absurdity.[228] For there is one thing that a man who has done wrong can always perform: *metanoia*, turning round. And the man who turns will find comfort in the verse: 'One gleam from the splendours of Thy Name, the All-Merciful, sufficeth to banish and blot every trace of sinfulness from the world, and a single breath from the breezes of the Day of Thy Revela-

immanent dimension. According to the Jewish faith the Messianic realm of peace is a realm of law and justice: 'And the work of righteousness shall be peace' (Isa. 32:17). According to Islámic tradition too, the promised Mahdi will 'fill the world with justice, as it is filled with injustice' (Ignaz Goldziher, *Vorlesungen über den Islam*, p.221) and found a theocratic rule. A system of justice without government is a *contradictio in adiecto*, for law and justice must necessarily be based on a society structured by rule.

220. On the subject as a whole, Schaefer, *The Light Shineth in Darkness*, pp.93–100.

221. Hebrew 'berith', in the Septuagint Greek 'diatheke', was translated by Luther as 'covenant' or 'testament'. Compare Gen. 6:18; 9:8–17; 15:18; 17:1–9; 19; Deut.5:1–3; 1 Chr.16:15–25; Ps.105:9–10; Acts 3:25; Qur'án 2:111–23; 4:59–82; the Báb, Qayyúmu'l-Asmá', ch.91 (*Selections*, p.68).

222. Compare Gen. 9:13–15.

223. Bahá'u'lláh, *Gleanings* 134:3.

224. Bahá'u'lláh, *The Hidden Words*, Arabic No.5; compare Zech. 1:3 and Mal. 3:7.

225. Qur'án 35:8.

226. Compare 'Abdu'l-Bahá, *Some Answered Questions*, chs.65 and 84.

227. Bahá'u'lláh, Aṣl-i-Kullu'l-Khayr, *Tablets*, p.156.

228. As both Paul and the Protestant theology based on him would have (Rom. 7:18ff.; Gal. 2:16), although the O.T. states tersely 'Sin lieth at the door. And unto thee shall be his desire; and thou shalt rule over him.' (Gen. 4:7.)

tion is enough to adorn all mankind with a fresh attire.'[229]

Thus the receipt of God's grace does not take place *sola fide*, through faith alone, but through faith and works. The 'freedom of a Christian'[230] proclaimed by Martin Luther is not the freedom of the Bahá'í, which is primarily bound up with God through the execution of the law[231] and thereby sanctified, as it says in the Gospel: 'Not every one that saith unto me, Lord, Lord, shall enter into the kingdom of heaven; but he that doeth the will of my Father which is in heaven',[232] and: 'But if thou wilt enter into life, keep the commandments.'[233]

That is why divine law is so highly prized in Bahá'u'lláh's writings. The laws of God are not the expression of a divine arbitrary will to suppress and overpower human nature. They 'are not imposition of will, or of power, or pleasure, but the resolutions of truth, reason and justice'.[234] They are 'the lamps of My loving providence among My servants, and the keys of My mercy for My creatures', the 'highest means for the maintenance of order in the world and the security of its peoples'.[235] That is why true freedom consists 'in man's submission unto My commandments, little as ye know it . . . The liberty that profiteth you is to be found nowhere except in complete servitude unto God, the Eternal Truth. Whoso hath tasted of its sweetness will refuse to barter it for all the dominion of earth and

---

229. Bahá'u'lláh, *Epistle to the Son of the Wolf*, p.10.

230. In his work published under this title in 1520 Luther spoke of the Christian who 'is free from all things and over all things so that he needs no works to make him righteous and save him' (p.356), 'who is justified and saved by faith because of the pure and free mercy of God' (p.360). 'It is clear, then, that a Christian has all that he needs in faith and needs no works to justify him; and if he has no need of works, he has no need of the law; and if he has no need of the law, surely he is free from the law . . . This is that Christian liberty, our faith, which does not induce us to live in idleness or wickedness but makes the law and works unnecessary for any man's righteousness and salvation' (pp.349–50). The extreme nature of Luther's position on this decisive question is shown by his advice to Melanchthon: '*Pecca fortiter, sed fortius fide!*' – despite Jesus's warning that it will not be the man who breaks the Commandments but 'whosoever shall do and teach them' who shall be great in the Kingdom of Heaven (Matt. 5:19) and his unambiguous statement: 'If a man love me, he will keep my words . . . He that loveth me not keepeth not my sayings.' (John 14:23–4.)

231. It is not possible to go into more detail here about the concrete commandments and prohibitions which make up the law of Bahá'u'lláh and which were revealed in the book of laws, the Kitáb-i-Aqdas (see also p.220). 'The two pillars that sustain the revealed Law of God' (Shoghi Effendi, *Bahá'í Procedure*, p.5) are, as far as the individual is concerned, the daily prayer – a ritual obligatory prayer – and fasting. Bahá'í fasting 'is essentially a period of meditation and prayer, of spiritual recuperation, during which the believer must strive to make the necessary readjustments in his inner life, and to refresh and reinvigorate the spiritual forces latent in his soul' (Shoghi Effendi, *Bahá'í Procedure*, p.6). The fasting period is the month ''Alá', which runs from 2–20 March, preceding New Year's Day (Naw-Rúz) on 21 March. In the nature of Islámic fasting, it consists of abstention from food and drink from sunrise to sunset. (See also Grossmann, *Der Bahá'í und die Bahá'í-Gemeinschaft*, pp.73ff.)

232. Matt. 7:21.

233. Matt. 19:17; compare further Matt. 23:2–3; 5:17.

234. 'Abdu'l-Bahá, *Paris Talks*, ch. 47, p.154.

235. Bahá'u'lláh, Kitáb-i-Aqdas, *Synopsis*, No.1, pp.11–12 (= *Gleanings* 155:3,2); see also Kalimát-i-Firdawsíyyih, 9th Leaf, *Tablets*, p.69.

heaven.'[236] The law is a manifestation of the grace of Almighty God who desires to lead man to the true destination of his being: 'Whatever duty Thou hast prescribed unto Thy servants of extolling to the utmost Thy majesty and glory is but a token of Thy grace unto them, that they may be enabled to ascend unto the station conferred upon their own inmost being, the station of the knowledge of their own selves.'[237]

236. Bahá'u'lláh, Kitáb-i-Aqdas, *Synopsis*, No.16, p.25 (= *Gleanings* 159:4).
237. Bahá'u'lláh, *Gleanings* 1:5.

11. The Responsibility of Man

The Question of Death

Man is the only creature that knows he is mortal and that death is the inevitable end of his earthly existence. '*Incerta omnia, sola mors certa*' wrote St. Augustine, and in the medieval hymn of St. Gall there is a line that fittingly describes man's situation: '*Media vita in morte sumus.*' In the midst of life man bears the signs of his own death. Is there any hope for him beyond its barrier?

The answer to the question whether the death of our bodily nature also means the complete destruction of our spiritual reality or progression to another stage of existence depends on our view of life and the answer to the basic question: 'What is man?' Now that God has been declared 'dead', it is modern science and philosophy that determine the popular Weltanschauung.

Scientific thinking tends to reduce man to his biological, chemical and anatomical elements. Accordingly, death is regarded as nothing more than a natural, biological occurrence, the final, irrevocable and absolute end of human existence. Thus for many the question of life after death has become irrelevant. But science can only investigate one aspect of man; it cannot explore his inmost essence. The problem of death cannot be solved by mere reason or scientific research. Empirical studies cannot help us, for experimentation is impossible. Science can only 'anticipate death or follow on its heels. It does not *encounter* death face to face.' [1]

Philosophical thought can make the immortality of man seem probable and understandable and has indeed done so for many centuries. Plato for-

1. Eberhard Jüngel, 'Der Tod als Geheimnis des Lebens', in Ansgar Paus, *Grenzerfahrung Tod*, p.10.

mulated a philosophy of immortality which is still current today: the soul of man is immortal; death is its liberation from the prison of the body. In the modified form given to them by Aristotle, Plato's teachings on immortality were taken up in the theology of Thomas Aquinas. However, philosophers can only speculate on this problem; they cannot know anything about it on the basis of their own experience. Thus a characteristic of modern philosophy is its abstinence from anything metaphysical and its orientation towards a fundamental scepticism.[2] For this kind of thinking the problem of immortality is no longer a subject of philosophical study. Metaphysics have been supplanted by science, and philosophical statements about death may not be made independently of the knowledge obtained by science. In this light the philosopher Walter Kamlah wrote: 'Death is a catastrophe by which a living creature that has lived for a certain time ceases to live for all time, and this catastrophe destroys every living creature, including man, sooner or later.'[3]

Moreover, in view of the 'death of God', it is not surprising that the possibility of life after death has become increasingly irrelevant for people in general. The question of our destiny, the nature and meaning of death, like the question of our origin and the meaning of life, is put to one side and pushed out of our consciousness.[4] Death, that inescapable and decisive event which is part of every man's life, has no place in the thinking of modern man. With the belief in God, the belief in an eternal life also disappeared.[5] Terms such as 'death', 'life after death', the 'hereafter', are considered out of place and disturbing in a time like ours that is hostile to transcendence; they are avoided in conversation.[6] Such questions do not fit into modern secular thinking anymore. Modern man does not want to hear

---

2. According to the philosopher Wilhelm Weischedel all philosophizing must start out from the basic experience of 'radical doubting': 'Everything that presents itself as a certain truth is drawn into this whirlpool. Everything that seems to be certain and sure is made to tumble.' Our age must be seen as the 'age of complete scepticism' (*Skeptische Ethik*, pp.35–9).

3. *Meditatio mortis*, pp.12ff.

4. See Max Scheler, 'Tod und Fortleben' (Death and Life after Death), *Gesammelte Werke*, Vol.X, *Schriften aus dem Nachlaß*, Vol.I, Berne 1957; Georg Scherer, *Das Problem des Todes in der Philosophie*, pp.24ff.

5. Feuerbach describes the connection: 'The belief in personal immortality is perfectly identical with the belief in a personal God . . . The doctrine of immortality is the final doctrine of religion; its testament, in which it declares its last wishes.' (*The Essence of Christianity*, ch.XVIII, pp.171,173.)

6. There seems to be a gradual change on the way. Questions concerning our origin and our destination are being asked more and more clearly as shown by the books published recently (Johannes Hemleben, *Jenseits* (The Hereafter), Hamburg 1975; the volume published by Piper Publishing Company, *Was ist der Tod?* (What is Death?), München 1975; Ansgar Paus (ed.), *Grenzerfahrung Tod* (Death, A Border-line Experience), Suhrkamp-Taschenbuch 430, Frankfurt 1978, contains eleven talks held during the Salzburg University Weeks in 1975; Georg Scherer, *Das Problem des Todes in der Philosophie* (The Problem of Death in Philosophy), Darmstadt 1979; Philippe Ariès, *L'homme devant la mort*, Paris 1977; = *The Hour of Our Death*, New York, Knopf, 1981; Gunther Stephenson (ed.), *Leben und Tod in den Religionen. Symbol und Wirklichkeit* (Life and Death in the Religions. Symbol and Reality), Darmstadt 1980). A further indication of the continuing hunger for immortality is the enormous response aroused by reports of 'out-of-body-experiences' that have been published recently. These are reports from patients who have 'returned' from the condition of clinical

or know anything about death. *Vita brevis*[7] reminds the believer of his transience and of how little time he has in which to act, but the person who lives only for the moment and is unaware of any goal beyond his earthly existence will regard the shortness of life as a justification for living more intensely and enjoying himself to the full, in the way Epicurus expresses it: 'So death . . . is nothing to us, since so long as we exist, death is not with us; but when death comes, then we do not exist',[8] or as expressed in the motto: 'Let us eat and drink; for tomorrow we die',[9] and, 'Après nous le déluge!'[10]

Killing and being killed is an entrenched characteristic of our society and one which is reinforced incessantly in depictions of violence on cinema and television screens; natural death, on the other hand, is made taboo, the thought of death is repressed and the last act which is in store for everyone is banished into the loneliness of sick-rooms,[11] and death (and thus life as well) has no meaning. The question of death is regarded no longer as a philosophical and religious question concerning the immortality of man, but, as 'natural death', is now a scientific and technological question concerning the prolongation of life by rational measures, the preservation of even partial life-processes, humane death, mercy killing and euthanasia, a matter of social politics and medical ethics, and as 'beautiful' death it is a cosmetic task for the undertakers.

And yet there are signs that the question of death cannot be repressed for long without adverse consequences. Fear of death, according to Heidegger, is a basic condition affecting the whole of our life. Psychoanalysis has shown that underlying many neuroses is the fear of death: 'In every neurosis', says the psychotherapist Achim Seidl, 'is hidden a vehement protest . . . against the harsh basic condition of death.'[12] One is inclined to draw the conclusion that the repression of death is one reason for the oft-noted susceptibility of modern man to neuroses. The question arises as to whether man is able to live a meaningful life at all when he eliminates the thought of death from his life. This thought is 'one of the possibilities that enables man to come to grips with himself and to discover the un-

death (Raymond A. Moody, *Life after Life: the Investigation of a Phenomenon, Survival of Bodily Death*, Boston, G. K. Hall, 1977; also: *Reflections on Life after Life*, Harrisburg, Stackpole Books, 1977; Johann Christoph Hampe, *Sterben ist doch ganz anders. Erfahrungen mit dem eigenen Tod* (Dying is Quite Different. Experiences with one's own death), Stuttgart, 1975; Karlis Osis and Erlendur Haraldsson, *At the Hour of Death*, New York, Avon, 1977). Although these reports are extremely interesting they do not constitute conclusive evidence for life after death.

7. Seneca, *De brevitate vitae*.

8. Ep. ad Men. No.125. Similarly the Roman poet Titus Lucretius Carus exclaimed in *De rerum natura* (On the Nature of Things) III, 830: 'Death then to us is nothing and concerns us not a whit.'

9. Isa.22:13; 1 Cor.15:32.

10. Attributed to the Marquise de Pompadour.

11. On the isolation and growing loneliness of dying cf. Elisabeth Kuebler-Ross, 'Menschlich sterben' (Humane Dying) in A. Paus, *Grenzerfahrung Tod*, pp.339ff.

12. *Psychosophie*, p.170. This is also confirmed by Gion Condrau, 'Todesfurcht und

changeable difference between himself and every possible social environment', to realize that 'he does not simply disappear in social structures and relationships'. [13]

Life as Preparation

The darkest of all secrets, death, was always the domain of religion. And even in the holy writings of the revealed religions this mystery has never been fully disclosed. [14] Even so, this is by no means a question of secondary importance. What we think of death determines our lives in a fundamental way. [15] The death of man and his continued existence on another plane of being constitute a central teaching of faith in all religions. Blaise Pascal writes: 'L'immortalité de l'âme est une chose qui nous importe si fort, qui nous touche si profondément, qu'il faut avoir perdu tout sentiment pour être dans l'indifférence de savoir de qui en est. Toutes nos actions et nos pensées doivent prendre des routes si différentes, selon qu'il y aura des biens éternels à espérer ou non, qu'il est impossible de faire une démarche avec sens et jugement, qu'en les réglant par la vue de ce point, qui doit être notre dernier objet.' [16] From quite a different viewpoint Arthur Schopenhauer comes to a similar conclusion: 'There are two points which not only concern every thinking man, but which also the followers of every religion have most at heart, and thus on which the strength and stability of religions rest. They are first the transcendent moral significance of our conduct, and secondly our continued existence after death. If a religion has taken care of these two points, everything else is secondary.' [17]

Like all religions the Bahá'í Faith promises that there will be a life beyond the threshold of death. Even though the Bahá'í Faith is focused on this life, is committed to this world, and has political aims that are manifested in striving to establish a just and humane social order and the unity of mankind, the Bahá'í is constantly aware that this world is only a passage, a preparation for another realm, and that man, as a creature designed to live for all eternity, must acquire in this world the personal structures which he will need in the next.

The human soul is created by God, and after death it returns to Him:

Todessehnsucht' (Fear of Death and Longing for Death), in A. Paus, *Grenzerfahrung Tod*, p.202.

13. Georg Scherer, *Das Problem des Todes in der Philosophie*, pp.18–19.

14. It is not disclosed in the Bahá'í Revelation either: 'The mysteries of man's physical death and of his return have not been divulged, and still remain unread.' (Bahá'u'lláh, *Gleanings* 164:1.)

15. The philosopher Georg Scherer, *Das Problem des Todes in der Philosophie*, p.3, also realizes this.

16. *Pensées*, 11, 898–194 (English edn p.156, see Appendix).

17. *Parerga and Paralipomena*, Vol.I, p.121. To be sure Schopenhauer's verdict is exaggerated. For the Bahá'í 'everything else' is by no means 'secondary': 'The beginning of all things is the knowledge of God.' (Bahá'u'lláh, *Gleanings* 2.) 'Know thou that first and foremost in religion is the knowledge of God.' (The Báb, Dalá'il-i-Sab'íh, *Selections*, p.117.)

'Verily, we are God's, and to Him shall we return.'[18] That the body is a cage and life a condition of suffering and purification from which death liberates us is a view which the Bahá'í Faith shares with all other world religions. Many philosophers from the time of antiquity up to the nineteenth century have professed this belief. Life on earth is only the embryonic state of our existence, and death is the birth into a new life, not the final end, but a transformation 'in which, as illustrated by the metamorphosis of the butterfly, the other life breaks forth out of the earthly life'.[19] 'Abdu'l-Bahá makes it clear that the death of the body does not affect the soul: 'To consider that after the death of the body the spirit perishes is like imagining that a bird in a cage will be destroyed if the cage is broken.' When the cage is broken, 'the bird will continue and exist . . . In truth, from hell it reaches a paradise of delights'.[20] However, 'Abdu'l-Bahá stresses the fact that the spirit does not dwell in the body of man because 'it is freed and sanctified from entrance and exit, which are bodily conditions. The connection of the spirit with the body is like that of the sun with the mirror.' When the mirror is broken, 'it will cease to reflect the rays of the sun'.[21]

Two concepts that are associated with death and are widely accepted must be discussed in this context: the concept of reincarnation or metempsychosis[22] which is found in Hinduism, Buddhism and many ancient philosophers,[23] and which surprisingly is finding disciples again in the Western world; and the Christian teaching of the raising of the dead, the resurrection of the flesh at the Last Judgement. Both views are unequivocally rejected in Bahá'u'lláh's writings.

Man is placed for one time only into an earthly physical life in which he acquires what he will need in the worlds of God after the death of his body. There is no cycle of rebirths or of eternal recurrence of everything that happens.[24] The hereafter is not a kind of 'soul bank' for this world. Nor is there a general raising of the dead in the sense of a resurrection of the flesh on the Day of Judgement, as the creed of the Church teaches – a teaching which, despite its scientific impossibility, still has its theological defendants.[25] The re-assembly of the natural body as a material, molecular entity, an idea that defies all reason, does not take place.

The teaching of the resurrection of the flesh is based on a fundamental

18. Qur'án 2:151.
19. Johannes Lotz, 'Der Tod in theologischer Sicht', in A. Paus, *Grenzerfahrung Tod*, p.79.
20. *Some Answered Questions*, ch.61.
21. ibid. ch.61; cf. also Bahá'u'lláh, *Gleanings* 82:8.
22. Also known as the transmigration of souls. Cf. 'Abdu'l-Bahá, *Some Answered Questions*, ch.81; see also Rúhíyyih Rabbání, *Prescription for Living*, pp.73–5.
23. Pythagoras, Empedocles (cf. Arthur Schopenhauer, *Parerga and Paralipomena*, Vol.I, p.36).
24. Jamshed Fozdar in *Buddha Maitrya Amitabha has appeared*, New Delhi, 1976, pp.92–146, deals exhaustively from a Bahá'í point of view with the teaching of reincarnation in the Far Eastern religions. See also 'Abdu'l-Bahá, *Promulgation*, pp.167ff.
25. e.g. Johannes Lotz, 'Der Tod in theologischer Sicht', in A. Paus, *Grenzerfahrung Tod*, p.82.

misunderstanding to which Islámic theologians have also succumbed, namely that whenever 'death' and 'life' are mentioned in the holy writings physical death and earthly life are meant.[26] But the words of Jesus: 'Let the dead bury their dead'[27] should have caused people to be somewhat more reserved in considering the literal interpretation of the words 'death' and 'life' to be the correct one.

In the Kitáb-i-Íqán Bahá'u'lláh has dealt thoroughly with the real inner meaning of this terminology, which is also used in the Qur'án:[28] 'By the terms "life" and "death", spoken of in the scriptures, is intended the life of faith and the death of unbelief.'[29] The 'resurrection' is the spiritual rebirth through which man attains true life: 'Wert thou to attain to but a dewdrop of the crystal waters of divine knowledge, thou wouldst readily realize that true life is not the life of the flesh but the life of the spirit. For the life of the flesh is common to both men and animals, whereas the life of the spirit is possessed only by the pure in heart who have quaffed from the ocean of faith and partaken of the fruit of certitude. This life knoweth no death, and this existence is crowned by immortality.'[30] Those who have awakened to this spiritual life have attained unto the ' "resurrection" and have entered into the "paradise" of the love of God. And whosoever is not of them, is condemned to "death" and "deprivation", to the "fire" of unbelief, and to the "wrath" of God.'[31]

The 'Last Day', the 'Day of Judgement', is the coming of the new Manifestation of God; the trumpet blast announced in the Gospels and the Qur'án is the call of Bahá'u'lláh resounding for all in heaven and on earth. The day of resurrection is the salvation ushered in by Bahá'u'lláh's coming, in which mankind is spiritually renewed and revived. The Last Judgement is a spiritual event[32] affecting all mankind whereas the individual himself experiences his personal 'judgement day'[33] at his own death.

The return of man to God does not mean that he becomes a part of the world-spirit, nor that he loses his individuality. The personality of the individual is preserved and he is aware of how he lived and what he did. In its essence the soul of man is a 'sign of God', a 'heavenly gem whose reality the most learned of men hath failed to grasp, and whose mystery no mind,

26. e.g. I Cor.15:1ff; 20–22, 27, 54, 55.
27. Matt. 8:22; John 8:52.
28. 35:20–1; 6:122; cf. also p.110 n.3.
29. p.114.
30. op. cit., p.120.
31. op. cit., p.118. This meaning of 'resurrection' can already be found in the writings of the Báb: 'True resurrection from the sepulchres means to be quickened in conformity with His Will, through the power of His utterance . . . The Day He revealeth Himself is Resurrection Day which shall last as long as He ordaineth.' (*Selections*, p.158.)
32. See pp.219ff.
33. See pp.200ff.

however acute, can ever hope to unravel'.[34] After its separation from the body it enters the next world, 'in the degree of purity to which it has evolved during life in the physical body'.[35] If it has been faithful to God, it will 'reflect His light', otherwise 'it will become a victim of self and passion, and will, in the end, sink in their depths'.[36]

Life in the coming world is not static but dynamic. There is progression and retrogression.[37] The soul 'after its separation from the body, will continue to progress until it attaineth the presence of God, in a state and condition which neither the revolution of ages and centuries, nor the changes and chances of this world, can alter . . . Blessed is the soul which, at the hour of its separation from the body, is sanctified from the vain imaginings of the peoples of the world. Such a soul liveth and moveth in accordance with the Will of its Creator, and entereth the all-highest Paradise.'[38] The nature of the soul after death 'can never be described, nor is it meet and permissible to reveal its whole character to the eyes of men'.[39] 'When the soul attaineth the Presence of God, it will assume the form that best befitteth its immortality and is worthy of its celestial habitation.'[40] While man in the physical world can work on his personal salvation through his works and with divine grace (contrary to the teachings of Martin Luther), progression in the coming world takes place *sola fide* and *sola gratia*.[41]

For him who has believed in God and His signs and who has led a righteous life, death is 'a messenger of joy'.[42] In the Qur'án is revealed: 'Every soul shall taste of death. Then to us shall ye return. But those who shall have believed and wrought righteousness will we lodge in gardens with palaces, beneath which the rivers flow[43] . . . No vain discourse shall they hear therein, but only "Peace"!'[44] Were the station of the true believers in the next world to be made known, they would be 'so filled with gladness as to wish for death, and beseech, with unceasing longing, the one true God . . . to hasten their end'.[45] Death is the gateway to everlasting life: 'Death proffereth unto every confident believer the cup that is life indeed. It bestoweth joy, and is the bearer of gladness. It confer-

34. Bahá'u'lláh, *Gleanings* 82:1.
35. 'Abdu'l-Bahá, *Paris Talks*, ch.20, p.66.
36. Bahá'u'lláh, *Gleanings* 82:1.
37. 'In the other world to cease to progress is the same as to decline.' ('Abdu'l-Bahá, *Some Answered Questions*, ch.63.)
38. Bahá'u'lláh, *Gleanings* 81.
39. Bahá'u'lláh, ibid.
40. Bahá'u'lláh, ibid.
41. 'The progress of man's spirit in the divine world, after the severance of its connection with the body of dust, is through the bounty and grace of the Lord alone, or through the intercession and the sincere prayers of other human souls, or through the charities and important good works which are performed in its name.' ('Abdu'l-Bahá, *Some Answered Questions*, ch.66.)
42. Bahá'u'lláh, *The Hidden Words*, Arabic 32.
43. 29:57–8.
44. 19:63.
45. Bahá'u'lláh, *Gleanings* 164:1.

reth the gift of everlasting life.'[46]

The unbeliever also continues to live after the death of his body, but he is deprived of the heavenly bounties: 'The souls of the infidels, however, shall – and to this I bear witness – when breathing their last be made aware of the good things that have escaped them, and shall bemoan their plight, and shall humble themselves before God. They shall continue doing so after the separation of their souls from their bodies.'[47] But they are not barred from redemption. They can progress in the next world and gain God's forgiveness through prayer, especially through the intercession of souls who are near to God in both this and the coming world.[48]

The writings of Bahá'u'lláh make it quite plain that there is a hierarchy of souls in the next world. All will have a station according to their 'faith and their conduct': 'They that are of the same grade and station are fully aware of one another's capacity, character, accomplishments and merits. They that are of a lower grade, however, are incapable of comprehending adequately the station, or of estimating the merits, of those that rank above them. Each shall receive his share from thy Lord.'[49] And on the nature of the spiritual realms is written: 'Every heart is filled with wonder at so bewildering a theme, and every mind is perplexed by its mystery. God, alone, can fathom its import[50] . . . The world beyond is as different from this world as this world is different from that of the child while still in the womb of its mother.'[51]

'Abdu'l-Bahá has developed this analogy of earthly life with life in the womb:[52] 'In the beginning of his human life man was embryonic in the world of the matrix. There he received capacity and endowment for the reality of human existence. The forces and powers necessary for this world were bestowed upon him in that limited condition. In this world he needed eyes; he received them potentially in the other. He needed ears; he obtained them there in readiness and preparation for his new existence. The powers requisite in this world were conferred upon him in the world of the matrix, so that when he entered this realm of real existence he not only

---

46. Bahá'u'lláh, *Gleanings* 164:2.

47. Bahá'u'lláh, *Gleanings* 86:3. See also Qur'án (17:74): 'And he who has been blind here, shall be blind hereafter, and wander yet more from the way.'

48. 'Abdu'l-Bahá, *Some Answered Questions*, ch.62.

49. Bahá'u'lláh, *Gleanings* 86:2. See also Qur'án (17:22): 'See how we have caused some of them to excel others! but the next life shall be greater in its grades, and greater in excellence.'

50. Bahá'u'lláh, *Gleanings* 82:11.

51. Bahá'u'lláh, *Gleanings* 81.

52. This comparison can also be found in Seneca's writings: 'The dragging years of mortal life are but a training for the life that's better and longer. For ten months we're carried in our mother's womb, which prepares us not for itself but for that place into which we're discharged, it seems, when at length we're fit to draw breath and live unshielded. So too throughout the period that stretches from babyhood to age, we're ripening for another birth. A new beginning, a new estate waits for us . . . But that day, which you dread as your last, is the birthday of the eternal.' (*Seneca's Letters to Lucilius*, Vol.II, p.198, Nos. 23, 24, 26.)

possessed all necessary functions and powers but found provision for his material sustenance awaiting him.

'Therefore in this world he must prepare himself for the life beyond. That which he needs in the world of the kingdom must be obtained here. Just as he prepared himself in the world of the matrix by acquiring forces necessary in this sphere of existence, so likewise the indispensable forces of the divine existence must be potentially attained in this world.'

'What is he in need of in the kingdom which transcends the life and limitation of this mortal sphere?[53] That world beyond is a world of sanctity and radiance; therefore it is necessary that in this world he should acquire these divine attributes. In that world there is need of spirituality, faith, assurance, the knowledge and love of God. These he must attain in this world so that after his ascension from the earthly to the heavenly kingdom he shall find all that is needful in that life eternal ready for him.'[54]

On Suicide

If the reason for our existence on earth is that we are to develop ourselves in order to be able to partake of the coming world of light, love and justice,[55] it is easy to understand why suicide has been forbidden by God and is looked upon as a grave wrong.[56] Suicide signifies a lack of respect for God-given life; it is an act of disbelief. A person who lays hands on himself shortens the period during which he can work on perfecting himself by means of his own actions and thereby rejects the God-given possibility of development.[57] It is not surprising that there have been more and more defenders of the right to take one's own life since the Enlightenment;[58]

53. Heaven, Hell and Paradise are not the places of abode for the departed but are metaphors for the state of being close to God or being far removed from Him. Bahá'u'lláh has dealt with the objection of Muslims who interpret the writings literally and say that the promised day has not come since Paradise and Hell have not been made visible: 'They say: "Where is Paradise, and where is Hell?" Say: "The one is reunion with Me; the other thine own self, O thou who dost associate a partner with God and doubtest."' With regard to the importance of His coming for the salvation of man He revealed: 'Paradise is decked with mystic roses, and hell hath been made to blaze with the fire of the impious.' (*Epistle to the Son of the Wolf*, pp.132–3.) On this subject see Bahá'u'lláh, *Kitáb-i-Íqán*, pp.44–5 and 76–7 and J. E. Esslemont, p.176ff.
54. *The Promulgation of Universal Peace*, pp.225ff.
55. It has already been explained that our purpose in life does not consist solely of the selfish search for our own salvation.
56. Qur'án 4:33; 'Suicide is one of the greatest sins in Islám because it is a flagrant breach of Allah's trust.' ('Abdul Hamíd Ṣiddíqí, *Commentary on Muslim, Kitáb al-Ímán*, ch.XLVIII). Cf. Bahá'u'lláh, *Epistle to the Son of the Wolf*, pp.108ff; 'Abdu'l-Bahá in *Star of the West*, Vol.XII, p.280. Suicide is also forbidden in Canon Law (can.1240) and by Protestant ethics. Buddhism and Judaism strongly condemn suicide. The voluntary sacrifice of one's life for others or martyrdom are judged quite differently.
57. Just as abortion deprives the foetus of the possibility to develop.
58. For instance Montesquieu, Voltaire, Schopenauer ('On Suicide', in *Parerga and Paralipomena*, Vol.II, ch.XIII, pp.306ff). Nietzsche hated the death 'which stealeth nigh like a thief, – and yet cometh as master'. He praised 'the voluntary death, which cometh unto me because I want it' (*Thus Spake Zarathustra*, 'Voluntary Death'. First Part, p.75). Jean Améry in his book *Hand an sich legen*, Stuttgart 1976, pleads for the right to commit suicide.

nor is it astonishing that today Christian theologians are becoming more reserved in condemning suicide. How much opinions have changed is shown by the fact that Swedish scientists have demanded the establishment of suicide clinics, in which people who are tired of living can take their own lives under the supervision of a doctor. The same request was made in Denmark. In the British Parliament a bill was recently proposed that would make it possible for the incurably ill to demand their own death in clinics with the costs covered by health insurance.[59] Up to now these demands have been unable to win popular endorsement but they are a convincing sign of the spreading disbelief, the loss of the religious concept of man and the belief in a supernatural world; they also indicate an attitude that views life as something that exists only between birth and death. If our individuality dies with our death, if our spiritual existence is extinguished when we lose our bodies, then it may seem fascinating 'that we have a real possibility of not having to take part in a world which revolts us' or of 'not being forced to live, which is the cruellest form of resignation' (Jean Améry).

The plea for suicide is ultimately the logical consequence of the emancipation movement which characterizes modern times. From the standpoint of the complete autonomy and absolute self-determination of man, death, which comes upon us, seems to be the utmost contradiction to freedom. Men gain radical freedom for themselves when they die 'at a moment of their own choosing'.[60] This kind of thinking is the ultimate consequence of man's self-worship. He wants to be like God[61] and even rule over death. The steadily increasing rate of suicides in the Western and Eastern industrial nations[62] is the spiritual outcome of materialism and nihilism.

The Hour of Truth

If life on earth is a passageway, a preparation for a life in a spiritual world and death is an 'open gate' to this new life, then it is clear that the way one lives is not at all a matter of indifference. As all sacred writings testify, the individual is responsible for his deeds: According to the teachings of Buddha two things 'dog' man's 'steps, like a shadow in pursuit' when death catches up with him: 'Man's merits and the sins he here hath wrought.'[63] It is impossible for him to flee from his bad deeds and thoughts: 'Not in the sky, not in the midst of the sea, not if we enter into the clefts of the

---

59. Erwin Ringel, 'Suizid und Euthanasie', pp.277ff. In particular, the British organization 'EXIT' demands legalization of suicide on request.
60. Herbert Marcuse, *Eros and Civilization*, p.237.
61. Gen. 3:5.
62. Every day in the world more than a thousand people die by their own hand. The number of suicide attempts is eight times higher (Erwin Ringel, 'Suizid und Euthanasie', op.cit., pp.241ff.).
63. Samyutta-Nikaya, Part I, p.98.

mountains, is there known a spot in the whole world where a man might be freed from an evil deed.'[64] Hence, 'let him make good store for life elsewhere. Sure platform in some other future world, rewards of virtue on good beings wait'.[65]

According to Christ all who 'do iniquity' will be gathered and 'cast . . . into a furnace of fire': 'There shall be wailing and gnashing of teeth. Then shall the righteous shine forth as the sun in the kingdom of their Father. Who hath ears to hear, let him hear.'[66] And in the Qur'án is revealed: 'And every man's fate have we fastened about his neck: and on the day of resurrection will we bring forth to him a book which shall be proffered to him wide open: "Read thy Book: there needeth none but thyself to make out an account against thee this day!"'[67] Bahá'u'lláh also says that death is the hour of truth: 'For every act performed there shall be a recompense according to the estimate of God.'[68]

The messengers of God were sent to guide men 'to the straight Path of Truth . . . that they may, at the hour of death, ascend, in the utmost purity and sanctity and with absolute detachment, to the throne of the Most High'.[69] Men should always be aware that this hour will come: 'Bring thyself to account each day ere thou art summoned to a reckoning; for death, unheralded, shall come upon thee and thou shalt be called to give account for thy deeds.'[70] 'Set before thine eyes God's unerring Balance and, as one standing in His Presence, weigh in that Balance thine actions every day, every moment of thy life. Bring thyself to account ere thou art summoned to a reckoning, on the Day when no man shall have strength to stand for fear of God, the Day when the hearts of the heedless ones shall be made to tremble.'[71] All good and bad done by man in this earthly life is known to the divine judge: 'O heedless ones! Think not the secrets of hearts are hidden, nay, know ye of a certainty that in clear characters they are engraved and are openly manifest in the holy Presence[72] . . . O friends! Verily I say, whatsoever ye have concealed within your hearts is to Us open and manifest as the day; but that it is hidden is of Our grace and favour, and not of your deserving.'[73]

Here it is obvious that the attitude of the believers of bygone ages towards death was right: Life was seen from the perspective of death – the hourglass was the reminder, the *memento mori*, the constant and vivid

64. Dhammapada, No.127.
65. Samyutta-Nikaya, Part I, p.98.
66. Matt. 13:41–3.
67. 17:14–15.
68. Bahá'u'lláh, Súriy-i-Vafá, *Tablets*, p.189.
69. *Gleanings* 81.
70. Bahá'u'lláh, *The Hidden Words*, Arabic 31; cf.also Matt. 7:19–23.
71. Bahá'u'lláh, *Gleanings* 114:12; cf. also the Báb, *Selections*, p.162.
72. Bahá'u'lláh, *The Hidden Words*, Persian 59.
73. ibid. Persian 60. Cf. also *Gleanings* 77: 'Every act ye meditate is as clear to Him as is that act when already accomplished.'

representation of our transitoriness and the proof of how relative is earthly longing for happiness. For the Bahá'í, too, this is the right attitude, for death, which terminates this earthly life, is at the same time the gateway to true life into which we are born. At death we reap what we have sown in this transitory life. Man is suddenly faced with what he has done on earth, with the divine perfections he has acquired, in a word with what he is: '*Omnia mea mecum porto.*'[74] Here his responsibility for his earthly life is shown: 'It is clear and evident that all men shall, after their physical death, estimate the worth of their deeds, and realize all that their hands have wrought. I swear by the Day Star that shineth above the horizon of Divine power! They that are the followers of the one true God shall, the moment they depart out of this life, experience such joy and gladness as would be impossible to describe, while they that live in error shall be seized with such fear and trembling, and shall be filled with such consternation, as nothing can exceed.'[75]

When man crosses the threshold of death he is given reward or punishment according to how he has lived: 'He who shall present himself with good works shall receive a tenfold reward; but he who shall present himself with evil works shall receive none other than a like punishment: and they shall not be treated unjustly.'[76] The reward in the next world is 'the eternal life which is clearly mentioned in all the Holy Books, the divine perfections, the eternal bounties, and everlasting felicity'.[77] Punishment consists of being far from God and bereft of heavenly gifts. Even the doer of bad deeds goes into the other world, however he sinks, according to his deserts, to 'the lowest degrees of existence' and 'is considered as dead by the people of truth'.[78] This is the spiritual death often mentioned in the holy writings; however, he who can show faith and good works arises to new spiritual life.

On the Innocence Mania

If there is no life after death, and joy and suffering can be experienced only in this life, then the only justice there is consists in that which man grants man on earth, the only place he exists. This idea implies the view that all injustice and all crime can only be expiated on earth or never. In this widespread conviction, namely that man has no transcendental responsibility, can be found the basic reason for the increase of crime in recent decades. If everything is over when we die, and when in addition the legitimation of punishment by the state is doubted or even disputed, man really has little

74. Cicero, *Paradoxa*, I, 1, 8.
75. Bahá'u'lláh, *Gleanings* 86:3–4.
76. Qur'án 6:161.
77. 'Abdu'l-Bahá, *Some Answered Questions*, ch.60, p.224.
78. 'Abdu'l-Bahá, ibid, p.225.

reason to abstain from anything he is tempted to do just because the law forbids it.

In the light of the truth proclaimed in all religions and enjoined again by Bahá'u'lláh, that man must account for his good and bad deeds at his death, this attitude proves to be a profound error of grave consequence. The same applies to the dominant tendency[79] today to contest the idea that man has free will, that he is free to act, thereby acquitting him of any kind of guilt or responsibility. This error is the last consequence of an atheistic and materialistic concept of man; it takes away not only his freedom but also his dignity. If there are no objective values, or if man is unable to orient himself by them, if they did exist, then the animal, certain and secure in its instincts, is superior to man. The instincts serve to preserve its life; man on the other hand, free of values and instincts, has no such protection.

This kind of thinking is totally incompatible with religion. It is undeniable that man is strongly influenced by his drives, by pressures, and by the actual deplorable conditions of society. He is by no means completely free, but is affected by manifold biological, psychological and sociocultural conditions. However, in contrast to a mere creature of nature, he is not biologically determined by his drives and instincts. Rather, he can choose and form his needs. Despite the determining factors he has a genuine scope of action to decide against the needs of his lower nature and for the ethical imperatives. Of course, the basic drives and desires, which include hate, are a part of nature, but man, even from a biological standpoint, is innately a cultural being. His original drives need to be restrained and sublimated.[80] This dependence of the basic drives on cultural guidance and control, and the necessity of canalizing them and concentrating them on goals beyond those of the self, represent the basic insight of recent German philosophical anthropology (Scheler, Gehlen).[81] Thus the recourse to biology[82] instead of to religious and metaphysical values (the validity of which has been shattered) misses the point. All moral commandments are, as Leszek Kolakowski pointed out, 'to a certain extent contrary to nature; after all they would be superfluous if their tasks were fulfilled by the instincts anyway'.[83] Nothing is more opposed to the nature of man than the love of one's enemy,[84] which is more than just not hating

---

79. cf. pp.49ff.

80. Helmut Schelsky, *Soziologie der Sexualität*, p.26.

81. With regard to sexuality cf. the remarks on pp.175ff.

82. The psychoanalyst Esther Harding writes: 'The quest for . . . a deeper appreciation of reality stands today as a guiding principle, replacing the discarded "submission to moral law".' (*The Way of all Women*, p.268.)

83. 'Erziehung zum Haß – Erziehung zur Würde' (Education towards Hatred – Education towards Dignity). A talk held at the conferment of the German book trade's peace prize in 1977. Printed in *Süddeutsche Zeitung* of 17.10.1977.

84. The claim first made by the father of the church Tertullian (*Ad Scapulam* 1) that Jesus's com-

him and which is demanded by all religions. Kolakowski counters the objection that this demand violates nature to such an extent that it cannot be generally binding: 'One can only reply with a very simple answer: it is certain that there are and will be only very few who really come up to this demand; it is on the shoulders of these few, however, that the structure of our civilization is based, and the little that we are able to accomplish is achieved thanks to them.'[85] Even the supposedly inescapable compulsions of society are no excuse for a deviation from the moral demands. Social conditions do not compel; they only make one inclined to follow a certain path.[86] Without doubt one who believes he has a transcendental responsibility has greater motivation to act, despite the individual and social conditions that determine human behaviour, than one who knows nothing of such perspectives and who associates the 'Day of Judgement' with the institutions of the state.[87]

Free will is something that each of us can experience. That man has the freedom to choose between good and evil is a truth that all religions proclaim. Just as everyone is able to recognize God and His Manifestations,[88] everyone has also the capacity to obey the will of God as it is manifested in His law: 'God will not burden any soul beyond its power', states the Qur'án,[89] and 'Abdu'l-Bahá said: 'Man has the power both to do good and to do evil.'[90] It would be in contradiction to the concept of God's justice[91] and be absolutely unacceptable to religious thought to imagine that God, the law-giver, provides men with an absolute rule of conduct and imposes upon them the duty 'to testify unto that which the Lord hath revealed, and follow that which He hath ordained in His mighty Book',[92] but that at the same time, as Creator, He has not endowed them with the

mandment to love one's enemy (Matt. 5:44) was peculiar to Christianity is erroneous, but widely spread and hard to eradicate. Friedrich Heiler ('Einheit und Zusammenarbeit der Religionen', pp.11ff.) has proved with a large number of quotations, that all the world religions of the earth, even the pre-Christian ones, have this commandment. Hinduism demands that its followers love their enemies, just as Laotse does: 'Recompense injury with kindness' (*The Tâo Teh King*, Part II, 63:1, p.106). The love of one's enemy plays an important part in Buddhism (Dhammapada 5); it was not unknown to pre-Christian Judaism and has a firm place in Islám. (On the whole subject see Hans Haas, *Idee und Ideal der Feindesliebe in der nichtchristlichen Welt* (The Idea and Ideal of Loving One's Enemy in the Non-Christian World), Leipzig 1927.)

85. 'Erziehung zum Haß – Erziehung zur Würde', ibid.
86. 'The fault, dear Brutus, is not in our stars,/But in ourselves, that we are underlings.' (Shakespeare, *Julius Caesar*, Act I, Scene ii.)
87. 'Dread of the penalties maketh people desist only outwardly from committing vile and contemptible deeds, while that which guardeth and restraineth man both outwardly and inwardly hath been and still is the fear of God.' (Lawh-i-Dunyá, *Tablets*, p.93.)
88. See Bahá'u'lláh, *Gleanings* 75.
89. 2:286.
90. *Paris Talks*, ch.18, p.60.
91. 'Everything Thou doest is pure justice, nay, the very essence of grace.' (Bahá'u'lláh, *Epistle to the Son of the Wolf*, p.10.)
92. Bahá'u'lláh, Aṣl-i-Kullu'l-Khayr, *Tablets*, p.155.

ability to fulfil the law.[93] In this context Kant's statement holds true: 'Thou canst, for thou shouldst.' When we know that according to the law of God we *should* do a certain thing, we also know that we *can* do it, even if it is not certain that we will fulfil our duty at the actual moment of test.

Therefore no one has to steal, no one has to commit adultery or get drunk or take drugs, etc. The theory that denies all human responsibility because man is bound by the compulsions of society and his own drives and therefore has no freedom to act, the concept that makes every deed an outcome of unlucky social circumstances with the result that the 'guilty person' can no longer be blamed for his acts, is a logical consequence of atheism. Dostoevsky was referring to this consequence when he had Ivan Karamazov say: 'If God does not exist, then everything is permitted. If there is no God, then nothing matters.' This means that when man is his own law-giver, as Jean-Paul Sartre teaches, and acknowledges no higher responsibility than the state courts, he can justify any crime. Our recent history bears clear witness to this.

Finally, something should be said on the equality of man in the eyes of God. God judges regardless of the rank of the person. The king and the beggar, the banker and the worker are all equal before Him. But there is no religious equality, in the sense that believers and unbelievers, good and bad, are also equal before God. 'Shall he then who is a believer be as he who sinneth grossly? They shall not be held alike' states the Qur'án.[94] This claim of equality, which would make a mockery of every kind of justice, is also refuted by Bahá'u'lláh: 'Let no one imagine that by Our assertion that all created things are the signs of the revelation of God is meant that . . . all men, be they good or evil, pious or infidel, are equal in the sight of God.'[95] Even in the ability of man to partake of the heavenly blessings there is no equality: 'The whole duty of man in this Day is to attain that share of the flood of grace which God poureth forth for him. Let none, therefore, consider the largeness or smallness of the receptacle. The portion of some might lie in the palm of a man's hand, the portion of others might fill a cup, and of others even a gallon-measure.'[96]

---

93. This is not the place to discuss Paul's thesis that it is impossible to fulfil the law (Rom. 7:18ff.) or the aspects of the Protestant teachings on justification. I refer to my comments in *The Light Shineth in Darkness*, pp.95ff.
94. 32:18.
95. *Gleanings* 93:7.
96. Bahá'u'lláh, *Gleanings* 5:4.

12. The New Man

His Necessity

The two great nineteenth-century philosophers, Friedrich Nietzsche and Karl Marx, were expecting the coming of a new man. Nietzsche, who called for an end to the Christian 'slave morality' and a return to the 'innocence of existence', foresaw the coming of 'superman'. Marx proclaimed the end of morality as soon as society was sufficiently moral for man to be able to dispense with morality, the State and religion. The departure from Christianity heralded by both these thinkers and now put into practice by countless people 'in fact gave rise to the decline of the old morality without creating a new social ethos: the birth of the new man is now more questionable than ever';[1] and yet it becomes clearer with every day that the survival of mankind is ultimately not a question of technology but of the concepts of values and goals of individuals and peoples[2] and of the coming of a new human consciousness. This is being more and more distinctly recognized today. Albert Einstein had already pronounced judgement in his time: 'Our world is threatened by a crisis of such dimensions that it seems to have outstripped those who have the most important decisions for good or ill within their power. The unleashed might of the atom has changed everything, except our thinking. We are consequently moving towards an unparalleled catastrophe. We shall need a substantially new way of thinking if mankind is to survive.'[3] A 'time of consummate means and chaotic ends' was how he summed up our era.[4]

---

1. Erich Kellner, in *Religionslose Gesellschaft*, Foreword, p.11.
2. Anyone who thinks: 'First comes the grub, then the morals' (Bertolt Brecht, *Threepenny Opera*, Second Threepenny Finale) may be able to observe in the not too distant future that without morals there will be no more 'grub'.
3. Quoted from Josef Rattner, *Psychologie des Vorurteils*, p.10, with list of sources.
4. Quoted from J. Schwartländer, 'Der Tod und die Würde des Menschen', p.10.

The American scholar Grover Foley also sees the basic problem of our existential crisis not in technology but in man himself, who is technologically 'a giant, morally a dwarf',[5] who has 'the knowledge of the atomic age and the emotional maturity of Neanderthal': 'We have become gods before we have learned to be men.'[6] Foley demands a 'total change in our goals and values, as sweeping as an old-fashioned religious conversion'[7] and asks: 'Who will create a new man for us?'[8] His reference to an 'old-fashioned religious conversion' shows that he does not expect this far-reaching change to come from science. He states with resignation: 'The theory that the final solution lies solely in the creation of new men is not exactly encouraging – in fact it is more disquieting than all the other facts. Compared with the task of changing the sons of Adam, splitting the atom looks like child's play.'[9] Foley looks towards new values, ethics and religion. This recognition is growing. Carl Friedrich von Weizsäcker calls for a 'comprehensive change of consciousness comprising the whole person,'[10] and Erich Fromm sees, as already described, man's one chance of survival in a religiously motivated, radical change of consciousness, in new thinking, in a new man.[11]

The new man on whom alone we can place our hopes if we want to escape the lemming-like urge towards self-destruction, the paranoid desire for extinction and the pre-programmed catastrophe, is a man capable of surviving, adapted to the new conditions. He will certainly not be the 'emancipated personality', the human being who is alienated from all norms and religious convictions, without morality and *Weltanschauung*. For what is already there can indeed be destroyed with the arsenal of negative attitudes at his disposal, such as distrust, conflict seeking, negative criticism and impatience for action,[12] but nothing new can be built with it.

Nor can science create the new man for us. There are some crazy notions about the possibility of breeding a new type of human being by biological means, for instance through tampering with the genes, or, as Heinrich Himmler vainly imagined in the SS organization, by means of racial selec-

---

5. 'A race of inventive dwarfs, who can be hired for anything' (Bertolt Brecht, *Galileo*, Scene 14). [Translator's note: The translation of this quotation was missing from the English version. The sentence above has been translated from the German original.]

6. 'Sind wir am Ende?', p.741.

7. op. cit., p.749.

8. op. cit., p.747.

9. ibid.

10. *Wege in der Gefahr*, p.137ff.

11. *To Have or to Be?* pp.201–2.

12. 'The widespread differences that exist among mankind and the prevalence of sedition, contention, conflict and the like are the primary factors which provoke the appearance of the satanic spirit. Yet the Holy Spirit hath ever shunned such matters. A world in which naught can be perceived save strife, quarrels and corruption is bound to become the seat of the throne, the very metropolis, of Satan.' (Bahá'u'lláh, Lawh-i-Maqṣúd, *Tablets*, p.177.)

tion. These ideas derive from a materialistic concept of man which reduces man to his biological nature and animal instincts. Gene manipulation or the delusion of racial selection are incapable of contributing to the case in point, which is that of a substantially new way of thinking: *'Mens agitat molem'* [13] – 'The spirit shapes the body for its dwelling.' [14]

Science can neither bring about a change of consciousness nor discern new standards of value, let alone set absolute standards. It is the revealed religions that have always succeeded in effecting a change in man. Each one of them has brought about such a change and produced a new type of man, has reorientated the life of the community towards new goals and values, thereby overcoming what had been undermining society; namely, antagonistic thinking on the central questions of life, the pluralism of un-committed opinions and the non-obligatory character of all norms and goals.

Spiritual Rebirth

Bahá'u'lláh tells us the only thing which has the power to produce this change: 'The Word of God, alone, can claim the distinction of being en-dowed with the capacity required for so great and far-reaching a change.' [15] Like all the prophets before him, he summons man to change and pro-claims that the Kingdom of God must first be built in the heart of man. [16] The basic condition of any change for the better on earth is the transforma-tion of the individual. Altering the political and social structures of mankind will produce a lasting improvement in our sick world only if the individual also makes positive changes in his thinking, feeling and doing. The basis for this change is the spiritual rebirth of man demanded by Bahá'u'lláh: 'O ye who are as dead! The Hand of Divine bounty proffereth unto you the Water of Life. Hasten and drink your fill. Whoso hath been re-born in this Day, shall never die; whoso remaineth dead, shall never live.' [17]

This rebirth [18] is a total reversal, the beginning of a new life with God, the submission of a person's whole life to the requirements of God an-nounced by the divine Manifestation. Only this total change can create the new man. Faith is the tree, works are the fruit. How does this complete change in the life of a human being come to pass? 'Abdu'l-Bahá gives the answer: 'First, through the knowledge of God. Second, through the love of God. Third, through faith. Fourth, through philanthropic deeds. Fifth, through self-sacrifice. Sixth, through severance from this world. Seventh,

13. Virgil, *The Aeneid*, book VI, 727.
14. Friedrich v. Schiller, *Wallenstein*, Act 3, scene 13.
15. *Gleanings* 99.
16. 'For, behold the kingdom of God is within you.' (Luke 17:21.)
17. *Gleanings* 106:3.
18. Compare also 'Abdu'l-Bahá, *Some Answered Questions*, ch.60.

through sanctity and holiness. Unless he acquires these forces and attains to these requirements he will surely be deprived of the life that is eternal. But if he possesses the knowledge of God, becomes ignited through the fire of the love of God, witnesses the great and mighty signs of the kingdom, becomes the cause of love among mankind, and lives in the utmost state of sanctity and holiness, he shall surely attain to second birth, be baptized by the Holy Spirit and enjoy everlasting existence.'[19]

The New Ethos

What are these 'fruits', which man is supposed to bear? They are indeed none other than those named by the early prophets: 'The purpose of the one true God in manifesting Himself is to summon all mankind to truthfulness and sincerity, to piety and trustworthiness, to resignation and submissiveness to the Will of God, to forbearance and kindliness, to uprightness and wisdom. His object is to array every man with the mantle of a saintly character, and to adorn him with the ornament of holy and goodly deeds.'[20] The Báb himself appealed to his disciples: 'O My beloved friends! You are the bearers of the name of God in this Day. You have been chosen as the repositories of His mystery. It behoves each one of you to manifest the attributes of God, and to exemplify by your deeds and words the signs of His righteousness, His power and glory. The very members of your body must bear witness to the loftiness of your purpose, the integrity of your life, the reality of your faith, and the exalted character of your devotion . . . The days when idle worship was deemed sufficient are ended. The time is come when naught but the purest motive, supported by deeds of stainless purity, can ascend to the throne of the Most High and be acceptable unto Him.'[21] The followers of Bahá'u'lláh are to instruct people by means of their exemplary lives: 'The companions of God are, in this day, the lump that must leaven the peoples of the world. They must show forth such trustworthiness, such truthfulness and perseverance, such deeds and character that all mankind may profit by their example.'[22]

This is not the place to set forth even the rudiments of Bahá'u'lláh's moral teaching, so great is the wealth of the verses which call all men to a new life and to untarnished conduct. Outstanding among the Bahá'í virtues are the love of God,[23] charity,[24] the love of mankind,[25] kindness to

19. *The Promulgation of Universal Peace*, p.226.
20. Bahá'u'lláh, *Gleanings* 137:4.
21. Quoted from Nabíl-i-A'ẓam, *The Dawn-Breakers*, pp.92ff.
22. Bahá'u'lláh, quoted from Shoghi Effendi, *The Advent of Divine Justice*, p.19.
23. Bahá'u'lláh, *Gleanings* 123:3; *The Hidden Words*, Arabic 4–10, 38; *Kitáb-i-Íqán*, p.131; Qur'án 35:16; 'Abdu'l-Bahá, *Some Answered Questions*, ch.84, and *Paris Talks*, ch.27, p.82: 'By the fire of the Love of God the veil is burnt which separates us from the Heavenly Realities, and with clear vision we are enabled to struggle onward and upward, ever progressing in the paths of virtue and holiness, and becoming the means of light to the world.'
24. Bahá'u'lláh, Lawḥ-i-Ḥikmat, *Tablets*, p.138; Aṣl-i-Kullu'l-Khayr, *Tablets*, p.156; 'Abdu'l-

animals, 'how much more unto his fellow-man, to him who is endowed with the power of utterance',[26] mercy,[27] kindliness,[28] sincerity,[29] truthfulness,[30] honesty,[31] patience and steadfastness,[32] purity and chastity,[33] cleanliness,[34] humility,[35] unselfishness,[36] self-knowledge,[37] freedom from prejudice,[38] justice,[39] righteousness,[40] hospitality,[41] courtesy,[42] submissiveness to the Will of God,[43] meekness,[44] modesty and contentment,[45] detachment,[46] steadfastness in His Faith,[47] impartiality,[48]

Bahá: 'To be as one soul in many bodies, for the more we love each other, the nearer we shall be to God.' (Quoted from J. E. Esslemont, *Bahá'u'lláh and the New Era*, p.73.)

25. Bahá'u'lláh, *Gleanings* 43:4, 6; 117; 132:1, 5; cf. pp.229ff.

26. Bahá'u'lláh, *Kitáb-i-Íqán*, p.194; 'Abdu'l-Bahá, *Selections*, No.137 and No.138.

27. Bahá'u'lláh, *Epistle to the Son of the Wolf*, p.29; Lawḥ-i-Ḥikmat, *Tablets*, p.138.

28. Bahá'u'lláh, *Gleanings* 132:5.

29. Bahá'u'lláh, *Gleanings* 130: Tablet of Ṭarázát, Fifth Ṭaráz, *Tablets*, p.39.

30. Bahá'u'lláh, *Gleanings* 114:3; 126:2; 134:2; 136:5; 137:4; 139:8. Lawḥ-i-Ḥikmat, *Tablets*, p.138. In contrast to the view of the founder of a modern State that 'speaking the truth is for the petit bourgeois', if a particular aim justifies the use of lies, according to 'Abdu'l-Bahá truthfulness 'is the foundation of all human virtues. Without truthfulness progress and success, in all the worlds of God, are impossible for any soul. When this holy attribute is established in man, all the divine qualities will also be acquired.' (Quoted from *The Divine Art of Living*, p.78.)

31. Bahá'u'lláh, *Gleanings* 136:6; 137:3. Kitáb-i-Aqdas, *Synopsis*, p.49. The virtue of honesty has always been rare. Schopenhauer writes: 'Instances of this sort can be found, beyond all doubt; only the surprise, the emotion, and the high respect awakened, when we hear of them, testify to the fact that they are unexpected and very exceptional. There are in truth really honest people: like four-leaved clover, their existence is not a fiction.' (*The Basis of Morality*, p.143.) 'To be honest, as this world goes, is to be one man picked out of ten thousand', says Hamlet (Act II, scene ii).

32. Bahá'u'lláh, *Gleanings* 66:10, 11; 115:4, 134:1, 2; 136:3; 143:1; *The Hidden Words*, Arabic 48.

33. Bahá'u'lláh, *Gleanings* 60:3; 131:4; 134:2; 136:1, 5, 6; 141:3, 4; *Epistle to the Son of the Wolf*, p.23; Lawḥ-i-Ḥikmat, *Tablets*, p.138; see also Shoghi Effendi, *The Advent of Divine Justice*, p.19; for further details see pp.175ff.

34. Kitáb-i-Aqdas, *Synopsis*, p.51; 'Abdu'l-Bahá, *Selections*, No.129; Báb, The Persian Bayán 5:14, *Selections*, p.80.

35. 'Humility exalteth man to the heaven of glory and power, whilst pride abaseth him to the depths of wretchedness and degradation' (Bahá'u'lláh, *Epistle to the Son of the Wolf*, p.30; compare also *Gleanings* 66:7); *The Hidden Words*, Arabic 68; Kalimát-i-Firdawsíyyih, third leaf, *Tablets*, p.64.

36. Bahá'u'lláh, *Gleanings* 136:1 and 161:2.

37. Bahá'u'lláh, Tablet of Ṭarázát, first Ṭaráz, *Tablets*, p.35; also *Gleanings* 90, where the utterance of Imám 'Alí is quoted in this connection: 'He hath known God who hath known himself.' (*Kitáb-i-Íqán*, p.102.)

38. Bahá'u'lláh, *Words of Wisdom and Communes*, p.10; 'Abdu'l-Bahá, *Selections*, No.202.

39. Bahá'u'lláh, *The Hidden Words*, Arabic 2; *Epistle to the Son of the Wolf*, p.13; *Gleanings* 100:6; Kitáb-i-Aqdas, *Synopsis*, p.50; Tablet of Ṭarázát, third and fifth Ṭaráz, *Tablets*, pp.36 and 39.

40. Bahá'u'lláh, *Gleanings* 131:4.

41. 'Abdu'l-Bahá, *Paris Talks*, ch.1, p.15.

42. Bahá'u'lláh, *Epistle to the Son of the Wolf*, p.50; Lawḥ-i-Dunyá, *Tablets*, p.88; *Gleanings* 139:8.

43. Bahá'u'lláh, *Gleanings* 68:2; 134:2; 137:4; 160:2 – 3.

44. Bahá'u'lláh, *Gleanings* 130; *The Hidden Words*, Persian 48.

45. Bahá'u'lláh, *The Hidden Words*, Arabic 18, 24, 52 – 3; Persian 50; *Gleanings* 134:2.

46. Bahá'u'lláh, *The Hidden Words*, Arabic 16, 23, 54 – 6; Persian 40, 47, 75; *Epistle to the Son of the Wolf*, p.12; *Gleanings* 14:18; 46:4; 72:2; 100:1; 121:4, 6; 144:1; 149; 153:4; Aṣl-i-Kullu'l-Khayr, *Tablets*, p.155.

47. Bahá'u'lláh, *Kitáb-i-Íqán*, p.233; *Gleanings* 134:3; Tablet of Tajallíyát, second Tajallí, *Tablets*, p.51.

48. Bahá'u'lláh, Tablet of Ṭarázát, third Ṭaráz, *Tablets*, pp.36 – 7; Kitáb-i-Aqdas, *Synopsis*, p.50.

keeping of agreements,[49] charitableness,[50] moderation in all things,[51] self-surrender,[52] trustworthiness,[53] forbearance,[54] thankfulness,[55] piety,[56] unity, union and concord amongst men,[57] wisdom.[58]

Bahá'u'lláh insistently warns people not to commit anything 'which will bring shame upon you'; to 'eschew all manner of wickedness', to be not of the 'mischief-makers', to beware 'lest ye encroach upon the substance of your neighbour';[59] and 'to be untainted by anything from which the Concourse on high may be averse'.[60] A good character is the means 'whereby men are guided to the Straight Path'. Its light 'surpasseth the light of the sun and the radiance thereof. Whoso attaineth unto it is accounted as a jewel among men.'[61] The faithful should be 'true reminders of the virtues of God'.[62]

To be avoided above all things are envy,[63] covetousness,[64] malice,[65] haughtiness,[66] sloth and idleness,[67] unseemly talk, backbiting and calumny,[68] cursing and reviling,[69] craftiness and suspicion,[70] cruelty to animals,[71] tyranny,[72] hate, strife, dissension and rancour,[73], pride,

'Abdu'l-Bahá, *Some Answered Questions*, ch.15.
49. Bahá'u'lláh, *The Hidden Words*, Arabic 29; 'Abdu'l-Bahá, *Some Answered Questions*, ch.15.
50. Bahá'u'lláh, *The Hidden Words*, Arabic 57.
51. Bahá'u'lláh, *Gleanings* 110; 114:9; 118:2; 163:2, 3. For further details see pp.217ff.
52. Bahá'u'lláh, *Gleanings* 160:2.
53. Bahá'u'lláh, *Gleanings* 128:9; 134:2; Tablet of Ṭarázát, fourth Ṭaráz, *Tablets*, p.37.
54. Bahá'u'lláh, *Gleanings* 134:2.
55. ibid.
56. Bahá'u'lláh, Tablet of Ṭarázát, third Ṭaráz, *Tablets*, p.37.
57. Bahá'u'lláh, Ishráqát, sixth and ninth Ishráq, *Tablets*, pp.127, 129; Lawḥ-i-Ḥikmat, *Tablets*, p.138. In the Kitáb-i-Aqdas is revealed: 'Be ye as the fingers of one hand, the members of one body' (*Synopsis*, No.11, p.17).
58. Bahá'u'lláh, Lawḥ-i-Ḥikmat, *Tablets*, p.138. Bahá'u'lláh's praise of wisdom is in the Kalimát-i-Firdawsíyyih, fifth leaf, where he calls wisdom 'the greatest gift' and 'the most wondrous blessing . . . It is man's unfailing protector', 'the foremost teacher in the school of existence' (*Tablets*, p.66).
59. Bahá'u'lláh, *Gleanings* 128:8, 9.
60. Bahá'u'lláh, *Gleanings* 141:3.
61. Bahá'u'lláh, Tablet of Ṭarázát, third Ṭaráz, *Tablets*, p.36; cf. also Ishráqát, fourth Ishráq, *Tablets*, p.126.
62. Bahá'u'lláh, Lawḥ-i-Ḥikmat, *Tablets*, p.138.
63. Bahá'u'lláh, *The Hidden Words*, Persian 6, 42.
64. Bahá'u'lláh, *The Hidden Words*, Persian 50.
65. Bahá'u'lláh, *The Hidden Words*, Persian 42.
66. Bahá'u'lláh, *The Hidden Words*, Persian 47.
67. Bahá'u'lláh, Bishárát, twelfth Glad-Tidings, *Tablets*, p.26.
68. *Gleanings* 7:1; Bishárát, thirteenth Glad-Tidings, *Tablets*, p.27, Kitáb-i-'Ahd, *Tablets*, p.219; *The Hidden Words*, Arabic 27; Persian 44, 66; *Kitáb-i-Íqán*, p.193.
69. Bishárát, thirteenth Glad-Tidings, *Tablets*, p.27; Tablet of Ṭarázát, fifth Ṭaráz, *Tablets*, p.38; Ishráqát, eighth Ishráq, *Tablets*, p.129.
70. Bahá'u'lláh, Lawḥ-i-Ḥikmat, *Tablets*, p.138.
71. Bahá'u'lláh, Kitáb-i-Aqdas, *Synopsis*, p.47.
72. Bahá'u'lláh, *The Hidden Words*, Persian 64; Báb, The Persian Bayán 5:19, *Selections*, p.79.
73. Bahá'u'lláh, *Gleanings* 96:3; 128:5, 9, 10; 136:4; 139:5; 153:6; *Epistle to the Son of the Wolf*, p.55; Bishárát, thirteenth Glad-Tidings, *Tablets*, p.27; Lawḥ-i-Ḥikmat, *Tablets*, p.138; Kitáb-i-Aqdas, *Synopsis*, pp.48, 50; Kitáb-i-'Ahd, *Tablets*, pp.222, 221; 'Abdu'l-Bahá, *Will and Testament*, pp.9, 13.

hypocrisy and fanaticism,[74] adultery and homosexuality.[75]

In the *Epistle to the Son of the Wolf* Bahá'u'lláh describes the qualities to which he who treads the path of the knowledge of God should aspire:

Be generous in prosperity, and thankful in adversity.
Be worthy of the trust of thy neighbour,
and look upon him with a bright and friendly face.
Be a treasure to the poor, an admonisher to the rich,
an answerer to the cry of the needy,
a preserver of the sanctity of thy pledge.
Be fair in thy judgement,
and guarded in thy speech.
Be unjust to no man,
and show all meekness to all men.
Be as a lamp unto them that walk in darkness,
a joy to the sorrowful,
a sea for the thirsty,
a haven for the distressed,
an upholder and defender of the victim of oppression.
Let integrity and uprightness distinguish all thine acts.
Be a home for the stranger,
a balm to the suffering,
a tower of strength for the fugitive.
Be eyes to the blind,
and a guiding light unto the feet of the erring.
Be an ornament to the countenance of truth,
a crown to the brow of fidelity,
a pillar of the temple of righteousness,
a breath of life to the body of mankind,
an ensign of the hosts of justice,
a luminary above the horizon of virtue,
a dew to the soil of the human heart,
an ark on the ocean of knowledge,
a sun in the heaven of bounty,
a gem on the diadem of wisdom,
a shining light in the firmament of thy generation,
a fruit upon the tree of humility.
We pray God to protect thee
from the heat of jealousy
and the cold of hatred.
He verily is nigh,
ready to answer.[76]

74. Bahá'u'lláh, Kitáb-i-Aqdas, *Synopsis*, p.50.
75. Bahá'u'lláh, Kitáb-i-Aqdas, *Synopsis*, p.47.

It stands to reason that this is not meant to represent a simple catalogue of virtues, a mere summary of individual values, but an order of values, a value hierarchy.[77] At the top of this hierarchical order stand the two central values of love and justice, love as the central value of a personal ethic and justice as the central value of the world of order. All other values are forms of these central values and subordinate to them. The virtues cannot be isolated from each other. They stand in a relationship of tension to one another, qualifying, supporting and delimiting each other, and it is the constant task of those who live according to these values to take care that this harmonic order is not disturbed by a shift of emphasis, as has happened in the past.[78] The balance of the virtues, as Plato taught, is the decisive element in a good and happy life.

The Work Ethic

As a divine lawgiver, Bahá'u'lláh laid down a large number of supreme standards for individual and social ethics. What follows will simply convey an impression of the moral values which go to make up the new man. A detailed description would be beyond the scope of this book. Nor can Bahá'u'lláh's society-oriented laws be treated here. It is self-evident that the individual virtues are ultimately also of relevance to social ethics because they are reflected in social reality. Some of Bahá'u'lláh's laws addressed to the individual have a direct effect on society. For instance, the strict prohibition of all intoxicating drinks and drugs, especially opium,[79] has an effect both directly for the benefit of the person and for the good of a society no longer in control of alcoholism and the drug problem.

The work ethic also has a far-reaching effect on both the individual and society. Man spends a considerable portion of his life working; the most essential part of social life consists in the creation of material and intellectual goods. Cultural values can be created and maintained only by work. Performance is a universal principle: 'Performance is striven for and rewarded in every social structure, in every value hierarchy.'[80] It is

---

76. pp.93–4; see also *Gleanings* 130.

77. cf. also Bahá'u'lláh, *Gleanings* 134:2.

78. As for instance in the commandment of chastity.

79. Kitáb-i-Aqdas, *Synopsis*, p.47. On this subject 'Abdu'l-Bahá says: 'Opium fasteneth on the soul, so that the user's conscience dieth, his mind is blotted away, his perceptions are eroded. It turneth the living into the dead. It quencheth the natural heat. No greater harm can be conceived than that which opium inflicteth. Fortunate are they who never even speak the name of it; then think how wretched is the user. O ye lovers of God! In this, the cycle of Almighty God, violence and force, constraint and oppression, are one and all condemned. It is, however, mandatory that the use of opium be prevented by any means whatsoever, that perchance the human race may be delivered from this most powerful of plagues.' (*Selections*, No.129.) Intoxicants are also forbidden in Buddhism. In the 'tenfold course', binding on every Buddhist, it is said: 'The training in aversion from places of wanton use of wine, spirits and strong drink I undertake.' (Khuddaka-Patha, 2, *The minor anthologies of the Pali Canon*, p.141.) With regard to the ban on alcohol in Islám compare also Qur'án 2:216; 4:46; 5:92–3.

80. Helmut Schelsky, *Die Arbeit tun die anderen*, p.251.

therefore of great importance to know what meaning man sees in his work and what motives guide him in it.

Now in the last twenty years the Western democracies have begun to doubt whether work represents an autonomous existential value, transcending the mere support of life. A resentment against performance has grown up. [81] With the insatiable pressure towards a higher standard of living and increasing luxury, the value of work has become relative. The question therefore arises whether there is any purpose in continuing to hanker after material goods for their own sake, or whether it would not be desirable to give man greater leisure in the form of shorter working hours. There were also inevitable repercussions when optimism about progress gave way to disillusionment with regard to our technical civilization and industrial culture, in which the burdens simply grow and grow. Whereas in the past people were always spurred on by the hope of a better future, this generation now fears that the future may be worse than the present or that there will be no future at all. Thus leisure became elevated into a value in itself, without answering the question as to what man should put into it and how much of it he can actually endure. [82] Performance-inhibiting factors such as these encouraged a development leading to a 'work significance crisis' in which work declines into the hasty 'job' and is regarded as a necessary evil, the most hated source of income.

Labour discipline has retrogressed everywhere, not only in the capitalist countries. The countries with a socialist economy are also increasingly suffering from the decline in working morality. Complaints of 'loafing' are among the regularly recurring major criticisms within the Communist system. The 'new man', working spontaneously because of proletarian commitment and higher motivation than money-earning, has not yet arrived. It has to be realized in this context that in the Welfare State the net of social security has been so tightly knotted that work often seems scarcely worthwhile any more. Social security and the removal of industrial enslavement [83] is a proud achievement of the labour movement, an indispensable milestone in the humanization of the world. Nevertheless, the Welfare State can continue to function permanently only if the individual uses it morally. Social security without a corresponding working morality gives rise to parasitism, [84] to people living on the public and doing nothing, or by doing little, obtaining a higher income from social security

81. On the vilification of work, see H. Schelsky, *Die Arbeit tun die anderen*, pp.244–59.

82. On the same subject: Thomas Chorherr, *Der Freizeitschock. Das Leben in der Urlaubsgesellschaft*, Vienna 1980.

83. When 'Abdu'l-Bahá was staying in San Francisco in 1912, he told the American people: 'Between 1860 and 1865 you did a wonderful thing; you knocked the shackles from chattel slavery; but today you must do a much more wonderful thing: you must destroy industrial slavery.' (Quoted from *Star of the West*, Vol.VII, No.15, p.147.)

84. See Alfred Bosch, *Die Schmarotzer breiten sich aus. Parasitismus als Lebensform* (Spongers are on the Increase, Parasitism as a Way of Life), Freiburg, Herder Bücherei Initiative, Vol.9543, 1981.

than if they were working full-time. [85] This danger is universally recognized; [86] the question is simply: how to overcome it?

The most natural characteristic of man is laziness, [87] and apart from the mere securing of existence, the constant mobilization of highly motivating forces is needed in order to overcome this tendency towards idleness. Without a moral attitude towards work, without a work ethic, these forces are not available. A mechanical, inwardly uncommitted attitude towards work is not enough. To be properly done, work demands application from within, regardless of its character. The refuse collector who does not empty the rubbish bins properly, the factory worker who is negligent in inserting the screws, the policeman who takes no notice of infringements because they are a nuisance to him, the waiter who serves badly and churlishly – all of them contribute to making life unenjoyable and glum for everyone. And the more responsible the work, the more prejudicial are the effects of inadequate and unreliable work, not to speak of professions such as nursing and the care of the old and handicapped, which are inconceivable without the idea of service to one's neighbour.

The work ethic cannot be enforced by law. Inner submission cannot be produced to order. The work ethic can only arise from a person's inner responsibility; it is unjustifiable without reference to religion. That is why work has always been the object of moral evaluation in all religions. [88] There are numerous statements by Bahá'u'lláh on this subject. In the first place he showed that it is man's duty to learn and practise a profession, that he should earn his living and that of his family by the work of his hands or his head, and that idleness, sloth and laziness are misdemeanours, that is, sins, for which man is responsible. In the Kalimát-i-

---

85. Jürgen Eick sees the real class antagonism in the exploitation of the 'producers of additional output' by the socially secure. He quotes the Dutch socialist Pollak: 'Today half of mankind has to slave itself to death so that the others can loaf about' ('Die zweigeteilte Gesellschaft', in *Frankfurter Allgemeine Zeitung* of 6.1.1973).

86. The constitution of the People's Republic of China contains the statement: 'If any would not work, neither should he eat', a maxim which is taken, not from Karl Marx, but from the Apostle Paul (II Thess.3:10).

87. 'When the traveller, who had seen many countries and nations and continents, was asked what common attribute he had found everywhere existing among men, he answered, "They have a tendency to sloth." ' (Nietzsche, *Schopenhauer as Educator*, I, p.1.).

88. In Judaism work in all forms is a 'service'. Work was expected of man even in Paradise as the fulfilment of a divine command (Gen. 2:15). In Christianity, work is the expression of grateful love of God (Col. 3:23). In Catholicism work is regarded as the moral exercise of virtue. The motto derived from Benedict of Nursia 'ora et labora' elevated work to the rank of prayer. The *vita contemplativa* faces the *vita activa*. For Benedict work is essentially service to others. Martin Luther, too, saw work as 'worship' and also as service to one's neighbour. The same is true of Calvin, whose idea that the Christian must prove himself in profession, commerce and craft by proficiency and reliability to the honour of God, put his stamp on the Puritan work morality and, as Max Weber showed (*The Protestant Ethic and the Spirit of Capitalism*, London 1950), contributed to the birth of the 'spirit of capitalism'. On the whole subject see *Die Religion in Geschichte und Gegenwart*, 3rd edn, Vol.I, pp.534–45.

Maknúnih[89] Bahá'u'lláh says: 'The best of men are they that earn a livelihood by their calling and spend upon themselves and upon their kindred[90] . . . Ye are the trees of My garden; ye must give forth goodly and wondrous fruits, that ye yourselves and others may profit therefrom. Thus it is incumbent on every one to engage in crafts and professions, for therein lies the secret of wealth, O men of understanding!'[91] Elsewhere he says: 'It is enjoined upon every one of you to engage in some form of occupation, such as crafts, trades and the like.'[92] Laziness is sharply condemned: 'Waste not your time in idleness and sloth. Occupy yourselves with that which profiteth yourselves and others . . . The most despised of men in the sight of God are those who sit idly and beg.'[93] The idea that man should bear fruit is a much used, recurrent theme in the writings of Bahá'u'lláh, which is of importance to the whole of his doctrine of virtue, but especially in connection with work: 'The basest of men are they that yield no fruit on earth. Such men are verily counted as among the dead, nay, better are the dead in the sight of God than those idle and worthless souls . . . Trees that yield no fruit have been and will ever be for the fire.'[94] Bahá'u'lláh expressly forbade begging.[95] He was accordingly pronouncing judgement on all forms of parasitical life. If man is to live by the work of his hands and welfare is to be gained by work,[96] then the idle pauper and the rich loafer are equally rejected.

According to Bahá'u'lláh work is a fundamental fulfilment of human existence and an essential sign of personality development. But it is still more: Bahá'u'lláh exalted it to the status of the service of God: 'We have graciously exalted your engagement in such work to the rank of worship unto God, the True One.'[97] Work, like prayer, is worship, which endows it with a quality which it does not possess in the profane sphere. Worship without surrender is impossible; if the work is to be done in the spirit of service to God, it must be done with inner surrender, thus becoming a sacred work, performed with a pure heart, inward collectedness, and from love and joy: 'The man who makes a piece of notepaper to the best of his ability, conscientiously, concentrating all his forces on perfecting it, is giving praise to God . . . All effort and exertion put forth by man from the fullness of his heart is worship, if it is prompted by the highest motives and

---

89. *The Hidden Words*. The title does not refer to a hidden verbal sense but is an allusion to the hidden book of Fátimáh, daughter of the prophet Muhammad. (cf. Adib Taherzadeh, *The Revelation of Bahá'u'lláh*, vol.I, Oxford 1974, pp.71ff.)
90. Persian 82.
91. Persian 80; cf. Aṣl-i-Kullu'l-Khayr, *Tablets*, p.155.
92. Bishárát, twelfth Glad-Tidings, *Tablets*, p.26.
93. Bishárát, ibid.
94. Bahá'u'lláh, *The Hidden Words*, Persian 81, 80.
95. Kitáb-i-Aqdas, *Synopsis*, p.47.
96. cf. Ṭarázát, first Ṭaráz, *Tablets*, p.35.
97. Bishárát, twelfth Glad-Tidings, *Tablets*, p.26.

the will to do service to humanity.'[98] Work is therefore also service to one's neighbour, for 'This is worship: to serve mankind and to minister to the needs of the people[99] . . . Service in love for mankind is unity with God. He who serves has already entered the kingdom and is seated at the right hand of his Lord.'[100] As long as the purpose of the work is not exclusively that of ensuring existence, but extends to being of service to God and man, then it is obvious that an important driving force becomes available here which can motivate the faithful and overcome the slothfulness which is described as their most natural feature. At the same time, the rank allotted to work in the teachings of Bahá'u'lláh opens up a new assessment of work activities: even the type of work which is unavoidably monotonous participates in the meaning of work. In a future Bahá'í society the very lowliest services, which are no less important to the common good than the works of the intellect, are those which will take on a new value. The caring professions, too – those least able to be performed without a loving devotion to one's neighbour, will once again be supported by an ethic which for centuries enabled man to sacrifice himself for his fellows.[101]

Moderation

In this connection it is worth examining the rank allocated by Bahá'u'lláh to the virtue of moderation. Cherished by the philosophers and poets of antiquity[102] and the wise men of China,[103] this principle is given outstanding significance by Bahá'u'lláh. In the Kalimát-i-Firdawsíyyih he says: 'In all matters moderation is desirable. If a thing is carried to excess, it will prove a source of evil.'[104] In connection above all with freedom and civilization, Bahá'u'lláh exhorted rulers to adopt the virtue of moderation, since both freedom and material civilization in excess 'exercise a pernicious influence upon men'.[105] Total freedom leads to anarchy and turns into tyranny. Material civilization which runs to extremes leads to over-

---

98. 'Abdu'l-Bahá, speech in London, quoted from *Paris Talks*, English edition, p.176.

99. 'Abdu'l-Bahá, op. cit., p.177.

100. 'Abdu'l-Bahá, quoted from *Pattern of Bahá'í Life*, p.39.

101. For an examination of the purpose of work see Rúḥíyyih Rabbání, *Prescription for Living*, pp.84ff.

102. *Méden agán* = not too much (translated by Terence as *Ne quid nimis*) is said by Plato to have been an inscription on the Temple of Apollo in Delphi. The hexameter by Horace *Est modus in rebus, sunt certi denique fines* from the *Satires* I, 1, 106, is well-known. Plato included moderation, *sophrosyne*, among the four cardinal virtues: wisdom, courage, moderation and justice. For Aristotle, in the Stoa (*temperantia*), and for Thomas Aquinas, moderation retained a central significance. Thomas Aquinas added to the four cardinal virtues a further three: faith, love and hope. Catholic moral theology counts moderation among the fundamental natural virtues of man. Literature: Joseph Pieper, *The four cardinal virtues; prudence, justice, fortitude, temperance*, Notre Dame, Ind., 1966. Another basic work on ethics is O. Fr. Bollnow, *Wesen und Wandel der Tugenden*, Berlin 1980.

103. 'How perfect is the virtue that accords with the Golden Mean!' (Confucius, *The Analects*, VI, XXVII.)

104. Ninth leaf, *Tablets*, p.69.

105. Bahá'u'lláh, *Gleanings* 110; Kitáb-i-Aqdas, *Synopsis*, No.16, pp.24–5; see also p.158.

industrialization and this, as Bahá'u'lláh predicted more than a hundred years ago when the industrialization of the world was in its early stages and could still have been brought under control, ends in the environmental destruction which we are now witnessing with bewilderment: 'The civilization, so often vaunted by the learned exponents of arts and sciences, will, if allowed to overleap the bounds of moderation, bring great evil upon men. Thus warneth you He Who is the All-Knowing. If carried to excess, civilization will prove as prolific a source of evil as it had been of goodness when kept within the restraints of moderation. Meditate on this, O people, and be not of them that wander distraught in the wilderness of error. The day is approaching when its flame will devour the cities, when the Tongue of Grandeur will proclaim: "The Kingdom is God's, the Almighty, the All-Praised!"'[106]

The world has lost the wisdom of moderation, and this loss is the true cause of the ecological misery. It is not that technology and industry are evil in themselves, but that an excess of them is threatening to devour us. Since the consequences are unpredictable, scientists today are becoming increasingly aware of this threat. Erwin Chargaff writes: 'We have lost entirely this sense of measure, of reticence, of knowing one's own boundaries. Man is only strong when he is conscious of his own weakness. Otherwise, the eagles of heaven will eat his liver, as Prometheus found out. No eagles of heaven any more, no Prometheus: now we get cancer instead – the prime disease of advanced civilizations.'[107]

When Bahá'u'lláh says 'All other things are subject to this same principle of moderation',[108] this also applies to the virtues themselves. Everything is wrong in excess, even virtue: 'To go beyond the mark is as bad as to fall short of it',[109] says Confucius. Exaggeration of the virtues led via chastity to celibacy and Victorian prudery, via the commandment of detachment from the earthly world to ascetic rejection of the world and monasticism; via the demand for women's equality to an aggressive, man-hating and in extreme cases even Lesbian feminism; via faith in God, the Islámic *tawakkul*, to the inactive quietism and fatalism of the *mutawakkilún*.[110] Generosity, practised to excess, becomes squandering; hence the prophet Muḥammad warned the faithful: 'And to him who is of kin render his due, and also to the poor and to the wayfarer; yet waste not wastefully, for the wasteful are brethren of the Satans . . . And let not thy hand be tied up to the neck; nor yet open it with all openness.'[111] Exaggerated piety degenerates into sanctimoniousness, bigotry and fanaticism, im-

106. *Gleanings* 163:2.
107. *Heraclitean Fire*, p.155.
108. *Gleanings* 163:3.
109. *The Analects*, XI, XV.
110. See Goldziher, *Vorlesungen über den Islam*, pp.151ff.
111. Qur'án 17:28–9, 31.

moderate uprightness into self-righteousness, courtesy into falseness, servility and sycophancy, boundless courage turns into bravado; dutifulness without ethical foundations and concepts of order without metaphysical reference-points lead straight to the crimes committed in the concentration camps.

Even the highest values in the value hierarchy, love and justice, degenerate when practised to excess. Justice, exercised in accordance with the tenet *Fiat iustitia, pereat mundus*, descends into fanatical *kohlhaasian*[112] persecution, and unbridled love leads to indulgence. When it oversteps the bounds of justice it becomes, as Emil Brunner aptly remarks, sentimentality and emotionalism, leading to the disintegration of order: 'Love which is not just in the world of institutions is sentimentality. And sentimentality, feeling for feeling's sake, is the poison, the solvent which destroys all institutions of justice.'[113] The generally observable one-sided tendency to concentrate on the central value of 'love' while completely ignoring all the other values, and justice in particular, ultimately leads to a complete subjectivity over values, and to the end of the objective value order.[114] The fact that even the norms of ethics have inherent limitations was known to Confucius: 'Courtesy uncontrolled by the laws of good taste becomes laboured effort, caution uncontrolled becomes timidity, boldness uncontrolled becomes recklessness, and frankness uncontrolled becomes effrontery.'[115]

The 'Balance' – the New Yardstick

The divinely ordained status of the new order of values emerges clearly from Islámic eschatology. The prophet Muḥammad promised that on the Day of Judgement a balance would be set up on which all the deeds of men, all their faults and works would be weighed.[116] When Bahá'u'lláh appeared and claimed that he himself had ushered in the 'hour' promised by Muḥammad, the Muslims, who thought of the 'balance' in a literal sense, objected that the promise had not yet been fulfilled, because the balance had not been set up. In an ode in which Bahá'u'lláh examines the

---

112. 'But the sense of justice turned him into a brigand and murderer.' This is the epigraph to the novella *Michael Kohlhaas* by Heinrich v. Kleist (1777–1811), one of the most brilliant of German dramatists and perhaps the greatest of German novella authors. This novella describes the fate of a horse dealer whose life is plunged into chaos through violence and injustice. Because governmental institutions fail to support or defend his civil rights, he seeks to secure them for himself, using whatever means are necessary, even criminal ones. In the process he turns into an arsonist and a murderer and meets a tragic end.

113. *Justice and the Social Order*, p.129.

114. See pp.180ff.

115. *The Analects*, VIII, II.

116. On the 'balance' see Qur'án 7:7–8; 21:48; 42:16–17; 55:6; 57:25; 23:104; 101:6–7; also the Hadíth collection of 'Alí al-Muttaqi al-Hindi (d.A.H. 975 = A.D. 1567), *Kanzúl 'Ummál*, published by Muíd-Khan, rev.edn, Haiderabad 1971 (Osmania Oriental Publication Bureau) Vol.18, pp.24–8.

many objections based on Islámic eschatology of those who rejected his mission, he writes: 'They say: "We see not the Balance". Say: "Surely, by my Lord, the God of Mercy! None can see it except such as are endued with insight." ' [117] Bahá'u'lláh maintains that the Balance has been set up: 'The All-Merciful is come invested with undoubted sovereignty. The Balance hath been appointed, and all them that dwell on earth have been gathered together', [118] and unequivocally states that this means the new Book of God, the tabernacle of the new morality.

The Kitáb-i-Aqdas (Most Holy Book), revealed by Bahá'u'lláh in 1873 in 'Akká, 'during the full tide of His tribulations, at a time when the rulers of the earth had definitely forsaken Him' [119] is regarded by the Bahá'ís as the central book of the new 'Book of God'. They see in it the law prophesied by Isaiah [120] deriving from Zion, the 'new heaven' and the 'new earth' seen by John, the 'holy city' descended from heaven, the 'new Jerusalem', the 'bride', the 'tabernacle of God with men'. [121] Bahá'u'lláh himself had already announced this in the *Kitáb-i-Íqán* [122] and adorned it with high attributes: 'the source of true felicity', 'the quickener of mankind', 'the mightiest stronghold', 'the Straight Path', [123] 'the Lamp of God for the whole world', [124] 'the standard of justice,' [125] 'the Unerring Balance'. [126]

The book, God's directions for the new mankind, the Charter of Bahá'u'lláh's World Order, [127] is a framework of the highest norms and values of morality and justice. Its laws are supreme guiding standards for all Bahá'í legislation, especially for that of the Universal House of Justice [128] which in the course of time, after the full enforcement of the laws of the Kitáb-i-Aqdas, will promulgate the supplementary laws which the world community needs. Besides the actual laws, the book contains exhortations and warnings to the spiritual and secular rulers, prophecies and elucidations on central questions of faith such as the infallibility of the manifestations of God, the essence of divine law, the boundaries of freedom and the like. The book is at the same time the divine constitutional document, because it lays down the legislative and administrative institutions of the world community and anticipates the later ministry of

117. *Epistle to the Son of the Wolf*, p.132; cf. also Ishráqát, *Tablets*, pp.117–19.
118. *Gleanings* 17:1; also 114:12; 129:5; 135:4.
119. Shoghi Effendi, *The Promised Day is Come*, p.24.
120. Isa.2:2–3.
121. Rev.21:1–3; Bahá'u'lláh, *Kitáb-i-Íqán*, pp.198–9; 'Abdu'l-Bahá, *Some Answered Questions*, ch.13; Shoghi Effendi, *God Passes By*, pp.213ff.
122. p.201.
123. Compare Shoghi Effendi, *God Passes By*, pp.215ff.: *Gleanings* 110.
124. Bahá'u'lláh, Kitáb-i-Aqdas, *Synopsis*, p.7.
125. Bahá'u'lláh, *Gleanings* 88.
126. Compare Shoghi Effendi, *God Passes By*, p.215.
127. Shoghi Effendi, *The Promised Day is Come*, p.24.
128. See p.244.

'Abdu'l-Bahá as successor and plenipotentiary interpreter of the revealed Word.[129] The Kitáb-i-Aqdas is therefore the principal source of Bahá'í constitutional law.[130] The laws it contains are supplemented by numerous additional regulations in the Tablets[131] Ishráqát, Bishárát, Tarázát, Tajallíyát, Kalimát-i-Firdawsíyyih, Lawh-i-Aqdas, Lawh-i-Dunyá, Lawh-i-Maqsúd, etc.

It should be no surprise that Bahá'u'lláh's standards are not strictly systematic, as we expect of our modern legal technique. The history of religion shows that the laws of God have never come down in the form of a rational, systematically structured design of general, abstract norms. It would therefore be wrong to apply the yardstick of our modern legal system, as Rosenkranz does when he calls the Kitáb-i-Aqdas 'a hotch-potch of instructions'.[132] This criticism fails to recognize that founders of religions were never systematic. Their doctrines are not logically developed systems of intellectual enlightenment. As Rosenkranz stresses elsewhere,[133] the essence of religion lies in the irrational, the numinous. Neither the laws of the Old Testament nor those of the Qur'án stand in a systematic context; it was only the theologians and lawyers who systematized them. The Kitáb-i-Aqdas is not a codified book of law, nor would Bahá'u'lláh have it so: 'Think not that We have revealed unto you a mere code of laws. Nay, rather, We have unsealed the choice wine with the fingers of might and power.'[134] The eschatological event, the setting up of the 'Balance', was announced by Bahá'u'lláh in challenging words: 'Say: O leaders of religion! Weigh not the Book of God with such standards and sciences as are current amongst you, for the Book itself is the unerring balance established amongst men. In this most perfect balance whatsoever the peoples and kindreds of the earth possess must be weighed, while the

---

129. Compare Shoghi Effendi, *God Passes By*, pp.214–15.

130. See also Udo Schaefer, thesis: 'Die Grundlagen der Verwaltungsordnung der Bahá'í', Heidelberg 1957.

131. Translation of the Arabic word *lawh*, which literally means 'table', and has a sublime significance in Arabic when writing is referred to. *Lawh* is then used exclusively for Holy Scriptures. If a *lawh* is in the form of a letter, it is translated by 'epistle', 'tablet' or 'letter' (e.g. Lawh-i-Ibn-i-Dhib = *Epistle to the Son of the Wolf*). The use of the word 'table' is also known in the Judeo-Christian tradition: God himself wrote the Ten Commandments on two tables of stone (compare Exod. 24:12; 31:18; 32:15–16; Isa. 30:8; Hab. 2:2). In the Qur'án *lawh* can be found in Sura 85:22; the plural *'alwáh* in 7:142; 7:149; 7:153.

132. *Die Bahá'í*, p.32.

133. op. cit., p.56.

134. Kitáb-i-Aqdas, *Synopsis*, No.1, p.12 (= *Gleanings* 155:5). The book was first published in print in Bombay in 1890. The oriental Bahá'ís have this book and live in accordance with it as far as the laws of personal status are concerned. Only a small part is available at present in an authentic translation from the Arabic, namely the sections translated into English by Shoghi Effendi (compare *Gleanings* 37; 56; 70; 72; 98; 105; 155; 159. See also the list in *Synopsis*, pp.29–30). In 1973 the Universal House of Justice published the translated parts of the work and a survey of the subjects on which directions were given in this work (*Synopsis and Codification of the Laws and Ordinances of the Kitáb-i-Aqdas*, Haifa 1973). As noted in the introduction, the complete translation of the book will be appear-

measure of its weight should be tested according to its own standard, did ye but know it.'[135] . . . 'Say: This is the infallible Balance which the Hand of God is holding, in which all who are in the heavens and all who are on the earth are weighed, and their fate determined, if ye be of them that believe and recognize this truth. Say: Through it the poor have been enriched, the learned enlightened, and the seekers enabled to ascend unto the presence of God. Beware, lest ye make it a cause of dissension amongst you. Be ye as firmly settled as the immovable mountain in the Cause of your Lord, the Mighty, the Loving.'[136]

The Balance is therefore a symbol, the sign of a new yardstick, revealed by God on the Day of Judgement. The revelation, the Book of God, the newly proclaimed values, are therefore the measure of all morality:[137] 'Know verily that the essence of justice and the source thereof are both embodied in the ordinances prescribed by Him who is the Manifestation of the Self of God amongst men, if ye be of them that recognize this truth. He doth verily incarnate the highest, the infallible standard of justice unto all creation. Were His law to be such as to strike terror into the hearts of all that are in heaven and on earth, that law is naught but manifest justice.'[138]

On the Genealogy of Ethical Norms

What is justice? Like Pilate's question 'What is truth?'[139] this is one of the eternal questions of mankind. The legal philosopher Hans Kelsen comments that no other question has caused the most exalted minds from Plato to Kant to ponder so deeply, that no other question has cost so much precious blood, so many bitter tears, and he states: 'And yet this question has no more been answered today than it ever was.'[140] The verses of Bahá'u'lláh quoted here are the answer to this question of justice. They are the theological pivot of the establishment of all law and all personal morality on earth.

Thus the bedrock of basic ethical values lies in the divine revelation. There is no moral law independent of God, no natural law to which God is bound. The assumption that there is such a preordained natural order of morality independent of God would in the Qur'ánic sense be _shirk_, the greatest sin of all, which God does not forgive.[141] The divine will alone

---

ing 'in due course'.
135. Kitáb-i-Aqdas, *Synopsis*, No.14 = *Gleanings* 98:1.
136. Kitáb-i-Aqdas, *Synopsis*, No.21 = *Gleanings* 70:3.
137. Compare Schaefer, *The Light Shineth in Darkness*, pp.73ff.
138. Bahá'u'lláh, *Gleanings* 88.
139. John 18:38.
140. *Was ist Gerechtigkeit?*, p.1.
141. 'God truly will not forgive the joining of other gods with Himself. Other sins He will forgive to

decides what is good and evil: 'But God doth what He will',[142] 'He shall not be asked of his doings'.[143] For the kind of religious thinking based on a monotheistic revealed religion, this voluntaristic view is the logically compelling one. For the Mosaic religion, the Torah is the revealed basic law of the moral world pure and simple.[144] For the Muslim the Qur'án and the *sunna*[145] of the prophet[146] is the quintessence of all morality and all law. Paul, too,[147] and Augustine and Duns Scotus,[148] deriving from him, supported this view: 'But there is no higher law above God, His will first creates every law there is, that is why His action is as He proceeds, always and necessarily right and ordered . . . God acts, as He acts, always justly. He is bound to no previous ideal order but all laws are contingent ordinances of God's will.'[149] Calvin also sees the source of all law in the unfathomable will of God: '*Adeo enim summa est iustitiae regula Dei voluntas, ut quidquid eo ipso quod vult iustum habendum est.*'[150] Therefore all obligation is founded, not, as Thomas Aquinas taught,[151] in being, but in the will of God. It is not reality but divine law which is the fundament of ethics. Ethics should not be guided by things as they are but by standards relating to supreme values. The role of reason in the sphere of revealed morality is to recognize the emphases of prescribed, supreme values and their relationship of tension to one another and to reify these values in the multiplicity of practical life and changing historical situations.

The view upheld here is in direct contradiction to the moral philosophy of Immanuel Kant. According to Kant the demands of the categorical imperative are recognized only by reason. God is not the creator of the moral law; the moral order is above Him. His existence is simply a postulate of practical reason to complete – not to lay the foundations of! – the moral law. Therefore, to Kant, religion is simply the continuation of moral philosophy to the 'knowledge of all our duties as divine

---

whom He will: but he who joineth gods with Gods, hath erred with far-gone error.' (Qur'án 4:116; compare also 31:12). Compare also Goldziher, *Vorlesungen über den Islam*, pp.41 and 107; also in this context Exod. 20:4.

142. Qur'án 2:254; 14:32.

143. Qur'án 21:23; compare the comments on pp.152ff.

144. 'For monotheistic rationalism, natural religion and, similarly, natural law cannot be a sufficient foundation; for it, the only foundation is the unique God. The latter, however, becomes identical with morality.' (Hermann Cohen, *Religion of Reason out of the Sources of Judaism*, p.353.)

145. The exemplary life of the prophet, all his utterances and actions, as passed on by means of the hadíth. See Goldziher, *Vorlesungen über den Islam*, pp.36ff.

146. 'All conditions of private and public life are the subjects of a religious doctrine of duty.' (Goldziher, op.cit., p.50.)

147. Rom. 9:14ff.

148. (1270–1308) op. Oxoniense I d.44 qu.un.n.1; II d.7 qu.un.n.18.

149. Hans Welzel, *Naturrecht und materiale Gerechtigkeit*, p.72.

150. *Institutio*, III, 23, 2.

151. Compai : J. Pieper, *The Human Wisdom of St. Thomas*, p.10, No.46.

commandments'.[152] According to Kant, morality leads 'directly to religion, by means of which it expands to the idea of a despotic moral legislator without man'.[153] The development described at the beginning of this book, the emancipation *from* morality in secular society, proves the opposite: that it is not morality which leads to religion, but religion to morality, and that the structure of morality collapses when its foundation, religion, is destroyed.

Catholic morality also drew the norms of a moral life from the source of divine revelation and from natural law recognized by reason. In the encyclopedia *Christliche Religion* published by Fischer in 1957, Heinrich Fries referred to revelation and described an exclusively interpreted philosophical moral doctrine as 'completely inappropriate' to the supernatural salvation of man.[154] By now a fundamental change has taken place in Catholic moral theology under the influence of secular thought. There are no longer any unalterable Christian standards of morality. Ethical concepts are autonomous and recognized by reason. According to the Catholic moral theologian Alfons Auer, teaching in Munich, the 'autonomy of morality' is 'not only a possible approach for the theologian but, at least in present-day society, the only sensible one'.[155] His thesis: 'Man achieves certain knowledge of his being and thus also of the moral order through his reason . . . The rationality of the moral arises from the rational nature of man . . . The rationality of the moral implies its autonomy.' Man can 'perfectly well understand the complete nature of his existence in the world and therefore also the decisive core of morality without the express knowledge of God'.[156] The yardstick for the recognition of genuine values, for the distinction between good and evil, according to Auer, lies in the 'consonance or dissonance' of our behaviour patterns 'with the fundamental dynamic of evolution'.[157] But how can anyone know so precisely what is truly consonant with this fundamental dynamic?

The Tübingen Catholic theologian Herbert Haag also considers that man finds out from his knowledge of historical and social conditions 'how to direct his life so that it succeeds' and sums up: 'The younger moral theologians are agreed that as far as content is concerned there can be no specifically Christian morality. The moral behaviour of a Christian in no

152. *Religion within the Limits of Reason Alone*, Section 4, Part 1, p.170.

153. op. cit. Prologue to first edition, IX, p.6.

154. p.34.

155. *Autonome Moral und christlicher Glaube*, p.12.

156. op. cit., pp.28–30. The obvious question as to why, in that case, such a pluralism of the most widely varying opinions prevails today on the problem of good and evil, why there are such divergent opinions about euthanasia, abortion, birth control, violence, marriage, homosexuality and so forth, and why all the reasonable people who think so differently cannot reach a consensus on such vital matters, apparently does not irritate him.

157. *Autonome Moral und christlicher Glaube*, p.72, with reference to L. Monden, *Sünde, Freiheit und Bewußtsein*, Salzburg 1968, pp.94–7.

way differs from the moral behaviour of a non-Christian living under the same cultural and social conditions. Therefore the moral awareness of the Christian is based on the *Humanum*.'[158] In Auer's view the articulation of moral obligations is possible only 'in the dialogue of the sciences'.[159] Since the different disciplines of the humane sciences mediate a knowledge of principles which is often superseded after only a decade, Auer sees 'the entire misery of ethics and moral theology made plain'. For the creative development of ethical consciousness in the light of scientific knowledge, which is constantly changing and never free of ambiguity, leads to a 'continuous state of ethical reflection' which only a few people 'can achieve without the risk of neurosis'.[160] The question then is whether anything specifically Christian is left in the Christian moral doctrine. The answer is: 'The horizon of sense and the motivation of the moral.'[161]

The international congress of German moral theologians in Munich in September 1979 also reflects this theological reorientation, described there by Auer as an 'historically due development'.[162] This change of view in fundamental theological problems shows to what an extent the once intractable positions of Catholic and 'modern' thought, which in the twenties were still leading to violent controversy,[163] have been levelled out by the incursion of modernism and the constant advance of secularization.

For evangelical theology, too, the Christian ethos does not mean living under the law of revealed and absolute norms but 'quite simply the life lived in the recognition of the reality of God and in community with Him. Everything else follows from the fact that we can be together with Him in His love.'[164] The Protestant theologian Eberhard Jüngel accordingly professes the view 'that the Christian ethos is not guided by a value ethic', because 'living from truth' is the same in the Gospel as 'existing in love'.[165]

As things are, Christian moral theology finds itself in a dual dilemma. On the one hand, the de-Christianization of the formerly Christian world has advanced to such an extent that the modern Christian is no longer prepared to accept prescribed norms without rational justification, which means that judgement has already been pronounced on norms that are less

---

158. 'Vor dem Bösen ratlos?' In *Zur Debatte*, themes of the Catholic Academy in Bavaria, 1979, Issue 2.
159. *Autonome Moral und christlicher Glaube*, p.47.
160. op. cit., pp.46–7.
161. Alfons Auer, *Autonome Moral und christlicher Glaube*, Foreword; similarly Herbert Haag, see Note 158; on the whole subject see also: Franz Böckle, *Fundamentalmoral*, Munich 1977.
162. *Süddeutsche Zeitung* of 24.9.1979.
163. Compare Messer and Pribilla, *Katholisches und modernes Denken*.
164. Rudolf Stählin, in *Christliche Religion*, Das Fischer-Lexikon, p.81.
165. 'Wertlose Wahrheit', in Carl Schmitt, E. Jüngel, S. Schelz, *Die Tyrannei der Werte*, pp.5, 47ff.

accessible to rational justification.[166] On the other hand, Christian theology is the captive of its standpoint of exclusivity and finality. Since the sum total of the divine was made manifest to mankind through Jesus Christ, it has to manage with what it has. Social ethics which are dependent on the changing times cannot be founded on Biblical norms which were fashioned to suit completely different conditions.[167] For the Christian, they can only be rationally conceived. The traditional values of personal ethics have become worn out in the course of two thousand years and have grown so diffuse as a result of many divergent interpretations that there is obviously a great temptation, instead of continuing to support them in a fundamentalist way, to provide a rationally founded, autonomous morality with a Christian meaning and Christian motives. There is one more thing which has to be recognized in this context: anyone who is once convinced of the possibility of an autonomous rational ethic and who is not irritated by the current pluralism of values and the disappearance of ethical ideas, will also be unable to see any necessity at all for new guidance from God, a new Revelation.

Bahá'u'lláh's teaching of a progressive, cyclically returning Manifestation opens up a new dimension of thought on the history of salvation and a new concept for the laying down of ethical norms. Therefore the new Book of God is at the same time a judgement on the old religions, as it purifies the genuine and true from the false and untrue, from human additions and misunderstandings, and at the same time it is a judgement on the moderns. In his Epistle to Pope Pius IX Bahá'u'lláh revealed: 'Verily, the day of ingathering is come, and all things have been separated from each other. He hath stored away that which He chose in the vessels of justice and cast into fire that which befitteth it.'[168]

Purification and Personal Development

Now the Christian and also the Jew, Muslim, Hindu and follower of Buddha will recognize himself in these values and ask himself where the special nature of the new morality promulgated by Bahá'u'lláh lies. This justifiable question cannot be dealt with here in the detail it requires. The answer lies in the idea already discussed, the idea of the progressive divine revelation, the idea of the impulse. The progressive revelation of God is conditioned by changing conditions on earth, by the difference in the

---

166. The virtue of chastity (for further details see pp.176ff.) cannot, for instance, be conclusively derived either from the knowledge of the humane sciences or from anthropological ideas. There are norms which are not amenable to logically imperative proof.

167. Islámic theology is in a similar dilemma: either it interprets norms which no longer fit the times (in particular the Qur'ánic penal regulations), or it remains fundamentalist and continues to practise what arouses revulsion and horror today, thus involuntarily contributing to the general disenchantment with religion.

168. *The Proclamation of Bahá'u'lláh*, p.86.

spiritual capacity of acceptance by men,[169] by the process of abrasion to which all religions are subject and by the exhaustion of the original shaping force which has come down to mankind with every divine revelation. The change in our social reality demands a change in the divine social norms and vice versa. The law and social institutions such as marriage and family have undergone various different versions in the different religions.[170] The norms revealed by Bahá'u'lláh for the new society also differ from those of the past. But the values which man is supposed to realize as an individual being are independent of historical change: 'Know thou that in every age and dispensation all divine ordinances are changed and transformed according to the requirement of the time, except the law of love, which, like a fountain, always flows and is never overtaken by change.'[171] Love stands here *pars pro toto* for the eternal values which belong to the central core of the one, indivisible religion of God, over the millennia. It is in this sense that 'Abdu'l-Bahá says that the Bahá'í religion is 'no new way to happiness'.[172] The values in the (individual) catalogue of virtues of Bahá'u'lláh are not new. The central values which men are called upon to acquire are the same as in all previous religions, and will remain the same in the future although they may be differently expressed and may occupy different positions in the hierarchy of values. In Bahá'u'lláh's revelation too, purified of their encrustations, deformations, misinterpretations, exaggerations, shifts in emphasis, and provided with new linguistic raiment, new force, new sense and new emphases, they are the pillars of individual morality. In Bahá'u'lláh's revelation these old, original values have been presented in an incomparably richer form than in the past – not least because they have been passed on in an unbroken tradition.

In this connection it is necessary to counter a misunderstanding which may have arisen in reading the introductory chapters. The criticism of the collapse of the religious value order[173] does not imply any nostalgia for the conditions of bygone days. There will be no restoration of what is past, for the hour of the aeon, and hence of the old order, is over. The Bahá'í is therefore no 'reactionary' straining against the unstoppable march of history. His gaze is directed at the future, not at the past. He knows the aim of history, and he knows that the foundations of morality have to be laid anew. To transmit the original values, which are simultaneously the

169. 'I have yet many things to say unto you, but ye cannot bear them now.' (John 16:12.)
170. St. Augustine also spoke of that true justice 'which judgeth not according to custom, but out of the most rightful Law of God Almighty, by which the fashions of several places and times were so disposed, as was fittest both for those times and places' and 'because God commanded them one thing then, and these another thing now for certain temporal respects; and yet those of both ages were servants to the same righteousness' (*Confessions*, III, 7).
171. Bahá'u'lláh, quoted from Esslemont, *Bahá'u'lláh and the New Era*, p.163.
172. Compare pp.125ff.
173. Compare comments on pp.32ff.

new ones, and anchor them in the consciousness of man, as soon as it has become clear what a poor basis the secular substitute values are for a fulfilled life and a stable society, will be a work of education accomplished over generations for mankind, the fruit of which will be the new man.

These values are in need of a new force, for together with the faith in which they were rooted, from which they were transmitted and kept alive in society, the values themselves have died away and are no longer an undisputed reality in our society. A new sense is needed because just as the concepts of Christian Faith have been deprived of sense, so central value concepts are being deprived of sense in their turn: 'The word is torn and tattered,' wrote Romano Guardini,[174] and Paul Tillich once suggested in relation to this subject that the Church ought to impose a thirty-year period of silence on all the fundamental religious words.[175] As an example: the commandment of chastity, which had already pushed the commandment to love into second place by the third century A.D., leading to the bedevilment of the instinctual area and the defamation of woman, and to celibacy, was invalidated by secular society and is now, despite the encyclical *Humanae vitae*, disputed within the Church. The current debate on the point shows how far theology has now moved from this former core of Christian morality[176] and how much a new signpost is needed.

The point emerges even more clearly from another example. The commandment to love, rightly put forward by Christians as the *Summmum bonum*, the quintessence of all morality, has had limitations imposed on it over the centuries: to people, race, religion or party. And where love is practised only within boundaries, it produces inward integration, but outward hatred. The wars of religion, the Crusades, the treatment of the Jews in Europe and particularly in Germany in our own century, or of the members of the black race in the United States and South Africa are examples of the way in which Christ's commandment to love one another has been distorted and limited in the course of history.

All-Embracing Love of Mankind

Bahá'u'lláh has torn down all the barriers set up by prejudice and supersti-

---

174. *The End of the Modern World*, p.102.

175. Verification in H. Zahrnt, *The Question of God*, p.300. Similarly, Jacob Burckhardt said that 'the whole range of possible theological standpoints has already been tried out . . . If theology understood its own advantage it would rather be silent for the next thirty years' (quoted from Löwith, *Meaning in History*, p.29.) The same idea can be found in Hölderlin: 'All that is divine has too long been in use, And all heavenly powers spurned and stale.' (*Dichterberuf, Werke*, Vol.IV, p.146.)

176. I refer to the discussion in Erich Kellner (ed.), *Sexualität ohne Tabu und christliche Moral*. Gespräche der Paulus-Gesellschaft, München, Mainz 1970. The Marburg theologian Siegfried Keil protested against the sexual morality of the Church at a meeting in 1966 of the Tutzing Evangelical Academy on the theme: 'Against the general sexual obligation', declaring that the Church's only chance as the traditional guardian of morals lay in obtaining advice from the relevant disciplines, sociology, medicine and psychology, and throwing the old morality overboard; it was foolish to talk of eternal yardsticks in matters of sexual morality. Responsible free love must be met half-way; even an unmarried woman should not be forbidden physical love and child-bearing.

tion in the past and proclaimed an all-embracing, great, selfless love for the whole of undivided humanity: 'It is incumbent upon every man, in this Day, to hold fast unto whatsoever will promote the interests, and exalt the station, of all nations and just governments. Through each and every one of the verses which the Pen of the Most High hath revealed, the doors of love and unity have been unlocked and flung open to the face of men. We have erewhile declared – and Our Word is the truth – : "Consort with the followers of all religions in a spirit of friendliness and fellowship." Whatsoever hath led the children of men to shun one another, and hath caused dissensions and divisions amongst them, hath, through the revelation of these words, been nullified and abolished . . . Of old it hath been revealed: "Love of one's country is an element of the Faith of God."[177] The Tongue of Grandeur hath, however, in the day of His manifestation proclaimed: "It is not his to boast who loveth his country, but it is his who loveth the world." Through the power released by these exalted words He hath lent a fresh impulse, and set a new direction, to the birds of men's hearts, and hath obliterated every trace of restriction and limitation from God's holy Book.'[178] 'That one indeed is a man who, today, dedicateth himself to the service of the entire human race . . . The earth is but one country, and mankind its citizens.'[179] 'The utterance of God is a lamp, whose light is these words: Ye are the fruits of one tree, and the leaves of one branch.'[180] 'Ye are all the leaves of one tree and the drops of one ocean.'[181]

Surrender to God demands a life of service to our neighbours. But our neighbour is every man, humanity, one and undivided: 'O son of men! If thine eyes be turned towards mercy forsake the things that profit thee and cleave unto that which will profit mankind.'[182] Everything that is done in the spirit of this service to mankind is a service to God.[183] The idea that the value of all action will be judged according to the good of humanity as a whole stands supreme in the value scale of the Bahá'í ethic. The fateful, disastrous group morality which calls for the preferential treatment of the group's own members (family, race, nation, class) must be overcome.

The seed of this idea was undoubtedly already present in the religions of the past, but it was never expressed in this form and – this is the decisive point – never generally and constantly practised. In this limitless love of

177. This refers to the revelation of Muhammad.
178. Bahá'u'lláh, *Gleanings* 43:6; Lawh-i-Dunyá, *Tablets*, pp.87–8.
179. Bahá'u'lláh, Lawh-i-Maqṣúd, *Tablets*, p.167 (= *Gleanings* 117).
180. Bahá'u'lláh, *Gleanings* 132:3; compare also Iṣhráqát, sixth Iṣhráq, *Tablets*, p.127; Lawḥ-i-Ḥikmat, *Tablets*, p.138.
181. Iṣhráqát, eighth Iṣhráq, *Tablets*, p.129; compare also Biṣhárát, *Tablets*, p.27.
182. Kalimát-i-Firdawsíyyih, third leaf, *Tablets*, p.64.
183. Compare Esslemont, *Bahá'u'lláh and the New Era*, pp.98ff.

humanity proclaimed by Bahá'u'lláh there is also a purification and further development of religion in the sphere of individual morality, the
'novelty' of the Bahá'í religion, to which its theological critics have often
been curiously blind.[184]

What Motivates People?

The acquisition of these virtues, these 'fruits of the tree of man',[185] by the
followers of Bahá'u'lláh, which is closely connected with the victory of the
Cause of God,[186] is an exalted goal, and the way to it is steep. Even purely
humanistic thinking may share many of these values and recognize that our
world would be a better place to live in if people lived according to this
ideal. But what encourages man to do good and avoid evil, to make efforts,
to try to control his desire for domination and vengeance, his lust, instincts
and envy, to love his neighbour or even his enemy, to sacrifice himself for
others, for whom he may have little feeling, to exercise mercy, to be honest
and sincere and so on? What is there which can motivate human beings to
do all this, to be a 'good person',[187] if our existence is useless and vain, if
there is no goal transcending man, no authority superior to him, and if we
are justified in saying: 'Let us eat and drink, for tomorrow we die'?[188]
Marion Countess Dönhoff wrote, surely referring to the reality of our society: 'If man is the measure of all things, if he is not compelled to see his
own significance as relative in comparison with a higher one, then it is
difficult to see why the one who promises a better future should not knock

184. I have already discussed this 'blindness' elsewhere (*The Light Shineth in Darkness*, pp.59–61,
144–9) pointing out that we are faced here with a phenomenon of religious history. Until now Christians have not succeeded in convincing the Jews that Jesus brought something fundamentally new,
transcending Moses.

185. Bahá'u'lláh, *Epistle to the Son of the Wolf*, p.26.

186. 'In this Revelation the hosts that can render it victorious are the hosts of praiseworthy deeds and
upright character. The leader and commander of these hosts hath ever been the fear of God, a fear that
encompasseth all things and reigneth over all things.' (Bahá'u'lláh, Ishráqát, the fourth Ishráq,
Tablets, p.126.)

187. As Brecht puts it: 'To be a good man – what a nice idea!/ And give the poor your money?
That is fine!/ When all mankind is good, His Kingdom's near!/ Who would not like to bask in Light
Divine?/ To be a good man – what a nice idea!/ But there's the little problem of subsistence:/ Supplies are scarce and human beings base./ Who would not like a peaceable existence?/ But this old
world is not that kind of place.' (*The Threepenny Opera*, Act one, first Threepenny Finale). Brecht is
right. Where conditions are such that part of mankind lives in darkness ('For some of them are in
darkness and the others are in light'), bereft of the naked right to have 'bread to eat and not a stone',
the capacity of man for 'being good' is intolerably limited. These conditions have to be removed. But
Brecht is wrong in believing that the natural goodness of human beings will automatically come into
force as soon as society has the desired structure. Changed social conditions will change nothing as
regards the fact that 'supplies are scarce and human beings base', unless at the same time man works
with all his strength and regardless of the conditions, to overcome his baseness. The accuracy of the
statement 'only the well-to-do live pleasantly' (Brecht, *The Threepenny Opera*, Act II, scene 3) is obvious. But the expectation that being well-to-do would automatically make everyone into a 'good man'
is daily contradicted by experience. Furthermore, it would be extraordinary if morality applied only to
fair-weather conditions and did not have to stand up to the storms of life as well. On this whole subject
see pp.139ff.

188. I Cor. 15:32.

out the brains of anyone who stands in the way of that future.'[189]

What motivates the Bahá'í to fulfil the commandments of Bahá'u'lláh is love for Bahá'u'lláh and fear of God. 'Abdu'l-Bahá has pointed out that it is impossible to love all men, without exception, for themselves alone. Man is capable of such love only 'in God, and for God',[190] in the consciousness that everything that bears a human face is God's creation. This basic direction, this conversion of the heart, makes it possible for man to be committed to his neighbour even where no one else is ready to help: 'Love the creatures for the sake of God and not for themselves. You will never become angry or impatient if you love them for the sake of God. Humanity is not perfect. There are imperfections in every human being and you will always become unhappy if you look toward the people themselves. But if you look toward God you will love them and be kind to them, for the world of God is the world of perfection and complete mercy. Therefore do not look at the shortcomings of anybody; see with the sight of forgiveness. The imperfect eye beholds imperfections. The eye that covers faults looks towards the Creator of souls. He created them, trains and provides for them, endows them with capacity and life, sight and hearing; therefore they are the signs of His grandeur.'[191]

Without a common father there can be no genuine brotherhood among men. That is why 'living for others' (which has often been quoted as a human goal since Feuerbach) and all humanist attempts at self-redemption must fail without a vertical direction.[192] Nietzsche himself recognized 'that love of man without some sanctifying ulterior objective is one piece of stupidity and animality more, that the inclination to this love of man has first to receive its measure, its refinement, its grain of salt and drop of

189. *Die Zeit* of 29.11.1974.
190. 'Abdu'l-Bahá, *Paris Talks*, ch.9, p.38.
191. Quoted from *The Divine Art of Living*, pp.115–16.
192. Feuerbach, who criticizes belief in Heaven as well as belief in God, sees man as a member of a species, finding fulfilment and 'immortality' in everyone living for mankind: 'He therefore who lives in the consciousness of the species as a reality, regards his existence for others, his relation to society, his utility to the public, as that existence which is one with the existence of his own essence – as his immortal existence.' (*The Essence of Christianity*, ch.XVIII, p.170; compare also his statements on love of humanity, pp.245–66.) But this 'existence for others' is a theory without force, producing no valid basis for a practical ethic. Jacques Chouleur rightly comments on this: 'Il n'y a cependant pas de vraie fraternité sans commune paternité, aurait dit Monsieur de la Palice, et c'est justement l'absence de ce père commun qui met en péril les structures de la famille humaniste. Les religions, elles, proposent à tous les hommes une fraternité effective fondée sur l'acceptation d'un père commun, et peu importe qu'on l'appelle Jehovah ou Allah ou d'autres noms encore. Les églises naivement modernistes qui s'efforcent de minimiser cette "dimension verticale" pour ne retenir que celle, horizontale, du service du prochain, se brisent sur la fatale contradiction d'une fraternité sans paternité commune.' ('La foi mondiale Bahá'ie: religion de l'avenir?', p.1.) Seventy years ago the pedagogue F. W. Förster saw that 'existence for others' in practice draws its motivation from faith: 'Anyone capable of that higher kind of love, although he no longer has a religion in the old sense, is capable of it only because the old Song of Songs of divine love and limitless mercy from his religious education continue to echo unconsciously within him.' ('Die pädagogische Unentbehrlichkeit der religiösen Moralbegründung' in *Hochland*, I, 1908/09, p.35).

amber from a higher inclination': 'To love men for the sake of God – that has been the noblest and most remote feeling attained to among men up till now.'[193]

Fear of God, responsibility to God, mentioned just now, is the weapon in this battle which the believer must wage with his own wishes and urges, 'that can render him victorious, the primary instrument whereby he can achieve his purpose. The fear of God is the shield that defendeth His Cause, the buckler that enableth His people to attain to victory. It is a standard that no man can abase, a force that no power can rival. By its aid, and by the leave of Him Who is the Lord of Hosts, they that have drawn nigh unto God have been able to subdue and conquer the citadels of the hearts of men.'[194]

The highest morality of man is not to act for the sake of reward in heaven or from fear of punishment, but with the pure intention of serving God. In the Persian Bayán the Báb revealed: 'Worship thou God in such wise that if thy worship lead thee to the fire, no alteration in thine adoration would be produced, and so likewise if thy recompense should be paradise . . . That which is worthy of His Essence is to worship Him for His sake, without fear of fire, or hope of paradise.'[195]

A Religion of Joy

Every fragmentary description contains the danger of abbreviation and distortion; thus the above discussion of this subject might awaken in the reader the impression that the life of a Bahá'í is nothing but a strict fulfilment of duty under the yoke of the law; that to live as a Bahá'í means to live 'in sackcloth and ashes'.[196] Nothing could be further from the truth. The Bahá'í religion is a religion of joy. Joy actually plays a central role in the message of Bahá'u'lláh. Joy, of course, is not identical with pleasure. It seems necessary to emphasize this because we live in a world of 'joyless pleasures'.[197] Fromm defines the difference: 'The pleasures of the radical hedonists, the satisfaction of ever new cupidities, the pleasures of contemporary society produce different degrees of excitements. But they are not conducive to joy. In fact, the lack of joy makes it necessary to seek ever new, ever more exciting pleasures.' In contrast to this, joy 'is the concomitant of productive activity. It is not a "peak experience", which culminates and ends suddenly, but rather a plateau, a feeling state that accompanies

193. *Beyond Good and Evil*, No.60.

194. Bahá'u'lláh, *Gleanings* 126:4; compare also Ishráqát, fourth Ishráq, *Tablets*, p.126.

195. 7:19, *Selections*, pp.77, 78. This idea is also to be found in the work of the earliest woman mystic of Islám, Rabia, who lived in Basra in the eighth century. (Anneliese Schimmel, 'Der Beitrag der islamischen Mystik zur Einheit der Religionen', in *Gemeinschaft und Politik*, published by the Institute of Geosociology and Politics, Bad Godesberg 1957, Issue 12, p.48.).

196. Compare Isa. 58:5; Matt. 11:21.

197. Fromm, *To Have or to Be?*, p.116.

the productive expression of one's essential human faculties. Joy is not the ecstatic fire of the moment. Joy is the glow that accompanies being.'[198]

In his writings Bahá'u'lláh constantly stresses that man was created for joy, and that cheerfulness and serenity should shine from his face:[199] 'O Son of Man! Rejoice in the gladness of thine heart, that thou mayest be worthy to meet Me and to mirror forth My beauty.'[200] 'O Son of Spirit! With the joyful tidings of light I hail thee: rejoice!'[201] A man should look at his neighbour 'with a bright and friendly face'[202] and not wear a morose and sullen expression.[203] And 'Abdu'l-Bahá said: 'Believers must show their belief in their daily lives, so that the world might see the light shining in their faces. A bright and happy face cheers people on their way.'[204] 'With hearts set aglow by the fire of the love of God and spirits refreshed by the food of the heavenly spirit you must go forth as the disciples nineteen hundred years ago, quickening the hearts of men by the call of glad-tidings, the light of God in your faces, severed from everything save God . . . Let the love and light of the kingdom radiate through you until all who look upon you shall be illumined by its reflection.'[205] 'I want you to be happy . . . to laugh, smile and rejoice in order that others may be made happy by you.'[206] So it is above all the properties of human warmth and cordiality which should be unfolded, and chilly formality, fear of contact and unrelatedness which have to be overcome by us.

Nor does the severance demanded mean that man should not rejoice in the beauties of this world. The Prophet Muḥammad himself rebuffed ascetic fanatics: 'O ye who believe! Interdict not the healthful viands which God hath allowed you; go not beyond this limit. God loveth not those who

---

198. Fromm, *To Have or to Be?*, p.117.

199. Compare Esslemont, *Bahá'u'lláh and the New Era*, pp.98–9.

200. *The Hidden Words*, Arabic 36.

201. *The Hidden Words*, Arabic 33.

202. Bahá'u'lláh, *Epistle to the Son of the Wolf*, p.93 (= *Gleanings* 130).

203. A study of early church history shows that this cannot be taken as a matter of course. Tertullian, Origen and Cyprian vied with each other in asceticism. 'Not content with forbidding the faithful to enjoy themselves, Basil even forbids them to laugh. The Christian is supposed to express grief over the failure of existence by lowered eyes, unkempt hair, shabby clothes and the like. Gregory of Nyssa compares the whole of life with a "dirty sediment". Laktanz senses a weapon of the devil even in the scent of a flower. And for Zeno of Verona the greatest boast of Christian virtue is "to tread nature underfoot."' (Karl-Heinz Deschner, *Abermals krähte der Hahn*, pp.194ff., with index of sources.) Even Islám, which from the beginning was incomparably more world-orientated than church Christianity, fell under the influence of neo-Platonic speculations into ascetic fanaticism and views permeated by contempt for everything earthly. They did not hesitate to think up a suitable ḥadíth: 'Your existence is a sin with which no other sin can be compared.' (Compare Ignaz Goldziher, *Vorlesungen über den Islam*, p.154, with references to sources.) The later ban on music can also be included in this context. Although there is not a single motive for this in the whole Qur'án, all four of the Sunni law schools forbade music. However, the ban was largely ignored. (For further details see H. M. Balyuzi, *Muḥammad and the Course of Islám*, pp.309–11.)

204. Quoted from *The Pattern of Bahá'í Life*, p.56.

205. *The Promulgation of Universal Peace*, p.8; compare also Bahá'u'lláh, *Tablets*, p.257.

206. op. cit., p.218.

outstep it. And eat of what God hath given you for food, that which is lawful and wholesome: and fear God, in whom ye believe.'[207] Bahá'u'lláh also warns against extremes: 'Should a man wish to adorn himself with the ornaments of the earth, to wear its apparels, or partake of the benefits it can bestow, no harm can befall him, if he alloweth nothing whatever to intervene between him and God, for God hath ordained every good thing, whether created in the heavens or in the earth, for such of His servants as truly believe in Him. Eat ye, O people, of the good things which God hath allowed you, and deprive not yourselves of His wondrous bounties.'[208] Bahá'u'lláh expressly rejected ascetic escapism: 'O concourse of monks! Seclude not yourselves in your churches and cloisters. Come ye out of them by My leave, and busy, then, yourselves with what will profit you and others. Thus commandeth you He Who is the Lord of the Day of Reckoning. Seclude yourselves in the stronghold of My love. This, truly, is the seclusion that befitteth you, could ye but know it. He that secludeth himself in his house is indeed as one dead. It behooveth man to show forth that which will benefit mankind. He that bringeth forth no fruit is fit for the fire. Thus admonisheth you your Lord; He, verily, is the Mighty, the Bountiful.'[209]

But the imperishable joy and peace of the human heart cannot be found in the perishable objects of this world, but only in that spiritual kingdom whose gates are open to everyone:[210] 'O Son of Man! Wert thou to speed through the immensity of space and traverse the expanse of heaven, yet thou wouldst find no rest save in submission to Our command and humbleness before Our Face.'[211]

Deed and Example

It is always easier to talk about high ideals than to live by them. Man's inclination not to follow up verbal professions of high ideals with deeds has always been great. Yet Bahá'u'lláh tells us quite clearly and trenchantly what is at stake: our life, our deeds. The idea that man must produce fruits and that he must not fruitlessly waste these days which will never return is a predominant and recurrent theme in Bahá'u'lláh's doctrine of virtue: 'O My Servant! The basest of men are they that yield no fruit on earth. Such men are verily counted as among the dead, nay better are the dead in the sight of God than those idle and worthless souls.'[212] 'The essence of faith is

---

207. Qur'án 5:89–90.
208. *Gleanings* 128:4.
209. *Epistle to the Son of the Wolf*, p.49; compare also Bishárát, the eighth Glad-Tidings, *Tablets*, p.24.
210. Compare 'Abdu'l-Bahá, *Paris Talks*, ch.35, pp.109ff.
211. Bahá'u'lláh, *The Hidden Words*, Arabic 40. Similarly St. Augustine: 'Tu nos fecisti ad te, et cor nostrum inquietum est, donec requiescat in te.' (*Confessions* I, 1.)
212. Bahá'u'lláh, *The Hidden Words*, Persian 81.

fewness of words and abundance of deeds; he whose words exceed his deeds, know verily his death is better than his life.'[213] 'Let deeds, not words, be your adorning.'[214]

The proclamation of a new morality loses all conviction if the behaviour of the faithful is in contradiction to it. This earns Bahá'u'lláh's condemnation: 'Doth it beseem a man while claiming to be a follower of his Lord, the All-Merciful, he should yet in his heart do the very deeds of the Evil One? Nay, it ill beseemeth him.'[215] Mere lip-service is not to Bahá'u'lláh's liking: 'Beware, O people of Bahá, lest ye walk in the ways of them whose words differ from their deeds ... Let your acts be a guide unto all mankind, for the professions of most men, be they high or low, differ from their conduct. It is through your deeds that ye can distinguish yourselves from others.'[216] And 'Abdu'l-Bahá shows us why the situation in this world is so bad: 'What profit is there in agreeing that universal friendship is good, and talking of the solidarity of the human race as a grand ideal? Unless these thoughts are translated into the world of action, they are useless. The wrong in the world continues to exist just because people talk only of their ideals, and do not strive to put them into practice. If actions took the place of words, the world's misery would very soon be changed into comfort.'[217]

Basically, modern man respects only two things: convincing theories and observable facts. The convincing theory is available: the World Order of Bahá'u'lláh. The observable facts have to be brought forth by the Bahá'ís. Modern society, anchored in technical and mathematical matters, is not willing to lend an ear to an intellectualized doctrine: 'The world is tired of words; it wants example,' Shoghi Effendi says,[218] and it is for the Bahá'ís to give this example. 'As a matter of fact no one cares very much what we say,' writes Rúḥíyyih Rabbaní. 'Everyone is saying something these days, from every loudspeaker in the world, in Chinese, Czech, Spanish and so on, people are shouting good plans, good precepts, good ideas – many of them are in fact similar or identical with our Bahá'í plans, precepts and ideas – but they are, as we can see from the state of the world, largely ineffectual. Why? Because nothing goes behind them, there is no right action, no upright conduct backing them up and everyone knows it.'[219] Mark Twain comments sarcastically but with perfect truth: 'The trouble with world improvers is that they don't begin with themselves.' As long as the Bahá'í does not begin with himself but is swallowed up in the general current he has no chance of serving as a signpost, a lighthouse in this dark

213. Bahá'u'lláh, Aṣl-i-Kullu'l-Khayr, *Tablets*, p.156.
214. Bahá'u'lláh, *The Hidden Words*, Persian 5; also Persian 76.
215. Bahá'u'lláh, *Gleanings* 128:1.
216. Bahá'u'lláh, *Gleanings* 139:8.
217. *Paris Talks*, ch.1, p.16.
218. *Living the Life*, p.26.
219. *Success in Teaching*, p.12.

age. What characterizes a true believer is the total seriousness with which he acts upon the teaching of Bahá'u'lláh. This requires detachment from the world, from the pleasure-seeking society, the society of enjoyment, with its superficial pastimes, and it requires sacrifice. A person who adapts to the yardsticks of a moribund society and assimilates its way of life, who lacks the courage to show the flag, will go down with this society.

It is not easy to be a Bahá'í today: 'The road is stony, and there are many tests.'[220] To live as a Bahá'í in a society whose yardsticks have become blurred and among people whose goals are increasingly the hedonistic ones of following inclinations and satisfying instincts means swimming against the tide in many respects. This calls for courage. For instance, anyone who is living in a society where sociability is largely marked by sharing alcoholic drinks, indeed where drinking customs amount to a positive drinking urge, and who puts aside alcoholic liquors in accordance with the commandments of Bahá'u'lláh, will be regarded, in Europe at least, as an odd sectarian and cranky outsider. The Bahá'í must come to terms with this state of affairs. 'The indifference and scorn of the world matters not at all.'[221] In our transitional age the Bahá'í may on many occasions appear like a man 'whose watch keeps good time, when all the clocks in the town in which he lives are wrong. He alone knows the right time; but what use is that to him? For everyone goes by the clocks which speak false.'[222]

Experience has shown that someone who is promoting a novelty is exposing himself in some degree to ridicule. Mark Twain says: 'A man with a new idea will be regarded as a fool until the idea has been accepted', and it is 'the fear of making ourselves ridiculous', which, as André Gide put it, 'gives rise to our greatest cowardice'. Man's herd instinct is great. As Rúḥíyyih Rabbání rightly says, they are very like sheep in this respect: 'They all "baa" together, they all graze together and they all stampede together. For a Bahá'í not to be able to realize that through identifying himself with the most progressive, constructive movement in the whole world, he has risen above the herd and covered himself with distinction, is pitiful.'[223] As Schopenhauer comments, he who tries to promote human knowledge and insight 'is destined to always encounter the opposition of his age'. But such a one must take comfort 'from the certainty that, although prejudices beset his path, yet the truth is with him. And Truth does but wait for her ally, Time, to join her; once he is at her side, she is perfectly sure of victory, which, if today delayed, will be won tomorrow.'[224]

Yet it should be remembered that the situation of the Bahá'í today has

220. Shoghi Effendi, *Living the Life*, p.36.
221. 'Abdu'l-Bahá, *Paris Talks*, ch.38, p.118.
222. Arthur Schopenhauer, *Counsels and Maxims*, V, 27.
223. *Success in Teaching*, p.12.
224. *The Basis of Morality*, p.282.

two aspects, a positive as well as a negative.

The negative aspect arises from the fact that the Bahá'ís are what the sociologists call a 'cognitive minority' – a group of people whose view of the world differs significantly from the one generally taken for granted in their society. The status of a cognitive minority is thus invariably 'an uncomfortable one'.[225] The discomfort lies in the fact that one's knowledge is in need of social support and is thus 'vulnerable to social pressures'.[226] For the Bahá'í the result of this circumstance is the danger that the destructive forces of society will affect him and that he will become subject to the alluring power of the conduct which is customary and expected today. Because of this danger Shoghi Effendi warned the faithful to be always on guard 'lest the darkness of society become reflected in our acts and attitudes, perhaps all unconsciously'.[227] The Bahá'í can draw the strength to stand up to social pressure rather than to capitulate to it – a strength developed in different degrees in different people – from his faith in the message of Bahá'u'lláh and its ultimate victory.

The positive aspect of this situation lies in the fact that the faster the old virtues are eroded and the old systems of control are dismantled without substitution, the more, as a result, the disorganization of society becomes apparent, the sooner it will be possible to be distinguished from one's environment and to become an example and pattern to it. When the author joined the Bahá'í community more than thirty years ago he was disturbed by an utterance of 'Abdu'l-Bahá: 'Should any one of you enter a city, he should become a centre of attraction by reason of his sincerity, his faithfulness and love, his honesty and fidelity, his truthfulness and loving-kindness towards all the peoples of the world, so that the people of that city may cry out and say: "This man is unquestionably a Bahá'í, for his manners, his behaviour, his conduct, his morals, his nature, and disposition reflect the attributes of the Bahá'ís."'[228] How could this be? After all, one was surrounded by many righteous people who lived a good life and from whom one could with difficulty distinguish oneself. Today a generation is growing up which bears only the faintest stamp of the old values, if any. With the old virtues, the benefits they brought with them are also disappearing. Our world grows daily darker, our life more gloomy and joyless. Even such a virtue as courtesy,[229] which demands relatively little of

---

225. Peter L. Berger, *A Rumor of Angels*, pp.7, 8. On the whole subject: Peter L. Berger and Thomas Luckmann, *The Social Construction of Reality: a treatise in the sociology of knowledge*, Garden City, N.Y., Doubleday, 1966.
226. Peter L. Berger, *A Rumor of Angels*, p.10.
227. *The Bahá'í Life*, p.14.
228. Quoted from Shoghi Effendi, *The Advent of Divine Justice*, p.21.
229. 'I admonish you to observe courtesy. For above all else it is the prince of virtues . . . Whoso is endued with courtesy hath indeed attained a sublime station.' (Bahá'u'lláh, Lawḥ-i-Dunyá, *Tablets*, p.88.)

a person and is most obviously consonant with wisdom,[230] is disappearing to a deplorable extent in our daily life. Today the young man who is courteous, sincere and honest, refusing to live in concubinage, attracts attention. Even the complete development of a single virtue would be noticed in this society. Shoghi Effendi reports: 'How often the beloved Master[231] was heard to say: Should each one of the friends take upon himself to carry out, in all its integrity and implications, only one of the teachings of the Faith, with devotion, detachment, constancy and perseverance and exemplify it in all his deeds and pursuits of life, the world would become another world and the face of the earth would mirror forth the splendours of the 'Abhá Paradise.'[232]

There is no doubt that detachment from worldly things, the constant struggle towards self-knowledge and self-education, is an exalted goal demanding constant watchfulness and willingness to change. But it would be a great mistake if we were to be content with the idea that this goal was simply unattainable, just as nowadays the commandments of the Sermon on the Mount are described as an unfulfillable, 'enthusiastic, idealistic ethic'.[233] This goal is attainable, this ethic can be achieved. A man has lived it out before us and given us the example we are trying to emulate: 'Abdu'l-Bahá.[234]

230. 'It is a wise thing to be polite; consequently, it is a stupid thing to be rude. To make enemies by unnecessary and wilful incivility, is just as insane a proceeding as to set your house on fire.' (Arthur Schopenhauer, *Counsels and Maxims*, V, 36.) Elsewhere Schopenhauer says that politeness is the 'systematic disavowal of Egoism in the trifles of daily intercourse.' (*The Basis of Morality*, p.153.)

231. 'Abdu'l-Bahá.

232. *Living the Life*, p.1.

233. Gerhard Szczesny, *The Future of Unbelief*, p.52. The accusation of excessive moral demands, so persistently made by enlightened moderns against the requirements of religious ethics, is an old one. Even Confucius came to grips with it: 'Jan Ch'iu remarked: "It is not that I have no pleasure in your teaching, Sir, but I am not strong enough." "He who is not strong enough," answered the Master, "gives up half-way, but you are drawing the line already."' (*Analects*, VI, 10.)

234. Guidance on his life and significance in religious history from Shoghi Effendi, *God Passes By*, pp.237–320; the same author, *The World Order of Bahá'u'lláh*, pp.131–9; H. M. Balyuzi, *'Abdu'l-Bahá*, London 1971; Howard Ives, *Portals to Freedom*, Oxford 1974; Lady Blomfield, *The Chosen Highway*, Wilmette, Illinois 1975; Allan L. Ward, *239 Days. 'Abdu'l-Bahá's Journey in America*, Wilmette, Illinois, 1979; Helen S. Goodall and Ella Goodall Cooper, *Daily Lessons Received at 'Akká*, January 1908, Wilmette, Illinois, 2nd edn, 1979.

13. The Community of Bahá'u'lláh

The People of Bahá

It follows, then, that a Bahá'í should strive for human perfections, but he should strive as well for a humane society and a just social order, for the establishment of the kingdom of God on earth. A Bahá'í should not, therefore, like an Indian guru, lead a life of contemplation and self-engrossment in seclusion both from the trivialities and the real problems of society. Even as he is engaged in the changing and forming of himself in conformity with the demands of these new ethics, he should be engaged in changing society, in building up a new order and creating a better world. He cannot pursue and reach this goal alone, in isolation, but only as a member of a world-wide community. To be a Bahá'í means, therefore, to belong to the Bahá'í community, to the people of Bahá.

There is only one condition attached to this membership: the recognition of Bahá'u'lláh as manifestation of God and the unreserved acceptance of his teachings and commands.[1] No one who espouses his Faith is expected to show a specific measure of perfection. What really matters is that the individual has the sincere wish to live according to the teachings of Bahá'u'lláh and makes efforts to advance on the path of perfection. And only God knows the degree to which everyone of us is ready to progress spiritually.

Whoever becomes a Bahá'í must, therefore, be aware that the com-

1. Shoghi Effendi has defined the qualifications of a true believer: 'Full recognition of the station of the Forerunner, the Author, and the True Exemplar; unreserved acceptance of, and submission to, whatsoever has been revealed by their Pen; loyal and steadfast adherence to every clause of our Beloved's sacred Will; and close association with the spirit as well as the form of the present day Bahá'í administration throughout the world.' (*Bahá'í Administration*, p.90.)

munity he is joining is not a heavenly group of angelic beings but a community of imperfect people. And the more society disintegrates, the more will we find that it is not only the mellow seekers of truth who come to Bahá'u'lláh but also those 'that labour and are heavy laden'[2] – the rejected, the under-privileged, the oppressed, the hopeless, the addicts, the sick in body and soul. Bahá'u'lláh has come for them too. And just as Bahá'u'lláh never rejects a man on account of his imperfections, a believer is not allowed to reject another on account of the latter's failings: 'Among the sons of men some souls are suffering through ignorance, let us hasten to teach them; others are like children needing care and education until they are grown, and some are sick – to these we must carry Divine healing. Whether ignorant, childish or sick, they must be loved and helped, and not disliked because of their imperfection.'[3]

On no point is the Bahá'í Faith more unequivocable than in asking the believer to refrain from fault-finding and backbiting: 'O Son of Man! Breathe not the sins of others so long as thou art thyself a sinner. Shouldst thou transgress this command, accursed wouldst thou be, and to this I bear witness.'[4] The self-righteous – according to Confucius, the 'spoilers of morals'[5] – are exhorted by Bahá'u'lláh: 'O Son of Being! How couldst thou forget thine own faults and busy thyself with the faults of others? Whoso doeth this is accursed of Me[6]. . . . If the fire of self overcome you, remember your own faults and not the faults of My creatures, inasmuch as every one of you knoweth his own self better than he knoweth others.'[7] The true believer 'should forgive the sinful, and never despise his low estate, for none knoweth what his own end shall be'.[8] Bahá'u'lláh praises 'the righteous that mock not the sinful, but rather conceal their misdeeds, so that their own shortcomings may remain veiled to men's eyes'.[9]

Backbiting is a 'grievous error'; it 'quencheth the light of the heart, and extinguisheth the life of the soul'.[10] 'Abdu'l-Bahá asks us 'to be silent concerning the faults of others, to pray for them and to help them through kindness, to correct their faults', and 'to look always at the good and not at the bad'.[11] This attitude of tolerance and loving-kindness, which Jesus Christ so emphatically enjoined upon His followers,[12] is the only guarantee that in a community of people with such different backgrounds and education, love and harmony should prevail instead of strife and dissension.

2. Matt. 11:28.
3. 'Abdu'l-Bahá, *Paris Talks*, ch. 39, p.121.
4. Bahá'u'lláh, *The Hidden Words*, Arabic 27.
5. *The Analects*, XVII, XIII.
6. Bahá'u'lláh, *The Hidden Words*, Arabic 26.
7. ibid. Persian 66.
8. Bahá'u'lláh, *Kitáb-i-Íqán*, p.194.
9. *Gleanings* 145.
10. Bahá'u'lláh, *Kitáb-i-Íqán*, p.193.
11. Quoted by J. E. Esslemont, *Bahá'u'lláh and the New Era*, p.80.
12. cf. Matt. 7:1–5.

These exhortations and counsels concern the individual believer in his relationship with his fellow-men. The institutions of the community, on the other hand, are responsible for helping believers to correct their faults and for the protection of the community from law-breakers. Nor should the institutions look passively on if some believers should attempt to undermine the common cause or indeed aspire to destroy God's Cause from within. Bahá'u'lláh and 'Abdu'l-Bahá have made provisions for the protection of the divine Covenant, which is 'the Ark of Salvation',[13] 'the pivot of the oneness of mankind';[14] for the foundation of the community and its order is justice and not mercy.[15]

Whole-hearted Allegiance

It goes without saying that he who joins this community of the Greatest Name must relinquish the ties to the religious institution to which he has formerly belonged. This requirement is not a sign of narrow-minded partisanship; it is a logical consequence. No one can serve two masters at the same time. Unless he be a schizophrenic no one can expect a future return of Christ (as a Christian) and at the same time believe (as a Bahá'í) that Christ has already returned in the person of Bahá'u'lláh. And just as no one can be of the Jewish Faith and at the same time Christian or Muslim, nor even belong to two different denominations of one and the same religion, such as to both the Catholic and Protestant churches, so also the Bahá'í cannot be a member of another religious community. To leave the Church is therefore a logical act. It is also, as Shoghi Effendi emphasizes, an act of honesty even towards the community to which one has until now belonged: 'We as Bahá'ís can never be known as hypocrites or as people insincere in their protestations and because of this we cannot subscribe to both the Faith of Bahá'u'lláh and ordinary church dogma. The churches are waiting for the coming of Jesus Christ; we believe He has come again in the glory of the Father. The Churches teach doctrines – various ones in various creeds – which we as Bahá'ís do not accept, such as the bodily resurrection, confession, or in some creeds, the denial of the immaculate conception. In other words, there is no Christian church today whose dogmas we Bahá'ís can truthfully say we accept in their entirety. Therefore, to remain a member of the church is not proper for us, for we do so under

13. Shoghi Effendi, *God Passes By*, p.239.
14. 'Abdu'l-Bahá, quoted by Shoghi Effendi, op. cit., p.238.
15. See pp.182ff. Literature on the covenant: Bahá'u'lláh, Kitáb-i-'Ahd, *Tablets*, pp.217 – 24; 'Abdu'l-Bahá, *Will and Testament*, Wilmette, Illinois, 1944; Shoghi Effendi, *The World Order of Bahá'u'lláh*, 2nd edn, Wilmette, Illinois, 1974; *The Covenant of Bahá'u'lláh. A Compilation*, published by the National Spiritual Assembly of the British Isles, 2nd rev. edn, London 1963; *The Covenant and Administration*, published by the Bahá'í Publishing Committee, Wilmette, 1951; *The Power of the Covenant*, published by the National Spiritual Assembly of the Bahá'ís of Canada, 1977; Hermann Grossmann, *Das Bündnis in der Offenbarungsreligion*, 2nd edn, Hofheim-Langenhain 1981.

false pretence. We should therefore withdraw from our churches but continue to associate, if we wish to, with the church members and Ministers. Our belief in Christ, as Bahá'ís, is so firm, so unshakeable, and so exalted in nature that very few Christians are to be found nowadays who love Him and reverence Him and have the faith in Him that we have. It is only from the dogmas and creeds of the churches that we dissociate ourselves; not from the Spirit of Christianity[16] . . . No Bahá'í who wishes to be a wholehearted and sincere upholder of the distinguishing principles of the Cause can accept full membership in any non-Bahá'í ecclesiastical organization. For such an act would necessarily imply only a partial acceptance of the Teachings and Laws of the Faith, and an incomplete recognition of its independent status, and would thus be tantamount to an act of disloyalty to the verities it enshrines. For it is only too obvious that in most of its fundamental assumptions the Cause of Bahá'u'lláh is completely at variance with outworn creeds, ceremonies, and institutions. To be a Bahá'í and at the same time accept membership in another religious body is simply an act of contradiction that no sincere and logically-minded person can possibly accept. To follow Bahá'u'lláh does not mean accepting some of His teachings and rejecting the rest. Allegiance to His Cause must be uncompromising and whole-hearted.'[17]

Thus one is not disloyal to Christ. And as formerly the true Jew showed his fidelity to his Prophet Moses by accepting Jesus,[18] the sincere follower of Christ shows his faithfulness to Jesus by following Bahá'u'lláh unreservedly and with all his heart. He who finds this venture too hazardous, who wishes to take up this new commitment but for reasons of reputation, business or family is reluctant to sever old ties, has not really understood what it is all about. These words are meant for him: 'He that loveth father or mother more than me is not worthy of me; and he that loveth son or daughter more than me is not worthy of me[19] . . . I would thou wert cold or hot! So then because thou art lukewarm, and neither cold nor hot, I will spew thee out of my mouth,'[20] and 'No man, having put his hand to the plough, and looking back, is fit for the kingdom of God.'[21]

The Legal Structure of the Community – Necessity and Purpose

The Bahá'í community is essentially more than a call to religious unity, a

16. Through his secretary, quoted in *Principles of Bahá'í Administration*, p.30.
17. Shoghi Effendi, through his secretary, in *Directives from the Guardian*, No. 173, pp.64–5. For more comments by Shoghi Effendi on this question see *Bahá'í Procedure*, p.14, and *Messages to America*, pp.4–5.
18. 'Do not think that I will accuse you to the Father: there is one that accuseth you, even Moses, in whom ye trust. For had ye believed Moses, you would have believed me: for he wrote of me. But if ye believe not his writings, how shall ye believe my words?' (John 5:45–7.)
19. Matt. 10:37; cf. also Qur'án 80:33–7.
20. Rev. 3:15–16.
21. Luke 9:62.

forum in which the old world religions can meet or a kind of vanguard of a world parliament of religions. It is not a mere association of like-minded world-reformers, but God's new people, the people of the new covenant. Hence it is not a loose, amorphous, spiritualistic movement, no 'pneumatic anarchy' or 'pneumatocracy' (that is to say a community guided and governed solely by pseudo-prophetic inspirations of single believers who are supposed to be inspired by the Holy Ghost),[22] but a community governed by legal institutions. The believers are not only united by the bond of faith and love but also by the bond of law, a fact which is sometimes overlooked. It is important for whoever lives and works in this community to know its structure. A detailed description is beyond the purpose of this book, but the necessity and purpose of this structure, and its significance to the believer, may be briefly discussed.

This legal structure was not developed as a result of external necessity, but was given by Bahá'u'lláh as an integral element of His teachings. He has decreed that His community must be based on law and guided by institutions which are regarded as 'a channel through which His promised blessings may flow'.[23] This is the first time in the history of religion that the legal structure of the community has been explicitly revealed by the Manifestation of God rather than left entirely to the discretion of His followers. Bahá'u'lláh is 'the judge, redeemer, and unifier' and also the 'lawgiver of all mankind'.[24] He has given his community its unchangeable and absolute legal form, thus assuring that a dispute over the right kind of structure cannot split the community of God as has so often happened in religious history.

The necessity for a system of laws is obvious. To be able to assert itself and be active in this world, which is a world of order, the community of God must have a legal structure. The spirit of faith and the legal structure of the community guarantee the unity of the believers and provide protection against schism and disintegration. And were it not for this unity, the spiritual impulse bestowed upon mankind through the Revelation of

---

22. cf. Rudolf Sohm, *Kirchenrecht*, Vol. I, pp.20ff.; Rudolf Sohm, *Wesen und Ursprung des Katholizismus*, p.viii; Hans Barion, *Rudolf Sohm und die Grundlegung des Kirchenrechts*, p.9; Wilhelm Albert Hauck, *Rudolf Sohm und Leo Tolstoi*, p.78. Rudolf Sohm, referring to Matt. 18:20 'For where two or three are gathered together in my name, there I am in the midst of them') and John 3:8 ('The wind bloweth where it listeth, and thou hearest the sound thereof but canst not tell whence it cometh and whither it goeth: so is everyone that is born of the Spirit') strongly condemned the fact that in the course of its history the church assumed a structure based on law. According to him, this was the 'Church's Fall'. The community of Christ, as Sohm asserted, should be established only on faith and love and guided solely by the Holy Ghost. The order destined for the Church was that of a 'pneumatic anarchy'. Sohm's thesis is based upon his conviction that spirit and law are incompatible opposites (*Kirchenrecht*, Vol. I, pp.1 and 700). Critics of Bahá'í administration also share Sohm's misconception, namely, that spiritualistic, pneumatic concept of religion and of religious communities, as well as the assertion that law and spirit are opposed to one another.
23. Shoghi Effendi, *The World Order of Bahá'u'lláh*, p.9.
24. Shoghi Effendi, *God Passes By*, p.93.

The Imperishable Dominion

Bahá'u'lláh would be dispersed and the spiritual forces latent within the Word of God would be dissipated before they could even take effect. This protection against schism and sectarianism is guaranteed by the authenticity of the constitution of the Bahá'í community.

The legal institutions ordained by Bahá'u'lláh secure the continuity of divine authority and guidance. With the passing away of the Prophet the divine guidance of the people of God would otherwise have ceased. In the Book He left behind, divine guidance is to be found, but the Book has been revealed in such a manner that it may last over a long period of time and it therefore offers only a framework as far as social norms are concerned. As the times and conditions change, it becomes necessary to have complementary laws. The formulation of such laws cannot be dependent upon the more or less imperfect and above all uncontrollable guidance of individual believers. The divine guidance which governs the community must be objectively recognizable. In the Bahá'í Faith divine guidance continues in an objective way, with an institution upon which Bahá'u'lláh has conferred the charisma of infallibility, The Universal House of Justice, which has its seat in Haifa and leads the destinies of the Faith on the whole planet. The community order of Bahá'u'lláh is thus of a theocratic nature: God Himself rules His people, through His Messenger, His laws and His institutions.

The order of Bahá'u'lláh is not an end in itself or a substitute for a lack of spirit but the instrument for the protection and propagation of the Cause of God, the 'pattern for future society' and 'a supreme instrument for the establishment of the Most Great Peace'.[25]

Its Structures

Moreover, this order has a democratic constitution. Through it, the demand for democracy is really taken seriously. Bahá'u'lláh emphasizes the importance of the historical coming of age and hence the responsibility of modern man. Therefore no distinction is made in the Bahá'í Faith between clergy and laymen. There is no priesthood,[26] no impersonal jurisdiction which comes in between the believer and God and claims to confer grace, just as there are no sacraments. All legal power has been excluded from the realm of personal conscience. Bahá'u'lláh has expressly forbidden con-

25. Shoghi Effendi, *The World Order of Bahá'u'lláh*, p.19; *Messages to America*, p.96; *Bahá Administration*, p.80; cf. Udo Schaefer, 'Die Grundlagen der Verwaltungsordnung der Bahá'í' (Diss.) Heidelberg 1957, and A. L. Lincoln, 'The Politics of Faith', in *World Order, A Bahá'í Magazine* Wilmette, Illinois, Winter 1970/71.

26. Among the numerous statements by Bahá'u'lláh on the clergy (cf. *Kitáb-i-Íqán*, pp.15–16 26–31; 36–41; 76–81; 109; 122; 146–7; 169–72; 213–14; 225; 227–8, and Shoghi Effendi, *The Promised Day is Come*, pp.79–107) can be found the following verses: 'From two ranks amongst men power hath been seized: kings and ecclesiastics' (Bahá'u'lláh, quoted by Shoghi Effendi, op. cit. p.72) and 'O concourse of divines! Ye shall not henceforth behold yourselves possessed of any power inasmuch as We have seized it from you, and destined it for such as have believed in God, the One, the All-Powerful, the Almighty, the Unconstrained' (Bahá'u'lláh, in *The Proclamation of Bahá'u'lláh*

fession.[27] For these reasons alone it is wrong to say that the Bahá'í Faith is taking on the structure of a church (*Verkirchlichung*).[28] In its nature the Bahá'í community is not a 'church'. Besides, individuals have no power of jurisdiction or executive authority at all, but what is accepted is the principle of collective guidance. The guidance and administration of the community on the local, national and international levels have been given to the 'Houses of Justice' instituted by Bahá'u'lláh, their duties and prerogatives elucidated by 'Abdu'l-Bahá and their election vested in the body of the believers.[29] As these Houses of Justice are still at the embryonic stage of their development, they are called 'Spiritual Assemblies' on the local and national levels. They must be 'the trusted ones of the Merciful among men' and 'regard themselves as the guardians appointed of God for all that dwell on earth'.[30] But these assemblies do not constitute a 'council-system' in the anarchic sense of a 'basis-democracy', a kind of direct democracy, where a member of the institution is only a mouthpiece and can be recalled by the electors whenever they choose. In the Bahá'í Faith, neither the elected bodies nor their individual members are responsible to their electors. They have no imperative mandate, nor are they constantly supervised by the electors.

Bahá'í Elections

The democratic principle is realized with much greater consistency than in parliamentary democracy, for not only is each believer who is of age able to vote but also actually – not only in theory – eligible for election. The votes and deliberations of these institutions are religious acts. They must take place in a spirit of prayer and meditation. The elector should turn his heart to God, and, detached from all but Him, implore His guidance and help.[31] Then 'in that rarified atmosphere of selflessness and detachment',[32] 'without the least trace of passion and prejudice, and irrespective of any material consideration',[33] he should elect only those 'whom

p.80).

27. 'When the sinner findeth himself wholly detached and freed from all save God, he should beg forgiveness and pardon from Him. Confession of sins and transgressions before human beings is not permissible, as it hath never been nor will ever be conducive to divine forgiveness. Moreover, such confession before people results in one's humiliation and abasement, and God – exalted be His glory – wisheth not the humiliation of His servants.' (Bishárát, ninth Glad-Tidings, *Tablets*, p.24.)

28. See Gerhard Rosenkranz, *Die Bahá'í*, p.56, and Kurt Hutten, *Seher, Grübler, Enthusiasten*, p.319.

29. Of course the Bahá'í is obliged to be obedient towards these legal institutions. What is unusual is that these institutions are bodies and not individuals. Individual believers, even when they are members of the guiding bodies, have no authority and cannot claim the obedience of the rest of the believers. Since the order of Bahá'u'lláh is an example of and a model for the coming world order, it can be assumed that the time of monocratic forms of government is coming to an end.

30. Bahá'u'lláh, Kitáb-i-Aqdas, *Synopsis*, No. 5, p.13.

31. Shoghi Effendi, letter of 27.2.1923 to the Bahá'ís in Persia.

32. Shoghi Effendi, *Bahá'í Administration*, p.65.

33. Shoghi Effendi, op. cit., p.88.

prayer and reflection have inspired him to uphold'[34] and 'who can best combine the necessary qualities of unquestioned loyalty, of selfless devotion, of a well-trained mind, of recognized ability and mature experience'.[35] All electioneering, propagandizing, electoral lists, election proposals, endorsements and candidatures, formation of parties, party manifestos and party-controlled voting, in short, every attempt to influence the election and manipulate the electoral process – conventions which poison political life – are strictly proscribed. Such practices are contrary to the spirit of prayer, to the atmosphere of spiritual purity, humility and selflessness in which both election and consultation must take place, and lead to 'pernicious methods, such as intrigues, party politics and propaganda',[36] thereby destroying all spirituality. Above all, these methods of manipulating the polls are adjudged harmful and therefore not permitted by Bahá'í law because the believer's right to do only what prayer has inspired him to do would be impaired and the theocratic principle which is the basis of Bahá'u'lláh's order could not operate: 'The confirmation of God will be cut off.'[37]

A danger, common in present-day politics, is averted, namely that people who are more concerned with realizing their own personal ambitions than with the common weal push themselves into the foreground. Nothing corrupts political morals more and is more detrimental to the common weal than political ambition and the lust for power of those who are elected to democratic bodies. Anyone who wants to gain a political office or who has chosen politics as his profession is forced by his natural egoism to put himself in the foreground. He cannot avoid having his finger in as many pies as possible, slapping every famous football player on the back and promising every electoral group his personal attention. He must always be praising himself, constantly wooing the favour of the voters and continually supporting his own followers. In all decisions, even those on which the fortunes of the whole of mankind depend, he must continually have his own popularity rating in mind and must always be thinking of the next election. And from self-praise it is not a far cry to disparagement, humiliation or even defamation of rivals. In the long run this ruins the character and encourages demagogic practices, a danger of which Aristotle was aware.[38] Instead of the leisure and reflection that rulers desperately need, this system produces flustered, hectic activity. The candidates or delegates rush from one meeting to another and succumb to the temptation 'to formulate everything very simply and crudely in a form that

34. Shoghi Effendi, op. cit., p.136.
35. Shoghi Effendi, op. cit., p.88.
36. Shoghi Effendi in a letter of 30.1.1923 to the Bahá'ís in Persia.
37. Shoghi Effendi in a letter of 16.1.1932 to the Bahá'ís in Persia.
38. 'There is an impropriety in requiring that, to be eligible, a man should openly seek election. The man who deserves the office should have it whether he wants it or no . . . For no one would seek election as councillor unless he had such an ambition. Yet ambition and avarice are exactly the motives which lead men to commit nearly all intentional crimes.' (*Politics*, Book II, IX, §§ 27,28).

is easily comprehensible, just to call forth the appropriate cheers' and 'to supply an immediate answer in the manner of one who can pluck everything from beneath his coat sleeve with superior nonchalance'.[39] Politics thus deteriorates into a caricature. Parliamentary elections turn into 'an exciting soap opera, in which the hopes and aspirations of the candidates – not political issues – are at stake'. The suggestive methods of canvassing, the semi-hypnotic election campaign techniques, the appeal to the emotions and the emphasis given to attractive, likeable father figures (together with family clan) transform the elections into 'modern Roman spectacles', in which 'politicians, rather than gladiators, fight in the arena'.[40] One essential reason for the degeneration of parliamentary democracy[41] can be found in this election system, which in principle contradicts[42] the rational form of rule. Thus for the Bahá'ís the parliamentary system of elections is far from an exemplary model.

Bahá'í Consultation

Bahá'u'lláh praises consultation as the best method of decision-making: 'The heaven of divine wisdom is illumined with the two luminaries of consultation and compassion. Take ye counsel together in all matters, inasmuch as consultation is the lamp of guidance which leadeth the way, and is the bestower of understanding.'[43] Men should 'hold fast to the cord of consultation'.[44]

Now consultation is nothing new. Wherever councils have to make decisions, these decisions are preceded by consultation. The decisions of the courts are consulted upon, the parliaments and their committees consult upon bills, and consultation takes place at every general meeting of an

39. Hans Heigert, 'Wie Politiker sich selbst entmündigen' (How Politicians Ridicule Themselves) in *Süddeutsche Zeitung* of 11.12.1978.
40. Erich Fromm, *To Have or to Be?*, pp.183ff. Political metaphors are often taken from sport. When the Democratic Senator Edward Kennedy announced that he was going to run as a candidate for the presidency, one of the headlines was 'Edward Kennedy steigt in den Ring' (Edward Kennedy steps into the ring), *Süddeutsche Zeitung* of 8.11.1979.
41. Alexis de Tocqueville's criticism of this in his work *De la Démocratie en Amérique* (Paris 1835), which is based on the conditions he had studied in the United States shows that this is not a symptom of degeneration that has only appeared in our time, but is a feature inherent in the parliamentary system: 'For a long while before the appointed time has come, the election becomes the important and, so to speak, the all-engrossing topic of discussion. Factional ardor is redoubled, and all the artificial passions which the imagination can create in a happy and peaceful land are agitated and brought to light. The President, moreover, is absorbed by the cares of self-defense. He no longer governs for the interest of the state, but for that of his re-election; he does homage to the majority, and instead of checking its passions, as his duty commands, he frequently courts its worst caprices. As the election draws near, the activity of intrigue and the agitation of the populace increase; the citizens are divided into hostile camps, each of which assumes the name of its favorite candidate; the whole nation glows with feverish excitement; the election is the daily theme of the press, the subject of private conversation, the end of every thought and every action, the sole interest of the present.' (*Democracy in America*, Vol. I, pp.135–6.)
42. Helmut Schelsky, *Die Arbeit tun die anderen*, p.203.
43. Lawḥ-i-Maqṣúd, *Tablets*, p.168; cf. also Ishráqát, the third Ishráq, *Tablets*, p.126.
44. Lawḥ-i-Dunyá, *Tablets*, p.92.

association before decisions are made. What, then, is the special feature of Bahá'í consultation?

Bahá'í consultation differs in the attitude, the spirit and the method in which it is carried out. Like the Bahá'í elections it is an act of worship. In turning to God those who consult strive jointly to find the truth and to solve problems in the best way possible.

The prime requisites for those who take counsel together are 'purity of motive, radiance of spirit, detachment from all else save God, attraction to His Divine Fragrances, humility and lowliness amongst His loved ones, patience and long-suffering in difficulties and servitude to His exalted Threshold. Should they be graciously aided to acquire these attributes, victory from the unseen Kingdom of Bahá shall be vouchsafed to them'. [45] The members of Bahá'í institutions must take counsel together in such wise 'that no occasion for ill-feeling or discord may arise. This can be attained when every member expresseth with absolute freedom his own opinion and setteth forth his argument. Should anyone oppose, he must on no account feel hurt for not until matters are fully discussed can the right way be revealed.' [46] 'The first condition is absolute love and harmony amongst the members of the assembly . . . The second condition: they must, when coming together, turn their faces to the Kingdom on high and ask aid from the Realm of Glory. They must then proceed with the utmost devotion, courtesy, dignity, care and moderation to express their views. They must in every matter search out the truth and not insist upon their own opinion, for stubbornness and persistence in one's views will lead ultimately to discord and wrangling and the truth will remain hidden.' [47] The members of the assembly must take care in all circumstances never 'to belittle the thought of another'; rather they should 'with moderation set forth the truth'. [48] 'Differences of opinion in my community are a sign of divine grace', said the Prophet Muḥammad, [49] and 'Abdu'l-Bahá gives the reason: 'The shining spark of truth cometh forth only after the clash of differing opinions.' [50]

Such consultation is assuredly 'no easy skill to learn, requiring as it does the subjugation of all egotism and unruly passions, the cultivation of frankness and freedom of thought as well as courtesy, openness of mind, and whole-hearted acquiescence in a majority decision'. [51] Thus Bahá'í consultation is not *debate*, the confrontation of monologues that serve only to promote the speaker's personal image, but *communication*; it is the search for truth carried out by means of dialogue and with a sense of solidarity. Those who consult in this way are applying in the sphere of

45. 'Abdu'l-Bahá, *Selections*, No.43.
46. 'Abdu'l-Bahá, op. cit., No. 44.
47. 'Abdu'l-Bahá, op. cit., No. 45.
48. ibid.
49. Hadíth, quoted by Goldziher, *Vorlesungen über den Islâm*, p.48.
50. 'Abdu'l-Bahá, *Selections*, No.44.
51. The Universal House of Justice, *Wellspring of Guidance*, p.96.

social affairs the same method that the scientists employ in their investigation of nature. In the field of scientific research whoever is biased and scornful of other opinions must bear the consequences. In politics people still think they can get away with this attitude.

If we compare Bahá'í consultation with the consultation usual today in political bodies, then we see how great the difference is. Genuine consultation, where people strive together without prejudice to find the right way and the right goal, can only be found in rare and exceptional situations. Everywhere else views that have already been determined are maintained without modification, and those holding these views try to enforce them by pocketing the majority of votes. Parliamentary debates serve less to throw light upon matters than to enable the politicians to project their own personalities, find fault with others, make propaganda and seek confrontation. For the most part such exchanges are empty rituals. The voting results usually reflect the particular party lines; they can be calculated in advance and are therefore a mere farce, a caricature of true consultation.

In the Bahá'í community, on the other hand, every kind of obstructive oppositional activity including the formation of parties and pressure groups is excluded by Bahá'í law, because such groups aim at forcing results. In the same way and for the same reason that every kind of influence on the election and manipulation of the polls is ruled out, every kind of manipulation of the consultation and voting procedure is strictly forbidden. A decision that is arrived at by a majority of votes is binding upon all. There is no announcement of *dissenting votes*,[52] which endanger the ability of institutions to function and undermine their authority. There is no minority standpoint; and polemics and opposition to a decision that has been made, or even the attempt to obstruct it, are not permitted, for 'such criticism would prevent any decision from being enforced'.[53] A decision that has been made in mutual consultation can be re-considered and changed. But up to that point it must be faithfully respected and carried out. In cases where there is a conflict between the substantive rightness of a decision and the unity of the consulting body, the motto *'Melius est, ut scandalum oriatur, quam ut veritas relinquatur'*,[54] cannot be applied at all. 'Abdu'l-Bahá has quite clearly put the unity of those who take counsel before the substantive rightness of the decision: 'If they agree upon a subject, even though it be wrong, it is better than to disagree and be in the right, for . . . that will be the cause of a thousand wrongs, but if they agree . . . in unity the truth will be revealed and the wrong made right.'[55]

---

52. The public announcement of dissenting votes was taken over from American law and is an established practice in the decisions of the Federal Constitutional Court of Germany (§ 30 par. 2 of the Federal Constitutional Court Law).

53. 'Abdu'l-Bahá, *Selections*, No. 45.

54. A statement by Pope Gregory the Great (590–604) that goes back to St. Augustine, Hom. VII in Ezekiel.

55. Quoted in *Principles of Bahá'í Administration*, pp.48–9.

This attitude and this technique of consultation, to be practised not only within the institutions of the Faith but also by the believers in their daily lives, provide an excellent instrument for dealing with conflicts. It is the best possible method for producing the right decision. Here too the theocratic idea is evident: the result of consultation can only be inspired when every participant is open-minded and free from fixed ideas regarding the result.[56]

Material Means

It is obvious that a community of people with such far-reaching goals cannot exist or realize these goals without material means. The life of the community, the teaching work, the establishment of educational institutions and places of worship, the administration of the local, national and international community cannot be carried out without some source of income. How are these financial means raised? Who supplies the funding for the world-wide efforts to spread the message of Bahá'u'lláh, for providing literature in over 600 languages, for building houses of worship,[57] for the activity of the administrative bodies and the World Centre in Haifa, for the maintenance of Bahá'í holy places, for the representatives of the Bahá'í International Community in the United Nations?

Two fundamental principles determine Bahá'í law with respect to financial means. The first is that the local and national governing bodies and the World Centre are supported exclusively by the voluntary donations of enrolled believers. The financial basis is thus the believers' spirit of sacrifice. It is only through this 'that the Cause can prosper and its message embrace the whole world'.[58] Donating freely and generously 'is the sacred obligation of every conscientious and faithful servant of Bahá'u'lláh who desires to see His Cause advance'.[59] But this duty is not regulated by law. It is a moral not a legal duty. The believer is completely free as to the amount and the regularity with which he wishes to donate. He even has the right to decide how his donation is to be used. However, contributing to the community fund is not only a moral duty; it is also a privilege, a natural consequence of the believer's active rights.[60]

---

56. On the whole subject cf. 'Abdu'l-Bahá's talk at the Hotel Plaza in Chicago on 2nd May, 1912, in *The Promulgation of Universal Peace*, pp.72ff.; see also the essay by Penelope Walker, 'Consultation – the keystone of creative administration', in *World Order Magazine*, Summer 1976, pp.23ff.

57. Mashriqu'l-Adhkár. The first European House of Worship is in Hofheim-Langenhain, Taunus. The other Houses of Worship are in Wilmette, USA, Sydney, Australia, Kampala, Uganda, and Panama. The first House of Worship in 'Ishqábád was expropriated by the Soviet authorities after the Russian revolution. It has since been destroyed in an earthquake. Other Houses of Worship are being built in Western Samoa and New Delhi, India.

58. Shoghi Effendi, *Extracts from the Guardian's Letters on Bahá'í Funds and Contributions*, p.8.

59. Shoghi Effendi, *Bahá'í Administration*, pp.41–2.

60. This is shown by the fact that a believer who has been deprived of his administrative rights is not permitted to donate to the Faith.

The principle of voluntary giving is ensured by the prohibition of all kinds of direct or indirect compulsion: 'It should be made clear and evident to every one that any form of compulsion, however slight and indirect, strikes at the very root of the principle underlying the formation of the Fund ever since its inception.'[61] Thus only appeals of a general character 'carefully worded and moving and dignified in tone'[62] are permitted. Any direct appeal to donate and any form of collection which could be interpreted as a psychological compulsion to donate[63] are banned. Similarly the anonymity of the giver and absolute discretion concerning the amount donated are guaranteed. There are no collections as are usual in church. All services provided by the institutions, including marriages, burials, even the news bulletins, are free of charge. Visitors to the holy places, which in Israel are open to the general public, are asked neither for an admission fee nor for donations.

The second irrevocable legal principle is that from people, who have not 'identified themselves with the Faith'[64] no financial help, in whatever form,[65] is accepted. The practical reason for this is obvious. The refusal of money and other financial contributions from non-members is the surest guarantee against the danger that the Cause of God could become financially dependent on outsiders and perhaps corrupted by its backers. Shoghi Effendi stresses that the Bahá'í institutions 'can best function and most powerfully exert their influence in the world only if reared and maintained solely by the support of those who are fully conscious of, and are unreservedly submissive to, the claims inherent in the Revelation of Bahá'u'lláh'.[66] No one should be able to say in the days to come 'that so beauteous, so significant an Edifice has been reared by anything short of the unanimous, the exclusive, and self-sacrificing strivings of the small yet determined body of the convinced supporters of the Faith of Bahá'u'lláh'.[67]

The Proclamation of the Message

It is the indispensable obligation of a Bahá'í to share the teachings of Bahá'u'lláh. Today, as mankind stands on the precipice of its menacing self-destruction, each believer is called upon to distribute widely the divine remedy for the many sufferings and afflictions of a tormented

---

61. Shoghi Effendi, *Bahá'í Administration*, p.101.
62. Shoghi Effendi, ibid.
63. Shoghi Effendi, *On Bahá'í Funds and Contributions*, p.9.
64. Shoghi Effendi, *Bahá'í Administration*, p.182.
65. not even when it has been willed to the Faith
66. *Bahá'í Administration*, p.182.
67. Shoghi Effendi, *Bahá'í Administration*, p.183. On the whole subject cf. *Extracts from the Guardian's Letters on Bahá'í Funds and Contributions*, The Universal House of Justice, Haifa, Israel, January 1970; 'Some Thoughts on Giving', by Rúḥíyyih K͟hanum, *Bahá'í News*, Nos. 226/227, Wilmette, Illinois, 1949–50.

humanity – the message of Bahá'u'lláh. For only when the Word of God reaches men will they wake from their sleep and rise in spiritual rebirth. It is love of mankind and compassion for his neighbour that inspires a Bahá'í to carry out this difficult work in the vineyard of the Lord. It is the same love and compassion as that which caused the Prophets of God to take their difficult task upon themselves, as the Gospel relates: 'But when he saw the multitudes, he was moved with compassion on them, because they fainted, and were scattered abroad, as sheep having no shepherd. Then said he unto his disciples, the harvest truly is plenteous, but the labourers are few; pray ye therefore the Lord of the harvest, that he will send forth labourers into his harvest.'[68] Is not mankind today tormented and scattered like sheep that have no shepherd? The shepherd is at hand, He is Bahá'u'lláh, and His disciples must gather in the harvest: 'The field is indeed so immense, the period so critical, the Cause so great, the workers so few, the time so short, the privilege so priceless, that no follower of the Faith of Bahá'u'lláh, worthy to bear His name, can afford a moment's hesitation.'[69]

In the Bahá'í Faith no special class is appointed to disseminate the teachings. It is incumbent upon every believer, according to his capacities and opportunities, to proclaim the Word of God: 'O ye beloved of God! Repose not yourselves on your couches, nay bestir yourselves as soon as ye recognize your Lord, the Creator . . . Unloose your tongues, and proclaim unceasingly His Cause[70] . . . Teach ye the Cause of God, O people of Bahá, for God hath prescribed unto every one the duty of proclaiming His Message, and regardeth it as the most meritorious of all deeds.'[71] 'Abdu'l-Bahá has Himself emphasized the outstanding service performed by those who teach: 'Of all the gifts of God the greatest is the gift of Teaching. It draweth unto us the Grace of God and is our first obligation. Of such a gift how can we deprive ourselves? Nay, our lives, our goods, our comforts, our rest, we offer them all as a sacrifice for the Abhá Beauty[72] and teach the Cause of God.'[73]

The greatest blessings descend upon those 'that have forsaken their country for the purpose of teaching Our Cause': 'No act, however great, can compare with it, except such deeds as have been ordained by God, the All-Powerful, the Most Mighty. Such a service is, indeed, the prince of all goodly deeds, and the ornament of every goodly act.'[74] He who decides to leave his home for the Cause of God is advised to 'put his whole trust in

68. Matt. 9:36–8.
69. Shoghi Effendi, *The Advent of Divine Justice*, p.39.
70. Bahá'u'lláh, *Gleanings* 154:2.
71. Bahá'u'lláh, *Gleanings* 128:10.
72. i.e. Bahá'u'lláh.
73. *Will and Testament*, p.25.
74. Bahá'u'lláh, *Gleanings* 157:1.

God, as the best provision for his journey, and array himself with the robe of virtue'.[75]

'God hath prescribed unto every one the duty of teaching His Cause'[76] and Bahá'u'lláh continues by immediately explaining the conditions for successful teaching: 'Whoever ariseth to discharge this duty, must needs, ere he proclaimeth His Message, adorn himself with the ornament of an upright and praiseworthy character, so that his words may attract the hearts of such as are receptive to his call. Without it, he can never hope to influence his hearers.'[77] And in another passage He says: 'Such a deed is acceptable only when he that teacheth the Cause is already a firm believer in God[78] . . . Whoso ariseth among you to teach the Cause of his Lord, let him, before all else, teach his own self, that his speech may attract the hearts of them that hear him. Unless he teacheth his own self, the words of his mouth will not influence the heart of the seeker. Take heed, O people, lest ye be of them that give good counsel to others but forget to follow it themselves. The words of such as these, and beyond the words the realities of all things, and beyond these realities the angels that are nigh unto God, bring against them the accusation of falsehood.'[79]

'Wholly for the sake of God' and 'unrestrained as the wind' must the believer carry forward the message and show such 'steadfastness in the Cause of God, that no earthly thing whatsoever will have the power' to deter him from his duty, from guiding his 'neighbour to the law of God, the Most Merciful'.[80]

With Moderation, Tact and Wisdom

The importance ascribed by Bahá'u'lláh to the teaching task in general should not lead one to regard the Bahá'í teaching method as importunate proselytism. Bahá'u'lláh exhorts the believers to be 'guided by wisdom'[81] and to treat all people with patience, friendliness and good-will: 'If ye be aware of a certain truth, if ye possess a jewel, of which others are deprived, share it with them in a language of utmost kindliness and good-will. If it be accepted, if it fulfil its purpose, your object is attained. If anyone should refuse it, leave him unto himself, and beseech God to guide him. Beware lest ye deal unkindly with him. A kindly tongue is the lodestone of the hearts of men. It is the bread of the spirit, it clotheth the words with

75. Bahá'u'lláh, op. cit., 157:2.
76. Bahá'u'lláh, op. cit., 158. 'Whoso is unable, it is his duty to appoint him who will, in his stead, proclaim this Revelation, whose power hath caused the foundations of the mightiest structures to quake, every mountain to be crushed into dust, and every soul to be dumbfounded.' (op. cit., 96:3.)
77. Bahá'u'lláh, op. cit., 158.
78. Bahá'u'lláh, op. cit., 128:10.
79. Bahá'u'lláh, op. cit., 128:6.
80. Bahá'u'lláh, op. cit., 161:2,1.
81. Bahá'u'lláh, *Gleanings* 96:4; cf. also 136:4 and 'Abdu'l-Bahá, *Selections*, no. 213.

meaning, it is the fountain of the light of wisdom and understanding.'[82]

In the Lawḥ-i-Maqṣúd Bahá'u'lláh refers to the effect of words and the necessity of moderation: 'Human utterance is an essence which aspireth to exert its influence and needeth moderation . . . As to its moderation, this hath to be combined with tact and wisdom as prescribed in the Holy Scriptures and Tablets.'[83] And 'Abdu'l-Bahá reminds us that 'caution and prudence, however, must be observed even as recorded in the Book. The veil must in no wise be suddenly rent asunder.'[84] Both are important, the right occasion and the right word. One word is 'like unto springtime causing the tender saplings of the rose-garden of knowledge to become verdant and flourishing, while another word is even as a deadly poison. It behoveth a prudent man of wisdom to speak with utmost leniency and forbearance so that the sweetness of his words may induce everyone to attain that which befitteth man's station.'[85]

To force people to the path of God is foolish and runs counter to the command of wisdom. Patience and understanding are indispensable and proselytizing is to be avoided along with every other undignified or ostentatious way of presenting the new truth: 'O Son of Dust! The wise are they that speak not unless they obtain a hearing, even as the cup-bearer, who proffereth not his cup till he findeth a seeker.'[86] And just as He reproves the 'fearful' one who seeks 'to dissemble his faith', Bahá'u'lláh cannot 'sanction the behaviour of the avowed believer that clamorously asserteth his allegiance to this Cause. Both should observe the dictates of wisdom, and strive diligently to serve the best interests of the Faith.'[87]

Time and again Bahá'u'lláh urges the believers to respect those who insist on their own views: 'Whosoever desireth, let him turn aside from this counsel, and whosoever desireth, let him choose the path to his Lord', we read in the Tablet of Aḥmad, and in another passage he says: 'Let him who will, acknowledge the truth of My words; and as to him that willeth not, let him turn aside[88] . . . Should any man respond to thy call, lay bare before him the pearls of the wisdom of the Lord, thy God, which His Spirit hath sent down unto thee, and be thou of them that truly believe. And should any one reject thine offer, turn thou away from him, and put thy trust and confidence in the Lord, thy God, the Lord of all worlds.'[89] Thus conversion with the *Nürnberger-Trichter*[90] is as inappropriate as an 'awakening' or

---

82. *Epistle to the Son of the Wolf*, p.15 (= *Gleanings* 132:5).

83. *Tablets*, p.172.

84. *Will and Testament*, p.25.

85. Lawḥ-i-Maqṣúd, *Tablets*, p.173. See also Lawḥ-i-Siyyid-i-Mihdíy-i-Daháji, *Tablets*, pp.198–9.

86. Bahá'u'lláh, *The Hidden Words*, Persian 36.

87. *Gleanings* 163:5.

88. op. cit., 66:13.

89. op. cit., 129:2.

90. *Nürnberger-Trichter*: a funnel by means of which information is successfully crammed into the head of even the dullest dunce.

'rebirth' in the style of the 'Jesus-people' or other charismatic revivalist movements. 'Blind zeal can only do harm', a German proverb says. Sectarian proselytism is wrong, for it is based on the erroneous assumption that it lies within one's power to convince others of the truth provided one uses the right technique and is insistent enough. But in reality religious truth cannot be demonstrated like a mathematical theorem. Above all, he who sets out to 'convert' someone does not take the other seriously. Therefore, if they are to become Bahá'ís, people should not be 'converted', i.e. talked and pushed into the religion, nor should they be 'awakened', i.e. manipulated in such a way that their critical judgement is befogged. Rather they should be made acquainted with the message of Bahá'u'lláh and learn from the Bahá'í teachings as long as they so desire. From then on it is their concern alone whether they decide to become Bahá'ís or not. Only if a person has made this decision of his own free-will is there a good chance that he will not subsequently regret it.

Bahá'u'lláh emphatically warns his followers not to engage in vain disputes: 'Rid thyself of all attachment to the vain allusions of men, and cast behind thy back the idle and subtle disputations of them that are veiled from God. Proclaim, then, that which the Most Great Spirit will inspire thee to utter in the service of the Cause of thy Lord, that thou mayest stir up the souls of all men.[91] And in another passage He says: 'Beware lest ye contend with any one, nay, strive to make him aware of the truth with kindly manner and most convincing exhortation. If your hearer respond, he will have responded to his own behoof, and if not, turn ye away from him, and set your faces towards God's sacred Court, the seat of resplendent holiness.'[92]

Not arrogance and pride but selflessness and humility are the qualities which characterize a true Bahá'í teacher: 'Show forbearance and benevolence and love to one another. Should any one among you be incapable of grasping a certain truth, or be striving to comprehend it, show forth, when conversing with him, a spirit of extreme kindliness and good-will. Help him to see and recognize the truth, without esteeming yourself to be, in the least, superior to him, or to be possessed of greater endowments.'[93] Success does not justify a proud attitude either: 'Should such a man ever succeed in influencing any one, this success should be attributed not to him, but rather to the influence of the words of God, as decreed by Him Who is the Almighty, the All-Wise. In the sight of God he is regarded as a lamp that imparteth its light, and yet is all the while being consumed within itself.'[94]

Each teacher of the Faith is assured of divine assistance: 'Whoso openeth

91. Bahá'u'lláh, *Gleanings* 139:4.
92. Bahá'u'lláh, op. cit., 128:10.
93. Bahá'u'lláh, op. cit., 5:3.
94. Bahá'u'lláh, op. cit., 128:7.

his lips in this Day and maketh mention of the name of his Lord, the hosts of Divine inspiration shall descend upon him from the heaven of My name, the All-Knowing, the All-Wise.'[95] Whenever a Bahá'í arises to teach the Cause of God, God 'will cause the pure waters of wisdom and utterance to gush out and flow copiously from his heart'.[96]

The believer has the right to express his personal belief and understanding of the revealed text:[97] 'We should not restrict the liberty of the individual to express his own views so long as he makes it clear that these views are his own . . . This does not, however, mean that the absolute authority does not remain in the revealed Words. We should try and keep as near to the authority as we can and show that we are faithful to it by quoting from the Words of Bahá'u'lláh in establishing our points.[98] To discard the authority of the revealed Words is heretic and to suppress completely individual interpretation of those Words is also bad.'[99] The believers must strike a happy medium between 'extreme orthodoxy on the one hand, and irresponsible freedom on the other'.[100] Through frequent reading they must deepen themselves in their understanding and knowledge of the utterance of Bahá'u'lláh, so as to be able 'to give it to others in its pure form'.[101] However, the believer who is teaching the Faith has no authority: only the revealed Word and its authorized interpretation is authoritative.

It is not difficult to understand why Bahá'u'lláh has described teaching as 'the most meritorious of all deeds'[102] for the weal and woe of mankind depend on God's message reaching each and every one. 'Can any of us feel', writes Rúḥíyyih Rabbání, 'he can receive such a bounty and yet withhold it from others, rest quiescent in his own inner sense of security and leave others untaught and unhelped in these disastrous days the world is passing through? Today, if ever, must ring in our ears the battle cry of Mullá Ḥusayn,[103] "Mount your steeds, O heroes of God!"'[104]

95. Bahá'u'lláh, op. cit., 129:3.
96. Bahá'u'lláh, op. cit., 144:1.
97. Shoghi Effendi, *Principles of Bahá'í Administration*, p.44.
98. Bahá'u'lláh calls the holy verses 'the most potent elixir' (Lawḥ-i-Siyyid-i-Mihdíy-i-Dahají, *Tablets*, p.200).
99. Shoghi Effendi, quoted in *Bahá'í Procedure*, pp.17–18.
100. Shoghi Effendi, *Bahá'í Administration*, p.42.
101. Shoghi Effendi, quoted in *Principles of Bahá'í Administration*, p.11.
102. *Gleanings* 128:10.
103. The first disciple of the Báb, also known as the Bábu'l-Báb (cf. Nabíl-i-A'ẓam, *The Dawn-Breakers*, pp.47ff.)
104. *Success in Teaching*, p.14.

14. Prospects

Thus the world is like an oilpress: under pressure. If you are the dregs of the oil you are carried away through the sewer; if you are genuine oil you will remain in the vessel. But to be under pressure is inevitable. Observe the dregs, observe the oil. Pressure takes place ever in the world, as, for instance, through famine, war, want, inflation, indigence, mortality, rape, avarice; such are the pressures on the poor and the worries of the states: we have evidence of them . . . We have found men who grumble under these pressures and who say: 'How bad are these Christian times!' . . . Thus speak the dregs of the oil which run away through the sewer; their colour black because they blaspheme: they lack splendour. The oil has splendour. For here another sort of man is under the same pressure and friction which polishes him, for is it not the very friction which refines him?

This is what St. Augustine[1] wrote when he surveyed the decline of the old order, namely of the Roman Empire, which he personally experienced. We, too, are witnessing a storm of changes thundering down upon us. The world is out of joint,[2] the old order is being rocked to the foundations and the abyss which mankind is approaching looms nearer. The consequences of the dethronement of religion have been described, and evaluated as a process of decay. Destruction, decomposition and decay[3] are the signs which characterize the global condition.

Nevertheless, many changes with which we are confronted are, in the end, inevitable, necessary and beneficial. An economic system in which rich nations become increasingly richer and poor ones increasingly poorer is immoral and cannot endure. The process of freeing various peoples from colonial dependence on the West is a prerequisite for the coming world

1. Serm.ed.Denis XXIV, 11.
2. cf. Bahá'u'lláh, *Gleanings* 70:1.
3. Bahá'u'lláh speaks about the 'loathsome and foul-smelling odours from the world', caused by the evil deeds of men 'which brought upon them the retribution of God, in accordance with the basic principles of His divine rule' (Bahá'u'lláh, Lawḥ-i-Maqṣúd, *Tablets*, p.177).

commonwealth. So long as colonial and neo-colonial oppression exists and the different countries are not fully recognized as equal members in the family of nations, the world will know no peace. The suppression of one half of mankind by the other half, namely, of women by men, will be overcome in the foreseeable future. The emancipation of women, already initiated by the Báb[4] in the last century, cannot be held back. Racial discrimination, which has manifested itself in such ghastly events in our century, is being increasingly condemned and denounced. The increasingly pressing economic, ecological and demographic questions, as well as the problems of energy and food supply, are forcing the peoples of the world to give up the fetish of exclusive national sovereignty and co-operate on a world-wide[5] scale, because global economic interdependence has made problem-solving on a nation-state basis impossible. The world conferences in Stockholm on environmental issues, in Bucharest on food and agriculture, in Caracas on international maritime law, in Geneva on the fight against crime, in Copenhagen on women's rights, and the North-South Conference in Cancun, Mexico, are among the first attempts at world-wide co-operation among the states, even though their results, through the short-sightedness of politicians, are still disappointingly minimal. Without people being particularly aware of it, continents and countries are gradually shedding their insularity and becoming a world community, cemented by a common fate.

And finally, the desertion of religion, the collapse of values and the signs of social and cultural decomposition, devastating and disastrous as their results are, are also part of this inevitable and necessary process, because man, in his yearning to explore and experiment with everything, cannot otherwise be convinced of what it means 'to be cut off from Revelation' until 'the benefits of Revelation disappear'.[6] Not until secular messianism (an extreme form of humanism which believes in the self-sufficiency of man), not until all humanistic futuristic utopias, all human attempts at self-redemption, have failed, not until the idols of self-worship have proven powerless, will the essential purpose of man's existence and the bedrock of human culture become fully visible: 'Only when the year grows cold do we realize that the pine and the cypress are the last to fade.'[7]

The many signs (described at the outset of this book) of a change in trend towards a new religious consciousness, the rediscovery of religion as a 'constitutive part of man's consciousness' as 'the ground of a shared moral

---

4. One of His eighteen apostles was a woman, the poetess Qurratu'l-'Ayn, called Ṭáhirih, who appeared at the Conference of Badasht (1848) without a veil, a revolutionary act which caused a scandal. (cf. to this Shoghi Effendi, *God Passes By*, pp.31ff.; H. M. Balyuzi, *The Báb*, p.168.)

5. The transformation of the law of nations into a law of co-operation is impressively presented by Wolfgang Friedmann, *The Changing Structure of International Law*, New York 1964.

6. Romano Guardini, *The End of the Modern World*, p.125.

7. Confucius, *The Analects*, IX, XXVII.

order',[8] and the realization by many well-known scholars that the destructive disease of hedonism can be cured only by a new religious belief, are an inducement to hope that a new consciousness is emerging, a new receptivity to the signs of the times, to something new.

Erich Fromm looks towards the future. He keeps an eye out for an 'object of devotion',[9] but he lives in the hope that the religious spirit will materialize without institutionalized religion. Daniel Bell looks towards the past. He hopes for a resurrection of the old religions.

However convincing the analyses of Bell and Fromm and however impressive the insights, mankind would be lost if the continuation of its existence depended on the realization of either of these hopes, for the one is as improbable as the other. Fromm is acutely aware that the subjugation of selfishness, greed and egocentricity is one of the original and fundamental aims of religion. What he fails to recognize is that religion is much more than just this one aim, that it isn't even the essence of religion, and that without God it remains unattainable. Religious goals which are detached from a living, breathing relationship to God and which lack a motivating and transformative power remain abstract knowledge, not concrete reality. Nowhere does Fromm tell us where this new vision, this new object of devotion is to come from, which charismatic figure is to awaken mankind from its lethargy and lead it to new shores. Fromm's hope is no more than a wish, a dream, for nothing indicates that the teachings of the 'Great Masters', detached from their ancient roots could come to life anew, like a phoenix from the ashes. The loss of the centre of our lives, of the 'dimension of depth' (Paul Tillich) cannot be made good by man-made means. Unlike Baron Münchhausen,[10] mankind cannot pull itself out of the swamp of nihilism, materialism, hedonism and unbelief by its hair.

Neither has Bell's widely shared hope of a revival of old religions any facts on its side which suggest its fulfilment, other than a widespread yearning for spirituality and the longing to give life meaning. The old dogmas have broken down, the old values are no longer lived by, at any rate not by the majority of people. Attempts to breathe life into the old religions again, to raise them from the dead or to integrate them into our modern world by reformation will fail. The truth is that the Word has been 'torn and tattered',[11] the original impulse or revolutionary spirit ex-

8. Daniel Bell, *The Cultural Contradictions of Capitalism*, pp.169, 154.

9. *To Have or to Be?*, p.137.

10. Baron Karl Friedrich von Münchhausen (1720–97), a passionate hunter and military officer who, at the end of his adventurous life, loved to entertain his friends with the most incredible stories of war, hunting and travel exploits. These were published later as an anthology, which was enriched with motifs from earlier 'tall story' literature (Lukian, Rabelais, Swift, Holberg). The oldest edition, edited by Rudolf Raspe, was published in Oxford in 1785 under the title *Baron Münchhausen's Narrative of his Marvellous Travels and Campaigns in Russia*. In one of these tall stories, Münchhausen tells how he once fell into a swamp when he was out riding. He describes how he managed to save himself at the last minute by seizing his own hair and pulling himself out.

11. Compare ch.12, p.228 n.174.

tinguished, and the clock can never be turned back. Bahá'u'lláh prophesied that the vitality of man's belief in God would die out and that religion could be revived only through a new revelation: 'Nothing short of His wholesome medicine can ever restore it.'[12]

We stand at a historical turning-point, and the great turning-points in human history have always been connected with a human manifestation of the Eternal, the Timeless, the Unconditioned; each new beginning, involving the transformation of man and society, has been the result of the creative, regenerating impulse of a new revelation, the new Word of God.

Man cannot do with God as he chooses. He cannot, as Martin Heidegger once remarked,[13] 'think God into being'. Neither is it necessary to do so, for He has spoken to humanity through His Messenger Bahá'u'lláh. Assuming that God spoke to the people in the past and guided them, is it so improbable, so out of the question, that He could have done so again in this most decisive, most dangerous phase in the history of mankind? Are we to believe that God's redemptive intervention ceased with the appearance of Moses, Jesus or Muḥammad and that thereafter mankind was to be deprived of divine guidance? Can the idea of the uniqueness (and exclusivity) of revelation be considered more plausible and more logically compelling than the cyclical return of the manifested Word? Do not all the holy scriptures of the past point to the dawning of a new day? In 1949, the distinguished Jewish philosopher Martin Buber wrote in his book *For the Sake of Heaven*: 'No way can be pointed to in this desert night. One's purpose must be to help men of today to stand fast, with their soul in readiness, until the dawn breaks and a path becomes visible where none suspected it.'[14]

Anyone who is looking today for a new vision, a new object of dedication, should not disregard what millions today see as this new vision, a new 'focal point for all our strivings and the basis for all our effective . . . values',[15] – the revelation of Bahá'u'lláh; nor should they ignore the advice of the apostle Paul: 'Prove all things; hold fast that which is good.'[16] The message of Bahá'u'lláh is the only really new thing in the world which points to the future without effecting a complete break with the past. The past is assimilated into the future. Not 'one jot or tittle shall pass'[17] from the messages of the former prophets. The continuity of God's redemptive intervention and of human culture is manifested in the Bahá'í Revelation.

It is not the first time in history that a small 'minority indicates the course that historical development will take',[18] and that the truth of

---

12. Bahá'u'lláh, *Gleanings* 99.
13. In an interview with *Der Spiegel*, cf. issue 10, 1977, p.236.
14. p.xiii.
15. Erich Fromm, *To Have or to Be?*, p.138.
16. 1 Thess. 5:21.
17. Matt. 5:18.
18. E. Fromm, op. cit., p.76.

Muḥammad's words are confirmed: 'How oft, by God's will, hath a small host vanquished a numerous host!'[19] The turning-point passes without fanfare: 'Tout ce qui est grand se passe en silence' – a realization which also finds expression in Nietzsche's profound words: 'It is the stillest words which bring the storm. Thoughts that come with dove's footsteps guide the world.'[20] The renewal of the world is approaching on dove's feet.

Every single person must make a decision, for each one is called upon to take part in building a new world. The Cause of God, however, is independent of acceptance or rejection by the people: 'The Day-Star of His Cause shineth through every veil and His Word of affirmation standeth beyond the reach of negation.'[21] As in the days of earlier prophets, the 'City of God' will be built by those who follow His call.

In these dark times of unbelief, Bahá'ís derive their assurance and strength to proclaim the Message of the Almighty from their historical perspective and their unshakeable conviction that what seems utterly improbable[22] can become a reality if the will and power of God are behind it to give it the necessary impetus: 'And that our armies should procure the victory for them.'[23] Did not the Báb give his disciples, the Letters of the Living, a radiant promise of triumph as he sent them on their way to proclaim the new truth? 'Heed not your weaknesses and frailty; fix your gaze upon the invincible power of the Lord, your God, the Almighty. Has He not, in past days, caused Abraham, in spite of His seeming helplessness, to triumph over the forces of Nimrod? Has He not enabled Moses, whose staff was His only companion, to vanquish Pharaoh and his hosts? Has He not established the ascendancy of Jesus, poor and lowly as He was in the eyes of men, over the combined forces of the Jewish people? Has He not subjected the barbarous and militant tribes of Arabia to the holy and transforming discipline of Muḥammad, His Prophet? Arise in His Name, put your trust wholly in Him, and be assured of ultimate victory.'[24]

19. Qur'án 2:250.
20. *Thus spake Zarathustra*, 'The stillest Hour', Part III, p.162.
21. Bahá'u'lláh, Tablet of Ṭarázát, *Tablets*, p.33.
22. For instance, that the carpenter from Nazareth or the illiterate and uninfluential merchant from Mecca were to move and change the world.
23. Qur'án 37:173.
24. Quoted from Nabíl-i-A'ẓam, *The Dawn-Breakers*, p.94.

Appendix

p.42.   *bellum omnium contra omnes:*
         universal war, *lit.* war of all against all

p.42.   *L'imagination au pouvoir!*
         Imagination to power!

p.43.   *in sexualibus:*
         in sexual matters

p.47.   *homo sum; humani nil a me alienum puto:*
         I am a man; nothing human is foreign to me

p.49.   *fin de siècle:*
         end of the century

p.57.   *rien ne va plus:*
         Nothing works any more

p.58.   *La parole a été donnée à l'homme pour déguiser sa pensée:*
         Words have been given to man so that he can disguise his
         thoughts

p.68.   *homo consumens:*
         Man the consumer

p.73.   *homo brutalis:*
         Man the brutal

p.78.   *L'homme est une passion inutile:*
         Man is a useless passion

p.78.   *Il est absurde que nous soyions nés, il est absurde que nous
         mourions:*
         It is absurd that we are born; it is absurd that we die

p.83.   *consensus omnium:*
         by common consent

p.85   *credo quia absurdum:*
         I believe it because it is absurd

p.103.   *interior intimo meo:*
         More inward than my most inward part

p.105.   *Unio Mystica:*
         Mystical Union

p.113.   *sub specie aeternitatis:*
         from the view of eternity

p.114.   *ex oriente lux:*
         light from the Orient

p.117.   *conditio sine qua non:*
         lit. condition without which nothing; *hence* a prerequisite

p.121.   *telos:*
         goal

p.127.   *Orandum est, ut sit mens sana in corpore sano:*
         It is to be prayed for a sound mind in a sound body

p.134.   *civitas maxima:*
         the greatest State

p.137.   *dies irae:*
         the Day of Wrath

p.155.   *errare humanum est:*
         To err is human

p.157.   *anima naturaliter christiana:*
         The soul is naturally Christian

p.159.   *L'esprit de modération doit être celui du législateur; le bien politique, comme le bien moral, se trouve toujours entre deux limites:*
         The spirit of moderation ought to be that of the legislator; political, like moral good, lying always between two extremes

p.162.   *horribile dictu:*
         horrible to say

p.166.   *La plus belle ruse du diable est de nous persuader qu'il n'existe pas:*
         The cleverest trick of the devil is to persuade us that he does not exist

p.167.   *relinquitur igitur quod nomine mali significetur quaedam absentia boni:*
         The result is that by the name of evil is meant the absence of good

p.178.   *remedium peccati:*
         a remedy for sins

p.178.   *Les hommes s'occupent à suivre une balle et un lièvre; c'est la plaisir même des rois:*
         Men spend their time chasing a ball or a hare; it is even the sport of kings

p.179.   *La seule chose qui nous console de nos misères est le divertissement, et cependant c'est la plus grande de nos misères. Car c'est cela qui nous empêche principalment de songer à nous, et qui nous fait perdre insensiblement. Sans cela, nous serions dans l'ennui, et cet ennui nous pousserait à chercher un moyen plus solide d'en sortir. Mais le divertissement nous amuse, et nous fait arriver insensiblement à la mort:*
         The only thing that consoles us for our miseries is diversion. And yet it is the greatest of our miseries. For it is that above all which prevents us thinking about ourselves and leads us imperceptibly to destruction. But for that we should be bored, and boredom would drive us to seek some more solid means of escape, but diversion passes our time and brings us imperceptibly to our death

p.179.   *do ut des:*
         I give so that you may give

p.180.   *sola fide:*
         only by faith

p.182.   *Iustitia fundamentum regnorum:*
         Justice, the foundation of kingdoms

p.183.   *ultima ratio:*
         lit. the last reason; *hence* in the last resort

p.184.   *quid leges sine moribus vanae proficiunt?*
         What is the use of vain laws without ethics?

p.184.   *punitur quia peccatum est:*
         It is punished because a crime has been committed

p.186.   *nullum crimen, nulla poena sine lege:*
         lit. no crime, no punishment without law; *hence* a deed must be
         defined by the law as criminal in order to be considered as such

p.187.   *ne bis in idem:*
         lit. not twice for the same; *hence* one cannot be punished twice
         for the same deed

p.188.   *contradictio in adiecto:*
         a contradiction in terms

p.189.   *pecca fortiter, sed fortius fide*:
         Sin bravely, but more bravely believe

p.191.   *incerta omnia, sola mors certa:*
         Everything is uncertain, only death is certain

p.193.   *Après nous le déluge:*
         After us the Flood

p.194.   *L'immortalité de l'âme est une chose qui nous importe si fort,
         qui nous touche si profondément, qu'il faut avoir perdu tout
         sentiment pour être dans l'indifférence de savoir ce qui en est.
         Toutes nos actions et nos pensées doivent prendre des routes si
         différentes, selon qu'il y aura des biens éternels à espérer ou
         non, qu'il est impossible de faire une démarche avec sens et
         jugement, qu'en les réglant par la vue de ce point, qui doit être
         notre dernier objet:*
         The immortality of the soul is something of such vital import-
         ance to us, affecting us so deeply, that one must have lost all
         feeling not to care about knowing the facts of the matter. All
         our actions and thoughts must follow such different paths, ac-
         cording to whether there is hope of eternal blessings or not, that
         the only possible way of acting with sense and judgement is to
         decide our course in the light of this point, which ought to be
         our ultimate objective

p.197.   *sola gratia:*
         only by grace

p.201.   *memento mori:*
         Remember death

p.202.   *omnia mea mecum porto:*
         All I have I carry with me
p.208.   *mens agitat molem:*
         Immanent Mind makes the universe work
p.215.   *ora et labora:*
         Pray and work
p.215.   *vita contemplativa:*
         the contemplative life
p.215.   *vita activa:*
         the active life
p.217.   *est modus in rebus, sunt certi denique fines:*
         There is a measure in all things, finally there are certain limits
p.219.   *fiat iustitia, pereat mundus:*
         Let there be justice even if the world perishes
p.223.   *adeo enim summa est iustitiae regula Dei voluntas, ut quidquid*
         eo ipso quod vult iustum habendum est:
         The supreme rule of justice is the Will of God and everything
         that he wills must be accepted because he wills it
p.225.   *humanum:*
         the human dimension
p.227.   *pars pro toto:*
         a part for the whole
p.228.   *summum bonum:*
         the sum of goodness; the highest good
p.231.   However, there is no true fraternity without a common pa-
         ternity, as Monsieur de la Palice would have said, and it is
         precisely the absence of this common father which imperils the
         structures of the humanist family. The religions present
         everyone with an effective fraternity founded in the acceptance
         of a common father, no matter whether we call him Jehovah or
         Allah or some other name. The naively modernist churches
         which try to minimize this 'vertical dimension', retaining only
         the horizontal one of service to one's neighbour, founder on the
         fatal contradiction of a fraternity without common paternity
p.234.   *Tu nos fecisti ad te, et cor nostrum inquietum est, donec*
         requiescat in te:
         For thou hast created us for thyself, and our heart cannot be
         quieted till it may find repose in thee
p.249.   *melius est, ut scandalum oriatur, quam ut veritas relinquatur:*
         It is better that scandal break loose than that truth should be
         relinquished
p.260.   *Tout ce qui est grand se passe en silence:*
         Everything great happens in silence

Bibliography

'ABDU'L-BAHÁ. *Paris Talks. Addresses given by 'Abdu'l-Bahá in Paris in 1911–12.* London: Bahá'í Publishing Trust, 12th edn 1971. (Published by Bahá'í Publishing Trust, Wilmette, Illinois, under the title *The Wisdom of 'Abdu'l-Bahá.*)
— *The Promulgation of Universal Peace.* Talks Delivered by 'Abdu'l-Bahá during His Visit to the United States and Canada in 1912. Compiled by Howard MacNutt. Wilmette, Illinois: Bahá'í Publishing Trust, 2nd edn 1982.
— *The Secret of Divine Civilization.* Translated by Marzieh Gail in consultation with Ali-Kuli Khan. Wilmette, Illinois: Bahá'í Publishing Trust, 2nd edn 1970.
— *Selections from the Writings of 'Abdu'l-Bahá.* Compiled by the Research Department of the Universal House of Justice; translated by a Committee at the Bahá'í World Centre and by Marzieh Gail. Haifa: Bahá'í World Centre, 1978.
— *Some Answered Questions.* Collected and translated from the Persian by Laura Clifford Barney. London: 1908; Wilmette, Illinois: Bahá'í Publishing Trust, 4th rev. edn 1981.
— *Tablets of the Divine Plan, revealed by 'Abdu'l-Bahá to the North American Bahá'ís.* Wilmette, Illinois: Bahá'í Publishing Trust, rev. edn 1977.
— *Will and Testament of 'Abdu'l-Bahá.* Wilmette, Illinois: Bahá'í Publishing Committee, 1944.
Abrüstung und Weltfrieden (Disarmament and World Peace). A Declaration of the International Bahá'í Community with an introduction by Ulrich Gollmer. Hofheim-Langenhain: Bahá'í-Verlag, 1980.
ALTIZER, THOMAS J. J. and HAMILTON, WILLIAM. *Radical Theology and the Death of God.* Harmondsworth: Penguin Books, 1968.
ALTNER, GÜNTER. *Zwischen Natur und Menschengeschichte. Perspektiven für eine neue Schöpfungstheologie* (Between Nature and the History of Man. Perspectives for a new Theology of Creation). München: 1975.
— 'Zwischen zerbrochenen Ideologien' (Between Shattered Ideologies). *Überblick. Zeitschrift für ökumenische Begegnung und internationale Zusammen-*

arbeit. Stuttgart: September 1979.

AMEND, HERBERT. *Sexfront*. Frankfurt: 1970.

AMÉRY, JEAN. 'Provokationen des Atheismus' (Provocations of Atheism). *Wer ist das eigentlich - Gott?* Edited by Hans-Jürgen Schultz. München: 1969, pp.209f.

— *Hand an sich legen. Diskurs über den Freitod* (Killing oneself. Discourse on Voluntary Death). Stuttgart: 1976.

ANDERS, GÜNTHER. *Die Antiquiertheit des Menschen. Über die Bombe und die Wurzel unserer Apokalypseblindheit* (The Obsolescence of Man. Concerning the Bomb and the Roots of our Apocalypse Blindness). Vol.I. München: C. H. Beck, 1956.

— *Die Antiquiertheit des Menschen. Über die Zerstörung des Lebens im Zeitalter der dritten industriellen Revolution* (The Obsolescence of Man. On the Destruction of Life. in the Age of the third industrial Revolution). Vol. II. München: 1980.

ARISTOTLE. *The Politics of Aristotle*. Translated with an introduction, notes and appendixes by Ernest Barker, New York and London: Oxford University Press, 1958.

AUER, ALFONS. *Autonome Moral und christlicher Glaube* (Autonomous Moral and Christian Belief). Tübingen: 2nd edn 1977.

AUGUSTINE. *St. Augustine's Confessions with an English translation by William Watts*. 1631 in two volumes. RP London: Heinemann, 1960.

BÁB, THE. *Selections from the Writings of the Báb*. Compiled by the Research Department of the Universal House of Justice and translated by Habib Taherzadeh with the assistance of a Committee at the Bahá'í World Centre. Haifa: Bahá'í World Centre, 1976.

BACON, FRANCIS. *The Moral and Historical Works of Lord Bacon, including his Essays, Apophthegms, Wisdom of the Ancients, New Atlantis and Life of Henry the Seventh*. London: Henry G. Bohn, 1860.

BAHÁ'U'LLÁH. *Epistle to the Son of the Wolf*. Translated by Shoghi Effendi. Wilmette, Illinois: Bahá'í Publishing Trust, rev. edn 1976.

— *Gleanings from the Writings of Bahá'u'lláh*. Translated by Shoghi Effendi. Wilmette, Illinois: Bahá'í Publishing Trust, rev. edn 1978.

— *The Hidden Words*. Translated by Shoghi Effendi. London: Bahá'í Publishing Trust, 1949. Wilmette, Illinois: Bahá'í Publishing Trust, rev. edn 1954.

— *The Hidden Words. Words of Wisdom and Communes*. Chicago: Bahá'í Publishing Society, undated.

— Kitáb-i-Aqdas. Extracts translated by Shoghi Effendi in *Synopsis and Codification of the Kitáb-i-Aqdas, the Most Holy Book of Bahá'u'lláh*. Haifa: Bahá'í World Centre, 1973.

— *Kitáb-i-Íqán. The Book of Certitude*. Translated by Shoghi Effendi. Wilmette, Illinois: Bahá'í Publishing Trust, rev. edn 1974.

— *Prayers and Meditations by Bahá'u'lláh*. Translated by Shoghi Effendi. Wilmette, Illinois: Bahá'í Publishing Trust, 6th RP 1974; London: Bahá'í Publishing Trust, rev. edn 1978.

— *The Proclamation of Bahá'u'lláh to the Kings and Leaders of the World*. Haifa: Bahá'í World Centre, 1967.

— *Qad Iḥtaraqa'l-Mukhliṣun. The Fire Tablet*. London: Bahá'í Publishing Trust, 1980.

— *The Seven Valleys and The Four Valleys*. Translated by Ali-Kuli Khan (Nabílu'd-Dawlih), assisted by Marzieh Gail. Wilmette, Illinois: Bahá'í Publishing Trust, 5th edn 1978.

— *Tablets of Bahá'u'lláh revealed after the Kitáb-i-Aqdas*. Compiled by the Research Department of the Universal House of Justice and translated by Habib Taherzadeh with the assistance of a Committee at the Bahá'í World Centre. Haifa: Bahá'í World Centre, 1978.

BALYUZI, H. M. *'Abdu'l-Bahá. The Centre of the Covenant of Bahá'u'lláh*. London: George Ronald, 1971.

— *Bahá'u'lláh. The King of Glory*. Oxford: George Ronald, 1980.

— *Muḥammad and the Course of Islám*. Oxford: George Ronald, 1976.

BARTH, KARL. *Church Dogmatics*. Vol.I: *The Doctrine of the Word of God*. Edinburgh: T. & T. Clark, 1956.

BAUDELAIRE, CHARLES. *Les Fleurs du Mal*. Paris: Gallimard, 1972.

BAUSANI, ALESSANDRO. 'Originalliteratur der Bahá'í-Religion' (Original Literature of the Bahá'í Faith), *Informationstagung über die Baha'i-Religion 8./9. Oktober 1976 in Langenhain*. National Spiritual Assembly of the Bahá'ís of Germany, undated.

BELL, DANIEL. *The Cultural Contradictions of Capitalism*. London: Heinemann, 1976.

BEN CHORIN, SCHALOM. 'Terroristen über uns' (Terrorists Above Us). *Kultur und Leben. Zeitschrift für Tradition und Fortschritt*. Baden-Baden: April 1978, pp.7ff.

BENNETT, JOHN C. *Christian Social Ethics in a Changing World. An Ecumenical Theological Inquiry*. New York and London: Association Press, 1966.

Bergedorfer Gesprächskreis zu Fragen der freien industriellen Gesellschaft (Bergedorf Discussions on Questions concerning the Free Industrial Society). Hamburg.

— 'Ein anderer ''Way of Life'' — Ist der Fortschritt noch ein Fortschritt?' (Another 'Way of Life' — Is Progress still Progress?) 1977, *Protokoll* No. 56.

— 'Sprache und Politik. Können Begriffe die Gesellschaft verändern?' (Language and Politics. Can Concepts Change Society?) 1972, *Protokoll* No. 41.

— 'Wachstum und Lebenssinn — Alternative Rationalität?' (Growth and Purpose of Life — Alternative Rationalities?) 1978, *Protokoll* No. 61.

— 'Jugend und Gesellschaft. Chronischer Konflikt — Neue Verbindlichkeiten?' (Youth and Society. Chronic Conflict — New Commitment?) 1979, *Protokoll* No. 63.

BERGER, PETER L. *A Rumor of Angels. Modern Society and the Rediscovery of the Supernatural*. Garden City, New York: Doubleday & Company Inc., 1969.

Bhagavadgita, The. With an Introductory Essay, Sanskrit Text, English Translation and Notes by S. Radhakrishnan. London: Allen & Unwin, 1956.

BLANK, JOSEF. 'Die Ethik Jesu' (The Ethic of Jesus). Erich Kellner (ed). *Religionslose Gesellschaft. Gespräche der Paulus-Gesellschaft*. Wien: 1976, pp.163ff.

BONHOEFFER, DIETRICH. *Letters and Papers from Prison*. London: SCM Press Ltd, 1971.

BRAUN, HERBERT. *Gesammelte Studien zum Neuen Testament und seiner Umwelt* (Collected Studies on the New Testament and its Environment). Tübingen: 1962.

BRECHT, BERTOLT. *Galileo.* In BENTLEY, ERIC. *From the Modern Repertoire.* Series Two. Bloomington: Indiana University Press, 1949.

— *The Threepenny Opera.* In BENTLEY, ERIC. *From the Modern Repertoire.* Series One. Bloomington: Indiana University Press, 1949.

BRESCH, CARSTEN. 'Die Menschheit an der zweiten Schwelle der Evolution' (Humanity at the Second Threshold of Evolution). In Schatz, O. (ed). *Hoffnung in der Überlebenskrise.* Graz-Wien-Köln: 1979, pp.44ff.

BREZINKA, WOLFGANG. *Erziehung und Kulturrevolution. Die Pädagogik der Neuen Linken* (Education and Cultural Revolution. The Pedagogic of the New Left). München, Basel: 2nd edn 1976.

BRUNNER, EMIL. *Justice and the Social Order.* New York and London: Harper & Brothers, 1945.

BUBER, MARTIN. *For the Sake of Heaven.* New York: Harper & Row, 1953.

BÜCHMANN, GEORG. *Geflügelte Worte. Der Zitatenschatz des deutschen Volkes* (Winged Words. The Treasury of Quotations in the German Language). Berlin: 2nd edn 1972.

BÜCHNER, GEORG. *Danton's Death.* In BENTLEY, ERIC. *From the Modern Repertoire.* Series One. Bloomington: Indiana University Press, 1955.

BURCKHARDT, JACOB. *Reflections on History.* London: Allen & Unwin, 1943.

BUSCHBECK, MALTE. 'Was ersetzt uns den Fortschrittsglauben? Vom therapeutischen Nutzen der Apokalypse für die säkulare Gesellschaft' (What do we have as a Substitute for the Belief in Progress? On the Therapeutic Benefit of the Apocalypse for the Secular Society). *Süddeutsche Zeitung,* 14–15.6.1980.

CHARGAFF, ERWIN. *Heraclitean Fire. Sketches from a Life Before Nature.* New York: Rockefeller, 1978.

CHAUCHARD, PAUL. *Biologie et Morale.* Tours: Mame, 1959.

CHOULEUR, JACQUES. 'La Foie Mondiale Bahá'íe: Religion Planetaire de l'Avenir?' (The Bahá'í World Faith: The Religion of the Future?) *Annales Universitaires.* Faculté des lettres et sciences humaines, Avignon: November 1975.

CLAËSSON, BENT H. *Sexualinformation für Jugendliche* (Sexual Information for Juveniles). Frankfurt: 6th edn 1979.

CLAUSEWITZ, CARL VON. *On War.* Edited and translated by Michael Howard and Peter Paret. Princeton: Princeton University Press, 1976.

COHEN, HERMANN. *Religion of Reason out of the Sources of Judaism.* New York: Frederick Ungar, 1972.

COMFORT, ALEX. *Sex in Society.* London: Duckworth, 1963.

CONDRAU, GION. 'Todesfurcht und Todessehnsucht' (Fear of Death and Longing for Death). Paus, A. (ed), *Grenzerfahrung Tod.* Frankfurt: 1978, pp.201ff.

CONFUCIUS. *The Analects or The Conversations of Confucius with his Disciples and Certain Others.* London: Oxford University Press, 1958.

CUBE, FELIX VON. 'Nicht Wissenschaft und Atheismus sind inhuman, sondern dogmatische Ansprüche. Eine Stellungnahme zu dem Beitrag von Hugo Staudinger' (It is not Science and Atheism that are Inhuman, but Dogmatic Claims. Commentary on the Article by Hugo Staudinger). *Das Parlament,* supplement on politics and current affairs, 16.6.1979, pp.17ff.

DAHRENDORF, RALF. *Gesellschaft und Freiheit. Zur soziologischen Analyse der Gegenwart* (Society and Freedom. On the Sociological Analysis of the Present Time). München: 1961.

DESCHNER, KARL-HEINZ. *Abermals krähte der Hahn. Eine kritische Kirchengeschichte von den Anfängen bis zu Pius XII* (The Cock Crew Again. A Critical History of the Church from its Beginnings until Pius XII). Stuttgart: Hans E. Günther Verlag, 1962.

Dhammapada (Path of Virtue). In *Buddhaghosha's Parables*. London: Trübner & Co, 1870.

DIEM, HERMANN. *Dogmatics*. Edinburgh and London: Oliver and Boyd, 1959.

DIRKS, WALTER. 'Gottesglaube und Ideologiekritik' (Belief in God and Ideology Critiques). *Wer ist das eigentlich - Gott?* Edited by Hans-Jürgen Schultz. München: 1969, pp.220ff.

DÖNHOFF, MARION GRÄFIN. 'Leben ohne Glauben. Auf der Suche nach einem Wertsystem für die Industriegesellschaft' (Life without Belief. The Search for a System of Values for an Industrial Society). *Die Zeit*, 21.12.1979.

DOSTOEVSKY, FYODOR. *The Possessed*. Edited by Ernest Rhys. Everyman Library, 1931.

EBELING, GERHARD. 'Die nicht-religiöse Interpretation biblischer Begriffe' (The Non-religious Interpretation of Biblical Concepts), *Zeitschrift für Theologie und Kirche*. Vol. 52, 1955, p.331.

EICK, JÜRGEN. 'Die zweigeteilte Gesellschaft' (The Split Society). *Frankfurter Allgemeine Zeitung*, 6.1.1973.

EPICURUS. *The Extant Remains*. With short critical apparatus, translation and notes by Cyril Bailey. Hildesheim-New York: Georg Olms, 1975.

ESSLEMONT, J. E. *Bahá'u'lláh and the New Era*. London: Bahá'í Publishing Trust, rev. edn 1974.

FECHNER, ERICH. 'Zukunft ohne Ethos?' (Future without Ethics?). Kellner, E. (ed), *Religionslose Gesellschaft. Gespräche der Paulus-Gesellschaft*. Wien: 1976, pp.71ff.

FERGUSON, MARILYN. *The Aquarian Conspiracy. Personal and Social Transformation in the 1980s*. Los Angeles: J. P. Tarcher, 1980.

FETSCHER, IRING. 'Der Tod im Lichte des Marxismus' (Death in the Light of Marxism). A. Paus (ed). *Grenzerfahrung Tod*. Frankfurt: 1978.

FEUERBACH, LUDWIG. *The Essence of Christianity*. Translated from the second German edition. London: Trübner & Co, 1881.

FÖRSTER, F. W. 'Die pädagogische Unentbehrlichkeit der religiösen Moralbegründung' (The Pedagogical Inevitability of Religious Moral Justification). *Hochland I*. 1908–9.

FOLEY, GROVER. 'Sind wir am Ende? Amerikanische Zukunftsprognosen' (Are We at the End? American Prognoses). *Frankfurter Hefte. Zeitschrift für Kultur und Politik*. Edited by Walter Dirks and Eugen Kogon. Issue 10, October 1971.

FOZDAR, JAMSHED. *Buddha Maitrya Amitabha has Appeared*. New Delhi: Bahá'í Publishing Trust, 1976.

FRANKL, VIKTOR. 'Das existentielle Vakuum' (The Existential Vacuum). *Wissenschaft und Weltbild*. Issue 25, Vol.XI, 1972, p.88.

— 'Die Sinnfrage in der Psychotherapie' (The Question of Meaning in Psychotherapy), *Suche nach Sinn – Suche nach Gott*. Edited by A. Paus. Graz, Wien, Köln: 1978, pp.308–39.

FREDERICK THE GREAT. *Letters of Voltaire and Frederick the Great*. London: Routledge, 1927.

FREUD, SIGMUND. 'Leonardo da Vinci and a Memory of his Childhood'. *The Standard Edition of the Complete Psychological Works of Sigmund Freud*. Vol.XI. London: The Hogarth Press, 1910.

— 'Obsessive Acts and Religious Practices.' *Collected Papers*. Vol.II. London: The Hogarth Press, 1924.

— *Three Essays on the Theory of Sexuality*. London: Imago, 1949.

FRIEDRICH, HEINZ. *Kulturkatastrophe. Nachruf auf das Abendland* (Cultural Catastrophe. Obituary of the West). Hamburg: Hoffmann & Campe, 1979.

FRIES, HEINRICH and STÄHLIN, RUDOLF. *Gott ist tot? Eine Herausforderung – Zwei Theologen antworten* (God is Dead? A Challenge – Two Theologians Answer). München: 1968.

FROMM, ERICH, *To Have or to Be?* New York: Harper & Row, 1976.

GALTUNG, JOHAN. *Strukturelle Gewalt. Beiträge zur Friedens- und Konflikt-forschung* (Structural Violence. Contributions to Peace and Conflict Research). Reinbek: Rohwolt, 1975.

GEBSER, JEAN. *Abendländische Wandlung. Abriß der Ergebnisse moderner Forschung. Ihre Bedeutung für Gegenwart und Zukunft* (Western Trans-formation. Outline of the Results of Modern Research. Their Significance for the Present and the Future). Berlin: Ullsteinbook No. 107, 1965.

— *In der Bewährung* (On Probation). Bern, München: 1962.

GEISSLER, HEINER (ed). *Der Weg in die Gewalt – Geist und gesellschaftliche Ursachen des Terrorismus und seine Folgen* (Trends Towards Violence – Intellectual and Social Causes of Terrorism and its Consequences). München: 1978.

GERLITZ, PETER. *Die Religionen und die neue Moral. Wirkungen einer weltweiten Säkularisation* (The Religions and the New Morality. Effects of World-wide Secularization). München: 1971.

GOETHE, JOHANN WOLFGANG VON. *Correspondence between Goethe and Carlyle*. Edited by C. E. Norton. London: Macmillan, 1887.

— *Faust*. Part One. New York: Philosophical Library, 1958.

— *West–Eastern Divan*. London and Toronto: J. M. Dent & Sons Ltd, 1914.

GOLDZIHER, IGNAZ. *Vorlesungen über den Islam* (Lectures on Islám). Heidelberg: 3rd edn, 1963.

GOLLWITZER, HELMUT. *The Existence of God as Confessed by Faith*. London: SCM Press Ltd, 1965.

GREENE, THEODOR. 'The Historical Context and Religious Significance of Kant's *Religion*'. I. Kant, *Religion within the Limits of Reason alone*. New York: Harper & Row, 1960.

GRIFFEL, ANTON. *Der Mensch – Wesen ohne Verantwortung?* (Man, a Being Without Responsibility?). Regensburg: 1975

GROSSMANN, HERMANN. *Der Bahá'í und die Bahá'í-Gemeinschaft* (The Bahá'í and the Bahá'í Community). Oberkalbach: 2nd edn, 1973.

— *Umbruch zur Einheit. Gott, Mensch und Welt an der Schwelle einer neuen*

Ordnung (Upheaval to Unity. God, Man and the World on the Threshold of a New Order). Stuttgart: 1947.

GRUHL, HERBERT. *Ein Planet wird geplündert. Die Schreckensbilanz unserer Politik* (A Planet is Plundered. The Terrifying Outcome of Our Politics). Frankfurt: 1976.

GUARDINI, ROMANO. *The End of the Modern World. A Search for Orientation.* London: Sheed & Ward, 1957.

GÜNZLER, CLAUS. *Anthropologische und ethische Dimensionen der Schule* (Anthropological and Ethical Dimensions of the School). Freiburg, Munich: 1976.

HAAG, HERBERT. 'Vor dem Bösen ratlos?' (Helpless in the Face of Evil?). *Zur Debatte, Themen der Katholischen Akademie in Bayern.* Issue 2, 1979.
— 'Rettet den Teufel!' (Save the Devil!). *Süddeutsche Zeitung*, 12–13.3.1977.

HABERMAS, JÜRGEN. 'Erkenntnis und Interesse' (Knowledge and Interest). *Technik und Wissenschaft als 'Ideologie'.* Frankfurt: 1970, pp.146–68.

HACKER, FRIEDRICH. *Aggression. Die Brutalisierung der modernen Welt* (Aggression. The Brutalization of the Modern World). Reinbek: Rohwolt, 1973.

HAENSCH, DIETRICH. *Repressive Familienpolitik. Sexualunterdrückung als Mittel der Politik* (Repressive Family Politics. Sexual Oppression as a Political Instrument). Reinbek: Rohwolt, 1969.

HALBFAS, HUBERTUS. 'Gegen die Erziehung zum Gehorsam' (Against Education to Obedience). *Vorgänge. Zeitschrift für Gesellschaft und Politik.* No. 3, 1973, pp.54–60.

HARDING, ESTHER. *The Way of all Women. A Psychological Interpretation.* New York: Harper & Row, 1970.

HAUPTMANN, WALTER. 'Was läßt die Kriminologie vom Strafrecht über?' (Does Criminology Leave Anything of the Penal Law?). *Kriminalistik. Zeitschrift für die gesamte Kriminalwissenschaft.* Issue 1, 1980.

HEILER, FRIEDRICH. 'Einheit und Zusammenarbeit der Religionen' (Unity and Cooperation of the Religions). *Gemeinschaft und Politik.* Edited by Institut für Geosoziologie und Politik. Bad Godesberg: No. 12, 1957, pp.1–19.

HEINE, HEINRICH. 'Germany'. *The Poetical Works of Heinrich Heine.* Vol.III. London: Heinemann, 1917.
— 'Romances.' *The Poetical Works of Heinrich Heine. Now first completely rendered into English verse: in accordance with the original forms.* Translated by John Payne. Vol. 2. London: The Villon Society, 1911.

HELVÉTIUS, CLAUDE ADRIEN. *A Treatise on Man: His Intellectual Faculties and His Education.* B. Law and G. Robinson. London: 1777.

HILD, GOTTLIEB and AICHELIN, HELMUT. 'Staat – Kirche – Gesellschaft. Perspektiven und Hintergründe eines umstrittenen Verhältnisses' (State – Church – Society. Perspectives and Background of a Disputed Relationship). *Impulse.* Edited by the Evangelische Zentralstelle für Weltanschauungsfragen, Stuttgart. Issue 9, October 1975.

HÖFFE, OTFRIED. 'Herrschaftsfreiheit oder gerechte Herrschaft?' (Freedom from Domination or Just Rule?). *Frankfurter Allgemeine Zeitung*, 31.7.1977.

HÖLDERLIN, FRIEDRICH. *Poems and Fragments.* London: Routledge & Kegan Paul, 1966.

HORKHEIMER, MAX. *Die Sehnsucht nach dem ganz Anderen. Ein Interview mit Kommentar von H. Gumnior* (The Longing for Something Quite Different. An Interview with Commentary by H. Gumnior). Hamburg: 1970.

HUTTEN, KURT, *Seher, Grübler, Enthusiasten. Sekten und religiöse Sondergemeinschaften der Gegenwart* (Seers, Ponderers, Enthusiasts. Sects and Religious Groups of Today). Stuttgart: 10th edn, 1966.

IVES, HOWARD C. *Portals to Freedom*. Oxford: George Ronald, 1967.

JÜNGEL, EBERHARD. 'Der Tod als Geheimnis des Lebens' (Death as the Secret of Life). A. Paus (ed). *Grenzerfahrung Tod*. Frankfurt: 1978, pp.9ff.

JUNGK, ROBERT. *Die Zukunft hat schon begonnen. Amerikas Macht und Ohnmacht* (The Future has already begun. America's Power and Helplessness). Reinbek: Rohwolt, 1967.

KAMLAH, W. *Meditatio Mortis*. Stuttgart: 1977.

KANT, IMMANUEL. *Religion within the Limits of Reason Alone*. New York: Harper & Row, 1960.

KASUN, JACQUELINE. 'Turning Children into Sex Experts.' *The Public Interest*. Issue 55, 1980, pp.3–14.

KELLNER, ERICH (ed). *Experiment eines kritischen Christentums. Analysen, Modelle, Aktivitäten der Paulus-Gesellschaft* (Experiment of a Critical Christianity. Analyses, Models, Activities of the Paulus Society). Mondsee: undated.

— *Religionslose Gesellschaft. Sind wir morgen Nihilisten?* (Society without Religion. Will we be Nihilists Tomorrow?) *Gespräche der Paulus-Gesellschaft*. Wien: 1976.

— *Sexualität ohne Tabu und christliche Moral* (Sexuality without Taboo and Christian Morality). *Gespräche der Paulus-Gesellschaft*. München, Mainz: 1970.

KELSEN, HANS. *Was ist Gerechtigkeit?* (What is Justice?) Wien: 1953.

Khuddaka-Patha (The Text of the Minor Sayings). *The Minor Anthologies of the Pali Canon*. Re-edited and translated by Mrs Rhys Davids. London: Oxford University Press, 1931.

KLEIST, HEINRICH VON. *The Marquise of O. and Other Stories*. Translated with an introduction by Martin Greenberg. Preface by Thomas Mann. London: Faber & Faber, 1963.

— *Michael Kohlhaas: From an old Chronicle*. Translated from the German by James Kirkup. London, Glasgow: Blackie, 1967.

KÖNIG, FRANZ CARDINAL, 'Für ein Lächeln von Marx' (For a Smile from Marx). *Deutsche Zeitung*, 30.8.1974.

— 'Die gemeinsame Verantwortung von Religion und Wissenschaft für eine menschenwürdige Zukunft' (The Common Responsibility of Religion and Science for a Humane Future). O. Schatz (ed). *Hoffnung in der Überlebenskrise*. Graz, Wien, Köln: 1979, pp.30ff.

OESTLER, ARTHUR. *Janus. A Summing Up*. London: Hutchinson, 1978.

OESTLER, ARTHUR and SMYTHIES, J. R. *Beyond Reductionism. New Perspectives in the Life Sciences*. The Alpbach Symposium. London: Hutchinson, 1972.

OLAKOWSKI, LESZEK. *Main Currents of Marxism. Its Origin, Growth and Dissolution*. Oxford: Clarendon Press, 1978.

— *Traktat über die Sterblichkeit der Vernunft* (Treatise on the Mortality of Reason). München: 1967.

KÜNG, HANS, *Existiert Gott? Antwort auf die Gottesfrage* (Does God Exist? Answer to the Question about God), *München*: 1978.

LAO TSE, *The Tao Teh King. The Sacred Books of China, The Texts of Taoism.* First published by the Clarendon Press, 1891. Reprinted by Motilal Banarsidass, 1966.

LEHMANN, KARL, 'Vom Sinn der christlichen Existenz zwischen Enthusiasmus und Institution' (The Purpose of Christian Existence between Enthusiasm and Institution). A. Paus (ed). *Suche nach Sinn – Suche nach Gott.* Graz, Wien, Köln: 1978, pp.47–93.

LICHTENBERG, GEORG CHRISTOPH, *Aphorisms and Apophthegms.* In *The Lichtenberg Reader; Selected Writings.* Boston: Beacon Press, 1959.

LOBKOWICZ, NIKOLAUS and HERTZ, ANSELM. *Am Ende aller Religion? Ein Streitgespräch* (The End of All Religion? A Dispute). Zürich: 1976.

LOCKE, JOHN. *Some Thoughts concerning Education.* In *The Works of John Locke.* Vol.IX. London: 1823. Aalen: Scientia Verlag, RP 1963.

LÖW, REINHARD, KOSLOWSKI, PETER and KREUZER, PHILIPP (ed). *Fortschritt ohne Maß? Eine Ortsbestimmung der wissenschaftlich-technischen Zivilisation* (Progress without Measure? A Topography of the Scientific-technical Civilization). München: 1981.

LÖWITH, KARL. *Meaning in History. The Theological Implications of the Philosophy of History.* Chicago: The University of Chicago Press, 1949.

LORENZ, KARL. *Civilized Man's Eight Deadly Sins.* New York: Harcourt Brace Jovanovich, 1973.

LOTZ, JOHANNES, 'Der Tod in theologischer Sicht' (A Theological View of Death) A. Paus (ed). *Grenzerfahrung Tod.* Frankfurt: 1978, pp.73ff.

LUCRETIUS, TITUS CARUS. *On the Nature of Things.* Oxford: Basil Blackwell 1929.

LUTHER, MARTIN. 'The Freedom of a Christian.' *Luther's Works.* Vol. 31 (Career of the Reformer I). Edited by Harold J. Grimm. Philadelphia: Muhlenberg Press, 1957.

— 'The Christian in Society II'. *Luther's Works.* Vol. 45. Edited by Walther I. Brandt. Philadelphia: Muhlenberg Press, 1962.

— 'Table Talk.' *Luther's Works.* Vol. 54. Edited and translated by Theodore G. Tappert. Philadelphia: Fortress Press, 1967.

MAIER, HANS. *Kritik der politischen Theologie* (A Critic of Political Theology) Einsiedeln: 1970.

MARCUSE, HERBERT. *An Essay on Liberation.* Boston: Beacon Press, 1969.

— *Eros and Civilization. A Philosophical Inquiry into Freud.* Boston: Beacon Press, 1966.

— *One Dimensional Man. Studies in the Ideology of Advanced Industrial Society.* Boston: Beacon Press, 1964.

MARTIN, DAVID. *The Dilemmas of Contemporary Religion.* Oxford: Basil Blackwell, 1978.

— *A General Theory of Secularization.* Oxford: Basil Blackwell, 1978.

MARX, KARL. *Critique of Hegel's 'Philosophy of Right'.* Cambridge: University Press, 1970.

MARX, KARL and ENGELS, FRIEDRICH. *The German Ideology*. Moscow: Progress Publishers, 1964.

MAURACH, REINHART. *Deutsches Strafrecht. Allgemeiner Teil* (German Penal Law. General Section). Karlsruhe: 3rd edn, 1954.

MAUZ, GERHARD. *Das Spiel von Schuld und Sühne. Die Zukunft der Strafjustiz* (The Game of Guilt and Atonement. The Future of Criminal Justice). Köln: 1975.

MAWDUDI, ABULA'LA. *Towards Understanding Islam*. Leicester: The Islamic Foundation, 1980.

MECHLER, ACHIM, 'Der Verbrecher als Sündenbock der Gesellschaft' (The Criminal as Scapegoat of Society). *Zeitschrift für Rechtspolitik*. Issue 1, 1971.

MEHNERT, KLAUS. *The Twilight of the Young. The Radical Movements of the 1960s and their Legacy*. London: Secker & Warburg, 1976.

MESAROVIC, MIHAJLO and PESTEL, EDUARD. *Mankind at the Turning Point. The Second Report to The Club of Rome*. London: Hutchinson, 1975.

MESSER, AUGUST and PRIBILLA, MAX SJ. *Katholisches und modernes Denken. Ein Gedankenaustausch über Gotteserkenntnis und Sittlichkeit* (Catholic and Modern Thinking. An Exchange of Ideas on the Knowledge of God and Morality). Stuttgart: 1924.

METZ, JOHNANNES B. *Theology of the World*. London: Burns & Oates, 1968.

METZ, JOHANNES B. and HÖFLICH, E. 'Karl Marx für die Kirche. Eine Antwort auf Hans Maiers Polemik gegen die politische Theologie' (Karl Marx for the Church. An Answer to Hans Maier's Polemic Against the Political Theology). *Frankfurter Hefte*. Issue 24, 1969, pp.777ff.

MOLTMANN, JÜRGEN. *Theology of Hope. On the Ground and the Implications of a Christian Eschatology*. London: SCM Press, 1967.

MONOD, JACQUES. *Chance and Necessity. An Essay on the Natural Philosophy of Modern Biology*. London: Collins, 1972.

MONTESQUIEU, CHARLES-LOUIS. *The Spirit of Laws*. Berkeley: University of California Press, 1977.

MOSER, TILMANN. *Gottesvergiftung* (Poisoning by God). Frankfurt: Suhrkamp, 3rd edn, 1977.

MÜLLER, MAX. 'Weisen der Sinnerfahrung des Menschen von heute' (Modes of Human Perception in the Present Day). A. Paus (ed). *Suche nach Sinn – Suche nach Gott*. Graz, Wien, Köln: 1978, pp.9ff.

MÜLLER-SCHWEFE, HANS-RUDOLF. *Atheismus*. Stuttgart: 1962.

MUHAMMAD. *The Qur'án*. Translated from the Arabic by J. M. Rodwell. London: Dent, 1953.

NABÍL-I-A'ZAM (MUHAMMAD-I-ZARANDÍ). *The Dawn-Breakers. Nabíl's Narrative of the Early Days of the Bahá'í Revelation*. Translated and edited by Shoghi Effendi. Wilmette, Illinois: Bahá'í Publishing Trust, 1932.

Neue Juristische Wochenschrift. Frankfurt.

NIETZSCHE, FRIEDRICH. *The Antichrist*. New York: Knopf, 1927.

— *Beyond Good and Evil. Prelude to a Philosophy of the Future*. Harmondsworth: Penguin Books, 1975.

— *The Dawn of Day*. London: George Allen & Unwin, 1924.

— *Ecce Homo*. London: George Allen & Unwin, 1924.

— *The Genealogy of Morals*. Garden City: Doubleday, 1956.

— *Human – All-Too-Human. A Book for Free Spirits.* London: George Allen & Unwin, 1924.

— *The Joyful Wisdom.* London: George Allen & Unwin, 1924.

— 'Schopenhauer as Educator.' *The Complete Works of Friedrich Nietzsche.* Vol.V (Thoughts Out of Season, Part II). Edinburgh: T. N. Fowlis, 1909.

— *Twilight of the Idols.* Harmondsworth: Penguin Books, 1968.

— *The Will to Power.* London: Weidenfeld and Nicolson, 1967.

— *Thus Spake Zarathustra.* New York: Random House, undated.

OTTO, RUDOLF. *The Idea of the Holy. An Inquiry into the Non-Rational Factor in the Idea of the Divine and its Relation to the Rational.* Revised with additions. London: Oxford University Press, 6th RP 1931.

PANAHI, BADI. 'Die Bedeutung der Psychoanalyse für die Sozialwissenschaften' (The Significance of Psychoanalysis for the Social Sciences). Erlangen-Nürnberg (Diss.), 1974.

PASCAL, BLAISE. *Pensées.* Harmondsworth: Penguin Books, 1966.

PAUS, ANSGAR, *Grenzerfahrung Tod* (Death, a Borderline Experience). Edited on behalf of the Salzburg University Weeks. Frankfurt: Suhrkamp Taschenbuch No. 430, 1978.

— *Suche nach Sinn – Suche nach Gott* (Searching for Meaning – Searching for God), Graz, Wien, Köln: 1978.

PETRY, GERHARD. 'Das Ende der Theologie?' (The End of Theology?). *Kirche in der Zeit.* Issue 18. Düsseldorf: 1963.

PEUKERT, H. (ed). *Diskussion zur 'politischen Theologie'* (Discussion on 'political theology'). Mainz, München: 1969.

PIEPER, JOSEF. *The Human Wisdom of St. Thomas. A Breviary of Philosophy from the Works of St. Thomas Aquinas.* London: Sheed & Ward, 1948.

PLACK, ARNO. *Die Gesellschaft und das Böse. Eine Kritik der herrschenden Moral* (Society and Evil. A Criticism of the Prevailing Moral Code). München: 7th edn 1970.

— *Plädoyer für die Abschaffung des Strafrechts* (Plea for the Abolition of Penal Law). München: 1974.

PLANCK, MAX. *Religion und Naturwissenschaft* (Religion and Science). Leipzig: 8th edn 1941.

PLATO. *The Republic.* Harmondsworth: Penguin Books, 1955.

PROUDHON, PIERRE JOSEPH. *De la Creation de l'ordre dans l'Humanité ou Principes d'Organisation Politique.* Paris-Besançon: 1843.

RABBĀNĪ, RŪḤĪYYIH. *Success in Teaching.* Wilmette, Illinois: Bahá'í Publishing Trust, 1965.

RABELAIS, FRANÇOIS. *Gargantua and Pantagruel.* London: David Nutt, 1900.

RADBRUCH, GUSTAV. *Legal Philosophy.* In *The Legal Philosophies of Lask, Radbruch and Dabin.* Cambridge: Harvard University Press, 1950, pp.47–224.

RADHAKRISHNAN, SAVARPALLI. *Recovery of Faith.* London: George Allen & Unwin, 1956.

RATTNER, JOSEF. *Psychologie des Vorurteils* (Psychology of Prejudice). Zürich: 1971.

RATZINGER, JOSEF. 'Schöpfungsglaube und Evolutionstheorie' (Belief in Creation and the Theory of Evolution). *Wer ist das eigentlich–Gott?* Edited by Hans-Jürgen Schultz. München: 1969, pp.232ff.

REICH, WILHELM. *Die sexuelle Revolution. Zur charakterlichen Selbsterneuerung des Menschen.* Frankfurt: 7th edn 1971. (*The Invasion of Compulsory Sex-Morality.* New York: Farrar, Strauss & Giroux, 1971.)

RENDTORF, T. R. and TÖDT, H. E. *Theologie der Revolution. Analysen und Materialien* (Theology of Revolution. Analyses and Materials). Frankfurt: 2nd. edn 1968.

REVERS, WILHELM J. 'Die szientistische Einäugigkeit des modernen Realitäts-bewußtseins' (The Scientistic One-Eyedness of Today's Consciousness of Reality). O. Schatz (ed). *Hoffnung in der Überlebenskrise?* Graz, Wien, Köln: 1979, pp.198ff.

RINGEL, ERWIN. 'Suizid und Euthanasie' (Suicide and Euthanasia). A. Paus (ed). *Grenzerfahrung Tod*, Frankfurt: 1978, pp.277ff.

ROEGELE, OTTO B. 'Freiheit und Bindung in der gesellschaftlichen Kommunikation. Prolegomena zu einer Ethik der Kommunikationsberufe' (Freedom and Commitment in Social Communication. Prolegomena to an Ethic of the Communication Professions). *Freiheit des Menschen. Im Auftrag des Direktoriums der Salzburger Hochschulwochen.* Edited by A. Paus. Graz, Wien, Köln: 1974.

ROSENKRANZ, GERHARD. *Die Bahá'í. Ein Kapitel neuzeitlicher Religionsgeschichte* (The Bahá'ís. A Chapter of Modern Religious History). Stuttgart: 1949.

SANYUTTA NIKAYA. *The Book of the Kindred Sayings or Grouped Suttas.* Translated by Mrs Rhys Davids. London: Oxford University Press, undated.

SARTRE, JEAN PAUL. *L'être et le néant. Essai d'ontologie phénoménologique.* Paris: 18th edn 1949.

— *Being and Nothingness. An Essay on Phenomenological Ontology.* London: Methuen, 1966.

SCHAEFER, HANS. 'Der Mensch und das Ende seiner Menschlichkeit' (Man and the End of His Humaneness). *Was ist das – der Mensch? Beiträge zu einer modernen Anthropologie* (What is Man? Contributions to a Modern Anthropology). 12 lectures. München: R. Piper & Co, 1968.

— 'Die Sexualität und die Medizin. Ihr Stellenwert in der Gesellschaft und die Aufgabe der Ärzte' (Sexuality and Medicine. Its Status in Society and the Task of the Doctors). *Sexualmedizin.* Issue 6, No. 9, September 1977, pp.720ff.

— *Leib, Geist, Gesellschaft. Aspekte einer Biologie des Menschen* (Body, Spirit, Society. Aspects of a Biology of Man). München: 1971.

SCHAEFER, UDO. *The Light Shineth in Darkness. Five Studies in Revelation after Christ.* Oxford: George Ronald, 1977.

SCHATZ, OSKAR (ed). *Hoffnung in der Überlebenskrise?* (Hope in the Crisis of Survival?). Salzburger Humanismusgespräche. Graz, Wien, Köln: 1979.

SCHELSKY, HELMUT. *Die Arbeit tun die anderen. Klassenkampf und Priester-herrschaft der Intellektuellen* (The Others do the Work. Class Antagonism and the Priestly Domination by the Intellectuals). Opladen: 2nd edn 1977.

— *Soziologie der Sexualität. Über die Beziehungen zwischen Geschlecht, Moral und Gesellschaft* (The Sociology of Sexuality. On the Relationships between Sex, Morals and Society). Hamburg: 1955.

SCHERER, GEORG. *Das Problem des Todes in der Philosophie* (The Problem of Death in Philosophy). Darmstadt: 1979.

SCHILLER, FRIEDRICH VON. 'Hymn to Joy.' *The Poems and Ballads of Schiller.*

Translated by Sir Edward Bulwer Lytton. Leipzig: 1844.

— *The Robbers*. Translated with an introduction by F. J. Lamport. Harmondsworth: Penguin Books, 1979.

SCHIMMEL, ANNEMARIE. 'Der Beitrag der islamischen Mystik zur Einheit der Religionen' (The Contribution of Islamic Mysticism to the Unity of Religions). *Gemeinschaft und Politik*. Edited by the Institut für Geo-Soziologie und Politik. Bad Godesberg: Issue 12, 1957, pp.47ff.

SCHMIDT, REINER. 'Der geforderte Staat' (The Challenged State). *Neue Juristische Wochenschrift*. Stuttgart: 1980, p.161

— 'Der Verfassungsstaat im Geflecht der internationalen Beziehungen' (The Constitutional State in the Network of International Relationships). *Veröffentlichungen der Vereinigung der deutschen Staatsrechtslehrer*. Issue 36, pp.66ff.

SCHMIDTCHEN, GERHARD. *Befragte Katholiken – Zur Zukunft von Glaube und Kirche* (Questions to Catholics – On the Future of Faith and the Church). Freiburg: Herder, 1973.

SCHMITT, CARL, JÜNGEL, E. and SCHELZ, S. *Die Tyrannei der Werte* (The Tyranny of Values). Hamburg: 1979.

SCHNEIDER, HANS JOACHIM. 'Behandlung in Freiheit' (Treatment in Freedom). *Psychologie heute*, 9.9.1978. Weinheim-Basel: Beltz-Verlag.

SCHOEPS, HANS-JOACHIM. *Jüdisch-christliches Religionsgespräch in neunzehn Jahrhunderten* (Jewish-Christian Religious Dialogue in Nineteen Centuries). Frankfurt: 1949.

SCHOPENHAUER, ARTHUR. *Counsels and Maxims, Being the second Part of Arthur Schopenhauer's Aphorismen zur Lebensweisheit*. London: Swan Sonnenschein & Co, 1890.

— *Parerga and Paralipomena. Short Philosophical Essays*. 2 vols. Oxford: Clarendon Press, 1974.

— *The Basis of Morality*. London: Swan Sonnenschein & Co, 1903.

SCHREY, HEINZ HORST (ed). *Säkularisation* (Secularization). Darmstadt: 1981.

SCHULTZ, HANS-JÜRGEN (ed). *Wer ist das eigentlich – Gott?* (Who is God?). München: 1969.

SCHULZ, PAUL. *Ist Gott eine mathematische Formel? Ein Pastor im Glaubensprozeß seiner Kirche* (Is God a Mathematical Formula? A Clergyman and the Development of His Faith). Reinbek: Rowohlt, 1977.

SCHWARTLÄNDER, J. 'Der Tod und die Würde des Menschen' (Death and the Dignity of Man). J. Schwartländer (ed). *Der Mensch und sein Tod*. Göttingen: 1976.

SCHWENDTER, RUDOLF. *Theorie der Subkultur* (Theory of Subculture). Frankfurt: 1978.

SCHWIND, HANS (ed). *Ursachen des Terrorismus in der Bundesrepublik Deutschland* (Causes of Terrorism in the Federal Republic of Germany). Berlin: 1978.

SECKLER, MAX. 'Kommt der christliche Glaube ohne Gott aus?' (Is Christian Belief Possible without God?). *Wer ist das eigentlich – Gott?* Edited by Hans-Jürgen Schultz. München: 1969, pp.181ff.

SEIDL, ACHIM, *Psychosophie*. München: Lurz, 1978.

SEIFERT, MONIKA. 'Antiautoritäre Kindererziehung' (Anti-authoritarian Education). S. H. Fraiberg (ed). *Das verstandene Kind*. Hamburg: 1969, pp.305–17

SENECA. *Letters to Lucilius*. 2 vols. Oxford: Clarendon Press, 1932.
— *Moral Essays*. 3 vols. London: Harvard University Press, 1964.
SERVIER, JEAN. *Histoire de l'Utopie*. Paris: Gallimard, 1967.
SHAULL, RICHARD. 'Revolution in theologischer Perspektive' (Revolution from a Theological Perspective). T. R. Rendtorff and H. E. Tödt (ed), *Theologie der Revolution. Analysen und Materialien*. Frankfurt: 2nd edn 1968.
— 'Revolutionary Change in Theological Perception'. *Christian Social Ethics in a Changing World. An Ecumenical Theological Inquiry*. Edited by John C. Bennett. New York, London: 1966.
SHAULL, RICHARD and OGLESBY, C. *Containment and Change*. New York: 1967.
SHOGHI EFFENDI. *The Advent of Divine Justice*. Wilmette, Illinois: Bahá'í Publishing Trust, 1939.
— *Bahá'í Administration*. Wilmette, Illinois: Bahá'í Publishing Trust, rev. edn 1974.
— *Directives from the Guardian*. Compiled by Gertrude Garrida. New Delhi: Bahá'í Publishing Trust, 1973.
— *Extracts from the Guardian's Letters on Bahá'í Funds and Contributions*. Haifa: Bahá'í World Centre, 1970.
— *God Passes By*. Wilmette, Illinois: Bahá'í Publishing Trust, 7th RP 1974.
— *Messages to America 1932–1946*. Wilmette, Illinois: Bahá'í Publishing Trust, 1947.
— *The Promised Day is Come*. Wilmette, Illinois: Bahá'í Publishing Trust, rev. edn 1963.
— *The World Order of Bahá'u'lláh*. Wilmette, Illinois: Bahá'í Publishing Trust, 2nd rev. edn 1974.
SKINNER, B. F. *Beyond Freedom and Dignity*. Harmondsworth: Penguin Books, 1977.
SOHM, RUDOLF. *Kirchenrecht*. Bd.I: 'Die geschichtlichen Grundlagen' (Church Law. The Historical Foundations). Leipzig: 1892.
Star of the West. The Bahá'í Magazine. Published between 1910 and 1933 from Chicago and Washington D.C., by official Bahá'í agencies variously titled.
STAUDINGER, HUGO. 'Atheismus als politisches Problem' (Atheism as a Political Problem). *Aus Politik und Zeitgeschichte* (From Politics and Contemporary History). Supplement 24/79 to the weekly magazine *Das Parlament*, 16.6.1979.
STEINBUCH, KARL. *Maßlos informiert. Die Enteignung unseres Denkens* (Informed Beyond Measure. The Expropriation of Our Thinking). München, Berlin: 1978.
STIRNER, MAX. *The Ego and His Own. The Case of the Individual Against Authority*. New York: Dover Publications, 1973.
SZCZESNY, GERHARD. *The Future of Unbelief*. London: Heinemann, 1962.
TACITUS. *The Histories. The Annals in four volumes*. Vol. IV. London: Heinemann, 1962.
TALMON, J. L. *Political Messianism. The Romantic Phase*. London: Secker & Warburg, 1960.
— *The Origins of Totalitarian Democracy*. London: Secker & Warburg, 1952.
TAYLOR, GORDON RATTRAY. *How to Avoid the Future*. London: Secker & Warburg, 1975.
TENBRUCK, FRIEDRICH. 'Ethos und Religion in einer zukünftigen Gesellschaft'

(Ethics and Religion in a Future Society). In *Religionslose Gesellschaft. Sind wir morgen Nihilisten? Gespräche der Paulus Gesellschaft*. Edited by Erich Kellner. Wien: 1976.

— 'Friede durch Friedensforschung? Ein Heilsglaube unserer Zeit' (Peace through Peace Research? A Salvational Belief of Our Times). *Frankfurter Allgemeine Zeitung*, 22.12.1973.

THOMAS AQUINAS. *Summa Theologiae*. New York: McGraw-Hill, 1964–.

THE UNIVERSAL HOUSE OF JUSTICE. *Wellspring of Guidance*. Messages from the Universal House of Justice. Wilmette, Illinois: Bahá'í Publishing Trust, rev. edn 1976.

TIECK, HEINRICH (ed). *Wenn ein Blatt sich bewegt, kann auch der Ast erzittern. Gedanken chinesischer Weiser* (When a Leaf Moves, the Branch Might Begin to Tremble. Thoughts of Chinese Sages). Wien, Leipzig: 1939.

TOCQUEVILLE, ALEXIS DE. *Democracy in America*. New York: Knopf, 1948.

TOYNBEE, ARNOLD J. *Change and Habit. The Challenge of our Time*. London: Oxford University Press, 1966.

VIRGIL. *The Aeneid*. London: The Hogarth Press, 1961.

VOLTAIRE. *Letters of Voltaire and Frederick the Great*. London: Routledge, 1927.

WAGNER, RICHARD. *Richard Wagner's Prose Works*. London: Kegan, Trench, Trübner & Co, 1899.

WEISCHEDEL, WILHELM. *Skeptische Ethik* (Sceptical Ethics), Frankfurt: 1976.

WEIZSÄCKER, CARL FRIEDRICH VON. *Wege in der Gefahr* (Routes in a Time of Danger). München: 5th edn 1977.

WELZEL, HANS. *Naturrecht und materiale Gerechtigkeit* (Natural Law and Substantive Justice). Göttingen: 4th edn 1962.

WETZEL, F. X. *Das Goldene Katholikenbuch* (The Golden Book of Catholicism). ed. A. Fäh. 1914.

World Order. A Bahá'í Magazine. Published quarterly by the National Spiritual Assembly of the Bahá'ís of the United States. Wilmette, Illinois: 1966.

ZAHRNT, HEINZ. *The Question of God. Protestant Theology in the Twentieth Century*. London: Collins, 1969.

Compilations:

Bahá'í Procedure. Compiled by the National Spiritual Assembly of the Bahá'ís of the United States and Canada. 2nd edn, 1942.

Bahá'í World Faith. Selected Writings of Bahá'u'lláh and 'Abdu'l-Bahá. Wilmette, Illinois: Bahá'í Publishing Committee, 1943.

Principles of Bahá'í Administration. London: Bahá'í Publishing Trust, rev. edn 1976.

Living the Life. A compilation issued by the Universal House of Justice. Haifa: 1972. London: Bahá'í Publishing Trust, 1974.

The Covenant of Bahá'u'lláh. London: Bahá'í Publishing Trust, 1963.

The Divine Art of Living. Selections from Writings of Bahá'u'lláh and 'Abdu'l-Bahá, compiled by Mabel Hyde Paine. Wilmette, Illinois: Bahá'í Publishing Trust, 1944.

The Pattern of Bahá'í Life. A Compilation from Bahá'í Scripture with some passages from the Writings of the Guardian of the Bahá'í Faith. London: Bahá'í Publishing Trust, 1948.

ndex of Names

General Index